Advances in Latent Variable Mixture Models

Advances in Latent Variable Mixture Models

Edited by

Gregory R. Hancock

and

Karen M. Samuelsen

INFORMATION AGE PUBLISHING, INC.
Charlotte, NC • www.infoagepub.com

Library of Congress Cataloging-in-Publication Data

Advances in latent variable mixture models / edited by Gregory R. Hancock
and Karen M. Samuelsen.
    p. cm.
  Includes bibliographical references and index.
  ISBN-13: 978-1-59311-847-1 (pbk.) ISBN-13: 978-1-59311-848-8 (hardcover)
1. Latent structure analysis. 2. Latent variables. 3. Mixture distributions
(Probability theory) I. Hancock, Gregory R. II. Samuelsen, Karen M.
  QA278.6.A38 2007
  519.5'35–dc22   2007037392

Printed in the United States of America

CONTENTS

PART I

MULTILEVEL AND LONGITUDINAL SYSTEMS

PART II
MODELS FOR ASSESSMENT AND DIAGNOSIS

PART III
CHALLENGES IN MODEL EVALUATION

EDITORS' INTRODUCTION

Gregory R. Hancock
University of Maryland

Karen M. Samuelsen
University of Georgia

The Center for Integrated Latent Variable Research (CILVR) at the University of Maryland, as its name implies, has latent variable methods as its focus. The latent variable work conducted in affiliation with CILVR is integrated in two senses. First, from a methodological perspective, over the last decade or so the walls separating historically distinct latent variable methods have been coming down, with the relations among these methods becoming much more emphasized than their differences. As such, the integration of these latent variable methods is facilitating the capability to address existing research questions more appropriately and, more interestingly, to address entirely new families of research questions. This latter point relates to the second aspect of CILVR's integrated nature, that of joining this analytic synergy with applied domains across the social and behavioral sciences, and well beyond, thereby integrating the newly available tools with the research contexts most in need.

In addition to this methodological and applied integration, the goals of CILVR include methodological training and scholarly dissemination as relate to the full spectrum of latent variable methods. Toward this end, workshops are offered periodically (e.g., structural equation modeling, latent class analysis) and a latent variable conference series was started. The aim of such conferences is to bring together leading researchers who are focus-

Advances in Latent Variable Mixture Models, pages vii–ix
Copyright © 2008 by Information Age Publishing
All rights of reproduction in any form reserved.

ing on a specific aspect of latent variable methods, but where that focus is deemed to have far-reaching methodological and applied implications. The theme for the inaugural conference, held at the University of Maryland on May 18 and 19, 2006, was *Mixture Models in Latent Variable Research*. With mixture-related training workshops the day before and the day after the conference, the four-day event was designed to introduce its national and international attendees to some of the research questions that can be addressed using these methods, to raise awareness of some of the methodological issues and challenges therein, and to stimulate dialog among and between methodological and applied researchers. The topic of mixture models in latent variable research delivered on all counts.

The current volume, *Advances in Latent Variable Mixture Models*, contains chapters by all of the speakers who participated in the 2006 CILVR conference, providing not just a snapshot of the event, but more importantly chronicling the state of the art in latent variable mixture model research. The volume starts with an overview chapter by the CILVR conference keynote speaker, Bengt Muthén, offering a "lay of the land" for latent variable mixture models before the volume moves to more specific constellations of topics. Part I, *Multilevel and Longitudinal Systems*, deals with mixtures for data that are hierarchical in nature either due to the data's sampling structure or to the repetition of measures (of varied types) over time. Part II, *Models for Assessment and Diagnosis*, addresses scenarios for making judgments about individuals' state of knowledge or development, and about the instruments used for making such judgments. Finally, Part III, *Challenges in Model Evaluation*, focuses on some of the methodological issues associated with the selection of models most accurately representing the processes and populations under investigation.

It should be stated that this volume is not intended to be a first exposure to latent variable methods. Readers lacking such foundational knowledge are encouraged to consult primary and/or secondary didactic resources in order to get the most from the chapters in this volume. Once armed with that basic understanding of latent variable methods, we believe readers will find this volume incredibly exciting. Just as anyone who has purchased a new car soon notices every other identical make and model on the road, once an awareness of mixtures is raised a researcher cannot help but search for them everywhere. Mixture models are seductive, to say the least. And when the assumptions upon which they rest are reasonable, mixture models are illuminating and even empowering. Whether dealing with structural equation models, latent growth curves, item response theory, survival analysis, or a host of other cognitive developmental analytical frameworks, the notion that multiple subpopulations might be operating simultaneously starts to seem not only possible, but often quite likely. The current volume exposes the reader to the integration of mixtures with latent variable methods, providing exposure to exciting new analytical options for modeling complex theories. We look forward to the permeation of these methods throughout the applied literature for research questions as yet unanswered, and to these methods' continued development and evolution for research questions as yet unanswerable.

ACKNOWLEDGMENTS

We wish to acknowledge C. Mitchell Dayton, Chair of the Department of Measurement, Statistics and Evaluation at the University of Maryland, for his support in the creation of the Center for Integrated Latent Variable Research (CILVR) as well as in hosting the inaugural conference that gave rise to the current volume. We greatly appreciate the editorial assistance of Dongyang Li in the technical aspects of the chapters' preparation, and for the cover art inspiration of Jaehwa Choi. We thank George Johnson and his team at Information Age Publishing for their steadfast support in making this edited work a reality. And finally, the first editor wishes to acknowledge the constant support of his family: Goldie, Sydney, Quinn, and the newest addition to the mixture, Tate.

CHAPTER 1

LATENT VARIABLE HYBRIDS

Overview of Old and New Models

Bengt Muthén[1]
University of California, Los Angeles

LATENT VARIABLE HYBRIDS:
OVERVIEW OF OLD AND NEW MODELS

The conference that this book builds upon contained many different special topics within the general area of modeling with categorical latent variables, also referred to as *mixture modeling*. The many different models addressed at that conference and within this volume may overwhelm a newcomer to the field. In fact, however, there are really only a small number of variations on a common theme. This chapter aims to distinguish the different themes, show how they relate to each other, and give some key references for further study. Some new mixture models are also proposed.

Table 1.1 gives a summary of different types of latent variable models. An overview discussion of the models of Table 1.1 was presented in Muthén (2002). The entries of the table are types of models, with the rows dividing the models into cross-sectional and longitudinal and the columns dividing models into traditional models with continuous latent variables, models

Advances in Latent Variable Mixture Models, pages 1–24

TABLE 1.1 Model Overview

	Continuous latent variables	Categorical latent variables	Hybrids
Cross-sectional models	Factor analysis, SEM	Regression mixture analysis, Latent class analysis	Factor mixture analysis
Longitudinal models	Growth analysis (random effects)	Latent transition analysis, Latent class growth analysis	Growth mixture modeling

with categorical latent variables, and newer hybrids using both types of latent variables. The upper left cell includes conventional psychometric models such as factor analysis (FA) and structural equation models (SEMs). The bottom left cell contains the generalization to longitudinal settings, where the continuous latent variables appear in the form of random effects describing individual differences in development over time. The categorical latent variable column includes cross-sectional models such as latent class analysis (LCA), which in longitudinal settings generalizes to latent transition analysis (LTA). LTA is a longitudinal model in the class of auto-regressive models (also including "hidden Markov" models), where the status at one time point influences the status at the next time point. Another LCA-related model is latent class growth analysis (LCGA), where the outcomes are influenced by growth factors analogous to conventional random effects growth modeling. The current chapter gives an overview that emphasizes the last column of hybrid models, with the typical examples of factor mixture analysis (FMA) and growth mixture modeling (GMM). As will be discussed, these models present useful generalizations of the models in the other columns, allowing for both classification of subjects in the form of latent classes and determination of continuous latent scores within these classes. All analyses to be discussed can be carried out using maximum-likelihood estimation in the M*plus* program (Muthén & Muthén, 1998–2007).

Figure 1.1 gives a diagrammatic overview of hybrid latent variable models. The following sections will discuss the different branches of this diagram. A key distinction is made between models that specify measurement invariance and those that do not. In this case, invariance refers to measurement parameters being equal across the latent classes of the categorical latent variable(s). Measurement invariance with respect to observed groups such as gender is a well-known topic in psychometrics (see, e.g., Meredith, 1964, 1993). Simultaneous confirmatory factor analysis in several groups to study measurement invariance and group comparisons of latent variable distributions has been discussed in Jöreskog (1971) and Sörbom (1974). Measurement invariance is an important prerequisite for valid across-group comparisons of continuous latent variable constructs, giving a latent construct the same meaning and scale for proper comparisons across groups.

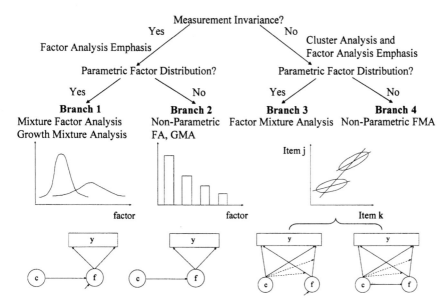

Figure 1.1   Overview of cross-sectional hybrids: Modeling with categorical and continuous latent variables.

Measurement invariance issues for latent groups are analogous and mixture analysis can be thought of as a multiple-group analysis, except with groups determined by the data and the model. With both continuous and categorical outcomes, the key factor analysis measurement parameters are the intercepts and the slopes in the regression of the outcome on the respective continuous latent variable. For example, with binary outcomes, a 2-parameter logistic regression model is typically used where in the item response theory (IRT) formulation the terms difficulty and discrimination are used for the two parameters, respectively. In IRT, measurement non-invariance is referred to as differential item functioning (DIF) and often focuses on the intercepts (difficulties) as in Rasch modeling.

As shown in the Figure 1.1 diagram, models with measurement invariance typically have a factor analysis (or IRT) focus. Here, the latent classes are used to describe heterogeneity among individuals in their continuous latent variable distributions. Separating heterogeneous classes of individuals is important when studying antecedents and consequences. For example, a covariate may have different influence on a factor for one class compared to another or a distal outcome may have different means or probabilities in different classes. As the diagram of Figure 1.1 shows, new branches are created by the choice of how to represent the continuous latent variable distribution. The typical approach is to make a parametric assumption such as normality as in the left-most branch, referred to as branch 1.

Branch 1: Hybrid Modeling With Measurement Invariance and Parametric Factor Distribution

The bottom of branch 1 displays two graphs. The top graph shows two factor distributions for two latent classes, differing in means and variances. The model diagram below denotes the categorical latent class variable as c, the continuous factor as f, and the observed items as y. Here, c influences f and f influences y. The regressions of the y items on f are either linear or non-linear (logit/probit) depending on the y scale. The regression of f on c is a linear regression. In line with dummy variables in linear regression, the different classes of c have different means for f. The short arrow pointing to f is a residual, indicating that c does not explain all the variation in f, but that there is also unaccounted for within-class variance. The measurement invariance specification is shown in the model diagram in that c neither influences y, nor changes the slopes in the regression of y on f.

Cross-Sectional Analysis

The following are some references to work in cross-sectional studies for branch 1, referring to the modeling as mixture factor analysis to emphasize the factor analysis aspects. Articles by McDonald (1967, 2003) on factor analysis represent pioneering work. Yung (1997) specifically studied measurement invariant mixture factor analysis and its maximum-likelihood (ML) estimation. Lubke and Muthén (2005) applied mixture factor analysis to continuous achievement data using ML via the M*plus* program. Lubke and Muthén (2007) did Monte Carlo studies of how well mixture factor model parameters could be recovered under different degrees of factor mean separation across latent classes. It was found that it is more difficult to recover a mixture solution if only the factor means change across classes than if the measurement intercepts change as well. In other words, the measurement invariant hybrid can be more difficult to work with in practice.

Longitudinal Analysis

Turning to longitudinal examples, measurement invariant models are far more commonly used. In the branch 1 model diagram, the y box now represents repeated measures over several time points of a univariate y variable and f would correspond to intercept and slope growth factors (random effects). The growth factor means change over the latent classes, and thereby give rise to different trajectory shapes. In the SEM approach to growth modeling, the time points at which the y items are measured are captured by fixed factor loadings and zero y intercepts. Measurement invariance is natural because the time points are the same across the latent classes. Compared to the mixture factor analysis model, such growth mixture models appear more successful in recovering parameter values. Figure 1.2 shows a hypothetical example

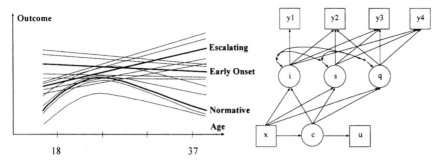

Figure 1.2   Growth mixture modeling of developmental pathways.

of three trajectory classes for an outcome studied over ages 18 to 37. In the graph on the left, the thick curves represent mean curves for each of the classes, while the thin curves represent individual curves within each class. The individual curves are variations on the curve shape themes represented by the mean curves. Defining the intercept growth factor i as the status at age 18, it is seen that the intercept i, the linear slope s, and the quadratic slope q have different means for the three classes. The model diagram of Figure 1.2 shows the mean differences of i, s, and q as arrows from c to i, s, and q.

Key references to growth mixture modeling include Verbeke and Lesaffre (1996) with applications to the development of prostate-specific antigen, Muthén and Shedden (1999) with application to the development of heavy drinking and alcohol dependence, Muthén et al. (2002) with application to intervention effects varying across trajectory classes for aggressive-disruptive behavior among school children, Lin, Turnbull, McCulloch, and Slate (2002) with application to prostate-specific antigen and prostate cancer, and Muthén (2004) with application to achievement development. Dolan, Schmittmann, Lubke, and Neale (2005) modify the model to study regime (latent class) switching. Muthén and Asparouhov (2007) give a recent overview with a technical description and an application to the development of criminal activity.

The Muthén (2004) analysis concerned mathematics achievement development in grades 7–10 in U.S. public schools. It was argued that poor development in this challenging topic was predictive of high school dropout, with antecedents of poor math development and dropout being found among variables capturing disengagement from school. In Figure 1.2 terms, x contains the antecedents and u is high school dropout. Figure 1.3 shows that the 20% classified as developing poorly in math have a drastically higher dropout rate than other students.

The Muthén (2004) analysis was carried out as two-level growth mixture modeling shown in diagram form in Figure 1.4. The top part of the figure labeled "Within" shows student variation, while the bottom part labeled "Between" shows variation across schools. This is a 3-level model with varia-

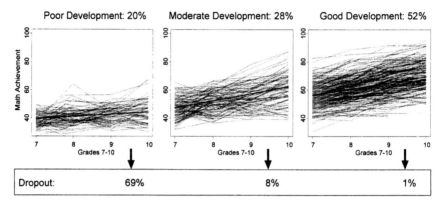

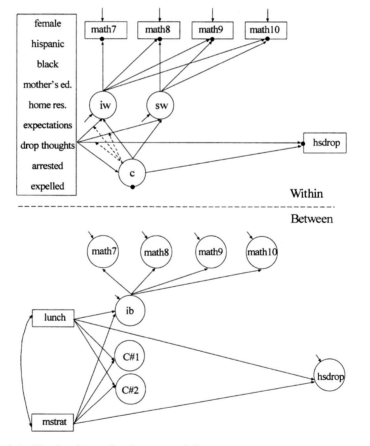

Figure 1.3 Growth mixture modeling: LSAY math achievement trajectory classes and the prediction of high school dropout.

Figure 1.4 Two-level growth mixture modeling.

tion across time as level 1, variation across student as level 2, and variation across school as level 3. The figure shows the M*plus* representation in "wide," multivariate form, transforming the model to two levels, Within and Between, where Within combines level 1 and level 2. The list of antecedents are shown in the box to the left in the Within part of the picture. Grade 7 measures of low schooling expectation and dropout thoughts were strongly related to both poor math development and dropout probability. The arrows from c to the intercept growth factor *iw* and the slope growth factor *sw* indicate that latent trajectory class membership influences the values of these growth factors. The arrow from *c* to high school dropout indicates that latent trajectory class membership influences the probability of this binary variable. The broken arrows from *c* to the arrows from the antecedents to the growth factors indicate that the antecedent influence varies across the latent trajectory classes. The math outcomes, the dropout outcome, and the latent class variable have filled circles attached to their boxes/circle indicating random intercepts, which vary across schools. On the Between level, these random intercepts are continuous latent variables. The math development on the Between level is captured by the random intercept *ib*, while the slope variance across schools is set to zero for simplicity. The latent class variable gives rise to two random intercepts, *c#1* and *c#2*, due to there being three classes. The regression of *ib* on the antecedents is a linear regression, the regressions of *c#1*, *c#2* on the antecedent are linear regressions, and the regression of *hsdrop* is a linear regression. Muthén (2004) found that a school-level covariate indicating quality of math teaching had a significant negative influence on being in the class of poor math achievement development and a positive influence on the within-class math achievement level. A school-level covariate indicating school neighborhood poverty had a positive influence on the probability of dropout.

Growth mixture modeling is also useful for outcomes with more complex distributions. The middle, left part of Figure 1.5 shows a commonly seen distribution of an outcome in longitudinal studies. A large portion of individuals is at the lowest point of the scale. A common reason is that these individuals at this time point have not yet started to engage in the activity studied. Examples of such outcomes include drinking and smoking among middle school students. A growth model approach that takes into account the large portion at zero was presented in Olsen and Schafer (2001). Figure 1.5 shows that the idea behind this modeling is to split the outcome in two parts. One part, labeled *u*, refers the binary outcome obtained by considering whether or not the individual engaged in the activity at the time point in question. The other part, labeled *y*, represents the amount of activity for those who engaged in the activity. At a time point where the person is not engaged in the activity, y is coded as missing. A parallel process growth

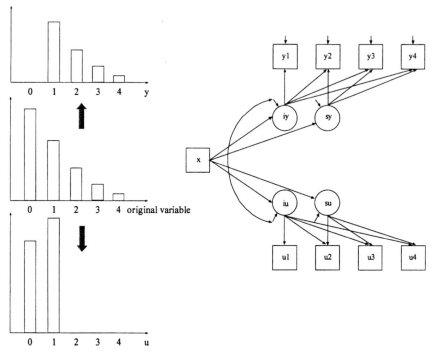

Figure 1.5 Two-part (semi-continuous) growth modeling.

model analyzes the two parts where the growth factors are correlated. The two parts may have different covariate influence.

The two-part growth model assumes that at a given time point individuals who just started to engage in the activity are at the same point in the growth process as individuals who started earlier. Individuals starting earlier may, however, be at a higher point in the growth process. To accommodate this, a mixture two-part model may be introduced as shown in Figure 1.6. A latent class variable cu influences the u part of the model, while the latent class variable cy influences the y part. In conclusion, it is clear that the models shown in Figures 1.4–1.6 can be seen as variations on the branch 1 theme of Figure 1.1.

Branch 2: Hybrid Modeling With Measurement Invariance and Non-Parametric Factor Distribution

In branch 2, the parametric latent variable distribution is replaced by a non-parametric approach using a flexible discretized representation of the distribution. This is illustrated at the bottom of branch 2 in the form of a

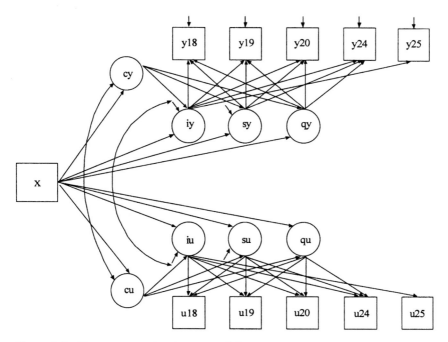

Figure 1.6 Two-part growth mixture modeling.

bar chart with four bars indicating a skewed distribution. The model diagram below the histogram shows that a mixture model can represent this where *c* influences *f*, but *f* has no within-class variability (there is no residual arrow pointing to *f*). Four classes of *c* results in four factor means for *f*. The positions of the four bars in the bottom graph represent scores on the latent variable distribution and are captured by the factor means in the four classes. The heights of the bars represent the class probabilities.

The relationship between the non-parametric approach and numerical integration is instructive and is illustrated in Figure 1.7 below. Numerical integration is necessary in maximum-likelihood estimation when a continuous latent variable has categorical indicators. With numerical integration, the latent variable distribution is also discretized, but the scores and the heights (called points and weights) are fixed, not estimated quantities. Figure 1.7 shows an example of a normal and a non-normal distribution, each with five points of support.

Cross-Sectional Analysis

Non-parametric estimation of latent variable distributions has both cross-sectional and longitudinal applications. In IRT applied to multiple-choice educational testing, Bock and Aitkin (1981) discussed the possibility of re-

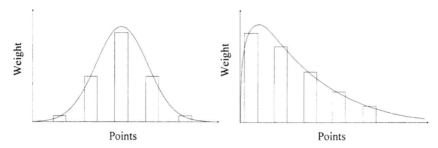

Figure 1.7 Non-parametric estimation of the random effect distribution using mixtures.

estimating the model with points and weights obtained from the posterior distribution, but suggested that this may not make much of a difference for the model parameters. This is also the experience of others (Robert J. Mislevy, personal communication), suggesting that the data commonly do not carry enough information about the particular form of the latent variable distribution. The normality assumption for the latent variable distribution may therefore be harmless in many applications, but perhaps not in cases where there is a strongly skewed or multimodal distribution. The non-parametric distribution shown in the histogram of branch 2 may be suitable for mental health applications where it is plausible that a large percentage of the population is unaffected. It is useful to try out such an alternative form and see if the likelihood improves to an important degree. An application to diagnostic criteria for alcohol dependence and abuse was studied in Muthén (2006), using the term latent class factor analysis.

Longitudinal Analysis

In longitudinal settings, Aitkin (1999) studied distributions of random effects in growth models, arguing that there it is hard empirically to find support for a normal distribution. He found that a few latent classes offered an adequate representation in several applications. Nagin and Land (1993) and Roeder, Lynch, and Nagin (1999) similarly argued for a non-parametric distribution of growth factors using the term "group-based" analysis, with application to groups of trajectories of criminal offenses. In some of Nagin's writings, however, the latent trajectory classes are given an interpretation as substantively meaningful subpopulations rather than seen as a mechanical way to non-parametrically represent a single population distribution (see Nagin, 2005). Figure 1.8 illustrates a unifying approach that does not seem to have been pursued by Nagin, namely using a combination of substantive and non-parametric classes. This example concerns analyses of the Cambridge data used in Nagin's research. Extending the analyses in Muthén, (2004), counts of biannual criminal convictions for youths aged

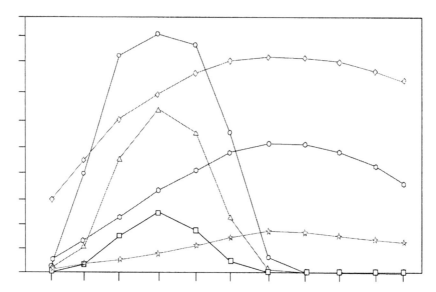

Figure 1.8   Three non-parametric classes within each of two substantive classes.

11–21 scored as 0, 1, and 2 for zero, one, or more convictions are analyzed using a quadratic growth model and six latent classes. The linear and quadratic growth factors were considered fixed, with zero variances. Figure 1.8 shows two substantively different latent classes of crime curves: early-peaking and late-peaking. Within each of these two classes, there are three variations: low, middle, and high. For each of the two substantive classes, the three variations are arrived at by using a three-class, non-parametric representation of the intercept growth factor in line with the branch 2 model diagram. Analogous to having the intercept factor random with a parametric intercept growth factor distribution, the linear and quadratic means were both held equal across the three non-parametric intercept classes. The non-parametric approach resulted in a skewed distribution for the intercept factor with more individuals in the low class as expected. An LCGA in line with Nagin's work would use six classes with no restrictions across classes on the linear and quadratic growth factor means.

Figure 1.9 compares three major approaches to growth modeling; hierachical linear modeling (HLM; see, e.g., Raudenbush & Bryk, 2002), growth mixture modeling (GMM; Muthén, 2004), and latent class growth analysis (LCGA; Nagin, 2005). LCGA and HLM are special cases of GMM. LCGA is a special case where there is no within-class variation so that the growth factor variances are all zero. In other words, there are no thin, individual curves in the graph implying that all individuals are the same within class. This in turn means that the within-class correlations across time are zero as

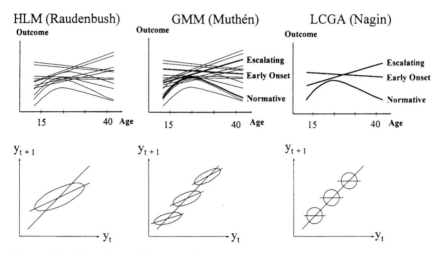

Figure 1.9 Growth modeling paradigms.

shown by the graph at the bottom right. HLM is a special case where there is only a single trajectory class. The thin, individual curves vary due to the growth factor variation. GMM allows more than one trajectory class as well as within-class variation, allowing non-zero within-class correlations across time. As mentioned above, GMM can be combined with a non-parametric representation of the growth factor distribution so that some latent classes have substantive meaning whereas others merely represent variation on the theme. A criminology application bridging the HLM, GMM, non-parametric GMM, and LCGA approaches is given in Kreuter and Muthén (2006).

Branch 3: Hybrid Modeling With Measurement Invariance and Parametric Factor Distribution

Going back up to the top of Figure 1.1, the first branching concerns measurement invariance or not. The non-invariant measurement branch often has a cluster analysis focus. Here, comparability of factor metrics across latent classes is not of importance, but the aim is to group individuals using a within-class model that is flexible. In some applications, however, the factor analysis focus is also present, although with no attempt to compare scores in different latent classes. The choice between a parametric and non-parametric latent variable distribution is available also here. The following discussion will focus on the parametric case of branch 3 given that there appears to be no literature on the non-parametric approach.

The bivariate graph of branches 3 and 4 shows two continuous items on the x and y axes, with the bivariate distribution of those two items displayed for two latent classes as two ellipses. Latent class analysis (LCA) specifies that the items are uncorrelated within each latent class, which means that the ellipses for the two classes in the figure would both have zero slopes. In contrast, the hybrid model of factor mixture analysis (FMA) allows the slopes to be estimated as non-zero. The branch 3 model diagram shows how this within-class correlation is represented. The factor f represents unobserved heterogeneity among individuals and because f influences all items the items have non-zero correlation within each class. Consider for example the measurement of depression by a set of diagnostic criteria. Here, f may represent environmental influence such as stress in a person's life, whereas c may represent genetically determined categories of depression. Therefore, f influences all items (say, diagnostic criteria) to varying degrees, such that the measurement slopes vary across items. Furthermore, the variance of the factor and the measurement parameters may be different in different classes.

The branch 3 measurement non-invariance is indicated in the model diagram by the arrows from c to the items, representing intercept differences, and by the broken arrows from c to the arrows from f to the items, representing slope differences. Using the depression example, the normative group of individuals who are not depressed may have smaller or a different pattern of measurement slopes (loadings) across the items due to being less influenced by stress or because stress has a different meaning for such individuals. Note that the model diagram does not include an arrow from c to f. This implies that the factor means in all classes can be standardized to zero, instead representing mean/probability differences across classes for an item by a direct arrow from c to the item. In cross-sectional analysis, the model in the diagram is referred to as an FMA model. LCA is a special case of FMA where f is absent, in other words has zero variance, so that only the arrows from c to the items are present.

Cross-Sectional Analysis

There are many cross-sectional examples of branch 3, referred to here as FMA models. The earliest application appears to be Blafield (1980), studying factor mixture analysis applied to Fisher's Iris data. Measurement parameters of slopes (factor loadings) were allowed to vary across classes to improve the classification, while measurement intercepts, factor means, and covariance matrices were class-invariant. Yung (1977) studied factor mixture models where all parameters were allowed to be class-varying. An application to the classic Holzinger-Swineford mental ability data was presented, resulting in a "mean-shift" model with non-invariant intercepts, invariant loadings, and invariant factor covariance matrix (factor means fixed at zero in all classes for identification given the class-varying intercepts). The generalization of factor mixture modeling to structural equation model mixtures has been studied in market research, for example by Jedidi, Jagpal, and DeSarbo (1997) with an application to market segmentation and customer satisfaction. Factor mixture work for continuous outcomes has also developed outside psychometrics. McLachlan and Peel (2000) discuss mixtures of factor analyzers where the within-class item correlations are described by an exploratory factor analysis (EFA) model. All measurement parameters are allowed to differ across the latent classes. The EFA model fixed the factor covariance matrix to an identity matrix (orthogonal factors) and let the residual variances vary across classes. McLachlan, Do, and Ambroise (2004) apply this model to microarray expression data, arguing that allowing for within-class correlation creates scientifically more meaningful clusters. In the most general case for continuous outcomes, FMA provides a within-class model with unstructured mean vector and covariance matrix, a commonly used model in finite mixture analysis. A classic example is the analysis of Fisher's Iris data as discussed in, for example, Everitt and Hand (1981).

A separate strand of factor mixture applications can be found in the IRT literature with a focus on categorical outcomes and applications to achievement testing. Mislevy and Verhelst (1990) used a mixture version of the 1-parameter Rasch model to classify individuals according to their solution strategies. Here, the measurement intercept (the "difficulty") varies across the latent classes, resulting in measurement non-invariance. Spatial visualization tasks can be solved by both rotational and by non-spatial analytic strategies, with item difficulties being higher for some items and lower for others depending on the latent class (strategy) the person belongs to. The authors also gave an example where the Rasch model holds for one latent class of individuals whereas the other class consists of those who guess at random. Mislevy and Wilson (1996) give an overview of mixture IRT models, including the Saltus model of Wilson (1989), distinguishing individuals with respect to different patterns of difficulties in line with theory of developmental psychology. For more recent work along the Saltus lines, see de Boeck, Wilson, and Acton (2005). The HYBRID model of Yamamoto (see Yamamoto & Gitomer, 1993) is a mixture model where an IRT model holds for one of the latent classes, whereas an LCA model model holds for other classes. Yamamoto and Gitomer apply this model to a test battery where several types of misunderstandings create item response patterns corresponding to latent classes. In the mixture IRT setting, measurement non-invariance is not a problem because the factor dimension of the different classes are recognized as different ability dimensions. Several chapters in this book describe further mixture IRT work.

Factor mixture analysis developments for categorical outcomes have also been made outside the IRT literature. Muthén (2006) and Muthén and Asparouhov (2006) considered dichotomous diagnostic criteria for substance use disorders, comparing LCA, FA/IRT, and FMA. FMA was chosen as the best model in both cases. Muthén, Asparouhov, and Rebollo (2006) applied FMA to alcohol criteria to provide latent variable phenotype modeling in a twin study of heritability.

Model testing is a challenging topic with mixture models in general and in particular with hybrid models. There are two reasons. First, it is difficult to test the model against data because no simple sufficient statistics such as mean vectors and covariance matrices exist. Second, comparing nested models, it is difficult to decide on the number of latent classes given that the regular likelihood ratio testing (LRT) does not give a chi-square test variable. For the second problem, Nylund, Asparouhov, and Muthén (in press) carried out a Monte Carlo simulation study of common indices such as the Bayesian Information Criterion (BIC), as well as the two newer approaches to LRT using non-chi-square distributions: Lo-Mendel-Rubin (LMR) and bootstrapped LRT (BLRT). The naïve LRT approach that incorrectly assumes a chi-square distribution was also studied (NCS). Table 1.2 shows how these four indices are able to pick the correct four classes for an LCA with 10 binary items. For each row, percentages are given for how frequently certain numbers of classes are chosen. It is seen that BIC tends to underestimate the number of classes, NCS tends to overestimate the number of classes, LMR falls in between, and BLRT does best. Research is needed on approaches for comparing models that differ not only in the number of classes, but also in the number of random effects (factors with non-zero variance).

To illustrate the previous points, the following is an FMA application in the area of diagnosing Attention Deficit Hyperactivity Disorder (ADHD). The analysis considers a UCLA clinical sample of 425 males ages 5–18. Subjects were assessed by clinicians through direct interview with the child (> 7 years) and through interview with mother about child using the KSADS instrument which has 9 inattentiveness items and nine hyperactivity items as shown in Table 1.3. The items were dichotomously scored. The research question concerned what types of ADHD are found in a treatment population. Table 1.4 shows model fitting results for three types of models: LCA, FA/IRT, and FMA. It is seen that the preferred LCA model is a 3-class model when

TABLE 1.2   Monte Carlo Simulation Excerpt from Nylund, Asparouhov, and Muthén (in press)

		BIC classes			NCS classes			LMR classes			BLRT classes		
	n	3	4	5	3	4	5	3	4	5	3	4	5
10-item	200	92	8	0	2	48	41	34	43	9	16	78	6
(complex	500	24	76	0	0	34	45	9	72	14	0	94	6
structure) with	1000	0	100	0	0	26	41	2	80	17	0	94	6
4 latent classes													

TABLE 1.3   The Latent Structure of ADHD

Inattentiveness items	Hyperactivity items
Difficulty sustaining attention on task/play	Difficulty remaining seated
Easily distracted	Fidgets
Makes a lot of careless mistakes	Runs or climbs excessively
Doesn't listen	Difficulty playing quietly
Difficulty following instructions	Blurts out answers
Difficulty organizing tasks	Difficulty waiting turn
Dislikes/avoids tasks	Interrupts or intrudes
Loses things	Talks excessively
Forgetful in daily activities	Driven by motor

TABLE 1.4   The Latent Structure of ADHD: Model Fit Results

Model	Log Likelihood	# parameters	BIC	BLRT p value for k–1
LCA—2c	–3650	37	7523	0.00
LCA—3c	**–3545**	**56**	**7430**	**0.00**
LCA—4c	–3499	75	7452	0.00
LCA—5c	–3464	94	7496	0.00
LCA—6c	**–3431**	**113**	**7547**	**0.00**
LCA—7c	–3413	132	7625	0.27
EFA—2f	**–3505**	**53**	**7331**	
FMA—2c, 2f	–3461	59	7280	
FMA—2c, 2f Class-varying factor loadings	**–3432**	**75**	**7318**	**χ^2-diff (16) = 58 $p < 0.01$**

judged by BIC, but is a 6-class model when judged by BLRT. The item profile plots corresponding to these two models are shown at the top of Figure 1.10. The items are arranged along the x axis with the nine inattentiveness items first, followed by the nine hyperactivity items. The 3-class model suggests a combined class, an inattentiveness only class, and a weakly defined hyperactivity only class. The 6-class model appears to show several variations on these three themes and is suggestive of a more dimensional representation. As seen in Table 1.4, an exploratory factor analysis (EFA) is a strong alternative to the LCA models. Here, EFA is the same as a two-dimensional IRT model, using 2-parameter logistic item characteristic curves. EFA has a better log-likelihood than the 3-class LCA for fewer parameters and a considerably better BIC than the 6-class model. Given these results, FMA is an

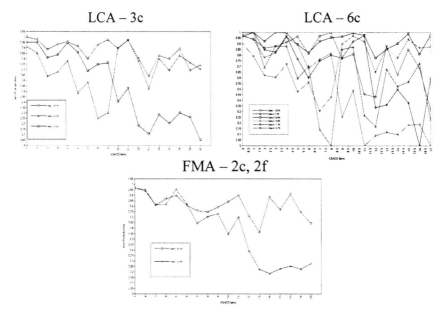

Figure 1.10 Item profiles for three-class LCA, six-class LCA, and two-class, two-factor FMA.

interesting alternative. As seen in Table 1.4, a 2-class FMA with 2 factors (one for inattentiveness and one for hyperactivity) has as good of a log-likelihood as the 6-class LCA but with far fewer parameters, and has a better BIC value than the EFA. Figure 1.10 shows that the hyperactivity only class disappears in the FMA model. The plot shows the mean probability of item endorsement, but it should be noted that variations in the item probabilities are produced within both classes as a function of the factor values.

Longitudinal Analysis

Longitudinal examples in branch 3 do not appear to have been published. Two different types of approaches can be considered. One model type is based on growth modeling where random effects influence an item measured at several time points. As seen when comparing the model diagrams in branches 1 and 3, this is different from the growth mixture modeling discussed in branch 1. The branch 3 model diagram shows that the latent class variable influences the items directly. Without the factor, this is an LCA model where the time structure is ignored and T repeated measures of the item is seen as T different items. This is a useful first analysis before turning to the branch 2 latent class growth analysis (LCGA) where growth factors govern the change over time in item means/probabilities. The LCA can be used to explore growth shapes in the data without impos-

Transition Probabilities

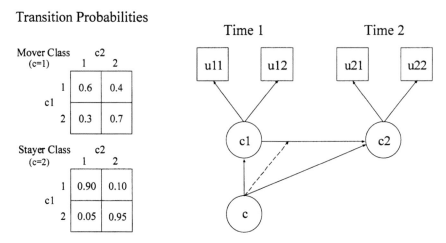

Figure 1.11 Latent transition analysis.

ing a particular growth function. As shown in the Figure 1.1 model diagram for branch 3, a factor may also be included to account for within-class correlations across time, allowing for a more flexible model in line with FMA. This factor does not have to be a growth factor where time determines the factor loadings, but a single-factor model with free factor loadings could for example be used.

Another longitudinal model type is based on auto-regressive modeling. As an example of the auto-regressive model type, latent transition analysis (LTA) considers several items measured at each of several time points to capture changes in a latent class variable. The latent class variable at one time point influences the latent class variable at the next time point in an auto-regressive fashion. Conventional LTA does not include a factor (factor variance is zero). A hypothetical example with two items measured at two time points is shown in Figure 1.11. LTA is an auto-regressive model in the sense that the time 2 status of the latent class variable $c2$ is dependent on the time 1 status of the latent class variable $c1$. Top left of Figure 1.11 is a hypothetical transition probability table (see "Mover Class"). For examples, individuals starting in the $c1 = 1$ class have the probability 0.4 to transition to the $c2 = 2$ class. The probabilities in each row of the table sum to one. The bottom table for the "Stayer Class" shows smaller probabilities for transitioning between classes. Conventional LTA does not include the latent class variable c at the bottom of the model diagram. Including this additional latent class variable makes it possible to distinguish between the latent classes of Movers and Stayers (see, e.g., Langeheine & van de Pol, 2002; Mooijaart, 1998).

Figure 1.12 shows a two-level extension of LTA by Asparouhov and Muthén (2008) in this volume. The application concerns aggressive-disruptive be-

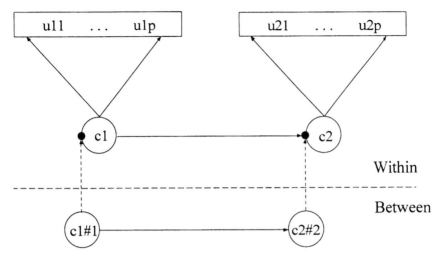

Figure 1.12 Two-level latent transition analysis.

havior in the classroom in Fall and Spring of first grade in Baltimore public schools (see also growth mixture modeling of these data in Muthén et al., 2002). The top part of the model diagram describes the within-level part of the model where the variables vary across students. The bottom part of the model diagram describes the between-level part of the model with variation across classrooms. The within-level shows filled circles next to the latent class variables c1 and c2, representing random intercepts. For example, the filled circle for c2 is the random intercept in the multinomial logistic regression of c2 on c1. On the between level, these random intercepts are continuous latent variables, shown as c1#1 and c2#1, representing the amount of classroom-level aggressive-disruptive behavior. On the between level, these two variables are connected via linear regression. Asparouhov and Muthén (2008) show that the classroom variation is large at both time points. The Fall between-classroom effect has a large impact on students' aggressive-disruptive behavior in the Fall. However, the effect also carries over into Spring, both through the individual level and through the classroom level.

A new model, which is a generalized, hybrid latent transition model will now be presented. This model includes f as shown in the Figure 1.1 model diagram of branch 3. A hypothetical example with p items at two time points is shown in Figure 1.13. At each time point, an FMA measurement model is specified with c having direct effects on the u's, and f describing continuous heterogeneity among individuals that reflects within-class correlation among the items. The latent class variable c2 is influenced by c1, but is also potentially influenced by f1. As shown by the vertical bars for the two latent classes in the bottom graph, individuals who at time 1 are low in the high

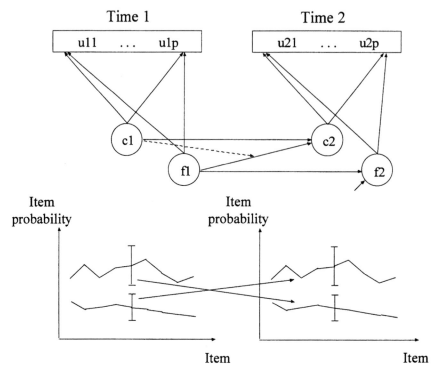

Figure 1.13   Factor mixture latent transition analysis.

class may be more likely to be in the low class at time 2 than individuals who are high in the high class. Similarly, individuals who are high in the low class may be more likely to be in the high class at time 2 than individuals who are low in the low class.

The FMA-LTA was applied to the data on aggressive-disruptive behavior in the classroom in Fall and Spring of first grade in Baltimore public schools referred to earlier. A model with two latent classes (high and low aggressive-disruptive behavior) and one factor dimension was found suitable for each of the two occasions. Table 1.5 shows the results of fitting the FMA-LTA versus the conventional LTA. It is seen that the log-likelihood is considerably better for FMA-LTA. Although this comes at the expense of 19 more parameters, the log-likelihood is so much better that this is more than compensated for. This advantage is reflected in the considerably better BIC value for the FMA-LTA model.

Table 1.6 shows the resulting estimates of the transition probability tables for the two model alternatives. The conventional LTA shows low probabili-

TABLE 1.5   Factor Mixture Latent Transition Analysis: Aggressive-Disruptive Behavior in the Classroom

Model	LogLikelihood	# parameters	BIC
Conventional LTA	−8,649	21	17,445
FMA LTA factors related across time	−8,012	40	16,306

TABLE 1.6   Estimated Latent Transition Probabilities, Fall to Spring

	Low	High
Conventional LTA		
Low	0.93	0.07
High	0.17	0.83
FMA-LTA		
Low	0.94	0.06
High	0.41	0.59

ties for transitioning from one class in Fall to a different class in Spring. In contrast, the FMA-LTA shows that there is a rather high probability (0.41) of transitioning from the high-aggressive class in Fall to the low-aggressive class in Spring.

CONCLUSION

This discussion has attempted to bring together seemingly disparate hybrid latent variable modeling efforts in many different application areas. The aim was to show that the various models are only slight variations on a few key themes. The critical aspects of the models are whether or not they specify measurement invariance and whether or not a parametric latent variable distribution is specified. By clearly showing the connections between different modeling branches and types of applications, researchers may be enabled to more easily learn from analysis experiences in neighboring fields. It is clear that much more methodological research is needed in this emerging research topic of mixture modeling and hopefully this chapter will stimulate such developments.

NOTE

1. This research was supported under grant K02 AA 00230 from NIAAA.

REFERENCES

Aitkin, M. (1999). A general maximum likelihood analysis of variance components in generalized linear models. *Biometrics, 55,* 117–128.

Asparouhov, T., & Muthén, B. (2008). Multilevel mixture models. In G. R. Hancock & K. M. Samuelsen (Eds.), *Advances in latent variable mixture models.* Charlotte, NC: Information Age Publishing, Inc.

Blafield, E. (1980). *Clustering of observations from finite mixtures with structural information.* Unpublished doctoral dissertation, Jyvaskyla studies in computer science, economics, and statistics, Jvasykla University, Jyvaskyla, Finland.

Bock, R. D., & Aitkin, M. (1981). Marginal maximum likelihood estimation of item parameters: Application of an EM algorithm. *Psychometrika, 46,* 443–459.

de Boeck, P., Wilson, M., & Acton, G. S. (2005). A conceptual and psychometric framework for distinguishing categories and dimensions. *Psychological Review, 112,* 129–158.

Dolan, C. V., Schmittmann, V. D., Lubke, G. H., & Neale, M. C. (2005). Regime switching in the latent growth curve mixture model. *Structural Equation Modeling: A Multidisciplinary Journal, 12,* 94–119.

Everitt, B. S., & Hand, D. J. (1981). *Finite mixture distributions.* London: Chapman and Hall.

Jedidi, K., Jagpal., H. S., & DeSarbo, W. S. (1997). Finite-mixture structural equation models for response-based segmentation and unobserved heterogeneity. *Marketing Science, 16,* 39–59.

Jöreskog, K. G. (1971). Simultaneous factor analysis in several populations. *Psychometrika, 36,* 409–426.

Kreuter, F., & Muthén, B. (2006). Analyzing criminal trajectory profiles: Bridging multilevel and group-based approaches using growth mixture modeling. Manuscript submitted for publication.

Langeheine, R., & van de Pol, F. (2002). Latent Markov chains. In J. A. Hagenaars & A. L. McCutcheon (Eds.), *Applied latent class analysis* (pp. 304–341). Cambridge, UK: Cambridge University Press.

Lin, H., Turnbull, B. W., McCulloch, C. E., & Slate, E. (2002). Latent class models for joint analysis of longitudinal biomarker and event process data: Application to longitudinal prostate-specific antigen readings and prostate cancer. *Journal of the American Statistical Association, 97,* 53–65.

Lubke, G. H., & Muthén, B. O. (2003). Performance of factor mixture models. Manuscript submitted for publication.

Lubke, G. H., & Muthén, B. O. (2005). Investigating population heterogeneity with factor mixture models. *Psychology Methods, 10,* 21–39.

Lubke, G. H., & Muthén, B. O. (2007). Performance of factor mixture models as a function of model size, covariate effects, and class-specific parameters. *Structural Equation Modeling, 14*(1), 26–47.

McDonald, R. P. (1967). Nonlinear factor analysis. *Psychometric Monograph No. 15.*

McDonald, R. P. (2003). A review of Multivariate taxometric procedures: Distinguishing types from continua. *Journal of Educational and Behavioral Statistics, 28*, 77–81.

McLachlan, G. J., Do, K-A., & Ambroise, C. (2004). *Analyzing microarray gene expression data.* New York: Wiley.

McLachlan, G. J., & Peel, D. (2000). *Finite mixture models.* New York: Wiley & Sons.

Meredith, W. (1964). Notes on factorial invariance. *Psychometrika, 19*, 187–206.

Meredith, W. (1993). Measurement invariance, factor analysis and factorial invariance. *Psychometrika, 58*, 525–543.

Mislevy, R. J., & Verhelst, N. (1990). Modeling item responses when different subjects employ different solution strategies. *Psychometrika, 55*, 195–215.

Mislevy, R. J., & Wilson, M. (1996). Marginal maximum likelihood estimation for a psychometric model of discontinuous development. *Psychometrika, 61*, 41–71.

Mooijaart, A. (1998). Log-linear and Markov modeling of categorical longitudinal data. In C. C. J. H. Bijleveld & T. van der Kamp (Eds.), *Longitudinal data analysis: Designs, models, and methods.* Newbury Park, CA: Sage Publications.

Muthén, B. (2002). Beyond SEM: General latent variable modeling. *Behaviormetrika, 29*, 81–117.

Muthén, B. (2004). Latent variable analysis: Growth mixture modeling and related techniques for longitudinal data. In D. Kaplan (Ed.), *Handbook of quantitative methodology for the social sciences* (pp. 345–368). Newbury Park, CA: Sage Publications.

Muthén, B. (2006). Should substance use disorders be considered as categorical or dimensional? *Addiction, 101* (Suppl. 1), 6–16.

Muthén, B., & Asparouhov. T. (2006). Item response mixture modeling: Application to tobacco dependence criteria. *Addictive Behaviors, 31*, 1050–1066.

Muthén, B., & Asparouhov, T. (2007). Growth mixture modeling: Analysis with non-Gaussian random effects. Forthcoming in Fitzmaurice, G., Davidian, M., Verbeke, G. & Molenberghs, G. (eds.), *Advances in Longitudinal Data Analysis.* Chapman & Hall/CRC Press.

Muthén, B., Asparouhov, T., & Rebollo, I. (2006). Advances in behavioral genetics modeling using Mplus: Applications of factor mixture modeling to twin data. *Twin Research and Human Genetics, 9*, 313–324.

Muthén, B., Brown, C. H., Masyn, K., Jo, B., Khoo, S. T., Yang, C. C., et al. (2002). General growth mixture modeling for randomized preventive interventions. *Biostatistics, 3*, 459–475.

Muthén, L. K., & Muthén, B. (1998–2007). *Mplus user's guide.* Los Angeles, CA: Muthén & Muthén.

Muthén, B., & Shedden, K. (1999). Finite mixture modeling with mixture outcomes using the EM algorithm. *Biometrics, 55*, 463–469.

Nagin, D. S. (2005). *Group-based modeling of development.* Cambridge, MA: Harvard University Press.

Nagin, D. S., & Land, K. C. (1993). Age, criminal careers, and population heterogeneity: Specification and estimation of a nonparametric, mixed Poisson model. *Criminology, 31*, 327–362.

Nylund, K. L., Asparouhov, T., & Muthén, B. (in press). Deciding on the number of classes in latent class analysis and growth mixture modeling: A Monte Carlo simulation study. *Structural Equation Modeling: A Multidisciplinary Journal.*

Olsen, M. K., & Schafer, J. L. (2001). A two-part random effects model for semi-continuous longitudinal data. *Journal of the American Statistical Association, 96,* 730–745.

Raudenbush, S. W., & Bryk, A. S. (2002). *Hierarchical linear models: Applications and data analysis methods* (2nd ed.). Thousand Oaks, CA: Sage.

Roeder, K., Lynch, K. G., & Nagin, D. S. (1999). Modeling uncertainty in latent class membership: A case study in criminology. *Journal of the American Statistical Association, 94,* 766–776.

Sörbom, D. (1974). A general method for studying differences in factor means and factor structure between groups. *British Journal of Mathematical and Statistical Psychology, 27,* 229–239.

Verbeke, G., & Lesaffre, E. (1996) A linear mixed-effects model with heterogeneity in the random-effects population. *Journal of the American Statistical Association, 91,* 217–221.

Wilson, M. (1989). Saltus: A psychometric model of discontinuity in cognitive development. *Psychological Bulletin, 105,* 276–289.

Yamamoto, K., & Gitomer, D. H. (1993). Application of a HYBRID model to a test of cognitive skill representation. In N. Fredriksen, R. Mislevy, & I. Beijar (Eds.), *Test theory for a new generation of tests.* Hillsdale, NJ: Erlbaum.

Yung, Y. F. (1997). Finite mixtures in confirmatory factor-analysis models. *Psychometrika, 62,* 297–330.

PART I

MULTILEVEL AND LONGITUDINAL SYSTEMS

.

CHAPTER 2

MULTILEVEL MIXTURE MODELS

Tihomir Asparouhov
Muthén & Muthén

Bengt Muthén
University of California, Los Angeles

INTRODUCTION

Multilevel statistical models allow researchers to evaluate the effects of individuals' shared environment on an individual's outcome of interest. Finite mixture models allow the researchers to question the homogeneity of the population and to classify individuals into smaller and more homogeneous latent subpopulations. Structural equation models allow the researchers to explore relations between observed variables and latent constructs. As researchers get more and more experience with these techniques they will inevitably want to use them within a unified framework that will enable them to combine all these ideas into a comprehensive statistical model that addresses all features present in the data. In this chapter we will describe a general statistical model that incorporates multilevel models, finite mixture models, and structural equation models into a very general and flexible

Advances in Latent Variable Mixture Models, pages 27–51
Copyright © 2008 by Information Age Publishing
All rights of reproduction in any form reserved.

modeling framework. The basis of this methodology was first implemented in M*plus* Version 3 (Muthén & Muthén, 2004), while the complete modeling framework described in this chapter became available in M*plus* 4.2 (Muthén & Muthén, 2006). Overall, the topic of multilevel mixture models is relatively new, although a number of articles have discussed similar frameworks and applications (see, e.g., Asparouhov, 2006; Bijmolt, Paas, & Vermunt, 2004; Vermunt, 2003; Vermunt & Magidson, 2005).

The goal of this chapter is to describe a two-level modeling framework that includes multiple latent variables. Each latent class variable can be either a within level variable, a between level variable, or a within-between level variable. The more general and flexible a statistical model is, the bigger the effort on the part of the researcher to interpret the model and the results in a practically meaningful way. In this chapter we will illustrate the general model with some specific simple examples and will describe the advantages of these models over conventional modeling techniques.

In Section 2 we describe the basic two-level mixture framework. In Section 3 we introduce the multiple class variables framework and describe a two-level latent transition analysis (LTA) model. In Section 4 we use the two-level LTA model to analyze students' behavior data and illustrate the modeling capabilities of this framework. In Section 5 we describe a two-level model with a between level latent class variable and compare this model to the model described in Section 2. We show that a between level latent class variable is a special case of the within-between latent class variable used in Sections 2 and 3. In Section 6 we describe a two-level model that incorporates both a within and a between latent class variables. In Section 7 we describe the grade of membership (GoM) model and show its advantages over latent class analysis (LCA) models. We also show how this model can be incorporated into the modeling framework described in Section 2. We illustrate the two- and three-class GoM model with an application to criminal offense data. The GoM modeling idea can be combined with most finite mixture models. In Section 8 we apply the GoM modeling idea to the factor mixture analysis (FMA) model. Thus, we incorporate the GoM, the IRT, and the LCA model into one general model. We illustrate the capabilities of this FMA-GoM model with a practical application using ADHD diagnostics data. In Section 9 we show that the 3PL guessing IRT model is a special case of the FMA-GoM model. Section 10 discusses the technical aspects of the estimation of the two-level mixture models.

THE BASIC TWO-LEVEL MIXTURE MODEL

In this section we will only consider two types of variables, categorical and normally distributed continuous variables. However, it is possible to incorporate other types of distributions and link functions as in the generalized linear models of McCullagh and Nelder (1989). Let y_{pij} be the pth observed dependent variable for individual i in cluster j. Suppose that C_{ij} is a latent categorical variable for individual i in cluster j which takes values $1,\ldots,L$. To construct a structural model for the categorical variables we proceed as in Muthén (1984) by defining an underlying normally distributed latent variable y_{pij}^* such that for a set of parameters τ_{ck}

$$[y_{pij} = k \mid C_{ij} = c] \Leftrightarrow \tau_{ck} < y_{pij}^* < \tau_{ck+1}. \tag{2.1}$$

A linear regression for y_{pij}^* is thus equivalent to a Probit regression for y_{pij}. Alternatively, y_{pij}^* can have a logistic distribution. A linear regression for y_{pij}^* will then translate to a logistic regression for y_{pij}. For continuous variables we define $y_{pij}^* = y_{pij}$.

Let $\mathbf{y}_{ij}^*$ be the vector of all dependent variables and let $\mathbf{x}_{ij}$ be the vector of all covariates. The structural part of the model is defined by

$$[\mathbf{y}_{ij}^* \mid C_{ij} = c] = \mathbf{v}_{cj} + \mathbf{\Lambda}_{cj}\mathbf{\eta}_{ij} + \mathbf{\varepsilon}_{ij} \tag{2.2}$$

$$[\mathbf{\eta}_{ij} \mid C_{ij} = c] = \mathbf{\mu}_{cj} + \mathbf{B}_{cj}\mathbf{\eta}_{ij} + \mathbf{\Gamma}_{cj}\mathbf{x}_{ij} + \mathbf{\xi}_{ij} \tag{2.3}$$

$$P(C_{ij} = c) = \frac{\exp(\alpha_{cj} + \mathbf{\beta}_{cj}x_{ij})}{\sum_c \exp(\alpha_{cj} + \mathbf{\beta}_{cj}x_{ij})}. \tag{2.4}$$

where $\mathbf{\eta}_{ij}$ contains normally distributed latent variables, $\mathbf{\varepsilon}_{ij}$ and $\mathbf{\xi}_{ij}$ are vectors of zero mean normally distributed residuals and $\mathbf{v}_{cj}$, $\mathbf{\Lambda}_{cj}$, $\mathbf{\mu}_{cj}$, $\mathbf{B}_{cj}$, $\mathbf{\Gamma}_{cj}$, α_{cj}, and $\mathbf{\beta}_{cj}$ are fixed or random model parameters. Some parameters have to be restricted for identification purpose. For example, the variance of $\mathbf{\varepsilon}_{pij}$ should be 1 for categorical variables y_{pij}. Also $\alpha_{Lj} = \beta_{Lj} = 0$.

The multilevel part of the model is introduced as follows. Each of the intercept, slope, or loading parameters in Equations 2.2 through 2.4 can be either a fixed coefficient or a cluster random effect, that is, a coefficient that varies across clusters. Let $\mathbf{\eta}_j$ be the vector of all such random effects and let $\mathbf{x}_j$ be the vector of all cluster level covariates. The between level model is then described by the following equation

$$\mathbf{\eta}_j = \mathbf{\mu} + \mathbf{B}\mathbf{\eta}_j + \mathbf{\Gamma}\mathbf{x}_j + \mathbf{\xi}_j \tag{2.5}$$

where $\mathbf{\xi}_j$ contains normally distributed residuals.

The above four equations comprise the definition of a simple multilevel structural mixture model. There are many extensions of this model that are available in the M*plus* framework. For example, observed dependent variables can be incorporated on the between level. Other extensions arise from the fact that a regression equation can be constructed between any two variables in the model. Such equations can be fixed or random effect regressions. Another interesting extension is to have all intercept and slopes parameters in Equation 2.5 vary across the latent class. This essentially amounts to interaction between the *C* variable and the random effect variables. Finally, the model described in this section can also be extended to include multiple latent class variables, as described in the following section.

MULTIPLE LATENT CLASS VARIABLES

In this section we describe the basic framework for a multilevel mixture model with multiple latent categorical variables C_1, C_2, and so forth. For simplicity, we will focus on the model with two latent categorical variables, C_1 and C_2; however, the framework easily extends to more than two class variables. One application of the multiple latent class variable framework is the latent transition analysis (LTA) model. The LTA model is used in longitudinal settings and C_t represents the latent class variable at time *t*. As in the previous section let $\mathbf{y}^*_{tij}$ be the vector of all dependent variables observed at time *t* and $\mathbf{x}_{tij}$ be the vector of all covariates at time *t*. The structural part of the model is given by

$$[\mathbf{y}^*_{tij} \mid C_{tij} = c] = \mathbf{v}_{tcj} + \mathbf{\Lambda}_{tcj}\mathbf{\eta}_{tij} + \mathbf{\varepsilon}_{tij} \tag{2.6}$$

$$[\mathbf{\eta}_{tij} \mid C_{tij} = c] = \mathbf{\mu}_{tcj} + \mathbf{B}_{tcj}\mathbf{\eta}_{tij} + \mathbf{\Gamma}_{tcj}\mathbf{x}_{tij} + \mathbf{\xi}_{tij} \tag{2.7}$$

where $\mathbf{\eta}_{tij}$ contains normally distributed latent variables and $\mathbf{\varepsilon}_{tij}$ and $\mathbf{\xi}_{tij}$ contain normal residuals. The multinomial logistic regression for the class variable C_1 at the first time point is given by

$$P(C_{1ij} = c) = \frac{\exp(\alpha_{1cj} + \beta_{1cj}x_{1ij})}{\sum_c \exp(\alpha_{1cj} + \beta_{1cj}x_{1ij})}. \tag{2.8}$$

The multinomial logistic regression for the second class variable C_2 includes C_1 as a covariate

$$P(C_{2ij} = d \mid C_{1ij} = c) = \frac{\exp(\alpha_{2dj} + \gamma_{dcj} + \beta_{2dj}x_{2ij})}{\sum_d \exp(\alpha_{2dj} + \gamma_{dcj} + \beta_{2dj}x_{2ij})}. \tag{2.9}$$

where c and d are the values of C_1 and C_2 and γ_{dcj} shows the effect of C_1 on C_2. Equations 2.8 and 2.9 form a recursive system of logit models (e.g., Agresti, 1996), and can be used to explore the dependence of C_2 on C_1. When there are more than two latent categorical variables, $C_1, \ldots, C_T$, the LTA models the dependence of C_t on the previous class variables $C_1, \ldots, C_{t-1}$. A first order Markov chain model is a special case of the LTA model which assumes that C_t depends only on C_{t-1} but not on earlier class variables.

As in the previous section, each of the intercept, slope, and loading parameters in Equations 2.6 through 2.9 can be either a fixed coefficient or a random effect. If η_j are all random effects and $\mathbf{x}_j$ are all cluster level covariates, Equation 2.5 again describes the cluster level structural model.

The multilevel framework described above allows us to study the effect of C_1 on C_2 on the individual level through Equation 2.9, but also on the cluster level by estimating the intercepts α_{2dj} and α_{1cj} as random effects and estimating a regression equation

$$\alpha_{2dj} = \mu + \beta \alpha_{1cj} + \varepsilon_{dcj}. \tag{2.10}$$

We illustrate this modeling technique with a practical example in the next section.

TWO-LEVEL LTA EXAMPLE

To illustrate the two-level LTA model we use data from the Baltimore study of aggressive and disruptive behavior in the classroom (see Muthén et al., 2002). The data to be analyzed consists of 10 Likert scale items known as the TOCA instrument. These items are teacher-rated student's behavior on the scale of 1 to 6. The resulting data are strongly skewed; for this reason, and to simplify our illustration, we convert all items to a binary scale (all values larger than 1 are recoded as 2). The statistical model that we present here is not intended to draw any substantive conclusions. We only illustrate the statistical methodology that could be useful in such applications. The model that we described, however, was suggested by Nicholas Ialongo (director of the Johns Hopkins Bloomberg School of Public Health) as an appropriate approach in these settings. We analyze the first grade data collected in the fall and in the spring. The 10 fall measurements, U_{1p}, $p = 1, \ldots 10$, are used to estimate a latent class model with two classes. Denote this class variable by C_1. Similarly, the 10 spring measurements, U_{2p}, $p = 1, \ldots 10$, are used to estimate a latent class model with two classes. Denote this class variable by C_2. Consequently, we combine the two models into a single model and estimate a transitional model from C_1 to C_2. Of particular interest is the effect of C_1 on C_2, which can be estimated in a logistic regression where C_2 is the dependent variable and C_1 is the predictor variable as in Equation 2.9. The structural part in the fall data is fairly similar to the structural part in the spring data so we estimate the joint model with a time invariant latent class model. In both the fall and the spring the first class contains the more disruptive students and the second class contains the less disruptive students. The model is described by the following equations:

$$P(U_{tp} = 2 \mid C_1 = c) = \pi_{cp} \tag{2.11}$$

$$P(C_1 = 1) = \frac{\exp(\alpha_1)}{\exp(\alpha_1) + 1} \tag{2.12}$$

$$P(C_2 = 1 \mid C_1) = \frac{\exp(\alpha_2 + \gamma I(C_1))}{\exp(\alpha_2 + \gamma I(C_1)) + 1}, \tag{2.13}$$

where $I(C_1)$ is an indicator variable for C_1, $I(C_1) = 1$ if $C_1 = 1$ and $I(C_1) = 0$ if $C_1 = 2$. Large values of γ will indicate a strong relation between C_1 and C_2. It is also possible to calculate the R^2 contribution of C_1 as a predictor of C_2:

$$R^2 = \frac{\gamma^2 P(C_1 = 1)(1 - P(C_1 = 1))}{\gamma^2 P(C_1 = 1)(1 - P(C_1 = 1)) + \pi^2 / 3}. \tag{2.14}$$

The term $\pi^2/3$ represents the variance of the error term with the logistic distribution.

The model described so far, however, will not allow us to evaluate the classroom effects on individual behavior. Previous analysis of the Baltimore data has shown that the average level of aggressive/disruptive behavior in the classroom strongly influences individual aggressive behavior development. To incorporate the classroom effects we estimate α_1 and α_2 as normally distributed classroom level random effects. These random effects will allow us to model the differences between the classrooms. For example, large α_1 values correspond to classrooms with a large number of disruptive students. In addition, we can estimate a regression equation between the two random effects

$$\alpha_{2j} = \mu + \beta \alpha_{1j} + \varepsilon_j, \tag{2.15}$$

where μ and β are fixed coefficients and ε_j is a mean zero normally distributed residual. Thus, the model will allow us to evaluate not only the individual effect of C_1 on C_2 in Equation 2.13, but also the direct effects of α_1 on C_1 in Equation 2.12, of α_2 on C_2 in Equation 2.13, and of α_1 on α_2 in

Equation 2.15. In addition, the total effect of α_1 on C_2 can be computed, which consists of two indirect effects: via C_1 and via α_2.

The results of this two-level LTA are presented in Table 2.1 and Figure 2.1. Table 2.1 contains the probability profiles for the two classes and all 10 TOCA instruments. It is clear that the two classes are very well separated. For the fall, data class 1 contains 46% of the students, while for the spring, data class 1 contains 52% of the students. The probability of switching from class 1 to class 2 is only 7% while the probability of switching from class 2 to class 1 is 18%.

TABLE 2.1 Probability Profiles for the Two Classes

	Parameter (Class)	
	π_{1p} $(C_t = 1)$	π_{2p} $(C_t = 2)$
Stubborn	0.92	0.36
Breaks Rules	0.96	0.29
Harms Others	0.73	0.03
Breaks Things	0.59	0.03
Yells at Others	0.82	0.18
Takes Others' Property	0.78	0.07
Fights	0.73	0.08
Lies	0.81	0.10
Teases Classmates	0.90	0.24
Trouble Accepting Authority	0.78	0.12

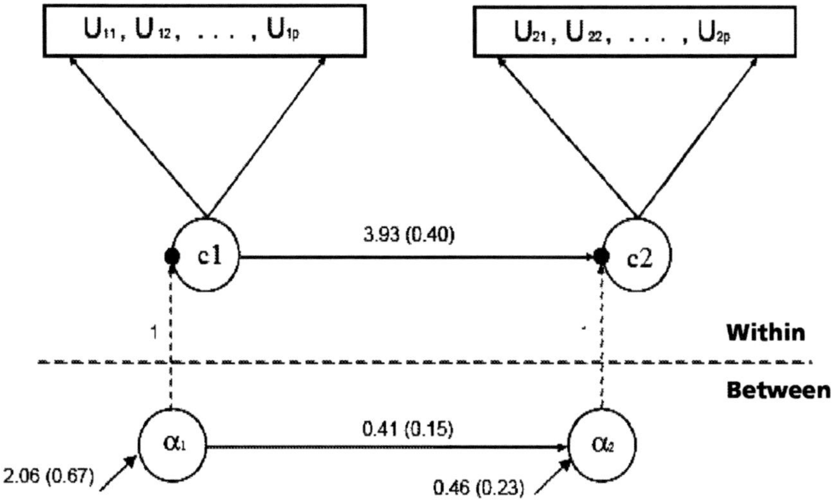

Figure 2.1 Two-level latent transition model.

Figure 2.1 shows the structure of the model and the estimated regression paths between C_j and α_j. As in Equation 2.14 we can compute the proportion of explained variance by this model. For example, the logistic regression equation from α_1 to C_1 shows that α_1 explains 39% of the variance of C_1. For C_2 this model explains 65% of the variance, 35% is explained by the classroom effect α_1, 25% is explained by the residual individual effect of C_1 (the part of C_1 that is unexplained by α_1), and 5% is explained by the residual classroom effect α_2 (the part of α_2 that is unexplained by α_1). Also, we can see that alone C_1 explains 41% of the variance of C_2, while the addition of the classroom effect α_2 explains now only 24% of the variance, which is a significant reduction from the fall classroom influence of 39%. This seems to indicate that much of the classroom influence has occurred in the fall.

BETWEEN LEVEL CLASS VARIABLES

Models where the latent class variable is not an individual level variable but is a cluster level variable are also of interest. Such models will allow us to explore population heterogeneity that is caused by cluster level variables. For example, when heterogeneity in students' performance is caused by heterogeneity among teachers the latent class variable in the model should be a cluster level variable. Small modifications in the model described in Section 2 are needed to accommodate between level class variables. The first modification is that

$$C_{ij} = C_j, \tag{2.16}$$

which essentially is a stochastic type equality constraint that guarantees equality between the class variables within a cluster of observations. The second modification is that Equation 2.4 should be replaced by

$$P(C_j = c) = \frac{\exp(\alpha_c + \beta_c x_j)}{\sum_c \exp(\alpha_c + \beta_c x_j)}, \tag{2.17}$$

because only between level covariates can be used as class predictors. Note also that the intercepts and slopes in Equation 2.17 are not random as we now have only one such equation per cluster, which makes it very hard to model these parameters as random effects. A between level class variable allows a more flexible structural model on the between level. In the between level structural model all parameters, including the residual variance covariance matrix, can be class specific:

$$\eta_j = \mu_c + B_c\eta_j + \Gamma_c x_j + \xi_j. \qquad (2.18)$$

In multilevel mixture models, estimating a between level class variable is actually easier than estimating a two-level model with a within level class variable. For example, the forward-backward algorithm (see Vermunt, 2003) is not needed when the class variable is on the between level; one can use a simple EM estimation approach as done by Muthén and Shedden (1999). However, it is not clear in general if between level heterogeneity is feasible to estimate in many practical applications with relatively small sample size on the between level. Between level sample size of 100 clusters or less is a rather common situation in multilevel data sets. The key question in modeling between level class variables is whether the within level observed variables can be used directly to identify the classes. If that is not the case, the within level observed data would be used simply to measure the between level random effects which will consequently identify the classes. In that case we will have a rather limited sample size to identify the classes, namely the between level sample size. An alternative way to pose this question is how to construct models with between level latent class variables where the within level data can contribute directly to the class formation and identification, which will produce more reliable models with more accurate parameter estimates.

The answers to the above questions will be illustrated with the following simulation study. We generate and estimate four different two-class mixture models and evaluate the stability of the estimation by the mean squared error (MSE) of parameters α_1 in Equation 2.4. The smaller the MSE of α_1 the easier it is to recover the heterogeneity in the population. We use a simple two-class mixture model for a two-level random effect regression

$$Y_{ij} = \mu_{cj} + \beta_{cj}X_{ij} + \varepsilon_{ij}, \qquad (2.19)$$

where μ_{cj} and β_{cj} are between level random effects with variance v and covariance 0. We vary the parameter v across the models. The means of μ_{cj} and β_{cj} are, respectively, 1 and 0.2 in class 1 and 0 and 0.8 in class 2. The residual variable ε_{ij} is a zero mean normally distributed variable with variance $\theta = 1$. The covariate X_{ij} is also a standard normal random variable. We vary the status of the C variable across the models. In Model 1 the variable is a within level variable and in Models 2 through 4 it is a between level variable. Table 2.2 summarizes the specification of the models and the MSE of the log odds ratio parameter α_1 in Equation 2.17. All models are generated and estimated with the correct specification. The sample size is 500 for all models, with 50 clusters of size 10 each. The two classes are of equal size. We generate 100 samples for each model.

TABLE 2.2   Model Specification and MSE of α_1

	C	v	MSE
Model 1	within	0.0	0.31
Model 2	between	0.0	0.10
Model 3	between	0.1	0.26
Model 4	between	0.2	0.44

The results of this simulation study show clearly that there are two competing forces moving in opposite directions when it comes to identifying between level class variables. The difference between Model 1 and Model 2 is only in the stochastic constraint in Equation 2.16. The fact that the class variables are constrained to be identical across clusters contributes greatly to easing the class identification process. The difference among Models 2 through 4 is in the variance of the between level random effects. As the variance increases, the advantage of the stochastic constraint in Equation 2.16 is lost due to the fact that the random effect means in the two classes are fewer and fewer standard deviation units apart, which makes the two classes overlap. The conclusion from this simulation study is that to produce reliable models with between level class variables the models should include a sufficient number of parameters that differ across classes and utilize the within level observed data directly. Such parameters are class-varying fixed effects or random effects with large variation across class but small variation across clusters. For example, a sound strategy would be to include significant between level random effects but to eliminate from the model between level random effects that are not significant and replace them with fixed effects that can vary across classes.

The next modeling issue we want to address is the situation when the researcher does not know *a priori* whether the latent class variable is a cluster level variable or an individual level variable. This is a substantively important question as it provides insight into the causation of the heterogeneity. We illustrate this issue with the following simulation study. We generate a sample according to a modification of Model 4 where the random slope variance is fixed to 0 while the random intercept variance is 0.2. We generate a sample of 100 clusters of size 10 for a total of 1,000 observations. Let us call this Model 5. We analyze the data according to this true model assuming that the class variable is a between level variable. We also analyze these data according to Model 6 where the latent class variable C is assumed to be a within level variable with a between level random intercept α_1. Model 6 would be the model of choice when the researcher is uncertain about the status of the latent class variable. In Model 6 we assume that the class variable is a within level variable, but with a between level component, so

TABLE 2.3   Parameter Estimates (standard errors) and Log-Likelihood Value

Parameter	True Value	Model 5	Model 6
μ_1	1.0	0.90(0.14)	0.90(0.13)
μ_2	0.0	0.13(0.13)	0.12(0.12)
β_1	0.2	0.25(0.07)	0.25(0.06)
β_2	0.8	0.81(0.07)	0.81(0.06)
θ	1.0	1.01(0.04)	1.01(0.04)
v	0.2	0.22(0.08)	0.22(0.08)
LL		−1517.6	−1517.6

essentially it is a variable that has both individual and cluster effect, that is, within and between level variable. The results of the analysis are presented in Table 2.3. The two estimated models have almost identical parameter estimates. For all parameters the true value is within the confidence limits. The variance of α_1 in Model 6 was estimated as 609 which can be used to compute the intraclass correlation (ICC) value for C:

$$ICC = \frac{Var(\alpha_1)}{Var(\alpha_1) + \pi^2/3} = 0.995. \tag{2.20}$$

This simulation shows that even if the latent class variable is a between level variable the data can be analyzed as if the variable is a between-within level variable as in Model 6.

Formal tests can be constructed to test whether the class variable is only a between level variable or it is a between-within level variable. Using the ICC value one can test whether this value is significantly different from 1 by constructing a confidence interval using the delta method or by using the bootstrap resampling method. Note, however, that because the ICC parameter is approaching its boundary value of 1, the delta method is not as reliable and should only be used as an approximation. This is because maximum likelihood estimation of bounded parameters does not follow the usual asymptotic theory of unbounded parameters. For practical purposes, however, an ICC value above 0.8 would be a good indication to pursue models where the class variable is only on the between level. In addition, the LRT test can be used to test for significant differences between the two models. That is because the two models are actually nested and Model 6 has one more parameter than Model 5. This additional parameter is the variance of α_1. Again, however, because of the boundary proximity the LRT test will not have the usual χ^2 distribution when the ICC approaches 1.

Finally, let us focus on the question of why Model 5 is nested within Model 6. When the variance of α_1 in Model 6 approaches infinity the model becomes equivalent to Model 5 because the variables C_{ij} are so highly correlated that

$$P(C_{i_1 j} \neq C_{i_2 j}) \approx 0; \qquad (2.21)$$

that is, the stochastic constraint in Equation 2.16 is mandated by the model. Figure 2.2 and Figure 2.3 also illustrate this point. In Figure 2.2 we plot the conditional class probability $P(C_{ij} = 1 \mid \alpha_1)$ on a standard scale of α_1, when the variance of α_1 is 100 and the mean is 0. Figure 2.3 shows this probability when the variance of α_1 is 10,000. It is clear from these plots that for most values of α_1 the conditional probability is either 0 or 1. This is especially so when the variance of α_1 is 10,000. When this probability is 0 or 1 then C_{ij} cannot vary across individuals in the cluster as it is completely determined by the value of the random effect α_1 in the jth cluster. When the variance of α_1 is large the influence of the random intercept α_1 on C_{ij} is large, which makes the class variables within a cluster so highly correlated that no variation of the class variables within the cluster is possible.

Table 2.4 summarizes the modeling possibilities for the latent class variables and the corresponding interpretation for the intercept variance parameter. Note, however, that when estimating a between level class vari-

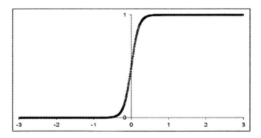

Figure 2.2 Conditional latent class probability, $\mathrm{Var}(\alpha_1) = 100$.

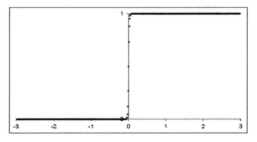

Figure 2.3 Conditional latent class probability, $\mathrm{Var}(\alpha_1) = 10,000$.

TABLE 2.4 Specification for Latent Class Variable Status

Status	Var(α_{qj})
Within	0
Between	huge
Within-Between	positive

able model there is a numerical advantage for directly specifying the class variable as a between level variable as in Model 5, rather than as a within-between level variable with large variance as in Model 6. Both approaches are possible in M*plus* 4.2. The advantage of the Model 5 approach is that it does not use numerical integration for the random effect α_{qj}. Model estimation with numerical integration will typically be more computationally demanding.

WITHIN AND BETWEEN CLASS VARIABLES

All three types of latent class variables given in Table 2.4 can be used simultaneously in a model. The variables can be measured and predicted by different observed variables, as in the two-level LTA model described in Section 3, or they can be measured and predicted by the same observed variables. Within level latent class variables can be measured and predicted only by within level observed variables. Between level latent class variables can be measured by within and between level observed variables but can be predicted only by between level observed variables. Within-between level latent class variables can be measured and predicted by within level observed variables, while the random effects a_{qj} can be measured and predicted by between level observed variables.

In this section we illustrate these modeling combinations by describing a model that includes both a within and a between latent class variable. Let C_{ij} be a latent class variable for individual i in cluster j which takes values $1,\ldots,L$. Let D_j be a between level latent class variable for cluster j which takes values $1,\ldots,M$. The within level model is

$$[\mathbf{y}_{ij}^{*} \mid C_{ij} = c, D_j = d] = \mathbf{v}_{cdj} + \mathbf{\Lambda}_{cdj}\mathbf{\eta}_{ij} + \mathbf{\varepsilon}_{ij} \tag{2.22}$$

$$[\mathbf{\eta}_{ij} \mid C_{ij} = c, D_j = d] = \mathbf{\mu}_{cdj} + \mathbf{B}_{cdj}\mathbf{\eta}_{ij} + \mathbf{\Gamma}_{cdj}\mathbf{x}_{ij} + \mathbf{\xi}_{ij}. \tag{2.23}$$

The multinomial logistic regression for the within class variable C_{ij} includes the between class variable D_j as a covariate,

$$P(C_{ij} = c \mid D_j = d) = \frac{\exp(\alpha_{cj} + \gamma_{cdj} + \boldsymbol{\beta}_{cj} x_{ij})}{\sum\limits_c \exp(\alpha_{cj} + \gamma_{cdj} + \boldsymbol{\beta}_{cj} x_{ij})}, \qquad (2.24)$$

where γ_{cdj} shows the effect of D on C. For identification purposes $\alpha_{Lj} = \beta_{Lj} = \gamma_{Ldj} = \gamma_{cMj} = 0$.

Each of the intercept, slope, or loading parameters in Equations 2.22 through 2.24 can be either a fixed coefficient or a cluster random effect. If $\boldsymbol{\eta}_j$ is the vector of all random effects, then the between level model is described by

$$[\boldsymbol{\eta}_j \mid D_j = d] = \boldsymbol{\mu}_d + \mathbf{B}_d \boldsymbol{\eta}_j + \boldsymbol{\Gamma}_d \mathbf{x}_j + \boldsymbol{\xi}_j. \qquad (2.25)$$

The model for the between level class variable D_j is also a multinomial logit regression

$$P(D_j = d) = \frac{\exp(\alpha_d + \boldsymbol{\beta}_d \mathbf{x}_j)}{\sum\limits_d \exp(\alpha_d + \boldsymbol{\beta}_d \mathbf{x}_j)}, \qquad (2.26)$$

where $\mathbf{x}_j$ contains the between level covariates.

THE GRADE OF MEMBERSHIP MODEL

In this section we show how to utilize the two-level mixture framework described in Section 2 to estimate the Grade of Membership (GoM) model. GoM is not a multilevel model, it is a single level model. The model is an extension of the latent class analysis (LCA) model that allows not only separation of individuals into classes that show similar outcomes but also allows for individuals to be modeled as partially members of several different classes. Individuals with such partial class membership will be those who, on some measurements, behave like the individual in one class while on some other measurements behave like individuals in another class. Partial class membership is a substantively useful concept for modeling individuals who are in a transitional state. For example, when modeling different levels of disability in the elderly, an individual can be classified as healthy or as disabled, but can also be in a state of deteriorating health; in this latter case the individual can be classified as partially healthy and partially disabled and the level of membership in each of the two classes can be specific to that particular individual. The GoM modeling idea also allows us to determine whether individuals transition from one class to another even when we have a cross-sectional sample rather than longitudinal. Observing individuals with partial membership at one point in time is an indication that individuals transition from one class to another.

In this chapter we follow the Erosheva (2002) exposition of the GoM model. For simplicity we assume that all observed variables are binary and that there are only two classes in the model; however, the model description below generally applies to any type of observed variables and any number of classes. Let Y_{ij} be the ith measurement for individual j. In the LCA model a class variable C_j is defined for each individual and the distribution of Y_{ij} is given by

$$P(Y_{ij} = 1 \mid C_j = c) = \Phi(\tau_{ic}), \tag{2.27}$$

where Φ is the standard normal distribution function and τ_{ic} is a threshold parameter. In the GoM model a latent class variable C_{ij} is defined specifically for the ith measurement of individual j. The distribution of Y_{ij} is given by

$$P(Y_{ij} = 1 \mid C_{ij} = c) = \Phi(\tau_{ic}). \tag{2.28}$$

The distribution of C_{ij} is given by

$$P(C_{ij} = 1) = f_j, \tag{2.29}$$

where f_j is a subject-specific random effect of some kind. Typically, f_j is given a Dirichlet prior which facilitates Bayesian estimation methods (see Erosheva, 2003), although other functional forms can be used as well. Here we will adopt the logistic regression equation that we have used in this chapter up to now. Let

$$P(C_{ij} = 1) = \frac{\exp(\alpha_{1j})}{1 + \exp(\alpha_{1j})}, \tag{2.30}$$

where α_{1j} is a normally distributed random variable. Equations 2.28 and 2.30 describe a simple GoM model. It is easy to see that this model is a special case of the two-level mixture model described in Section 2 where now the individual j takes the role of a cluster j and the multivariate vector of all measurements Y_{ij} is treated as univariate observations clustered in the individual j. Many statistical packages, including M*plus*, implement data transformation routine that converts the data from the original "wide-multivariate" format to "long-multilevel" format. Such transformation is applied here as well. It is easy to see now that the GoM model is equivalent to a univariate two-level mixture model. There is one complication in the GoM model that is not directly available in the two-level mixture model. This complication is the fact that the parameter τ_{ic} depends on i, that is, it varies across observations in the cluster. This complication, however, can easily be resolved by incorporating dummy variable for all measurements. Suppose that there are L measurements and N individuals in the sample. Define the dummy variables X_{qij} for $i = 1,\ldots,N$, $j = 1,\ldots,L$, and $q = 1,\ldots,L$:

$$X_{qij} = \begin{cases} 1 & \text{if } q = i \\ 0 & \text{otherwise} \end{cases}. \tag{2.31}$$

Each observation now consist of one dependent variable Y_{ij} and L independent variables X_{qij} for $q = 1,\ldots,L$. Equation 2.28 can now be written as

$$P(Y_{ij} = 1 \mid C_{ij} = c) = \Phi(\sum_{q=1}^{L} \tau_{qc} X_{qij}). \tag{2.32}$$

Note now that the parameters in Equation 2.32 are independent of i and thus the GoM model is part of the two-level framework described in Section 2.

The above formulation of the GoM model has the advantage that it can easily accommodate predictors $\mathbf{X}_j$ for the class allocation by adding a regression equation such as

$$\alpha_{1j} = \alpha_1 + \boldsymbol{\beta} \mathbf{X}_j + \varepsilon_j. \tag{2.33}$$

Equivalently, the predictors can be added directly in the multinomial logistic regression (Equation 2.30). It is also possible to add item specific covariates. This is done by adding a new covariate in Equation 2.32 which is the product of the dummy variable corresponding to that item and the covariate.

The above formulation of the GoM model also allows us to easily see that the LCA model is nested within the GoM model. In fact, the two class GoM model that we described above has just one more parameter than the 2 class LCA model. This parameter is the variance of the random effect variable α_{1j}. Note that the LCA is different from the GoM model only by the fact that it imposes the stochastic restriction (Equation 2.16), which basically means that all measurements for individual j can be in one and the same class. As we explained in the previous section the stochastic restriction is equivalent to fixing the variance of α_{1j} to infinity, or to a numerically large value. For GoM models with $K > 2$ classes, Equation 2.30 is replaced by

$$P(C_{ij} = c) = \frac{\exp(\alpha_{cj})}{1 + \sum_{c=1}^{K-1} \exp(\alpha_{cj})}, \tag{2.34}$$

where now there are $K-1$ random effects α_{cj} for $c = 1,\ldots,K-1$. The LCA class model with K classes is again nested within the GoM model with K classes, which has $K(K-1)/2$ more parameters, namely the variances and covariance parameters of the random effects α_{cj}. When the variances are fixed to large values and the covariances to 0 the GoM model becomes equivalent to the LCA model.

In the estimation of the GoM model the random effects α_{cj} are numerically integrated which makes the estimation more challenging when there is a large number of classes. To avoid this problem a more restricted model has been proposed by Hedeker (2003) and Vermunt (2003) which essentially adds a one factor analysis model without residuals on the random effects α_{cj}

$$\alpha_{cj} = \alpha_c + \lambda_c \eta_j, \qquad (2.35)$$

where η_j is a standard normal random effect and a_c and λ_c are fixed parameters. This model requires only one dimension of numerical integration and has $K-1$ more parameters, namely the loadings parameters λ_c. Note, however, that the LCA model is not nested within this more restricted GoM model. When $K = 2$ the restricted GoM (Equation 2.35) is equivalent to the unrestricted GoM.

It is possible to include other types of dependent variables in the above formulation of the GoM model. If the variables are continuous, for example, the dummy variable structure described above will produce item-specific class varying means. For polytomous variables taking d categories, the Probit equation (Equation 2.34) should be replaced with a multinomial logistic regression so that each dummy variable contributes $d-1$ parameters rather than 1 and all item probabilities are unconstrained and class specific.

We now illustrate the GoM model and compare it to the LCA model. We use the Antisocial Behavior (ASB) data taken from the National Longitudinal Survey of Youth (NLSY) that is sponsored by the Bureau of Labor Statistics. These data are made available to the public by Ohio State University, and include 17 antisocial behavior items that were collected in 1980 when respondents were between the ages of 16 and 23. The ASB items assessed the frequency of various behaviors during the past year, with 8 items addressing property offense, 5 items addressing personal offense, and 4 items addresing drug offense. The items were dichotomized (0/1) with 0 indicating that the offense had not occurred in the past year. A sample of 7,326 respondents has complete data on these antisocial behavior items.

Table 2.5 shows the log-likelihood values obtained for the two- and three-class LCA and GoM models. For the three-class GoM model we used the restricted model (Equation 2.35). For both the two- and the three-class mod-

TABLE 2.5   Log-Likelihood Comparison for the LCA and GoM Models

Status	2 class	3 class
LCA	−42625.7	−41713.1
GoM	−42159.1	−41554.6

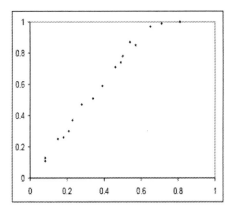

Figure 2.4   Seventeen item probability profiles for the offense prone class for GoM vs. LCA models.

els the GoM model improved the log-likelihood value substantially. The GoM estimation showed more dependence upon starting values than the LCA model. To obtain these results we used 30 randomized starting value sets and conducted a preliminary optimization using only 10 EM iterations. Complete convergence was then obtained for the five starting value sets that led to the highest log-likelihood values in the preliminary optimization. A good strategy for selecting starting values for the GoM model estimation is to use the LCA parameter estimates. The GoM model estimation is also more computationally demanding because it needs numerical integration for the random effects α_g and because the data are expanded to include the dummy variables.

In the two-class model both the LCA and the GoM model essentially split the population into a more offense-prone class and less offense-prone class. Figure 2.4 shows the probability profiles for the offense-prone class for the two models. Each of the plotted points represents an item, where the X coordinate is the LCA probability of occurrence and the Y coordinate is the GoM probability of occurrence. The probability profiles are different. The GoM probabilities in this class are all higher than the LCA probabilities. However, the correlation between the two sets of probabilities is 99%. The difference in the probability profiles is due to the fact that the two models identify the classes differently. In the LCA model the classes are identified by the average probability pattern in the class while in the GoM model the classes are identified by the extreme probability pattern that members are drawn to as they become closer and closer to being fully in that class.

COMBINING LCA, IRT, AND GoM MODELS

In this section we describe a model that incorporates the modeling capabilities of three types of models, namely the LCA, IRT, and the GoM model. The combination of LCA and IRT models is sometimes refereed to as factor mixture analysis (FMA) model or alternatively as mixture IRT model. This model was used, for example, by Qu, Tan, and Kutner (1996) to model residual correlations within a class. In Muthén (2006) and Muthén and Asparouhov (2006), FMA models were also explored as substantively important generalizations of the IRT and LCA models.

The following is a brief formulation of the FMA model. As in the previous section, for simplicity we assume that Y_{ij} is the ith binary observed variables for individual j. Let C_j be the latent class variable for individual j. The model is then described by the following two equations:

$$P(Y_{ij} = 1 \mid C_j = c) = \Phi(\tau_{ic} + \lambda_{ic}\eta_j) \tag{2.36}$$

$$P(C_j = c) = \frac{\exp(\alpha_c)}{1 + \sum_{c=1}^{K-1} \exp(\alpha_c)} \tag{2.37}$$

where η_j is a standard normal random effect and τ_{ic}, λ_{jc}, and α_c are fixed parameters. To generalize this model to include partial class membership into an FMA-GoM model, we proceed as in the previous section. Let C_{ij} be an item-specific latent class variable. The FMA-GoM model is described by the following equations:

$$P(Y_{ij} = 1 \mid C_{ij} = c) = \Phi(\tau_{ic} + \lambda_{ic}\eta_j) \tag{2.38}$$

$$P(C_{ij} = c) = \frac{\exp(\alpha_{cj})}{1 + \sum_{c=1}^{K-1} \exp(\alpha_{cj})} . \tag{2.39}$$

where α_{cj} are normally distributed random variables. As in the previous section, Equation 2.38 is equivalent to

$$P(Y_{ij} = 1 \mid C_{ij} = c) = \Phi(\sum_{q=1}^{L} \beta_{qc} X_{qij}) \qquad (2.40)$$

$$\beta_{qc} = \tau_{qc} + \lambda_{qc} \eta_j, \qquad (2.41)$$

This model is again a special case of the framework described in Section 2. All random effects α_{cj} and η_j are now numerically integrated. Just as the LCA model is nested in the GoM model, the FMA model (Equations 2.36 and 2.37) is nested within the FMA-GoM model (Equations 2.39 through 2.41). For example, for a two-class model the FMA-GoM model has just one more parameter.

For illustration, we estimate a two-class FMA-GoM model for a UCLA clinical sample of 425 males ages 5–18, all with ADHD diagnosis. The data consist of nine inattentiveness items and nine hyperactivity items, all dichotomously scored. For simplicity, we estimate the restricted FMA model where the factor loadings λ_{jc} are class invariant, $\lambda_{jc} = \lambda_i$. Table 2.6 shows the log-likelihood values and the number of parameters for the two-class LCA, FMA, and FMA-GoM models. In this example, the FMA improved the likelihood dramatically over the LCA model, however the FMA-GoM improved the likelihood only marginally. The ICC of the α_{1j} was estimated to be 0.86. Thus, in this example the concept of partial class membership is not supported by the data. The substantive conclusion appears to be that individuals are never in a transitional phase and are preset to be in one of the two classes.

One of the original applications of the FMA/Mixture IRT model involves the separation of individuals into classes based on similar responses to the various items. For example, individuals solve mental rotation problems using one of several solution strategies. The Mixture IRT model allows us to separate the population into classes that appear to be using the same solution strategy. Adding the GoM modeling idea to the Mixture IRT model will allow us also to model individuals who may use one strategy on one item but another strategy on a different item.

TABLE 2.6 Log-Likelihood Comparison for the LCA, FMA, and FMA-GoM Models

Model	Log-likelihood	Number of Parameters
LCA	–3650.0	37
FMA	–3502.4	56
FMA-GoM	–3501.7	57

THE THREE PARAMETER GUESSING IRT MODEL

In this section we show that the three parameter (3PL) guessing IRT model is a special case of the FMA-GoM model described in the previous section. The 3PL model is described by the following equation

$$P(Y_{ij} = 1) = g_i + (1 - g_i)\Psi(a_i(\eta_j - b_i)) \tag{2.42}$$

where Ψ is the normal or the logistic distribution function. Now let us consider the following FMA-GoM model with two classes:

$$P(Y_{ij} = 1 \mid C_{ij} = c) = \Psi(\tau_{ic} + \lambda_{ic}\eta_j) \tag{2.43}$$

$$P(C_{ij} = 1) = \frac{\exp(\alpha_{1j} + \sum_q \gamma_q X_{qij})}{1 + \exp(\alpha_{1j} + \sum_q \gamma_q X_{qij})}. \tag{2.44}$$

The difference between the model in Equations 2.38 and 2.39 and that directly above is that in the multinomial logistic regression on C_{ij} we have included covariates. Let us now constrain several of the parameters in the above model:

$$\alpha_{1j} = 0$$

$$\lambda_{i1} = 0$$

$$\tau_{i1} = 15.$$

The constant 15 above is chosen to be sufficiently high so that $\Psi(15) \approx 1$. This approximation holds for both the normal and the logistic distribution. Given these constraints we can simplify the above model:

$$P(Y_{ij} = 1 \mid C_{ij} = 1) = 1 \tag{2.45}$$

$$P(Y_{ij} = 1 \mid C_{ij} = 2) = \Psi(\tau_{i2} + \lambda_{i2}\eta_j) \tag{2.46}$$

$$P(C_{ij} = 1) = \frac{\exp(\gamma_i)}{1 + \exp(\gamma_i)}. \tag{2.47}$$

It is now easy to see that the model in Equation 2.42 is just a reparameterization of the model directly above in Equations 2.45 through 2.47. The parameters in the former are obtained from the parameters of the latter via the following equations:

$$g_i = \frac{\exp(\gamma_i)}{1 + \exp(\gamma_i)} \qquad (2.48)$$

$$a_i = \lambda_{i2} \qquad (2.49)$$

$$b_i = -\frac{\tau_{i2}}{\lambda_{i2}} \cdot \qquad (2.50)$$

TECHNICAL ASPECTS OF THE ESTIMATION

All models presented in this article were estimated with M*plus* Version 4.2. M*plus* uses maximum likelihood estimation with robust standard error estimation (see White, 1980).

The estimation of Multilevel Mixture Models presents a number of challenges. The maximum likelihood estimation of mixture models in general is susceptible to local maximum solutions. To avoid this problem M*plus* uses an algorithm that randomizes the starting values for the optimization routine. Initial sets of random starting values are first selected. Partial optimization is performed for all starting value sets which is followed by complete optimization for the best few starting value sets. It is not clear how many starting value sets should be used in general. Different models and data may require different starting value sets. Most results in this article were obtained by selecting 20 initial sets and completing the convergence process for the best five. One useful criterion for gauging the thoroughness of the starting value perturbation is that the best log-likelihood value is reached at least twice; however, even if this criterion is satisfied, it is no guarantee that the number of starting value sets is sufficient. A sound strategy to minimize the impact of the starting values of the optimization routine is to build Multilevel Mixture Models gradually starting with simpler models that have few random effects and classes. Consequently, one can use the parameter estimates from the simpler models for starting values for the more advanced models.

Another estimation challenge is the fact that most Multilevel Mixture Models require numerical integration techniques for some of the normally distributed latent variables in the model. Both adaptive and non-adaptive numerical integration can be performed in M*plus*. In general, adaptive numerical integration tends to be more accurate but it is also more unstable and frequently can fail during the optimization process. In such situations,

M*plus* will abandon adaptive integration and will use non-adaptive integration. Gauss-Hermite, trapezoid, and Monte-Carlo integration methods are implemented in M*plus*. It is well know that Gauss-Hermite is very dependent on the adaptiveness of the integration method and without it can produce very inaccurate results. This is not the case for the trapezoid integration method, which performs quite well even without adaptive integration. Given the instability of adaptive integration we prefer the trapezoid integration method over Gauss-Hermite, which is also the M*plus* default and the method we used for the results presented here. The Monte-Carlo integration method is appropriate when the number of integration dimensions is high (five or more). It is usually the least accurate integration method. Model parameterization is also a very important but largely unexplored component in the estimation of Multilevel Mixture Models. Certain parameterizations will facilitate faster convergence during optimization; see, for example, the PM-EX algorithm of Liu, Rubin, and Wu (1998). Another parameterization that generally improves convergence speed is the Cholesky parameterization (see Hedeker & Gibbons, 1996). This parameterization is available for all Multilevel Mixture Models in M*plus*. Another attractive feature of this parameterization is that, when it is used with non-adaptive quadrature, it can guarantee monotonically increasing likelihood in the EM-algorithm, which makes the convergence process very stable even with a small number of integration points and a large number of integration dimensions. The parameterization in the model can also affect the number of dimensions of the numerical integration, and therefore affect dramatically the computational speed. Ultimately, choosing the most optimal parameterization for a model is more difficult than choosing other technical options. M*plus* is very flexible and can be used with most parameterizations, especially since M*plus* can implement a separate auxiliary parameterization model in addition to the statistical model. There are other technical options related to numerical integration as well; see Muthén and Muthén (1998–2006) for more details. A sound strategy when selecting these technical options would be that they should not affect the estimation results, and if they do such effects should conform with the published literature on this topic.

CONCLUSION

In this chapter we described a modeling framework that incorporates three popular modeling techniques: multilevel modeling, structural equation modeling, and finite mixture modeling. This modeling framework has the potential of uncovering previously unexplored aspects of the data. Two-level analysis with multiple latent categorical variables was illustrated with a two-level latent transition analysis. We also described how heterogeneity can be modeled as a within, between, or a within-between phenomenon. We illustrated how the GoM modeling idea can be incorporated within a single level mixture model to allow partial class membership. The GoM models are estimated within the two-level mixture modeling framework. The M*plus* user's guide (Muthén & Muthén, 2006) has a number of other practical multilevel mixture examples as well as details on the M*plus* model specifications.

Another important application of this framework is the non-parametric hierarchical regression models. These models provide an alternative to the popular hierarchical regression models with normally distributed random effects by assuming a more realistic non-parameteric distribution instead. A detailed discussion on this topic is available in Muthén and Asparouhov (in preparation).

Two-level mixture models vary greatly in their complexity. In this chapter we illustrated most of the basic modeling principles. Researchers familiar with multilevel models and mixture models will find it easy to combine these modeling ideas. Sound modeling strategies should be used with these complex new models. Gradual model building, comparison with single class models and single level models should always be performed. The flexible modeling framework we described in this chapter will offers researchers many competing modeling strategies. Rigorous statistical techniques should be used to choose among these alternatives. In addition, researchers should promote models that have solid connections with substantive theory.

NOTE

1. This research was supported by SBIR grant R43 AA014564-01 from NIAAA to Muthén & Muthén. The research of the second author was also supported under grants R01 DA11796 from NIDA and K02 AA 00230 from NIAAA. The authors thank E. Erosheva for helpful comments on the earlier draft.

REFERENCES

Agresti, A. (1996). *An Introduction to Categorical Data Analysis*. New York: Wiley.

Asparouhov, T. (2006). General multilevel modeling with sampling weights. *Communications in Statistics: Theory and Methods, 35*, 439–460.

Bijmolt, T. H., Paas, L. J., & Vermunt, J. K. (2004). Country and consumer segmentation: Multi-level latent class analysis of financial product ownership. *International Journal of Research in Marketing, 21*, 323–340.

Erosheva, E. (2002). Partial membership models with application to disability survey data. In H. Bozdogan (Ed.), *Proceedings of Conference on the New Frontiers of Statistical Data Mining* (pp. 117–134). London: CRC Press.

Erosheva, E. (2003). Bayesian estimation of the grade of membership model. *Bayesian Statistics, 7*, 501–510.

Hedeker, D. (2003). A mixed-effects multinomial logistic regression model. *Statistics in Medicine, 22*, 1433–1446.

Hedeker, D., & Gibbons, R. D. (1996). MIXREG: a computer program for mixed-effects regression analysis with autocorrelated errors. *Computer Methods and Programs in Biomedicine, 49*, 229–252.

Liu, C. H., Rubin, D. B., & Wu, Y. N. (1998). Parameter expansion to accelerate EM—the PX-EM algorithm. *Biometrika, 85*, 755–770.

McCullagh, P., & Nelder, J. A. (1989). *Generalized linear models*. London: Chapman & Hall.

Muthén, B. (1984). A general structural equation model with dichotomous, ordered categorical, and continuous latent variable indicators. *Psychometrika, 49*, 115–132.

Muthén, B. (2006). Should substance use disorders be considered as categorical or dimensional? *Addiction, 101*(Suppl. 1), 616.

Muthén, B., & Asparouhov, T. (2006). Item response mixture modeling: Application to tobacco dependence criteria. *Addictive Behaviors, 31*, 1050–1066.

Muthén, B., & Asparouhov, T. (in preparation). *Non-parametric hierarchical regressions*.

Muthén, B., Brown, C. H., Masyn, K., Jo, B., Khoo, S. T., Yang, C. C., et al. (2002). General growth mixture modeling for randomized preventive interventions. *Biostatistics, 3*, 459–475.

Muthén, B., & Shedden, K. (1999). Finite mixture modeling with mixture outcomes using the EM algorithm. *Biometrics, 55*, 463–469.

Muthén, L. K., & Muthén, B. O. (1998-2006). *Mplus user's guide* (4th ed.). Los Angeles, CA: Muthén & Muthén.

Qu, Y., Tan, M., & Kutner, M. H. (1996). Random effects models in latent class analysis for evaluating accuracy of diagnostic tests. *Biometrics, 52*, 797–810.

Vermunt, J. (2003). Multilevel latent class models. *Sociological Methodology, 33*, 213–239.

Vermunt, J., & Magidson, J. (2005). Hierarchical mixture models for nested data structures. In C. Weihs & W. Gaul (Eds.), *Classification: The ubiquitous challenge* (pp. 176–183). Heidelberg: Springer.

White, H. (1980). A heteroscedasticity-consistent covariance matrix estimator and a direct test for heteroscedasticity. *Econometrica, 41*, 733–750.

CHAPTER 3

LONGITUDINAL MODELING OF POPULATION HETEROGENEITY

Methodological Challenges to the Analysis of Empirically Derived Criminal Trajectory Profiles[1]

Frauke Kreuter[2]
Joint Program in Survey Methodology,
University of Maryland, College Park

Bengt Muthén
University of California, Los Angeles

The question of how to model population heterogeneity in longitudinal data has been repeatedly discussed in criminological journals, especially in the context of modeling "criminal careers" as the variable of interest (e.g., Elliot, 1985; Farrington & West, 1993; Nieuwbeerta & Blokland, 2003; Tracy, Wolfgang, & Figlio, 1990). It has been recognized that there is variation in criminal trajectories and any analysis of the age-crime relationship requires a decision on how to model this variation. In Chapter 1 in this volume, Muthén briefly touched on different modeling approaches to capture ob-

Advances in Latent Variable Mixture Models, pages 53–75
Copyright © 2008 by Information Age Publishing
53

served heterogeneity around trajectory profiles. Here we will revisit and extend the examples mentioned. To do so we will use two well-known criminological data sets, the Philadelphia Cohort Study (Tracy et al., 1990) and the Cambridge data (Farrington & West, 1990). Both datasets have been used in the past to describe criminal activity as a function of age.

It is important to note that we are not seeking to provide the final analysis for either one of these datasets. Too many substantive decisions would have to be made that only criminologists could provide. Nonetheless, we will take this opportunity to discuss how the different modeling alternatives are related to each other, what the different modeling results for these applications are, how results from one model can be translated to another, and what further modeling opportunities the different models offer for substantive researchers.

In our analysis we focus on growth mixture models (Muthén, 2001, 2002, 2004; Muthén & Muthén, 1998–2006; Muthén & Shedden, 1999), nonparametric growth models (Aitkin, 1999; Hedeker, 2000; Heinen, 1996), and latent class growth models, also known as group-based trajectory models (e.g., Nagin & Land, 1993; Roeder, Lynch, & Nagin, 1999). The in-depth comparison of these models is important because it can help to answer a key question that substantive researchers have often asked in the past, that is, how to find a balance between mixture classes that are needed according to substantive theory and those needed to model variation around observed growth trajectories (e.g., Bushway, Brame, & Paternoster, 1999; Heckman & Singer, 1984; Nagin & Tremblay, 2005; Sampson & Laub, 2005).

POPULATION-BASED CONVICTION DATA

As mentioned above, we decided to use two data sets for our demonstration. The first includes data on convictions of 403 "boys" from Cambridge, England who were followed from ages 10 to 40 (Farrington & West, 1990).[3] The second dataset includes information on 13,160 males born in Philadelphia in 1958. Annual counts of police contacts are available from age 4 to 26 for this birth cohort. Strengths and limitations of these data have been discussed in various places (Brame, Mulvey, & Piquero, 2001; Moffitt, 1993; Nagin & Land, 1993) and will not be repeated here.

Both datasets share two characteristics. First, the aggregate age-crime curve follows the well-known pattern of increasing yearly convictions throughout the subjects' teenage years and decreasing annual conviction rates thereafter (Farrington, 1986; Hirschi & Gottfredson, 1983). Second, the outcome variable is extremely skewed with a large number of zeros at each point in time. Both characteristics can be seen in Figure 3.1. The upper panel of Figure 3.1 displays the average number of police contacts for

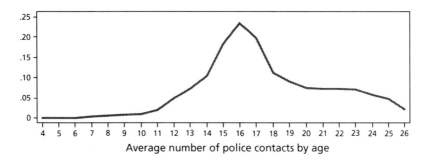

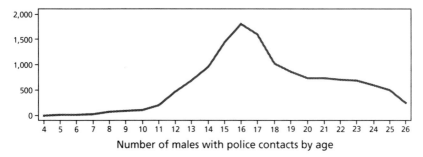

Figure 3.1   Distribution of police contacts over the ages 5 to 26 for the Philadelphia Cohort Study.

the Philadelphia data by age-groups. We see the average number of police contacts rise up to the age 16, where it peaks at an average of 0.23 police contacts for the entire cohort of 13,160 males.

The lower panel of Figure 3.1 displays the number of males with police contacts by age. We see that the change noted in the upper panel of Figure 3.1 is not just due to an increase in the number of contacts for a particular subset of males, but is also largely due to a changing number of males that experienced police contacts. At age 11, for example, 205 males, which is less than two percent of the entire cohort, had a police contact. At age 16, on the other hand, this number increased to 1800 males (13.7% of the cohort). But there are also a large number of males who never had any contact with the police. In the Philadelphia birth cohort roughly 60% had no recorded police contact in the recorded years between age six and age 26, about 15% had one police contact during this period, and the remaining quarter of the birth cohort shows between 2 and 57 police contacts. In any given year more than 90% of males in the 1958 cohort do not show any policy contact, except for the teenage years (15 through 17) where the number of non-offenders ranged between 86.3 % and 89%.

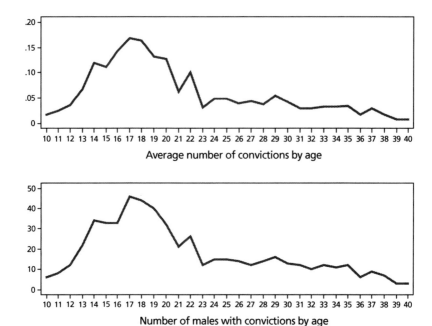

Figure 3.2 Distribution of convictions over the ages 10 to 40 for the Cambridge Study.

The distribution of convictions over time looks very similar for the Cambridge study (Figure 3.2), only a little less smooth due to the smaller number of cases. For the Cambridge males we see also an increase in early adulthood resulting in a peak at age 17 with an average of 0.17 convictions and a decline thereafter. The number of males engaged in crimes increased in a similar way. At age 11 roughly 2% (8 boys) were convicted, while at age 17 there were somewhat more than 10%. Here too most males show no convictions throughout the observational period. Overall, 60% of males in the Cambridge study were never once convicted, and in any given year anywhere between 88.8% and 98.5% of males had zero convictions.

For our modeling example several decisions were made to deal with the large amount of zeros in the outcome variable at each individual time point. Following Roeder et al. (1999) we decided to analyze the data grouped into bi-annual intervals,[4] and use zero-inflated Poisson models (Lambert, 1992; Nagin & Land, 1993) in all our analyses of the count outcome variable. These zero-inflated Poisson (ZIP) models were developed for situations in which the count outcome is equal to zero more often than one would expect assuming a Poisson distribution (Hall, 2000). The ZIP model is discussed in detail by Nagin and Land (1993) and Roeder et al. (1999), and will therefore not be explained any further. A brief model description can be found in the Appendix to this chapter.

COMPARISON OF THE MIXTURE MODELING APPROACHES

The key to the model comparison is a good understanding of the assumptions behind the different growth models, specifically the presence or absence of random effects, as well as a good understanding of non-parametric modeling of the distributions of those random effects. Before we discuss the results we will therefore review the specification of a different growth model using a general latent variable framework.[5] The use of this framework allows a straightforward comparison of the growth models, both in terms of equations and in terms of actual model specification. In our comparison of growth mixture models, we focus on their ability to capture the heterogeneity of trajectories. However, it should be noted that all assumptions underlying regression-based models still apply and need to be considered when applying these even more demanding techniques.

Underlying Concepts

In growth curve models, the development of the observed outcome variables over time is characterized as a function of age. Conventional growth modeling can be used to estimate the amount of variation across individuals in the growth parameters (intercepts and slopes) as well as average growth. In other words, in a conventional growth model the individual variation around the estimated average trajectory is expressed in growth parameters that are allowed to vary across individuals (Raudenbush & Bryk, 2002), and that variation of the growth parameters is assumed to take on a normal distribution (Hedeker & Gibbons, 1994). Substantively, it means that one assumes all people in the sample have the same expected criminal trajectory and that the individual variation around this expected trajectory is centered on the estimated intercept and slopes for the whole sample, with symmetric deviation on both sides (e.g., some individuals start their criminal careers earlier and some start later, but on average they start at the estimated intercept).

The normality assumption of the conventional growth model was challenged by Nagin and Land (1993). These authors adopted a model by Heckman and Singer (1984) that approximates an unspecified continuous distribution of unobserved heterogeneity with a linear combination of discrete distributions (Nagin, Farrington, & Moffitt, 1995). That is, different groups are used to capture the overall variation. Within the latent variable framework one would say the population consists of latent classes each of which has its own growth trajectory; we therefore refer to this approach as latent class growth analysis (LCGA). Over the last few years, LCGA has become attractive for quantitative criminologists and specialists in related fields (e.g., Blokland & Nieuwbeerta, 2005; Fergusson & Horwood, 2002; Haviland & Nagin, 2005; Piquero, Farrington, & Blumstein, 2003). The group-based modeling approach supports distinctions among subgroups having distinct offending trajectories. It also matches theories like the one proposed by Moffitt (1993) that differentiate between a large group of adolescence-limited offenders and a small subgroup of life-course persistent offenders. However, subgroups found in these latent-class-type models have not always matched theory, and there has been a tension regarding how to interpret the classes found (for a review see Raudenbush, 2005). Recently Nagin and Tremblay (2005) warned about the reification of the trajectory groups when their initial purpose was solely a statistical approximation of a complex continuous distribution. As Raudenbush (2005) pointed out:

> Perhaps we are better off assuming continuously varied growth *a priori* and therefore never tempting our audience to believe in the key misconception that groups of persons actually exist. We would then not have to warn them strongly against "reification" of the model they have been painstakingly convinced to adopt. (p. 136)

Looking at the models introduced by Muthén in Chapter 1 of this volume, the decision regarding how to model trajectories might not necessarily be an either/or. A growth mixture model (GMM) would allow for both—a mixed population as predicted by certain criminological theories of different subpopulation trajectories, and a variation in the growth parameters (and likewise the trajectories) within the groups. However, if random effects are allowed within the classes, the growth mixture model also relies on the normality assumption. A nonparametric version of a growth mixture (NP-GMM) can be employed instead, which does not rely on any distributional assumption for the random effects. Instead, the model is specified such that latent classes are used to capture the potentially non-normal distribution within the growth mixture classes. In this sense, the nonparametric growth mixture model resembles the latent class growth model. At the same time it allows for an explicit specification of "substantively meaningful" trajectory groups and groups that are needed solely to capture the variation in the growth factor(s).

Model Specifications

The similarities and differences between these models will become clearer with a closer look at the model specifications. Let us start with a simple model with no covariates other than age, where the age-crime relationship is described by a quadratic growth function. The outcome variable is a count (e.g., number of convictions) and the Poisson parameter λ can be expressed for each individual i at time point t as a linear combination of the time-related variable X with a linear slope parameter β_1 and a quadratic slope parameter β_2, $\ln(\lambda_{it}) = \beta_{0i} + \beta_{1i}x_t + \beta_{2i}x_t^2$. In this specification of a conventional growth model β_{0i} is a random intercept, and β_{1i} and β_{2i} are random slopes. That means that the values for the intercept and slopes are allowed to vary across individuals.

Let us assume for simplicity a conventional growth model with a random intercept factor and no random effects for the slope or quadratic term. The equation above would change to $\ln(\lambda_{it}) = \beta_{0i} + \beta_1 x_t + \beta_2 x_t^2$ with no i subscripts on β_1 and β_2. Substantively speaking, every observational unit shows the same development but starting from different values. One can think of this as a shift of the growth trajectories along the vertical axis in pictures like Figures 3.1 and 3.2. Using multilevel notation (e.g., Raudenbush & Bryk, 2002), the equation estimated at level two (the individual level) for the growth model with just a random intercept is $\beta_{0i} = \alpha_0 + r_{0i}$. In a latent variable framework, this random effect β_{0i} can be seen as a latent variable with a normal distribution. The latent variable captures the heterogeneity in the intercepts, and again, the normality assumption implies that the individual variation around the expected trajectory is centered on the estimated intercept for the whole sample, with symmetric deviation on both sides. But what if the assumption is violated and the random effects cannot be seen as being normally distributed? This issue will be discussed next in the context of nonparametric growth models.

Nonparametric Growth Models

In this case the distribution of the random effects can be left unspecified and will be estimated. For estimation the EM algorithm can be employed, and within the E-step numerical integration can be used. In numerical integration the integral is substituted by a finite weighted sum of mass points (nodes) as shown in Chapter 1, Figure 1.7 (left panel). If one were to approximate a normal distribution with numerical integration, Gauss-Hermite quadrature can be used. In this case nodes and weights of the nodes are known and fixed. However, if an unknown distribution needs to be approximated, the nodes (mass points) and weight of the nodes (masses) can be estimated. Together they provide the necessary parameters to capture the unknown distribution of the random effect (see Chapter 1, Figure 1.7, right panel; there the mass points determine the location of the bars, and the weight determines their height).

For our example of an age-crime relationship that is described by a quadratic growth function, the random effect of the intercept would now not longer be captured by $\beta_{0i} = \alpha_0 + r_{0i}$, but rather through N different nodes that would be called classes in the latent variable framework. The full estimation equation would be expressed by $\ln(\lambda_{it|c_i=n}) = \beta_{0n} + \beta_1 x_t + \beta_2 x_t^2$. The subscript i on the intercept growth factor is replaced with n indicating a particular class (*node*) in the unknown distribution. With this model specification there is now no longer any within-class variation in the intercept growth factor and there is no error term for the growth factors. Instead, there are k different growth factor means. Note that the "classes" do not have a substantive interpretation, but are needed as mass points to approximate the variation in intercepts.

Growth Mixture Model and Latent Class Growth Model

Let us step aside for a moment and consider general mixture-modeling applications. In such a model, be it a growth mixture model or a latent class growth model, the classes are usually perceived as being substantively different in their development. That is, not only do the intercept growth factor means differ across classes, but so too do their slope factor means. Thus, they too should have a subscript k, as indicated in the equations in Figure 3.3. In the growth mixture model, the growth factors, β_{0i}, β_{1i}, and β_{2i}, may vary randomly among individuals. However, in marked contrast to conventional growth models, these random effect models can be specified for k unobserved subpopulations or classes.

The key differences among the classes are typically found in the fixed effects α_0, α_1, and α_2, which may differ for each of the k classes of C but do not necessarily do so. Likewise, slopes and intercepts may have random effects, but do not necessarily do so. That said, if all variances in the growth factors, β_0, β_1, and β_2, are set to zero, a growth mixture model specification would look like the specification of a latent class growth model (group based tra-

Growth Mixture Model	Latent Class Growth Model
$\ln(\lambda_{it|c_i=k}) = \beta_{0ki} + \beta_{1ki} x_t + \beta_{2ki} x_t^2$	$\ln(\lambda_{it|c_i=k}) = \beta_{0k} + \beta_{1k} x_t + \beta_{2k} x_t^2$
$\beta_{0ki} = \alpha_{0k} + r_{0ki}$	$\beta_{0k} = \alpha_{0k}$
$\beta_{1ki} = \alpha_{1k} + r_{1ki}$	$\beta_{1k} = \alpha_{1k}$
$\beta_{2ki} = \alpha_{2k} + r_{2ki}$	$\beta_{2k} = \alpha_{2k}$

Figure 3.3 Specification of general growth mixture model and latent class growth model.

jectory model). If random effects are specified in a growth mixture model they are again latent variables with a normal distribution. Here the normality assumption implies now that for each latent class the individual variation around the expected trajectory is centered on the estimated intercept and slopes for the respective class, with symmetric deviation on both sides. Note that each individual has a probability of membership in each of the classes, and the individual's score on the growth factors can be estimated.

Nonparametric Growth Mixture Model

Having discussed the nonparametric version of a conventional growth model, and the similarities and differences in the latent class growth model and the growth mixture model, we can now combine the different elements and take a closer look at the nonparametric version of a growth mixture model. As the name indicates the nonparametric GMM does not rely on any distributional assumption for the random effects. Instead, the model is now specified such that additional latent classes are estimated to capture the potentially non-normal distribution within the growth mixture classes.

Consider, for example, a growth mixture model with random intercept (and no random effects on the linear and quadratic slope parameters): $\ln(\lambda_{it|c_i=k}) = \beta_{0ki} + \beta_{1k}x_t + \beta_{2k}x_t^2$, and $\beta_{0ki} = \alpha_{0k} + r_{0ki}$. A nonparametric version of this growth mixture model would use classes to capture the variation of the intercept within each of the k substantive classes established before. The overall trajectory shape of the k substantive classes will not change. That is, each substantive class is still defined by the same slope and quadratic term. However, there will now be n additional classes that differ only in the estimated intercept term and are used to capture the distribution of the random effect on the intercept.

It might be helpful here to look at the example model specification in Figure 3.4 (which resembles what would be specified in the M*plus* software). A quadratic growth model is specified for an observed outcome variable. The slope variance s and the variance q for the quadratic random effect are set to zero (s@0 and q@0). Only a random intercept is estimated in this growth mixture model. In the lower part of the first column of Figure 3.4 (labeled GMM) a mean intercept β_0 represented by [i], a slope β_1 represented by [s], and a quadratic term β_2 represented by [q] will be estimated for three substantive classes. This results in nine estimated growth parameters for the Poisson part of the growth mixture model, three for each class

A nonparametric version of the same growth mixture model is displayed in the middle column of Figure 3.4, labeled nonparametric GMM. Two latent class variables are specified in this model: *csub*, with three classes that capture the substantive different trajectories found in the GMM model,

GMM	Non-parametric GMM	LCGA
CLASSES = csub(3);	CLASSES = csub(3) cnp(2);	CLASSES = csub(5);
s@0; q@0;	model csub: 　%csub#1% 　　[s-q]; 　%csub#2% 　　[s-q]; 　%csub#3% 　　[s-q];	i@0; s@0; q@0;

Estimated Growth Parameters

GMM				Non-parametric GMM					LCGA—5 classes			
csub	[i	s	q]	csub	cnp	[i	s	q]	csub	[i	s	q]
1	1	2	3	1	1	1	2	3	1	1	2	3
2	4	5	6	1	2	4	2	3	2	4	5	6
3	7	8	9	2	1	5	6	7	3	7	8	9
				2	2	8	6	7	4	10	11	12
				3	1	9	10	11	5	13	14	15
				3	2	12	10	11				

Figure 3.4 Example model specification for GMM, NP-GMM, and LCGA.

and *cnp*, to capture the distribution of the random intercept. This second class variable is allowed to have two classes, which vary in their estimated intercept factor means but not in the slope or the quadratic means, as seen in the bottom half of Figure 3.4. For the first substantive class (csub=1) four parameters are estimated. The estimated value for the two intercepts varies across np-classes that capture the distribution of the random intercept; the value for the estimated slope and quadratic term does not (see the values 2 and 3 for both s and q). Note that by having the slope factor means for the linear and quadratic term [s q] be the same across the np-classes within each substantive class, the assumption is made that the linear and quadratic slope growth factors are uncorrelated with the intercept growth factor. This assumption is not made by the LCGA model, as outlined in the left column of Figure 3.4, where all growth factor means (intercept, slope and quadratic term) can be different across classes and all growth factor variances are set to zero. That said, a latent class growth model could give a result where the estimated slope factor means ([s] and [q]) vary across substantive classes without being correlated with the estimated mean intercept factor. An LCGA model could therefore lead to the same result as a nonparametric growth mixture model.

The model set-up shows the similarity between these models. But the similarity should not disguise the important theoretical implications of the different model specifications. We will come back to this point when we discuss the different interpretations of the model results for the two data examples in the next section.

APPLICATION OF THE THREE DIFFERENT
MODELING STRATEGIES

To discuss the different modeling results for the Cambridge data as well as the Philadelphia data, we will build on past results from Kreuter and Muthén (2006),[6] Roeder et al. (1999) as well as D'Unger, Land, McCall, & Nagin (1998). For both data sets we will select a set of growth models that have been shown to represent the data well. We start the comparison of the growth mixture, latent class growth, and nonparametric growth mixture solutions with a discussion of the model statistics followed by a comparison of the resulting mean trajectories, as well as the assignment of most likely class membership.

Discussion of Model Statistics

A common challenge for all of the latent variable models discussed here is the decision regarding the number of classes needed to best represent the data (see, e.g., McLachlan & Peel, 2000). Objective criteria for doing so have been a matter of some controversy. Kreuter and Muthén (2006) used a different set of statistics to evaluate different models for the Cambridge data. The comparison of the log-likelihood values was used as an indicator for the appropriate number of classes. However, this likelihood ratio test was not used as the sole decision criterion, since for these models it does not have the usual large-sample chi-square distribution due to the class probability parameter being at the border of its admissible space (Muthén, 2004). Therefore, the comparison of log-likelihood values was supplemented by alternative procedure like the Bayesian Information Criterion (BIC; Schwartz, 1978), new mixture tests like the likelihood-ratio test proposed by Lo, Mendell, and Rubin (LMR; 2001), and the bootstrap likelihood ratio-test (BLRT; McLachlan & Peel, 2000; Nylund, Asparouhov, & Muthén, 2007). Results from models fit to the Cambridge data and Philadelphia data are presented in Table 3.1, and described below.

Cambridge Data
For the Cambridge data, Kreuter and Muthén (2006) identified a three-class growth mixture model (GMM), a six-class nonparametric growth model (GM np) to fit the data best within each of these modeling types. A five-class latent class growth model (LCGA) was among the best fitting

TABLE 3.1 Growth Mixture Model, Nonparametric Representation of Growth Mixture Model, and Latent Class Growth Analysis (all with zero-inflation)

Model	Classes	LogL	Number of parameters	BIC	Entropy
Cambridge Data					
GMM (zip)	2 + 0	–1,454.7	12	2,981.5	0.493
GMM np zip	2 + 3 + 0	–1,444.4	15	2,978.8	0.660
LCGA (zip)	5	–1,441.0	22	3,014.0	0.814
Philadelphia Cohort Study '58 (subset n=1000)					
GMM (zip)	3	–3,173.6	15	6,450.8	0.238
GMM np zip	2 + 2 + 2	–3,172.4	18	6,469.2	0.704
LCGA (zip)	5	–3,177.1	22	6,506.1	0.817

models for this model type and will be used in the present comparison. For the three-class GMM, a model with two different developmental trajectories (labeled as GMM (zip) 2 + 0 in Table 3.1) showed the best fit. This model has 12 parameters: two parameters for class membership, three parameters (intercept, linear slope and quadratic slope) for both count trajectories, one for the intercept variance, two for the slope and a quadratic slope for the zero-inflation part of the model, and one parameter for the probability of being in the zero class at each point in time. The log-likelihood value for this model is –1,454.7 with a BIC of 2,981.5.

Of the different nonparametric GMM models, a nonparametric model with two support points (nodes) for intercept variation in one non-zero class and three in the other performed best using log-likelihood values, BIC and BLRT as indicators of model fit (labeled as *GMM np zip* in Table 3.1). This model, which has 15 parameters, yielded a log likelihood value of –1,444.4 and a BIC of 2,978.8. Among the LCGA models without a pre-specified zero class (indicated as *LCGA (zip)* in Table 3.1), both four- and five-class models performed well. The five-class solution, which has 22 parameters, has a log-likelihood value of –1,441 and a BIC of 3,014.

Philadelphia Data

The data from the *Philadelphia Cohort Study* were examined in a similar fashion. Following D'Unger et al. (1998), a random subset of 1000 observations was used for this model comparison. To keep the parallel with the Cambridge data results, we decided to use the results for the five-class latent class growth model (a solution found to fit the data best in the D'Unger et al., 1998 study). Also, while the six-class latent class growth model had a slightly better BIC value than the five-class model (6,504 vs. 6,506), the

LMR likelihood ratio test failed to reject a five-class model in favor of a six-class model. We matched these results to a three-class GMM model as well as a nonparametric GMM model with three substantive classes and two nonparametric classes.[7] A noticeable departure from the Cambridge data was that, in this case, specifying an explicit zero class was not necessary for any of these models; however, the outcome variable was specified as zero-inflated Poisson, just like it was in the models for the Cambridge data.

For the Philadelphia data the three-class GMM model has a likelihood of −3,173.6 with 15 parameters, resulting in a BIC value of 6,450.8 (see bottom half of Table 3.1). The nonparametric version of this GMM model, which has 18 parameters, has a slightly higher log-likelihood value of −3,172.4, resulting in a BIC of 6,469.2. The latent class growth model with five classes and 22 parameters has a log-likelihood value of −3,177.1.

We will look in detail at the results for the trajectories later in the chapter. For now, what is interesting to note at this point is that the log-likelihood values for the three models for each of these datasets are very similar. In fact, they are much more similar to each other than the results within one model type when different numbers of classes are used, or when the models are run without the zero-inflated Poisson specification (see Appendix). The biggest difference between the models is in the number of parameters used to achieve these likelihoods (with the lowest number in GMM and the highest in LCGA) and the values of entropy. Entropy is a measure used for the separation of the latent classes which is based on the posterior class membership probabilities (Muthén & Muthén, 1998-2006). Entropy measures capture how well one can predict class membership given the observed outcomes. Values range from 0 to 1, and high values are preferred. However, entropy measures are by definition a function of the number of classes. If one were to fit a model with as many classes as there are observations, entropy would necessarily be 1. We therefore do not want to overemphasize this value, but will come back to this difference in entropy when we compare class assignment and predictive power of the different models.

Lastly, it should be noted that all of these mixture models appear to have a considerably lower BIC values than the conventional growth model with a random intercept term. For the random subset of 1000 observations from the Philadelphia data, the BIC was 6,528.2 for a model with 7 parameters and a log-likelihood value of −3,239.8. The distribution of factor scores presented in the next section will illustrate this effect.

Factor Score Distribution

The two graphs in Figure 3.5 show the distribution of intercept factor scores for the conventional growth curve model and the growth mixture

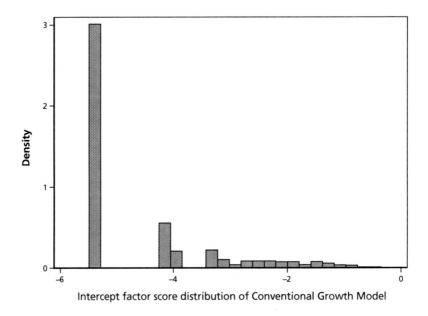

Figure 3.5 Distribution of intercept growth factor scores for the conventional growth model and the two biggest classes of the GMM model (class assignment according to most likely class membership) for the Philadelphia data.

model for the Philadelphia data. The picture on the bottom shows for the general growth mixture models a highly skewed distribution of the intercept growth factor. The three-class growth mixture model divides this distribution in three sub-classes. Displayed here are the intercept factors scores for the two biggest classes (roughly 40% and 44%; according to the most likely class membership 16.1% and 78.5%).

Looking at the bottom picture in Figure 3.5, we see that there is a high pile of intercept factor scores around zero (–15 on the log-scale) and another pile of factor scores that ranges from –9 to –3 on the log-scale with a mean and median at -6. In the nonparametric version of the growth mixture model these two distributions are represented with two additional subclasses for each of the mixture classes. The early and higher peaking class has two support points at –13.7 (with a weight of 3%) and –15.5 (with a weight of 17%), the late and very low peaking class has one support point at –5.6 (with a weight of 63%) and –2.6 (with a weight of 12%).

However, looking back at Table 3.1, the nonparametric version of the GMM has a very similar log-likelihood to the GMM and needs more parameters. It is therefore less parsimonious and does not fit the data better. The normality assumption for the random effect in the GMM model does not seem to be violated so much as to make a nonparametric representation necessary. For the Cambridge data, Kreuter and Muthén (2006) showed the quadrature points for the NP-GMM model and the related intercept factor score distributions. There, too, the nonparametric specification of the random effects in the GMM model appeared to be unnecessary.

Mean Trajectories

Growth model results are most often displayed with mean trajectory curves. Figure 3.6 shows the results for the Philadelphia Cohort study. The three mean trajectories from the GMM are shown in the upmost panel and the five mean trajectories for the LCGA are shown in the lowest panel. The results of both models capture three themes: a peak in mid-teenage years (age 15) with a steep decline, a peak in later teenage years (age 16/17) with a slower decline and very low peaking in early adulthood (age 19/20). The height of the GMM trajectories is notably lower than those of the LCGA, but one should not forget that additional variance terms are estimated for the GMM that allow for a variation around the means displayed here. One could display the GMM curves not just conditional on the mean but conditional on one standard deviation above and one standard deviation below

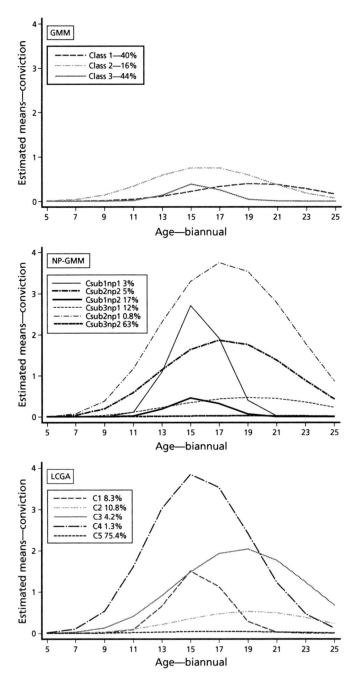

Figure 3.6 Mean trajectories for the three-class, its nonparametric GMM, and latent class growth model.

the mean for any given class. In this case the graphs would look more similar to the NP-GMM result.

Looking back to the model setup in Figure 3.4, the NP-GMM falls between GMM and LCGA. Like LCGA there is no variance estimated for the trajectory curves, or to phrase it differently, all random effects for intercept, slope, and quadratic terms are set to zero. However, the parameters for slope and intercept are constrained to be equal for some of the classes, which allows for a nonparametric representation of the variation of the intercept in the GMM model. The estimated classes that form the two solid lines in the NP-GMM graph of Figure 3.6 are variations on the trajectory shape represented with a solid line in the GMM graph of Figure 3.6. Likewise, the two short-dashed lines are variations of Class 1 in the GMM graph and the dot-dashed lines are variations of the dot-dash line in the GMM graph. For all three substantive classes the np-class with the larger estimated class size is marked with a thicker line in Figure 3.6.

The LCGA results follow similar themes with early and late peaking classes. However, there are shifts in form and location of the trajectories compared to the GMM and NP-GMM model results, as well as changes in the estimated class sizes. The two late-peaking classes in LCGA peak at age 19, not 17 as in the GMM and NP-GMM results. Additionally, the peak height of the earlier peaking class trajectories is different from those in the NP-GMM solution. For the Philadelphia data the early high peaking class in the LCGA has an estimated class size of little more than 1% (C 4) and occurs at age 15. In the GMM-NP the early high peaking class has an estimated class size of 3% (Csub1np1) and is not as high peaking as the LCGA class. The even higher peaking class with an estimated class size of almost 1% (Csub2np1) peaks at a later age. And, the LCGA has a late-peaking 4% class 3, peaking at 19, while GMM-NP has 2 later-peaking classes with 1 and 5%, both peaking at age 17.

For the Cambridge data the results for the NP-GMM and the LCGA model were very similar (Kreuter & Muthén, 2006). Figure 3.7 shows the estimated average number of convictions at each time point plotted in the LCGA estimates against the estimates for each time point in the NP-GMM model for each of the five LCGA classes. The dashed diagonal line is the identity line. Points fall on this line if the estimated means are exactly the same at each time point for both models. While there is some slight deviation from the identity line, this graph nevertheless shows the similarity in the model results for the Cambridge data (further modeling details can be found in Kreuter & Muthén, 2006).

For a substantive researcher attention should be paid to shape and location of the estimated trajectories. If the shape of the trajectories is the same for a set of classes and the only difference between the classes is in how high or low these trajectories start, then there is reason to check carefully

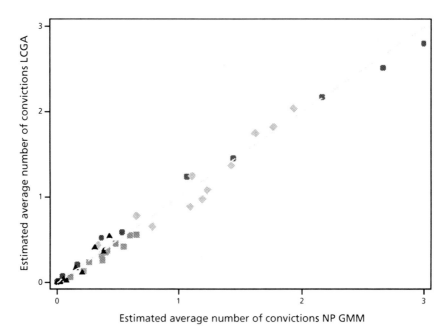

Figure 3.7 Cambridge data: LCGA estimated average number of convictions at each time point plotted against NP-GMM estimates for each time point for each of the five LCGA classes.

if this indicates that the classes are solely variations on the same theme (nonparametric ways to capture a random intercept effect) or if they really have substantive meaning. The latter can be guided by theory, but cannot be decided without extending the models. The relationship of the classes to antecedents and consequences can be information in this regard. For example, if the NP-GMM sub-classes that represent the distribution of the intercept factor scores of the GMM have different predictive power for a distal outcome, or if covariates predict the subclasses differently, then it would be reasonable to relax the restrictions on the growth factor means and move to an LCGA. On the other hand, LCGA might tempt the research to try a substantive interpretation for each of the LCGA classes whereas some of those classes are only needed to capture random variation in the growth factor(s) and GMM would come up with fewer substantively different classes. The model statistics for the Philadelphia cohort study suggest this, with GMM resulting in a higher log-likelihood and lower BIC value than the LCGA. But again, knowledge regarding the interpretation of the classes can only be gained in relating classes and growth factors to variables outside the model (antecedents and consequences).

One note of caution should be added here. So far we only discussed random variation around an estimated mean intercept trajectory. That is, we discussed that shifts along the vertical axis are a random effect that might call for a nonparametric representation. A similar thought can be brought up for shifts along the horizontal axis. For these example data sets this would mean that the number of convictions or police contacts in certain life periods is more predictive of later consequences than at which age those convictions or police contacts happen. This shows once again that successful modeling needs to combine substantive and technical knowledge.

SUMMARY

This chapter illustrates and compares three different modeling approaches for longitudinal data. The approaches considered include latent class growth analysis as well as parametric and nonparametric versions of growth mixture models. The analyses show that researchers might not want to make *a priori* decisions regarding whether to assume continuously varied growth or to rely entirely on substantive classes to capture the variation in growth. A growth mixture model where random effects are allowed within classes can be an alternative. Or, if the normality assumption is questioned, a nonparametric version may be considered.

For both the Philadelphia and Cambridge data we saw that mixture models are needed to summarize the developmental trajectories. We also saw that the variation in the intercept random effect of a GMM can be represented in a nonparametric way. The resulting estimates for the nonparametric model seem to fit the data slightly better than the other two mixture specifications for the Cambridge data. Note that in the Cambridge data the resulting trajectories for an LCGA model are very similar to the NP-GMM results. This is not the case for the Philadelphia data. The parametric and non-parametric version of the GMM model show very similar growth trajectories. However, the resulting trajectories of the LCGA differ in class sizes and slope compared to the parametric and non-parametric GMM.

In both cases, but in particular for the Philadelphia data, the next analysis step would be to try models that relate the growth factor variation in the GMM model, as well as the different classes in NP-GMM and LCGA, to distal outcomes or antecedents. If it is the case that the NP-GMM sub-classes have different predictive power regarding a distal outcome, for example, then this could be a sign that these classes represent more than a mere variation on a random intercept. In addition, the full Philadelphia data could be explored with models that allow for random linear and quadratic slopes (see Muthén & Asparouhov, 2007).

NOTES

1. We thank Tihomir Asparouhov, Shawn Bushway, John Laub, Katherine Masyn, Daniel Nagin, Paul Nieuwbeerta and the participants of the 2006 CILVR conference at the University of Maryland for stimulating discussions that shaped our perspective for this paper. Michael Lemay was of great help in data preparation and analysis.
2. The authors contributed equally to this chapter.
3. Eight boys died during the observational period and are not included in the analysis.
4. The Cambridge data were grouped into bi-annual intervals starting with age 10. The Philadelphia data were also grouped into bi-annual intervals starting with age 5. In addition, we reduced the age range for the Cambridge data to age 10–27.
5. For an overview of this modeling framework, see Muthén (2002). For a step-by-step introduction to applying latent variable models to longitudinal data, see Muthén (2004).
6. Please contact the first author for a copy of the manuscript. An update of the analysis will appear in the Journal of Quantitative Criminology.
7. Note that in the GMM model we allow for a random intercept only. A more detailed analysis of the full Philadelphia cohort study can be found in Muthén and Asparouhov (2007). Note that a model with random effect for the intercept and the linear slope fits the data better and changes the results somewhat. The analysis here is kept simpler for illustrative purposes.

REFERENCES

Aitkin, M. (1999). A general maximum likelihood analysis of variance components in generalized linear models. *Biometrics, 55,* 117–128.

Asparouhov, T., & Muthén, B. (2008). Multilevel mixture models. In G. R. Hancock & K. M. Samuelsen (Eds.), *Advances in latent variable mixture models.* Charlotte, NC: Information Age Publishing, Inc.

Berk, R. (2004): *Regression analysis: A constructive critique.* Thousand Oaks, CA: Sage.

Blokland A. A. J., & Nieuwbeerta, P. (2005). The effects of life circumstances on longitudinal trajectories of offending. *Criminology, 43,* 1203–1240.

Brame, R., Mulvey, E. P., & Piquero A.R. (2001). On the development of different kinds of criminal activity. *Sociological Methods & Research, 29,* 319–341.

Bushway, S., Brame, R., & Paternoster, R. (1999). Assessing stability and change in criminal offending: A comparison of random effects, semiparametric, and fixed effects modeling strategies. *Journal of Quantitative Criminology, 15,* 23–61.

D'Unger, A. V., Land, K. C., McCall, P. L., & Nagin, D. S. (1998). How many latent classes of delinquent/criminal careers? Results from mixed Poisson regression analyses. *American Journal of Sociology, 103,* 1593–1630.

Elliot, D. (1985). *National Youth Survey 1976–1980: Wave I–V.* Ann Arbor, MI: Behavioral Research Institute, Inter-University Consortium for Political and Social Research.

Farrington, D. (1986). *The Cambridge study on delinquency: Long term follow-up.* Cambridge, MA: Cambridge University Press.

Farrington, D. P., & West, D. J. (1990). *The Cambridge study in delinquent development: A long-term follow-up of 411 London males.* In H. J. Kerner & G. Kaiser (Eds.), *Kriminalitaet.* Berlin: Springer.

Farrington, D. P., & West, D. J. (1993). Criminal, penal and life histories of chronic offenders: Risk and protective factors and early identification. *Criminal Behaviour and Mental Health, 3,* 492–523.

Fergusson, D. M., & Horwood L. J. (2002). Male and female offending trajectories. *Development and Psychopathology, 14,* 159–177.

Hall, D. B. (2000). Zero-inflated Poisson and binomial regression with random effects: A case study. *Biometrics, 56,* 1030–1039.

Haviland, A., & Nagin, D.S. (2005). Causal Inference with Group-based Trajectory Models. *Psychometrika, 70,* 1–22.

Heckman, J., & Singer, B. (1984). A method for minimizing the impact of distributional assumptions in econometric models for duration data. *Econometrica, 52,* 271–320.

Hedeker, D. (2000). *A fully semi-parametric mixed-effects regression model for categorical outcomes.* Paper presented at the Joint Statistical Meetings, Indianapolis, IN.

Hedeker, D., & Gibbons, R. D. (1994). A random-effects ordinal regression model for multilevel analysis. *Biometrics, 50,* 933–944.

Heinen, T. (1996). *Latent class and discrete latent trait models: Similarities and differences.* Thousand Oaks, CA: Sage.

Hirschi, T., & Gottfredson, M. (1983). Age and the explanation of crime. *American Journal of Sociology, 89,* 552–584.

Kreuter, F., & Muthén, B. (2006). *Analyzing criminal trajectory profiles: Bridging multilevel and group-based approaches using growth mixture modeling.* Manuscript submitted for publication.

Lambert, D. (1992). Zero-inflated Poisson regression with application to defects in manufacturing. *Technometrics, 34,* 1–14.

Lo, Y., Mendell, N. R., & Rubin, D. B. (2001). Testing the number of components in a normal mixture. *Biometrika, 88,* 767–778.

McLachlan, G., & Peel, D. (2000). *Finite mixture models.* New York: Wiley.

Moffitt, T. (1993). Adolescence-limited and life-course-persistent antisocial behavior: A developmental taxonomy. *Psychological Review, 100,* 674–701.

Muthén, B. (2001). Latent variable mixture modeling. In G. A. Marcoulides & R. E. Schumacker (Eds.), *New developments and techniques in structural equation modeling* (pp. 1–33). Mahwah, NJ: Erlbaum.

Muthén, B. (2002). Beyond SEM: General latent variable modeling. *Behaviormetrika, 29,* 81–117.

Muthén, B. (2004). Latent variable analysis: Growth mixture modeling and related techniques for longitudinal data. In D. Kaplan (Ed.), *Handbook of quantitative methodology for the social sciences* (pp. 345–368). Newbury Park, CA: Sage.

Muthén, B. & Asparouhov, T. (2007). Growth mixture modeling: Analysis with non-Gaussian random effects. Forthcoming in Fitzmaurice, G., Davidian, M., Verbeke, G. & Molenberghs, G. (eds.), *Advances in Longitudinal Data Analysis*. Chapman & Hall/CRC Press.

Muthén, B., & Shedden, K. (1999). Finite mixture modeling with mixture outcomes using the EM algorithm. *Biometrics, 55*, 463–469.

Muthén, L., & Muthén, B. (1998–2006). *Mplus user's guide*. Los Angeles, CA.

Nagin, D. S., Farrington, D. P., & Moffitt, T. E. (1995). Life-course trajectories of different types of offenders. *Criminology, 33*, 111–139.

Nagin, D. S., & Land, K. C. (1993). Age, criminal careers, and population heterogeneity: Specification and estimation of a nonparametric, mixed Poisson model. *Criminology, 31*, 327–362.

Nagin, D. S., & Tremblay, R. E. (2005). Developmental trajectory groups: Fact or a useful statistical fiction? *Criminology, 43*, 873–904.

Nieuwbeerta, P., & Blokland, A. (2003). *Criminal careers in adult Dutch offenders* (codebook and documentation). Leiden: NCSR.

Nylund, K. L., Asparouhov, T., & Muthén, B. (2007). Deciding on the number of classes in latent class analysis and growth mixture modeling: A Monte Carlo simulation study. *Structural Equation Modeling: A Multidisciplinary Journal.*

Piquero, A. R., Farrington, D. P., & Blumstein, A. (2003). The criminal career paradigm: Background and recent developments. *Crime and Justice: A Review of Research, 30*, 359–506.

Raudenbush, S. W. (2005): How do we study "What Happens Next"? *The Annals of the American Academy of Political and Social Science, 602*, 131–144.

Raudenbush, S. W., & Bryk, A. S. (2002). *Hierarchical linear models: Applications and data analysis methods* (2nd ed.). Thousand Oaks, CA: Sage.

Roeder, K., Lynch, K. G., & Nagin, D. S. (1999). Modeling uncertainty in latent class membership: A case study in criminology. *Journal of the American Statistical Association, 94*, 766–776.

Sampson, R. J., & Laub, J. H. (2005). Seductions of methods: Rejoinder to Nagin and Tremblay's "Developmental Trajectory Groups: Fact or Fiction?" *Criminology, 43*, 905–913.

Schwartz, G. (1978). Estimating the dimension of a model. *The Annals of Statistics, 6*, 461–464.

Tracy, P., Wolfgang, M. E., & Figlio, R. M. (1990). *Delinquency careers in two birth cohorts*. New York: Plenum Press.

APPENDIX

Note that the ZIP model is already a special case of a finite mixture model with two classes. For the zero class a zero count occurs with probability one. For the non-zero class, the probability of a zero count is expressed with a Poisson process. The interesting feature for the ZIP, or its expression as a two-class model, is that the probability of being in the zero class can be modeled by covariates that are different from those that predict the counts for the non-zero class. The same is true when allowing for a zero class in the growth trajectory modeling.

More formally, for the present application this model can be represented as follows: At each individual time point a count outcome variable U_{ti} (the number of convictions at each time point t for individual i) is distributed as ZIP (Roeder et al., 1999).

$$U_{ti} \begin{cases} 0 \text{ with probability } \rho_{ij} \\ \text{Poisson}(\lambda_{ti}) \text{ with probability } 1 - \rho_{ij} \end{cases}.$$

The parameters p_{ti} and λ_{ti} can be represented with

$$\text{logit}(\rho_{ti}) = \log[\rho_{ti}/1 - \rho_{ti}] = X_{ti} \times \gamma_t$$

and

$$\log(\lambda_{ti}) = X_{ti}\beta_i.$$

CHAPTER 4

EXAMINING CONTINGENT DISCRETE CHANGE OVER TIME WITH ASSOCIATIVE LATENT TRANSITION ANALYSIS[1]

Brian P. Flaherty
University of Washington

This chapter is concerned with change in and associations between two categorical latent variables. Latent variables are useful in many circumstances, but two uses of latent variable models are central to this current work. The first is the use of latent variables to make inferences about unobservable (latent) characteristics. The second is as a data reduction technique. That is, associations among several measured variables may be accounted for by a smaller number of latent variables.

Perhaps the most familiar latent variable model is the factor model (Gorsuch, 1983), a continuous latent variable model. In contrast, this chapter concerns categorical latent variables. For example, suppose we had three binary items measuring some sensitive political issues:

- "Should personal income taxes be raised to fund public programs?"
- "Should same-sex couples be able to marry?"
- "Should marijuana be legalized?"

Advances in Latent Variable Mixture Models, pages 77–103
Copyright © 2008 by Information Age Publishing
All rights of reproduction in any form reserved.

Furthermore, let's say we believe there are two types of people in our sample: conservative and liberal. We believe these types (or classes) of people are responsible for the data we obtain. That is, we believe that membership in the conservative or liberal class is largely responsible for how one responds to these three items.

As another example, consider theoretical models of tobacco use onset (Flay, 1993; Leventhal & Cleary, 1980; Mayhew, Flay, & Mott, 2000). These models are comprised of states or stages corresponding to levels of cigarette smoking such as initiators, experimenters, regular users, and daily or perhaps dependent smokers. Other classes of cigarette smokers may also be of interest, for example, former smokers/quitters and chippers (Shiffman, Kassel, Paty, & Gnys, 1994). (Chippers are non-dependent smokers who smoke relatively few cigarettes intermittently.) As with the political items above, we could assume that the responses to a set of measures of tobacco use were largely due to membership in a specific tobacco use or tobacco experience class.

The latent class (LC) model (e.g., Clogg, 1995; Goodman, 1974; Lazarsfeld & Henry, 1968) is a statistical model for analyzing data of the sort just described. That is, the LC model is a model of an unobservable categorical variable that is assumed to account for the observed patterns of responses to a set of categorical measures. The LC model is a type of mixture model (Titterington, Smith, & Makov, 1985). Observed data are comprised of data from subgroups (i.e., the latent classes), and the LC variable indexes the different classes. Within the subgroups the probability distribution of the items differs. That is, members of one class may be highly likely to respond negatively to each of three items; members of a second class may be likely to reply positively to the first item, but negatively to the second and third; and members of a third class may be most likely to reply positively to all three items.

The original LC model, as discussed by Lazarsfeld and Henry (1968) and Goodman (1974), treated the latent classes as a static latent variable. That is, the LC to which someone belonged did not change. This static nature of the class memberships is a common feature of many typological theories, for example temperament (Stern, Arcus, Kagan, Rubin, & Snidman, 1995) and attachment (Ainsworth & Bell, 1970). However, one can also view the LC variable as dynamic (Collins & Cliff, 1990) and examine changes in class memberships over time (called latent transition analysis, LTA, or latent Markov models; Collins & Wugalter, 1992; Langeheine, 1994). Rather than belonging to a static class, or a class defined by a similar pattern of change, in this perspective people may belong to one class at Time t and a different class at Time $t + 1$. Stage theories of development, like Piaget's theory of cognitive development, are probably the best known examples of this perspective. These models are characterized by change among the levels of a latent categorical variable (qualitative change), rather than quantitative change of a continuous variable.

Consider the tobacco research mentioned above. If one views the latent classes as the current levels of tobacco use, examining change in the levels of tobacco use is a central interest to tobacco and prevention researchers. In part, LTA was designed to address questions of this sort.

In this chapter, we will provide an overview of LC and latent transition models, and then discuss an extension of latent transition models to the examination changes in two dynamic latent variables. This approach is referred to as associative latent transition analysis (ALTA). All three of these models (LC, LTA, and ALTA) are illustrated with data on tobacco and alcohol use from a nationally representative sample of U.S. adolescents.

LATENT CLASS MODEL

There is a vast literature on the LC model, and we will not attempt to review it all here. Overviews include Clogg (1995); Lanza, Flaherty, and Collins (2003), and McMutcheon (1987). As discussed in the introduction, the basic LC model is useful in situations where discrete classes of observations are important. Much substantive theory in tobacco and other drug use has been based upon a stage or class concept (Flay, 1993; Leventhal & Cleary, 1980). Because so much theoretical work in tobacco research involves classes of smokers, LC analysis (and related methods) can be quite useful for work in this area. In particular, the LC model corresponds nicely to the class structure commonly found in nicotine and tobacco use theory.

Latent Class Model, Parameters, and Assumptions

We will briefly review the LC model in this section. However, first we will link the LC model to the broader literature on mixture models. This literature often refers to components (the sub-groups being identified in the population), component weights (the proportions of the sub-groups in the population), and the component densities (the distributions of the characteristics within each component). Mixture models share a common mathematical form (McLachlan & Peel, 2000)

$$f(\mathbf{y}_j) = \sum_{i=1}^{C} \pi_i f_i(\mathbf{y}_j) \tag{4.1}$$

where $\mathbf{y}_j$ is the vector of data for observation j, C is the number of components in the population, π_i is the proportion of the population in component i, and $f_i(\mathbf{y}_j)$ is the within-component multivariate density function of the observed data. That is, $f_i(\mathbf{y}_j)$ describes how the measured characteristics are distributed within the sub-groups.

In the LC literature, the language is different than that found in the broader mixture modeling literature. Rather than components, the population is comprised of latent classes, and rather than component densities, the within-class distributions are referred to as the conditional response probabilities. As a categorical data model, the standard LC model only includes probability distributions.

As a mixture model, the mathematical formula for the LC model has the same form as Equation 4.1, but the specific distribution functions are given. In Equation 4.1, $\mathbf{y}$ is subscripted by j because every individual observation has potentially different data. In the LC model, frequency data are analyzed and the unit of analysis can be referred to as a response pattern ($\mathbf{W}$). If three dichotomous yes/no items were asked of a sample of individuals, the resulting data could have at most eight (2^3) different response patterns: (No, No, No), (Yes, No, No), (No, Yes, No), etc.. The goal of the LC model is to reproduce these observed response frequencies.

In addition to letting $\mathbf{W}$ denote a response pattern, we will use q to denote the number of measured items. The LC model is not limited to dichotomous items. $\mathbf{W}$ can include polytomous items as well. As such, the vector $\mathbf{r}$ (length q) contains the number of response categories for each of the items. We will also use C to denote the number of latent classes in the model. Given this notation, we can write the LC model as

$$\Pr(\mathbf{W}) = \sum_{c=1}^{C} \gamma_c \left(\prod_{j=1}^{q} \prod_{k=1}^{r_j} \rho_{jk|c}^{I(w_j=k)} \right) \tag{4.2}$$

where w_j denotes the jth response in $\mathbf{W}$; r_j denotes the jth element of the vector $\mathbf{r}$ (i.e., the number of response categories for item j); and $I(\cdot)$ is the indicator function. The indicator function is 0 when the argument (terms inside the parentheses) are false and 1 when the argument is true. It is used here to select the appropriate response probabilities.

Recall that in the general mixture model (Equation 4.1), there were essentially two types of parameters: component weights and the component distributions. In Equation 4.2, γ_c are the component weights, or LC proportions. These values are the proportions of the population in each of the latent classes. An unrestricted LC model estimates only $C-1$ LC proportions, because the sum of all the LC proportions is 1.0 and the Cth is equal to 1.0 minus the rest.

The distribution of the measured items within each class is the

$$\prod_{j=1}^{q} \prod_{k=1}^{r_j} \rho_{jk|c}^{I(w_j=k)}$$

term from Equation 4.2. Each

$$\rho_{jk|c}^{I(w_j=k)}$$

is the probability of making response k to item w_j conditional on membership in the cth latent class. If one of the tobacco items was the question, "Have you smoked 100 or more cigarettes?" then $\rho_{100+Yes|LC1}$ would be the probability that someone in LC 1 responded *Yes* to the 100+ cigarettes question. If LC 1 was a group of regular smokers, we would expect that probability to be high. In an unrestricted LC model, there are $\sum_{j=1}^{q} C(r_j - 1)$ estimated ρ parameters.

The LC model is a nonparametric model, in that it entails few overall assumptions and no distributional assumptions. It is assumed that the correct number of classes has been specified (i.e., C is correct) and that each person in the population is a member of one and only one LC (i.e., $\sum \gamma_c = 1.0$). Furthermore, it is assumed that people within a class are homogeneous, meaning that everyone in a LC shares the same response distributions.

The most critical assumption of the LC model, and it is shared with the common factor model, is the assumption of conditional independence. This means that once an observation's latent variable score is known, in this case the LC membership, then the item responses are statistically independent. Another way to state this is that LC membership is assumed to account for all item covariation.

When the factor and LC models were originally developed, conditional independence was an assumption. Now LC models, just like confirmatory factor models, may include residual item dependencies (Hagenaars, 1988). However, as has been discussed in the structural equation modeling literature, dependent residuals should only be included when substantively meaningful, not simply to improve the fit of the model (Hayduk, 1987; MacCallum, 1986).

Estimation and Identification

Numerous estimation procedures may be used for the LC model, but maximum likelihood estimation is the most frequently used, especially via an EM algorithm (Dempster, Laird, & Rubin, 1977). An important deficiency of the EM algorithm is that standard errors are not a by-product of the analysis. Bootstrapping (Efron & Tibshirani, 1993) and Bayesian simulation methods (Lanza, Collins, Schafer, & Flaherty, 2005) can be used to estimate the uncertainty of the parameter estimates.

One characteristic of the loglikelihood function of the unrestricted LC model is that it is multimodal. Ideally, the loglikelihood function is unimodal, meaning there is one best solution to the loglikelihood function. This is never the case for the LC model. One reason that the loglikelihood function is known to be multimodal is that the order of the latent classes is arbitrary. A different ordering of the classes corresponds to a different sub-space of the loglikelihood surface. This characteristic of the loglikelihood function is an important issue for simulation-based estimation routines (Gilks, Richardson, & Spiegelhalter, 1996). In that literature, this is referred to as the *label switching* problem. It is important to note, though, that reordering the classes does not change the interpretation or substantive implications of the results.

But separate from the solutions due to reordering the classes, these models often have multiple solutions to the loglikelihood that are not simply reorderings of the latent classes. This means that there are different sets of estimates that fit the data to varying degree in the same general region of the loglikelihood function. Becuase of this problem, referred to as multimodality, Goodman (1974) only discusses local identification, meaning that a solution is only identified in a region of the loglikelihood. This is often the best that can be achieved in these models.

It is important to check that LC models are identified, especially the large longitudinal models that will be discussed. But these identification problems can also occur in cross-sectional models. These different sets of estimates can often imply different substantive conclusions. In the extreme, two quite different solutions will have nearly the same fit to the data. When this happens, reducing the number of parameters can often eliminate this problem (see section below). Checking for these multiple plausible solutions is commonly accomplished by running multiple sets of start values and verifying that one solution is clearly better than any of the others. Ideally, this one "best" solution is also the result in most of the sets of start values run. An example of this is presented below.

Model Fit and Selection

Assessing model fit and model selection are thorny issues across a variety of latent variable modeling areas, including the LC model (see, e.g., Aitkin & Rubin, 1985; Bollen & Long, 1993; Collins, Fidler, Wugalter, & Long, 1993; Hu & Bentler, 1999). Recall that the standard LC model is reproducing the observed response pattern frequencies. As such, categorical data fit statistics may be used in this context. The degrees of freedom of the LC model is the number of response patterns minus the number of parameter estimates minus 1. Two of the most commonly used fit statistics for LC models are Pearson's X^2 and the likelihood ratio statistic (G^2) (Agresti, 1990), which, under ideal circumstances, can be compared to a χ^2 distribution with the appropriate degrees of freedom.

However, there is a difficulty in using these statistics for assessing absolute fit in any large contingency table analysis. When data are sparse (i.e., relatively low n compared with the number of response patterns), the expectation of both of these statistics is less than the degrees of freedom (Agresti & Yang, 1987; Read & Cressie, 1988). This results in the situation where a fit statistic will look good, but in fact that model does not fit well due to sparse data.

One solution that has been proposed to the problem of assessing the fit of the LC model with sparse data is to use only limited information in the two-way marginals (Reiser & Lin, 1999). This approach only assesses how well the two-way item interactions are reproduced, rather than the full contingency table. But if higher-order interactions are important, then this approach is not expected to work well (Reiser & Lin, 1999).

A more *ad hoc* approach when fitting large complex models is to proceed with an interpretable model that has a G^2 statistic at or less than the degrees of freedom. When there are several competing models, one can use BIC (Raftery, 1995; Schwarz, 1978) or cross-validation (Collins, Graham, Long, & Hansen, 1994) to choose the best of the set.

Nested model comparisons are comparisons between two or models, one of which is a submodel (i.e., more restrictive form) of the other. By their nature, nested model tests are based on fewer parameters and tend not to be as strongly affected by sparse data. As a result, the difference of the degrees of freedom for the nested model comparison tend to be reasonable for making a statistical conclusion regarding the fit of the submodel. (Note that models with different numbers of classes are not strictly nested and nested model comparisons may not work in those cases; see Lo, Mendell & Rubin, 2001 for a discussion.)

Parameter Restrictions

Above it was mentioned that one way to address identification problems is to reduce the model's size. Parameter restrictions are one way of accomplishing that. Parameter restrictions, as the name implies, restrict in some way the possible values an estimate can take. One common and useful form of parameter restriction is fixing an estimate to a specific value. In this case, the fixed value is not estimated and therefore removed from the loglikelihood function.

Another common type of parameter restriction is equality constraints. This restriction specifies that two or more parameters are to be estimated at the same value. These restrictions can be very useful in improving model interpretability, hypothesis testing and reducing model size. The work presented here makes extensive use of equality constraints.

Latent Class Illustration

In this section, we will interpret some cross-sectional results from a LC analysis. Consider the following three Yes/No items measuring recent tobacco use: a) "Have you ever tried cigarette smoking, even just 1 or 2 puffs?"; b) "Have you smoked cigarettes on any of the last 30 days?"; and c) "Have you ever smoked cigarettes regularly (at least 1 cigarette every day for 30 days)?".

Table 4.1 contains estimates from a LC analysis of these three items[2]. The first column of Table 4.1 contains the LC proportions. However, before looking at the LC proportions, one should interpret the latent classes to confirm that the model is sensible. The final three columns of Table 4.1 contain the conditional response probabilities of a *Yes* response to the three tobacco items. We see that people in the first LC were very unlikely to respond *Yes* to any of the items. For example, people in this LC were only 3% likely to reply *Yes* to the question about if they ever smoked cigarettes regularly.

Note the two superscripted values in the last column. The superscripts denote estimates with equality restrictions. In this analysis, the probability of replying *Yes* to the third tobacco item was constrained to be equal for the first two latent classes. The substantive implication of this restriction is that classes 1 and 2 have identical probability distributions for Item 3 responses. As these class members are all people with no or relatively little smoking experience, it seems reasonable to constrain their probabilities of responding to the item about ever smoking cigarettes regularly. Another way to think of this equality restriction is that classes 1 and 2 have identical error rates (3%) for this item.

Let's interpret the three latent classes. The first class is characterized by a low probability of an affirmative response to any of the tobacco questions. This class could be labeled a "Never smoked" or "Never tried" class. Members of the second class are virtually certain to say that they have tried cigarettes, but only 28% likely to indicate any smoking in the past 30 days and 3%

TABLE 4.1 Estimated Latent Class Probabilities and the Probabilities of Responding Yes to the Tobacco Items Conditional on Latent Class (the $\hat{\rho}$'s).

LC (Proportion)	Probability of a Yes Response		
	Ever Try	Past 30 Days	Ever Regular
LC 1 (0.45)	0.0	0.01	0.03[1]
LC 2 (0.38)	1.0[2]	0.27	0.03[1]
LC 3 (0.17)	1.0[2]	0.99	0.97

Note: Superscripts denote estimates that were constrained to be equal.

likely to report ever smoking every day for 30 days. This second class could be labeled a "Tried cigarettes" class. The third class is very likely to respond affirmatively to each item. A label for this class could be "Regular smokers." Finding the interpretation of the classes satisfactory, we should look at the LC probabilities (expressed as percentages in the first column of Table 4.1). The largest class is the "Never smoked" class. The "Regular smokers" is the smallest class, with only 17% of the sample. The results in Table 4.1 provide a sense of a cross-sectional latent class analysis, but are actually from a single time-point in the longitudinal model to be presented next.

LATENT TRANSITION ANALYSIS

As originally developed, the LC model does not include parameters that explicitly quantify change. However, one can reparameterize the LC model to explicitly model change. This longitudinal model is referred to as latent transition analysis (LTA; Graham, Collins, Wugalter, Chung, & Hansen, 1991; Collins & Wugalter, 1992) or latent Markov modeling (Langeheine, 1994).

LTA is referred to as a reparameterization of the LC model above. This means that the parameters of the LTA model are functions of the parameters of the LC model. One can go from one model to the other without altering the fit of the model to the data. Consider a situation where one has data from two assessments of the same individuals, and there are two different latent classes to which people can belong at each time. One could fit a cross-sectional LC model, where each of the four "latent classes" corresponded to the combinations of two classes at two times (see Figure 4.1). For example, the first of the four classes in the cross-sectional model is comprised of the people who were in LC 1 at both measurement occasions. In this four-class cross-sectional model, and apart from the conditional response probabilities, three LC proportions would be estimated.

Let's turn to modeling these hypothetical data longitudinally. Instead, one could fit a model where everyone starts out in one of the two classes and estimate transition probabilities for the class memberships at Time 2 (see Figure 4.2). In this model, one would estimate one LC proportion for Time 1—where did people start? Also, there would be two estimated transition probabilities—for example, if one started out in LC 1, how likely was

| LC 1 | LC 1 | LC 2 | LC 2 |
| LC 1 | LC 2 | LC 1 | LC 2 |

Figure 4.1 Diagram representing the latent class model based upon two latent classes at each of two measurement occasions.

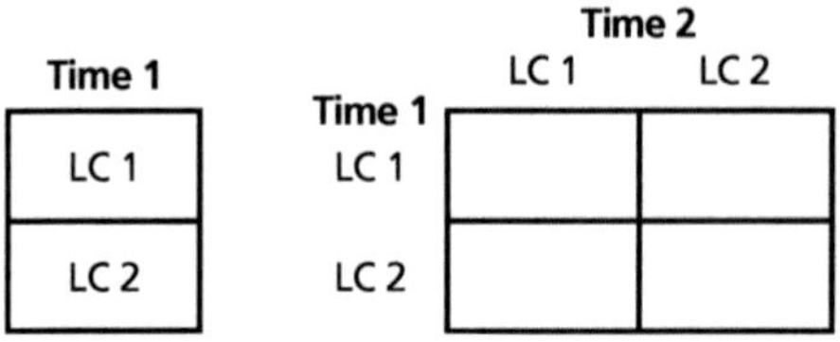

Figure 4.2 Diagram of the latent transition model with two latent classes at two times.

one to change? Notice that again in this LTA case, three parameters are being estimated, the same as the previous LC example.

If the unrestricted LTA model fits as well as an unrestricted latent class model, why do it? The answer is to make change explicit in the parameterization, which further allows one to easily test interesting yet complex hypotheses about change over time.

Latent Transition Model and Parameters

In presenting the LTA model and parameters, when possible we will use similar notation to that shown previously. An important difference between the notation for the LC model and the LTA model is that, in the longitudinal case, we have q items measured at each of T occasions. Therefore, the response pattern ($\mathbf{W}$) and the vector of the number of response categories ($\mathbf{r}$) are now both of $q \times t$ dimension. Instead of using C to index the number of latent classes, let $S_1, S_2, \ldots, S_T$ index the number of classes at each measurement occasion $t = 1, \ldots, T$. The latent transition model can be written as

$$\Pr(\mathbf{W}) = \sum_{s_1=1}^{S_1} \cdots \sum_{s_T=1}^{S_T} \delta_{s_1} \left(\prod_{j=1}^{q} \prod_{k=1}^{r_j} \rho_{1\,jk|s_1}^{I(w_{1j}=k)} \right) \times \prod_{t=2}^{T} \left(\tau_{s_t|s_{t-1}}^{(t-1)} \prod_{j=1}^{q} \prod_{k=1}^{r_j} \rho_{tjk|s_t}^{I(w_{tj}=k)} \right), \quad (4.3)$$

where w_{tj} denotes the jth response in $\mathbf{W}$ at Time t.

Recall from Figures 4.1 and 4.2 that the LTA model is taking the static LC approach (Figure 4.1) and splitting it into two pieces: the starting latent classes and subsequent transitions among the latent classes. In Equation 4.3, δ_{s_1} denotes the proportion of the population in LC S_1 at Time 1. The only other new parameter,

$$\tau_{s_t|s_{t-1}}^{(t-1)},$$

denotes the probability of changing from LC S_{t-1} at Time $t-1$ to LC S_t at Time t. In an unrestricted LTA model, there are S_1-1 estimates of δ parameters and $\sum_{t=2}^{T} S_{t-1}(S_t-1)$ estimates of τ parameters. The ρ parameters in Equation 4.3 have the same interpretation as in the traditional LC model, but now they can differ across time points. As the response probabilities can vary over time, there are T sets of ρ estimates in an unrestricted LTA model, where each occasion has the same number of ρ estimates as the LC model.

As a reparameterization of the LC model, the LTA model involves similar estimation, model checking, and fit assessment procedures and challenges. Note that the difficulties in assessing fit with sparse data mentioned previously are even more of an issue with these larger models, as the number of items is usually relatively large. However, simulation studies have investigated the effects of sparseness, and even with a great deal of sparseness, bias in parameter estimation may not be substantial (Collins & Tracy, 1997).

Latent Transition Illustration

As an illustration of the LTA model, consider the previous tobacco example extended to two measurement occasions. In this case, the three tobacco items have been asked of the sample twice. The first parameter estimates to examine are (again) the conditional response probabilities. The probabilities shown in Table 4.1 were actually the response probabilities from an LTA model in which equality restrictions were used to equate the conditional response probabilities longitudinally. This means that the probability of responding *Yes* to each item for each LC was restricted to be the same at both times. This ensures that the latent classes have the same interpretation across time. Furthermore, the LC proportions in parentheses of Table 4.1 are the estimates for the initial distribution of the classes.

The reason for the LTA parameterization is to study transitions among the latent classes. Table 4.2 shows the estimated transition probabilities for the tobacco data example. From this table, one sees that those who had not

TABLE 4.2 Estimated Transition Probabilities among Tobacco Classes

Time 1	Time 2 LC		
	LC 1	LC 2	LC 3
LC 1	0.82	0.15	0.03
LC 2	0.44	0.42	0.14
LC 3	0.07	0.08	0.85

tried cigarette smoking at Time 1 where 82% likely to remain in the "Never tried" LC. Correspondingly, 85% of Time 1 "Regular smokers" were likely to still be "Regular smokers" by Time 2. Interestingly, those who started in the "Tried cigarettes" class were 44% likely to change to the "No smoking" class and 42% likely to stay in the "Tried cigarettes" class. One could test if those transition probabilities were the same by fitting a model where those estimates were constrained to be equal, and comparing that restricted model to the full model. Additionally, the latent transition model can be extended to multiple groups which allows one to look at transition patterns broadly. For example, one could compare uptake of cigarette use between treatment and control groups.

ASSOCIATIVE LATENT TRANSITION ANALYSIS

As the latent transition model is a reparameterization of the LC model, so is the associative latent transition model. The latent transition model was formulated in order to study transitions in class memberships in one dynamic LC variable. The associative parameterization was formulated in order to facilitate examining conditional dependencies between two dynamic LC variables. Associative latent transition analysis (ALTA) makes specific conditional dependencies explicit and easy to test. As an example, consider the following two questions: a) If one progresses in tobacco use, is one more likely to also progress in alcohol use?; b) If one reduces one's tobacco use, is a parallel reduction in alcohol use also expected? These sort of associations between tobacco and alcohol use will be used to illustrate the associative latent transition model below.

Associative Model and Parameters

In the latent transition model, there is only one LC variable and people may change LC memberships over time. In the associative latent transition model, there are two dynamic latent class variables. The first may be thought of as the "predictor" LC variable and the second may be thought of as the "dependent" variable. That is, in the ALTA model one LC variable is conditioned on the other. It is not a cross-lagged model where influence is bi-directional. For simplicity, the predictor variable will be referred to as X and the dependent variable as Y.

As before, let **W** denote the full $q \times T$ response pattern. Recall that q is the number of measured variables at each time point, **r** is the number of response categories for the q items, and T is the number of measurement occasions. Furthermore, let $c_1 = 1,\ldots,C_1$ denote the latent classes in the X

latent class variable at Time 1, and let $d_1 = 1, \ldots, D_1$ denote the classes in Y at Time 1. In general, let C_t and D_t denote the number of latent classes in X and Y at Time t, $t = 1, \ldots, T$, respectively. Then the associative latent transition model can be written as

$$
\Pr(\mathbf{W}) = \sum_{c_1=1}^{C_1} \sum_{d_1=1}^{D_1} \cdots \sum_{c_T=1}^{C_T} \sum_{d_T=1}^{D_T} \alpha_{c_1} \beta_{d_1|c_1} \left(\prod_{j=1}^{q} \prod_{k=1}^{r_j} \rho_{1\,jk|c_1 d_1}^{I(w_{1j}=k)} \right) \times \qquad (4.4)
$$

$$
\prod_{t=2}^{T} \left(\varepsilon_{c_t|c_{t-1}d_{t-1}}^{(t-1)} \eta_{d_t|c_{t-1}c_t d_{t-1}}^{(t-1)} \prod_{j=1}^{q} \prod_{k=1}^{r_j} \rho_{tjk|c_t d_t}^{I(w_{tj}=k)} \right)
$$

The LTA model essentially "split" the LC formulation into two parts: initial LC memberships and transitions over time. The ALTA model is similarly refining how LC memberships are examined. Rather than one parameter for initial status, ALTA has two: α_{c_1} and $\beta_{d_1|c_1}$. (While going over the interpretation of the parameters, keep in mind that there are two dynamic LC variables here: X and Y, and that Y is conditioned on X.)

The α_{c_1} parameters are the unconditional class membership probabilities in the X variable at Time 1. In a model of tobacco and alcohol use, where alcohol use classes are conditional on tobacco use class membership, the α_{c_1} values are the initial tobacco class memberships. In an unrestricted ALTA model, there are $C_1 - 1$ estimates of α parameters.

The $\beta_{d_1|c_1}$ parameters are the probabilities of the latent classes in Y conditional on X class membership. In our example, these quantities are the estimates of each alcohol LC conditional on Time 1 tobacco LC membership. There are $C_1(D_1 - 1)$ estimates of β parameters in an unrestricted model.

The α and β parameters characterize the initial distribution of the latent classes. The remaining two parameter sets concern the longitudinal part of the model. The

$$
\varepsilon_{c_t|c_{t-1}d_{t-1}}^{(t-1)}
$$

parameters are the probabilities of X LC membership at Time t conditional on the pair of X and Y LC memberships at Time $t-1$. These parameters reflect the change on X given previous X and Y memberships. An unrestricted ALTA model includes $\sum_{t=2}^{T} C_{t-1} D_{t-1} (C_t - 1)$ estimates of ε parameters. In the context of the tobacco and alcohol example, these parameters quantify tobacco LC at Time 2, given both Time 1 class memberships. For example, these parameters could be used to compare the transition from "Tried cigarettes" to "Regular smoking" among people with no and some alcohol experience.

The

$$\eta^{(t-1)}_{d_t|c_{t-1}c_t d_{t-1}}$$

parameters are the probability of Y LC membership at Time t conditional on the X and Y pair of LC memberships at Time $t-1$ as well as the X membership at Time t. That is, how are both previous X and Y LC memberships and concurrent X membership associated with Y LC membership? Another way to think about these parameters is as quantifying how change in Y is associated with change on X. For example, how is change in alcohol use LC membership predicted by change and stability in tobacco class membership? There are $\sum_{t=2}^{T} C_{t-1} D_{t-1} C_t (D_t - 1)$ estimates of η parameters in an unrestricted ALTA model. Each of these parameters will be illustrated and discussed with an empirical example below.

As the ALTA model is a LC model, like LTA, it shares many of the same characteristics, features, and challenges of LC and latent transition models. For example, the other parameters in Equation 4.4 are conditional response probabilities (ρ terms) and their interpretation is the same as in the LC and latent transition models. Furthermore, there are the same number of conditional response probabilities in the ALTA model as in the LTA model. As was mentioned above, LTA models tend to be relatively large LC models because the items are assessed repeatedly. Correspondingly, ALTA models will tend to be large as well (even larger) because two sets of items (one for each LC variable) are assessed repeatedly. As such, difficulties in assessing absolute fit due to sparse data will be prevalent with ALTA models.

Illustrative Example

Theories of substance use onset often focus on stages of substance use. These stages are commonly defined in terms of the pattern, frequency and quantity of use. Typical stages are: "No use," "Tried" (meaning sampled a couple times), "Experimentation" (more frequent, but irregular use), and "Regular use."

In order to illustrate ALTA, we will examine the effects of tobacco use onset on alcohol use onset. Reciprocal and bi-directional effects of tobacco and alcohol use have been studied for many years (Sher, Gotham, Erickson, & Wood, 1996). In contrast to cross-lagged models, the ALTA parameterization orders the constructs. That is, the second LC variable is conditioned on the first. In other work on adolescent substance use onset, the "tobacco only" class has been found to be less stable than an "alcohol only" class. "Less stable" means that people transitioned out of a "tobacco only" class more often than those in an "alcohol only" class (Graham et al., 1991). For this reason, we are interested in treating tobacco as the predictor and alcohol as the response variable.

We will use data from the National Survey of Adolescent Health (Add Health; Udry, 2003). Specifically, we will look at the relation between the onsets of tobacco and alcohol use. One strength of using Add Health data for this is that it a nationally representative sample of people at a point in their lives when many have their first experiences with tobacco and alcohol.

However, one difficulty of using the Add Health data for this sort of analysis is that the items are not actually redundant indicators, as is typically preferred in a latent variable analysis of change. For example, rather than asking if someone has ever tried tobacco at each measurement occasion, in the Add Health Survey respondents were asked if they had ever tried tobacco at Time 1, but at Time 2 they were asked if they had tried tobacco since the prior interview.

One effect of these questions is that it essentially treats the responses as error free. That is, if the questions had been identical at each measurement occasion, then at Time 2 some respondents would have backtracked or claimed that they had never tried tobacco, when at Time 1 they had indicated that they had. One of these responses is incorrect, but we don't know which. The LC model is ideally suited for this sort of data because the conditional response probabilities can model inconsistent responding.

For the analysis here, since the items are not actually measuring life-time use, the models presented here are essentially recent use. As such, there is nothing inconsistent about saying that one had tried tobacco at Time 1, but not at Time 2. In this context, the no response at Time 2 simply means that they had not tried tobacco since the first assessment. As a result, these data appear to have little or no measurement error.

Data

The data used here are from the first two waves of the Add Health data (public use version). In 1994, 6504 U.S. students in grades 7 through 12 were surveyed, and in 1995, 4834 were reinterviewed. Our analysis uses data on all 6504 Time 1 respondents. For more information on the study, please see Harris et al. (2003).

Items

Three items for tobacco and alcohol use each were used in the LC analyses. The Time 1 tobacco items were: a) "Have you ever tried cigarette smoking, even just 1 or 2 puffs?"; b) "Have you ever smoked cigarettes regularly, that is, at least 1 cigarette every day for 30 days?"; and c) "During the past 30 days, on how many days did you smoke cigarettes?" The first two items were coded as *yes/no.* The past 30 day use item was recoded to indicate no past 30 day use versus any past 30 day use. As mentioned above, the parallel items at Time 2 for the two "ever use" items differed because they started with "Since [the last interview]...."

Three items were used in the analysis for Time 1 alcohol use. The first two were: a) "Have you had a drink of beer, wine, or liquor—not just a sip or a taste of someone else's drink—more than 2 or 3 times in your life?"; and b) "During the past 12 months, on how many days did you drink alcohol?" The third item was derived from two survey questions: a) "Over the past 12 months, on how many days did you drink five or more drinks in a row?"; and b) "Over the past 12 months, on how many days have you gotten drunk or 'very, very high' on alcohol?" These two items were coded as *yes/ no,* where a *yes* response to either of these questions gave the respondent a *yes* on the binary item used in the analysis. As with the tobacco items, the wording of the first alcohol item was different at Time 2 "Since [the last interview], have you had a drink..."

Analysis

In order to highlight the substantive features of the ALTA model, and keep the illustration straightforward, an overly simplistic model is presented. As a result, readers should focus on the sort of relations highlighted by the ALTA model, not on the substantive implications of this particular analysis.

The models presented here include three latent classes for tobacco and alcohol each. This number of classes was expected given the items and expectation based on many models of substance use onset: "No use," "Tried," "Experimentation," and "Regular use." However, the items used here do not provide much basis for distinguishing "Tried" from "Experimentation" classes, so the expected tobacco classes were: "No use," "Tried," and "Regular use." For alcohol, the expected classes were: "No use," "Recent use," and "Drunk/Binge." Furthermore, parameter equality restrictions (as shown above) were imposed on the conditional response probabilities both longitudinally and across several LC/item combinations in order to simplify and identify the models.

In order to examine the identifiability of the models, multiple sets of start values were run. The ALTA model was estimated with a Fortran 90 program written by the author. It is available free of charge, and is developed and supported by both the author and The Methodology Center at The Pennsylvania State University (http://www.methodology.psu.edu). The program fits the full ALTA model, including latent grouping variables for multiple groups analysis. Furthermore, it handles arbitrary patterns of missing data on the measured variables.

RESULTS

ALTA Model Fit and Identification

The full ALTA model has 88 parameters to estimate. Eighty are the substantive ALTA parameters: two α terms, six β terms, 18 ε terms, and 54 η terms. Only eight conditional response probabilities are estimated due to equality restrictions. Tables 4.1 and 4.3 show the conditional response probabilities for the tobacco and alcohol latent class variables, respectively.

The G^2 value of the full ALTA model is 1,335.8 with 4,007 degrees of freedom (df). In order to check if the ALTA model was identified, 1,000 sets of random start values were run. A total of 14 G^2 values were found and two did not converge (see Table 4.4). The mode corresponding to the lowest G^2 value (1,335.8) appears to be the largest mode in terms of support over the parameter space (Gelman, Carlin, Stern, & Rubin, 1995) as reflected by the largest number of sets of start values going to that solution, and it is a much lower value than the next lowest G^2 (5,538.2). Furthermore, the second and third G^2 values were degenerate solutions in that they had one empty LC. Given this pattern of results from the 1000 sets of start values, the model with the lowest G^2 was considered identified. Results from this full ALTA model are presented next.

Selected ALTA Model Estimates

The ALTA parameter estimates are discussed here. Only selected ε and η estimates will be presented.

TABLE 4.3   Probabilities of a Yes Response to the Alcohol Items Conditional on Latent Class Membership (the $\hat{\rho}$s).

	Probability of a Yes Response		
	Ever Try	Past 30 Days	Ever Regular
LC 1	0.0	0.00	0.0[3]
LC 2	1.0[4]	0.67	0.0[3]
LC 3	1.0[4]	1.00	1.0

Note: Superscripts denote estimates that were constrained to be equal.

TABLE 4.4   Fourteen Modes Found with 1,000 Sets of Start Values for the Full ALTA Model (df = 4,007)

G^2 Value	Number of solutions at each mode
1335.8	356
5538.2	77
5538.3	67
5737.1	86
6412.4	84
6491.4	73
9019.5	101
9845.0	39
10589.7	27
10600.8	3
10600.9	25
13598.1	15
14189.0	23
14433.1	22

Table 4.5 shows the distribution of the tobacco latent classes at Time 1. The majority of the sample was in the "No tobacco" LC at both times, but there appears to be an increase in the proportion of people in the "Regular tobacco" class.

Table 4.6 shows the Time 1 alcohol use LC distributions conditional on Time 1 tobacco use LC. If one was in the "No tobacco" LC at Time 1, one was also most likely to be in the "No alcohol" LC at Time 1. Among the Time 1 "Regular tobacco" use LC, the Time 1 alcohol use class membership probabilities are in the reverse order, but similar in magnitude. Among the members of the "Tried tobacco" LC at Time 1, there is little to no association between that LC and the alcohol use latent classes.

The first parameters reflecting change over time are the ε parameters, which describe how the pair of Time 1 LC memberships are associated with Time 2 tobacco use LC. Table 4.7 shows the ê estimates for those who were in the "No tobacco" LC at Time 1. Predominantly, those who started in the "No tobacco" LC were likely to remain there. One does see a decreasing trend in those probabilities as the level of Time 1 alcohol use LC increases.

The other estimates reflecting change over time are the η̂ estimates. These estimates are the Time 2 alcohol use LC membership probabilities conditional on Time 1 alcohol use LC and the Time 1 and Time 2 pair of tobacco use classes. Table 4.8 shows the η̂ estimates for those people in the

TABLE 4.5   The $\hat{\alpha}$s for Time 1 Tobacco Latent Classes

	Tobacco Use		
	No	**Try**	**Regular**
Time 1	0.45	0.38	0.17
Time 2	0.43	0.24	0.33

TABLE 4.6   The $\hat{\beta}$s for Time 1 Alcohol Use Latent Classes

	Time 1 Alcohol Use		
Time 1 Tobacco LC	**No**	**Try**	**Drunk**
No tobacco	0.71	0.19	0.10
Try tobacco	0.30	0.33	0.37
Regular tobacco	0.11	0.16	0.73

TABLE 4.7   The $\hat{\varepsilon}$s for Time 2 Tobacco Use Latent Classes Conditional on Time 1 No Tobacco Use and Time 1 Alcohol Use Latent Classes

	Time 2 Tobacco Use LC		
Alcohol LC	**No**	**Try**	**Regular**
No alcohol	0.85	0.13	0.02
Try alcohol	0.78	0.20	0.02
Drunk	0.67	0.24	0.09

TABLE 4.8   The $\hat{\eta}$s for People Starting in Time 1 No Tobacco and No Alcohol Use Classes

	Time 2 Alcohol Use		
Time 2 Tobacco LC	**No**	**Try**	**Drunk**
No tobacco	0.87	0.09	0.04
Try tobacco	0.65	0.15	0.20
Regular tobacco	0.44	0.06	0.50

Note: The rows are Time 2 tobacco class, and the estimates reflect the probability of Time 2 Alcohol use latent class conditional on the pair of Time 1 latent class memberships and Time 2 Tobacco use.

"No tobacco" and "No alcohol" classes at Time 1. If one remained in the "No tobacco" class at Time 2, then there was an 87% chance that person would also remain in the "No alcohol" LC. However, if one changed to the

"Tried tobacco" LC, then that person was over 20% less likely to also remain in "No alcohol." Notably, the probability of changing from "No alcohol" to the "Drunk" LC was five times greater among those who changed to "Tried tobacco" than for those who remained in the "No tobacco" LC.

An important group from a prevention perspective consists of those who make the largest jump in their use. Those individuals who changed from the "No tobacco" LC to "Regular tobacco use" were also most likely to make the transition from "No alcohol" to the "Drunk" LC. For this group of individuals in both no use latent classes at Time 1, it appears that changes in tobacco use are associated with change in alcohol use.

Hypothesis Testing

We next describe two examples of hypothesis testing. The first is a simple two parameter test focusing on examining if a particular reduction in alcohol use (i.e., Time 1 "Drunk" to Time 2 "No alcohol") depends upon the pattern of reduction in tobacco use (i.e., Time 1 "Tried tobacco" or "Regular tobacco" to "No tobacco"). The second illustrative hypothesis test is a larger, multiple parameter test, focusing on the association between the transition from Time 1 "No alcohol" to the Time 2 "Drunk" LC and the pattern of change in tobacco use LC memberships.

Is reducing to "No tobacco" from either the "Tried tobacco" or "Regular tobacco" latent classes equally associated with the transition from Time 1 "Drunk" to "No alcohol" at Time 2? In other words, are the rates that people change from "Drunk" to "No alcohol" independent of the pattern of reducing to "No tobacco" use? Or does the probability of the transition from "Drunk" to "No alcohol" depend on the pattern of reduction in tobacco use? In order to address this question, we need to compare two probabilities, the probability of changing from Time 1 "Drunk" to Time 2 "No alcohol" for a) those who changed from Time 1 "Tried tobacco" to Time 2 "No tobacco" (0.26) and b) those who changed from Time 1 "Regular tobacco" to Time 2 "No tobacco" (0.45). On the basis of the full model, it appears that those who reduced their tobacco use from "Regular tobacco" to "No tobacco" were almost twice as likely to also reduce their alcohol use from "Drunk" to "No alcohol" as those who reduced their tobacco use by changing from "Tried tobacco" to "No tobacco."

In order to test the hypothesis that the transition from the Time 1 "Drunk" LC to "No alcohol" at Time 2 does not depend on either of the patterns of reduction to "No tobacco" at Time 2, we can impose equality constraints on these two η estimates. When that is done, the constrained estimate is 0.29. The G^2 value from the constrained model is 1,343.36 with 1,408 df. This yields a $\Delta G^2 = 7.55$ with 1 df ($p = .006$). So, it appears that these probabilities should not be constrained to be equal and that the transition from the "Drunk" LC to "No alcohol" does depend on the pattern of the parallel reduction in tobacco use.

Next, consider a multi-parameter hypothesis focusing on whether the probability of changing from "No alcohol" to the "Drunk" LC depends on the combination of tobacco use latent classes over time, or if it only depends on Time 2 tobacco use LC. For example, is the probability of being in the Time 2 "Drunk" LC from "No alcohol" the same for these three tobacco use LC pairs: a) "No tobacco" → "No tobacco"; b) "Tried tobacco" → "No tobacco"; c) "Regular tobacco" → "No tobacco." Similarly, tobacco use transitions ending in the "Tried tobacco" and "Regular tobacco" latent classes will be compared. Table 4.9 shows the separate $\hat{\eta}$s for all patterns of tobacco use for those people who started in "No alcohol" and changed to the "Drunk" LC.

In order to test this hypothesis, the $\hat{\eta}$s are constrained to be equal within Time 2 tobacco LC. So, in Table 4.9 the 0.04, 0.08, and 0.11 are all constrained to be equal. Therefore, instead of estimating the nine values in the table, only three are estimated in the restricted model. The new G^2 value for the constrained model is 1,347.9 with 4,013 df, providing a $\Delta G^2 = 12.1$ with 6 df ($p = .060$). Table 4.10 contains the constrained $\hat{\eta}$s.

Had these been real substantive analyses, these results would be about the worst we could obtain. Based on the nested model test and the standard significance level of 0.05, the statistical conclusion is not clearly one way or another. If the constrained model had been clearly acceptable, then the implication would have been that the probability of membership in the

---

TABLE 4.9 The Probabilities of Time 2 Membership in the Drunk Latent Class for All Combinations of the Tobacco Use Latent Classes for Those Who Started in No Alcohol Use

Tobacco Class Transitions	
(Time 1, Time 2)	P(Drunk)
No tob, No tob	0.04
No tob, Try tob	0.20
No tob, Reg tob	0.50
Try tob, No tob	0.08
Try tob, Try tob	0.23
Try tob, Reg tob	0.55
Reg tob, No tob	0.11
Reg tob, Try tob	0.19
Reg tob, Reg tob	0.41

TABLE 4.10   Constrained η̂ Estimates from a Model Where the Probability of Membership in the Drunk Latent Class Only Depends on Time 2 Tobacco Use LC for Those People Starting in the No Alcohol Use LC

Time 2 Tobacco Class	P(Drunk)
No tobacco	0.05
Try tobacco	0.21
Regular tobacco	0.46

"Drunk" LC at Time 2 given Time 1 membership in the "No alcohol" LC depended only upon Time 2 tobacco use LC. On the other hand, if the constrained model clearly did not fit the data, the conclusion would have been that the transition from "No alcohol" to the "Drunk" LC indeed depended upon the pair of tobacco use latent classes. Hence in this case, change in alcohol use would be conditional on change in tobacco use.

DISCUSSION

A reparameterization of the LC model that focuses on the analysis of contingent change between two LC variables has been presented. This work follows from latent transition analysis. However, rather than modeling a single dynamic LC variable, the purpose of the ALTA parameterization is to make change and specific patterns of relations explicit in the model. This facilitates interpretation of the results as well as testing substantive questions via patterns of parameter restrictions. As illustrated, both specific and broad hypotheses of conditional change can be tested with ALTA.

The ALTA parameterization conditions one of the LC variables on the other. It is not a bi-directional model, as a cross-lagged regression model where each variable predicts the other. This parameterization is most appropriate for situations where there are reasons to condition one variable on another. In the current example, this ordering could perhaps be argued either way, however, this ordering was chosen by the author based on previous work in which tobacco use appeared to be associated with higher risk of subsequent alcohol use.

Though it was not discussed in this paper, the ALTA model in Equation 4.4 can be extended to a latent or manifest grouping variable. This allows one to compare contingent change between two groups, for example, treatment and control. Following the example used here, if escalation in tobacco use were found to be associated with escalation in alcohol use, an intervention aimed at slowing tobacco uptake could be found to also slow the rate of escalation among the alcohol use latent classes.

In addition to the ALTA model, the basic LC and latent transition model were presented and described. This chapter did not focus on the use of each of these models as measurement error models. When this is of interest, the conditional response probabilities are the primary means of assessing measurement quality (Clogg & Manning, 1996; Flaherty, 2002).

Any LC models, but especially large models such as LTA and ALTA, can have identification problems. In the empirical illustration, the problem of multiple modes was shown. While this problem was relatively well behaved, it becomes much more difficult when two or more solutions have similar fit. When this happens, one can reduce the model by imposing further parameter restrictions. This can often remove the multiple similar solutions. However, multiple solutions in general will probably always exist and it is important to confirm that the chosen solution is clearly the best of all the solutions.

Recommendations

Besides the recommendation to run multiple sets of start values to check model identification, there are some other recommendations about fitting these large models. If there is *a priori* theory about the number of classes and perhaps item class relations, then it can be relatively straightforward to select a model for a given problem. However, in the absence of clear theory, one must determine the number of classes for both LC variables in an ALTA model. One option is starting with separate LTA models in order to arrive at reasonable models of each process, including identifying measurement restrictions that may be necessary and/or desirable. That is, can a simple measurement model be used with the data? Does invariance hold over time, or do the response probabilities differ longitudinally? Once the individual LTA models are satisfactory, then one can move to the ALTA models.

Limitations

There are several limitations in the current work, primarily in what is understood about the model's behavior in real world applications. As mentioned, ALTA models tend to be quite large, but it is not clear how big is too big. Furthermore, how many respondents are necessary to fit these models? The difficulty in responding to these questions is that the answers are complex and related. For example, if measurement is very good (i.e., conditional response probabilities that are very close to 0.0 and 1.0), then fewer people will be necessary and more time points may be possible. Furthermore, if longitudinal restrictions on the transition parameters are reasonable, then model complexity is greatly reduced and fewer people may suffice or more time points may be possible.

On the other hand, if measurement is poor (i.e., conditional response probabilities approaching random), then very large samples, for example several thousand, may not be enough to identify a model slightly larger than the one presented here. This really should not be seen as a limitation of the model though, but rather one of poor measurement.

The current implementation of software to fit the ALTA model also suffers from some limitations. A very important one is that it does not currently produce standard errors for the parameter estimates. The only ways to address that omission right now are to either use nested model tests to evaluate all hypotheses of interest, or to bootstrap the standard errors.

Distinct benefits of this software are that it is free and it allows one to test quite complex hypotheses of change rather simply and directly. Other software packages such as M*plus* and ℓem may also fit these models.

While the ALTA model is a large LC model and entails all the challenges that go along with those models, it allows one to test very interesting hypotheses of conditional change between two dynamic LC variables. As developmental and longitudinal research move away from studying change in a single variable towards the study of change among multiple variables, models like ALTA should become increasingly valuable.

REFERENCES

Agresti, A. (1990). *Categorical data analysis*. New York: John Wiley & Sons.

Agresti, A., & Yang, M.-C. (1987). An empirical investigation of some effects of sparseness in contingency tables. *Computational Statistics and Data Analysis, 5*, 9–21.

Ainsworth, M. D., & Bell, S. M. (1970). Attachment, exploration, and separation: Illustrated by the behavior of one-year-olds in a strange situation. *Child Development, 41*, 49–67.

Aitkin, M., & Rubin, D. B. (1985). Estimation and hypothesis testing in finite mixture models. *Journal of the Royal Statistical Society, Series B, 47*, 67–75.

Bollen, K. A., & Long, J. S. (Eds.). (1993). *Testing structural equation models*. Newbury Park, CA: Sage.

Clogg, C. C. (1995). Latent class models. In G. Arminger, C. C. Clogg, & M. E. Sobel (Eds.), *Handbook of statistical modeling for the social and behavioral sciences* (pp. 311–359). New York: Plenum Press.

Clogg, C. C., & Manning, W. D. (1996). Assessing reliability of categorical measurements sing latent class models. In A. von Eye & C. C. Clogg (Eds.), *Categorical variables in developmental research: Methods of analysis.* (pp. 169–182). San Diego, CA: Academic Press.

Collins, L. M., & Cliff, N. (1990). Using the longitudinal Guttman simplex as a basis for measuring growth. *Psychological Bulletin, 108*, 128–134.

Collins, L. M., Fidler, P. L., Wugalter, S. E., & Long, J. D. (1993). Goodness-of-fit testing for latent class models. *Multivariate Behavioral Research, 28*, 375–389.

Collins, L. M., Graham, J. W., Long, J. D., & Hansen, W. B. (1994). Cross validation of latent class models of early substance use onset. *Multivariate Behavioral Research, 29*, 165–183.

Collins, L. M., & Tracy, A. J. (1997). Estimation in complex latent transition models with extreme data sparseness. *Kwantitatieve Methoden, 55*, 55–71.

Collins, L. M., & Wugalter, S. E. (1992). Latent class models for stage-sequential dynamic latent variables. *Multivariate Behavioral Research, 27*, 131–157.

Dempster, A. P., Laird, N. M., & Rubin, D. B. (1977). Maximum likelihood from incomplete data via the EM algorithm. *Journal of the Royal Statistical Society, Series B, 39*, 1–38.

Efron, B., & Tibshirani, R. J. (1993). *An introduction to the bootstrap.* Boca Raton, FL: Chapman and Hall/CRC.

Flaherty, B. P. (2002). Assessing the reliability of categorical substance use measures with latent class analysis. *Drug and Alcohol Dependence, 68S*, 7–20.

Flay, B. R. (1993). Nicotine addiction. In C. T. Orleans & J. Slade (Eds.), (pp. 360–384). New York: Oxford University Press.

Gelman, A., Carlin, J. B., Stern, H. S., & Rubin, D. B. (1995). *Bayesian data analysis.* London: Chapman & Hall.

Gilks, W. R., Richardson, S., & Spiegelhalter, D. J. (Eds.). (1996). *Markov chain Monte Carlo.* London: Chapman & Hall.

Goodman, L. A. (1974). Exploratory latent structure analysis using both identifiable and unidentifiable models. *Biometrika, 61*, 215–231.

Gorsuch, R. L. (1983). *Factor analysis* (2nd ed.). Hillsdale, NJ: Lawrence Erlbaum Associates.

Graham, J. W., Collins, L. M., Wugalter, S. E., Chung, N. K., & Hansen, W. B. (1991). Modeling transitions in latent stage-sequential processes: A substance use prevention example. *Journal of Consulting and Clinical Psychology, 59*, 48–57.

Hagenaars, J. A. (1988). Latent structure models with direct effects between indicators: Local dependence models. *Sociological Methods & Research, 16*, 379–405.

Harris, K. M., Florey, F., Tabor, J., Bearman, P. S., Jones, J., & Udry, J. (2003). *The National Longitudinal Study of Adolescent Health: Research design.* Available at http://www.cpc.unc.edu/projects/addhealth/design.

Hayduk, L. A. (1987). *Structural equation modeling with LISREL.* Baltimore: Johns Hopkins.

Hu, L., & Bentler, P. M. (1999). Cutoff criteria for fit indexes in covariance structure analysis: Conventional criteria versus new alternatives. *Structural Equation Modeling: A Multidisciplinary Journal, 6*, 1–55.

Langeheine, R. (1994). Latent variable Markov models. In A. von Eye & C. C. Clogg (Eds.), *Latent variables analysis. Applications for developmental research* (pp. 373–395). Thousand Oaks, CA: Sage Publications.

Lanza, S. L., Collins, L. M., Schafer, J. L., & Flaherty, B. P. (2005). Using data augmentation to obtain standard errors and conduct hypothesis tests in latent class and latent transition analysis. *Psychological Methods, 10,* 84–100.

Lanza, S. L., Flaherty, B. P., & Collins, L. M. (2003). Latent class and latent transition analysis. In I. B. Weiner, J. A. Schinka, & W. F. Velicer (Eds.), *Handbook of psychology: Vol 2. Research methods in psychology* (pp. 663–685). Hoboken, NJ: John Wiley & Sons.

Lazarsfeld, P. F., & Henry, N. W. (1968). *Latent structure analysis.* Boston: Houghton Mifflin.

Leventhal, H., & Cleary, P. D. (1980). The smoking problem: A review of the research and theory in behavioral risk modification. *Psychological Bulletin, 88,* 370–405.

Lo, Y., Mendell, N., & Rubin, D. B. (2001). Testing the number of components in a normal mixture. *Biometrika, 88,* 767–778.

MacCallum, R. (1986). Specification searches in covariance structure modeling. *Psychological Bulletin, 100,* 107–120.

Mayhew, K. P., Flay, B. R., & Mott, J. A. (2000, May). Stages in the development of adolescent smoking. *Drug and Alcohol Dependence, 59,* S61–S81.

McCutcheon, A. L. (1987). *Latent class analysis.* Thousand Oaks, CA: Sage Publications.

McLachlan, G., & Peel, D. (2000). *Finite mixture models.* New York: Wiley.

Raftery, A. E. (1995). Bayesian model selection in social research (with discussion). In P. V. Marsden (Ed.), *Sociological methodology* (pp. 111–196). Cambridge, MA: Blackwell.

Read, T. R. C., & Cressie, N. A. C. (1988). *Goodness-of-fit statistics for discrete multivariate data.* New York: Springer-Verlag.

Reiser, M., & Lin, Y. (1999). A goodness-of-fit test for the latent class model when expected frequencies are small. *Sociological Methodology, 29,* 81–111.

Schwarz, G. (1978). Estimating the dimension of a model. *The Annals of Statistics, 6,* 461–464.

Sher, K. J., Gotham, H. J., Erickson, D. J., & Wood, P. K. (1996). A prospective, high-risk study of the relationship between tobacco dependence and alcohol use disorders. *Alcoholism: Clinical and Experimental Research, 20,* 485–492.

Shiffman, S., Kassel, J. D., Paty, J. A., & Gnys, M. (1994). Smoking typology profiles of chippers and regular smokers. *Journal of Substance Abuse, 6,* 21–35.

Stern, H. S., Arcus, D., Kagan, J., Rubin, D. B., & Snidman, N. (1995). Using mixture models in temperament research. *International Journal of Behavioral Development, 18,* 407–423.

Titterington, D. M., Smith, A. F. M., & Makov, U. E. (1985). *Statistical analysis of finite mixture distributions.* New York: Wiley.

Udry, J. R. (2003). *The National Longitudinal Study of Adolescent Health (Add Health), Waves I & II, 1994–1996.* Chapel Hill, NC: Carolina Population Center, University of North Carolina at Chapel Hill.

NOTES

1. This work was supported by National Institute of Drug Abuse grants R01DA018673.
2. The estimates in Table 4.1 are actually based upon the longitudinal analysis, but we will treat them as cross-sectional results. This model as an unrestricted cross-sectional model based upon these three items would not be identified because there are more estimates than degrees of freedom.

CHAPTER 5

MODELING MEASUREMENT ERROR IN EVENT OCCURRENCE FOR SINGLE, NON-RECURRING EVENTS IN DISCRETE-TIME SURVIVAL ANALYSIS

Katherine E. Masyn
University of California at Davis

In the social sciences, research questions around specific behaviors, such as drug use or school drop out, and related events such as juvenile arrest, are often concerned with both the "if" and "when" of the behaviors and events. For example, it may be of interest to understand not only what predicts drug use but also what predicts the timing of first drug use, that is, the age of onset. It may also be of interest to understand how that drug use and its timing affects the likelihood of other negative life course outcomes. Survival analysis, sometimes called event history analysis, refers to a general set of statistical methods developed specifically to model the timing of events. This chapter concerns a subset of those methods dealing with events measured or occurring in discrete-time or grouped-time intervals.

Discrete-time survival analysis is distinguished from its counterpart, continuous-time survival analysis, by the time-scale on which the occurrence of

Advances in Latent Variable Mixture Models, pages 105–145

the event of interest is measured. On a continuous time-scale, an event can occur at any point in time and the exact timing of each event occurring in the sample is recorded such that no two people share the same event time (e.g., measuring event occurrence to the year, month, day, hour and minute). On a discrete time-scale, an event can occur at any point in time[1] but the timing of each event is recorded as occurring in one of a finite number of time intervals or time periods, where the number of intervals is notably fewer than the number of events observed in the sample (e.g., measuring event occurrence only to the year in a 10 year range). This time-scale distinction is necessary because the methods developed for continuous-time survival data do not directly apply to discrete-time survival data, just as regression techniques for continuous dependent variables do not directly apply to categorical outcomes.

As important as determining the time-scale for the event process is defining the nature of the event of interest. For this chapter, we limit ourselves to single, non-recurring events. This means that the event in question can happen once and only once to each individual. This also means that the event is of only one kind or type, meaning that we would consider the event of first juvenile arrest without distinguishing arrests for crimes against property from arrests for crimes against persons. All of what is presented here, however, can be extended to include recurring events and competing risks. We further assume that the duration of the event is short, even instantaneous, relative to the length of the discrete time periods into which time is divided. This means that an event occurrence would not span multiple time intervals but would occur within only one of the possible time periods.

Typically, when discrete-time survival analysis is applied, there is an implicit assumption that the "if" of the observed events is known with complete certainty. In some cases, this assumption might be quite reasonable, especially when dealing with truly definitive outcomes such as death. However, this assumption may be much less tenable when dealing with behavioral or clinical outcomes. Part of what may lessen the plausibility of this assumption is the means by which the event occurrence and timing thereof is assessed. In a retrospective study, each individual may be asked about the timing of an event, for example, "At what age did you have your first full drink of alcohol?" Even in prospective longitudinal studies we often must rely on the self-reports of behavior, such as, "How often did you drink alcohol in the last year?" For clinical outcomes, symptom level data may be collected every year and the occurrence of a clinical diagnosis (e.g., alcohol use disorder) is surmised from the reported symptoms. Techniques for dealing with error and bias in the reporting of event timing have been developed and applied (see, e.g., Gaskell, Wright, & O'Muircheartaigh, 2000). Much less attention has been given to measurement error in the assessment of the event occurrence. This chapter builds upon the limited amount of previous work done on this issue to further our understanding of the impact that measurement error in the determination of event occurrence can have on estimates related to the survival process, and to clarify a reformulation of the survival model as a latent Markov chain model that allows such error to be explicitly incorporated into the survival analysis.

The chapter begins with an overview of discrete-time survival analysis and the main quantities of interest when describing an event history process. The overview is followed by a detailed explanation of how a discrete-time survival analysis can be equivalently reformulated as a restricted Markov chain model. That model is then extended to include event indicators without measurement error and covariate predictors of the event process. The application of the model is illustrated with a real data example. The section after that explores the consequences of having measurement error on the event indicators for the parameter estimates related to the survival process. The chapter concludes with the presentation of a model with multiple event indicators at each time period and a discussion of model limitations and possible modeling extensions.

OVERVIEW OF DISCRETE-TIME SURVIVAL ANALYSIS

Suppose only events occurring in the time range $[a_0, a_J)$ may be observed for a given study with a random sample of n independent individuals[2] i, with $i = 1, 2, \ldots, n$. Suppose further that the time range is grouped into J time intervals, $t_j = [a_{j-1}, a_j)$, of equal width[3]. Let J_i be the final complete time period for which individual i is observed, where $J_i \leq J$ for all i. Usually, $J = \max_i(J_i)$. If an individual is lost to follow-up during a certain time period, say time period 5, then the last complete time period of observation for that individual would be $J_i = 4$. Assume for the purposes of this chapter that $a_0 = 0$ so that the beginning of the first time interval is the beginning of the survival process; that is, t_1 is the first time period for which individuals are at-risk for the event and, thus, no one has experienced the event prior to time period 1. Let T_i be the time period in which the event occurs for individual i. If $T_i \leq J_i$, then the event is recorded during the time that the individual is under observation and T_i is known. If $T_i > J_i$, then the event is not recorded during the time that the individual is under observation and the value of T_i is unknown to the researcher; that is, the value of T_i is missing. This kind of missingness is known as *right-censoring*. It is assumed that all individuals are at-risk for the event of interest and that if an individual is not observed to experience the event during the time that he or she is under observation, then he or she will experience the event at some later time, beyond J_i. The key feature of right-censored observations is that there is still some information available about T_i—even though the true value of T_i is unknown, it is known that $T_i > J_i$. This information does contribute something to our understanding of the survival process and can be included in the data analysis. For this chapter, we will limit our treatment of missing event time data to non-informative right-censoring, meaning that the time at which an individual is censored is not related to the event time for that individual $(T_i \perp J_i)$, conditional on observed covariates.

There are two main quantities of interest when describing a discrete-time event history process: the survival probability and the hazard probability. The survival probability is likely the most intuitive in understanding the nature of an event history process. The survival probability corresponding to time period j is defined as the probability of an individual "surviving" beyond the interval, j; that is, remaining event-free through time period j. We will denote the survival probability as $P_s(j)$ such that:

$$P_s(j) = \Pr(T > j). \tag{5.1}$$

The hazard probability, although perhaps less intuitive, is the quantity that we deal with most often in survival analysis since, as will be shown later, our models for the event history process are specified in terms of the hazard probabilities. The hazard probability corresponding to time period j is defined as the probability of an individual experiencing the event in time period j given that he or she had not experienced the event prior to time period j. We will denote the hazard probability as $P_h(j)$ such that:

$$P_h(j) = \Pr(T = j \mid T \geq j). \tag{5.2}$$

A specific survival probability can be computed from hazard probabilities using the following relationship:

$$P_S(j) = \Pr(T > j) \tag{5.3}$$
$$= \Pr(T \neq 1 \mid T \geq 1) \cdot \Pr(T \neq 2 \mid T \geq 2) \quad \Pr(T \neq j \mid T \geq j)$$
$$= \prod_{v=1}^{j} (1 - \Pr(v)).$$

It is useful to examine both the survival and hazard probabilities for the time periods under study. The hazard probabilities describe how the risk for an event changes over time while the survival probabilities reflect not only the cumulative risk impact on the population, but also quantify the proportion of the original population still susceptible to the risk defined by the hazard probability for each time period.

Given these definitions and the relationship between the survival and hazard probabilities, it is possible to construct the likelihood functions for both uncensored and right-censored observations in terms of the hazard probabilities. We will assume that all individuals in the sample are drawn from the same population, such that $T_i \sim T$ for all $i = 1, \ldots, n$. For an individual i whose event time T_i is observed (i.e., $T_i \le J_i$), the likelihood is given by:

$$l_i = \Pr(T = t_i) \tag{5.4}$$
$$= \Pr(T = t_i \mid T \ge t_i) \cdot \Pr(T > t_i - 1)$$
$$= P_h(t_i) \cdot P_S(t_i - 1)$$
$$= P_h(t_i) \cdot \prod_{v=1}^{t_i-1} (1 - P_h(v)).$$

For an individual i who is right-censored at J_i so that T_i is not observed (i.e., $T_i > J_i$), the likelihood is given by:

$$l_i = \Pr(T > j_i) \tag{5.5}$$
$$= P_S(j_i)$$
$$= \prod_{v=1}^{j_i} (1 - P_h(v)).$$

The full observed data likelihood can then be written as:

$$L = \prod_{i=1}^{n} \left[\left(P_h(t_i) \cdot \prod_{v=1}^{t_i-1} \left(1 - P_h(v)\right) \right)^{I(T_i \le j_i)} \cdot \left(\prod_{v=1}^{j_i} \left(1 - P_h(v)\right) \right)^{I(T_i > j_i)} \right]. \tag{5.6}$$

Note that the above likelihood may appear less compact than the conventional likelihood expression (see, e.g., Singer & Willet, 1993) where it is usually assumed that if T_i is observed, then $J_i = T_i$; that is, if the event is observed, then the time period in which the event occurs is the final time period of observation so that J_i represents either an event time or a censoring time. We do not make this assumption, which allows for the possibility that an individual may continue to be under observation even *after* the event has occurred. The reason for this becomes clearer in the sections that follow, but is a necessary consequence of probable error in the measurement of event occurrence. The maximum likelihood estimates for the $P_h(j)$ terms under the missing-at-random (MAR) assumption correspond to the same estimates under the assumption of non-informative right-censoring (Little & Rubin, 2002; Masyn, 2003; Muthén & Masyn, 2005).

The various approaches to discrete-time survival analysis differ primarily in the required format of the observed data and how the relationships between the hazard probabilities and covariates are specified. In his seminal 1972 paper, Cox suggested using a logistic regression to relate the discrete-time hazard probabilities to observed covariates. The use of logistic regression for discrete-time survival analysis has been studied further by Singer and Willet (1993, 2003) as well as many others including Prentice and Gloeckler (1978) and Allison (1982, 1984, 1995). Alternate approaches include multi-level ordinal multinomial regression (Hedeker, Siddiqui, & Hu, 2000), mixed Poisson models (Land, Nagin, & McCall, 2001), log-linear models (Laird & Oliver, 1981; Vermunt, 1997), latent class regression models (Masyn, 2003; Muthén & Masyn, 2005; Vermunt, 1997, 2002), multistate models (Lindeboom & Kerkofs, 2000; Steele, Goldstein, & Browne, 2004), and discrete-time Markov chain models (Tuma & Hannan, 1984; Van de Pol & Langeheine, 1990; Vermunt, 1997). This chapter explores in detail the formulation of a discrete-time event history process in a Markov chain framework for the reason that this formulation, of all those listed above, is the one that most readily accommodates the possibility of measurement error in event occurrence. This chapter also details a model specification that allows estimation of the proposed models in more advanced statistical modeling software packages, specifically M*plus* Version 4.2 (Muthén & Muthén, 2006). (For more information on continuous-time survival analysis in a Markov chain framework, see, e.g., Aalen & Johansen, 1978, and Andersen, 1988.)

DISCRETE-TIME SURVIVAL ANALYSIS AS A MARKOV CHAIN MODEL

The phrase *Markov chain* refers to a model for repeated measures of one or more discrete variables where change in a categorical outcome (latent or observed) over time is described through a set of transition matrices. The levels of the categorical outcome are referred to as *states* and the elements of the transition matrices are conditional probabilities for being in a specific state in one time period conditional on the occupied states in the prior time periods. (For more general information on Markov chain models, see, e.g., Langeheine & Van de Pol, 2002; Van de Pol & Langeheine, 1990; Vermunt, Langeheine, & Bockenholt, 1999.) In this section, we reframe the single, non-recurring event history process as a simple first-order Markov chain where the states occupied at each time period are directly observed and measured without error, and where the probability of being in a specific state in one time period is only dependent upon the state occupied in the time period immediately preceding the time period in question.

In order to reformulate an event history process as a Markov chain, we must first define the *states* that may be occupied in any given time period. For a single, non-recurring event, there are three states: pre-event, event, and post-event. The event state is occupied during the time period in which the event occurs. As in the previous section, we will assume that the first time period begins at $a_0 = 0$ so that all individuals occupy a pre-event state prior to the first time period. From one time period to the next, an individual may either remain in a pre-event state or may transition to the event state. As stated before, we assume that the nature of the event is such that its duration is always contained within a single time period. Thus, once an individual occupies an event state for a given time period, he or she will automatically transition into a post-event state in the next time period where he or she will remain for all subsequent time periods. The post-event state, in Markov chain terms, would be referred to as an *absorbing* state. This means that for a single, non-recurring event, individuals may not occupy an event state more than once.

Let E_j represent the categorical outcome variable for time period j with three categories corresponding to the three potential states. The expressions below formalize the state definitions:

$$E_j = \begin{cases} 0 \text{ (pre-event)} & \text{if } T > j \\ 1 \quad \text{(event)} & \text{if } T = j \\ 2 \text{ (post-event)} & \text{if } T < j \end{cases} \qquad (5.7)$$

where $j = 1, 2, \ldots, J$. As explained previously, changes in the categorical outcome, in this case, E, across time periods are described through a set of transition matrices. The elements of each transition matrix are conditional probabilities, denoted τ, where $\tau_{k(j)|m(j-1)}$ is the probability of an individual occupying state k in time period j given that he or she occupied state m in time period $j - 1$. That is:

$$\tau_{k(j)|m(j-1)} = \Pr(E_j = k | E_{j-1} = m). \qquad (5.8)$$

The transition matrices are denoted $\mathbf{T}$, where $\mathbf{T}_{(j)(j-1)}$ is the $M \times K$ transition matrix containing the conditional probabilities for states $(1,\ldots,K)$ in time period j given each state $(1,\ldots,M)$ in time period $j - 1$. In our case, there are three states that may be occupied during any given time period,[4] and so a general representation of each transition matrix can be given by:

$$
\begin{array}{cc}
 & E_j \\
\begin{array}{c} E_{j-1} \end{array} &
\begin{array}{ccc} 0 & \quad 1 & \quad 2 \end{array}
\end{array}
$$

$$
\mathbf{T}_{(j)(j-1)} = \begin{array}{c} 0 \\ 1 \\ 2 \end{array}
\begin{pmatrix}
\tau_{0(j)|0(j-1)} & \tau_{1(j)|0(j-1)} & \tau_{2(j)|0(j-1)} \\
\tau_{0(j)|1(j-1)} & \tau_{1(j)|1(j-1)} & \tau_{2(j)|1(j-1)} \\
\tau_{0(j)|2(j-1)} & \tau_{1(j)|2(j-1)} & \tau_{2(j)|2(j-1)}
\end{pmatrix}. \qquad (5.9)
$$

Note that the elements across each row the transition matrix must sum to one. That is:

$$\sum_{k=1}^{K} \tau_{k(j)lm(j-1)} = 1.$$ (5.10)

In order for the above transition matrix to properly reflect the nature of the three states as we defined them above, certain restrictions must be placed on the transition probabilities. Once an individual experiences the event, he or she cannot return to a pre-event state. Therefore:

$$\tau_{0(j)|1(j-1)} = \Pr(E_j = 0 \mid E_{j-1} = 1) = \Pr(T > j \mid T = j-1) = 0.$$ (5.11)

We also assume that occupation in an event state does not extend beyond one time period. Thus:

$$\tau_{1(j)|1(j-1)} = \Pr(E_j = 1 \mid E_{j-1} = 1) = \Pr(T = j \mid T = j-1) = 0.$$ (5.12)

And once in an event state, the individual automatically transitions to a post-event state where he or she remains for the rest of time. Therefore:

$$\tau_{2(j)|1(j-1)} = \Pr(E_j = 2 \mid E_{j-1} = 1) = \Pr(T < j \mid T = j-1) = 1;$$

$$\tau_{0(j)|1(j-1)} = \Pr(E_j = 0 \mid E_{j-1} = 1) = \Pr(T > j \mid T = j-1) = 0;$$

$$\tau_{0(j)|2(j-1)} = \Pr(E_j = 0 \mid E_{j-1} = 2) = \Pr(T > j \mid T < j-1) = 0;$$ (5.13)

$$\tau_{1(j)|2(j-1)} = \Pr(E_j = 1 \mid E_{j-1} = 2) = \Pr(T = j \mid T < j-1) = 0;$$

$$\tau_{2(j)|2(j-1)} = \Pr(E_j = 2 \mid E_{j-1} = 2) = \Pr(T < j \mid T < j-1) = 1.$$

Since an individual cannot move to a post-event state without first occupying an event state, we also have:

$$\tau_{2(j)|0(j-1)} = \Pr(E_j = 2 \mid E_{j-1} = 0) = \Pr(T < j \mid T > j-1) = 0.$$ (5.14)

Inserting the above restrictions into the general transition matrix, we obtain the following:

$$
\mathbf{T}_{(j)(j-1)} =
\begin{array}{c c}
 & E_j \\
E_{j-1} &
\begin{array}{c c c}
\quad 0 \quad & \quad 1 \quad & \quad 2 \quad \\
\end{array} \\
\begin{array}{c} 0 \\ 1 \\ 2 \end{array}
&
\left(
\begin{array}{c c c}
\tau_{0(j)|0(j-1)} & \tau_{1(j)|0(j-1)} & 0 \\
0 & 0 & 1 \\
0 & 0 & 1 \\
\end{array}
\right).
\end{array}
$$ (5.15)

Since each row sums to 1, we then have:

$$\tau_{0(j)|0(j-1)} = 1 - \tau_{1(j)|0(j-1)}.$$ (5.16)

Substituting in our definitions for E_j gives:

$$\tau_{1(j)|0(j-1)} = \Pr(E_j = 1 \mid E_{j-1} = 0) = \Pr(T = j \mid T > j-1) = P_h(j), \text{ and}$$ (5.17)

$$\tau_{0(j)|0(j-1)} = 1 - P_h(j).$$

The transition matrix can now be written in terms of the hazard probabilities as:

$$
\begin{array}{c}
& & E_j \\
& E_{j-1} & 0 & 1 & 2 \\
\mathbf{T}_{(j)(j-1)} =
& \begin{array}{c} 0 \\ 1 \\ 2 \end{array}
& \left(\begin{array}{ccc}
1 - P_h(j) & P_h(j) & 0 \\
0 & 0 & 1 \\
0 & 0 & 1
\end{array}\right).
\end{array}
$$ (5.18)

For each time interval j with $j > 1$, there is an associated transition matrix, $\mathbf{T}_{(j)(j-1)}$ as defined above. For the first time interval, $j = 1$, there is no transition matrix. It is assumed that at the beginning point of the first time interval, everyone is in a pre-event state. Thus, the only two states that an individual may occupy in the first interval is a pre-event state or an event state. Here, the marginal probabilities rather than transition probabilities map onto the hazard probabilities where:

$$\Pr(E_1 = 0) = \Pr(T > 1) = 1 - P_h(1);$$
$$\Pr(E_1 = 1) = \Pr(T = 1) = P_h(1);$$ (5.19)
$$\Pr(E_1 = 2) = \Pr(T < 1) = 0.$$

Instead of a transition matrix, define a 1×2 vector of the initial marginal probabilities, $\mathbf{\Pi}_{(1)}$, where:

$$\mathbf{\Pi}_{(1)} = \begin{bmatrix} \pi_0 & \pi_1 \end{bmatrix} = \begin{bmatrix} 1 - P_h(1) & P_h(1) \end{bmatrix}.$$ (5.20)

The first transition matrix, $\mathbf{T}_{(2)(1)}$, is then a 2×3 matrix rather than a 3×3 matrix given by:

$$
\begin{array}{c}
 E_2 \\
\end{array}
$$

$$
\mathbf{T}_{(2)(1)} =
\begin{array}{c}
0 \\ 1
\end{array}
\left(
\begin{array}{ccc}
1 - P_h(2) & P_h(2) & 0 \\
0 & 0 & 1
\end{array}
\right).
\tag{5.21}
$$

with column labels E_1 $\;0$, E_2: 1 and 2.

In Markov chain models, it is possible to compute the transition probabilities for ending in a particular state in time period j given a starting state in time period $j - p$ by multiplying the transitions matrices between $j - p$ and j. That is:

$$
\mathbf{T}_{(j)(j-p)} = \mathbf{T}_{(j-p+1)(j-p)} \cdot \mathbf{T}_{(j-p+2)(j-p+1)} \cdots \mathbf{T}_{(j)(j-1)}.
\tag{5.22}
$$

Further, the probabilities of ending in a particular state in time period j given an initial starting state are given by:

$$
\mathbf{T}_{(j)(1)} = \mathbf{\Pi}_{(1)} \cdot \mathbf{T}_{(2)(1)} \cdot \mathbf{T}_{(3)(2)} \quad \mathbf{T}_{(j)(j-1)}.
\tag{5.23}
$$

As an example, the transition probabilities in our case from initial state (pre-event) to time period 3 can be expressed as:

$$
\mathbf{T}_{(3)(1)} = \mathbf{\Pi}_{(1)} \cdot \mathbf{T}_{(2)(1)} \cdot \mathbf{T}_{(3)(2)}
\tag{5.24}
$$

$$
= \begin{bmatrix} 1 - P_h(1) & P_h(1) \end{bmatrix} \cdot
\begin{bmatrix}
1 - P_h(2) & P_h(2) & 0 \\
0 & 0 & 1
\end{bmatrix} \cdot
\begin{bmatrix}
1 - P_h(3) & P_h(3) & 0 \\
0 & 0 & 1 \\
0 & 0 & 1
\end{bmatrix}
$$

$$
= \begin{bmatrix}
\left(1 - P_h(1)\right) \cdot \left(1 - P_h(2)\right) \cdot \left(1 - P_h(3)\right) \\
\left(1 - P_h(1)\right) \cdot \left(1 - P_h(2)\right) \cdot \left(P_h(3)\right) \\
\left(1 - P_h(1)\right)\left(P_h(2)\right) + P_h(1)
\end{bmatrix}^{T}.
$$

Notice that the first element, $T^{(1)}_{(3)(1)}$, of the resultant vector, $\mathbf{T}_{(3)(1)}$, is the survival probability for time period 3. More generally:

$$
T^{(1)}_{(j)(1)} = \prod_{v=1}^{j}\left(1 - P_h(v)\right) = P_S(j),
\tag{5.25}
$$

$$
T^{(2)}_{(j)(1)} = \left(\prod_{v=1}^{j-1}\left(1 - P_h(v)\right)\right) \cdot P_h(j) = P_S(j-1) \cdot P_h(j).
$$

ESTIMATING THE DISCRETE-TIME SURVIVAL ANALYSIS AS A MARKOV CHAIN MODEL

To understand the identification and likelihood construction for the discrete-time survival analysis model for a single, non-recurring event in a Markov chain model framework, it is useful to consider the information available from a complete sample with no missing data during the observation period. This does not mean there are no missing event times, only that all of the right-censoring occurs at the end of the final time period of observation. As an example, take a study with six periods of observation. The possible observed chains for a complete data set are listed in Table 5.1 below.

For six time periods of observation, there are seven potential complete chains. In general, for J time periods, there are $J + 1$ possible observed chains for the complete data. With the complete data, all observations could be summarized into a single frequency table. Since the frequencies must add to the total sample size, that is,

$$\sum_{j=1}^{J+1} n_j = n,$$

there are J degrees of freedom available for parameter estimation in a model. Each transition matrix, as defined in the previous section, has exactly one unknown value, $P_h(j)$. There are $J - 1$ transition matrices needed to describe the chain across J time periods along with the initial state probabilities vector, also with one unknown value, $P_h(1)$, resulting in J unknown values. Not surprisingly then, the discrete-time survival Markov chain without covariates and without restrictions on the hazard probabilities across time is a just-identified, fully saturated model that reproduces the observed chain frequencies exactly in the complete observations case.

TABLE 5.1   Frequency Table of Observable Chains for Complete Data

E_1	E_2	E_3	E_4	E_5	E_6	f
1	2	2	2	2	2	n_1
0	1	2	2	2	2	n_2
0	0	1	2	2	2	n_3
0	0	0	1	2	2	n_4
0	0	0	0	1	2	n_5
0	0	0	0	0	1	n_6
0	0	0	0	0	0	n_7

The last chain in Table 5.1 represents individuals under observation for all six time periods who do not experience the event during the entire length of observation. These individuals are right-censored in that we do not know their exact event times, only that $T > 6$, but the observations are complete in that we do know their event states for all six periods. Suppose, however, that there are incomplete data in the sense that some individuals are right-censored prior to the end of the study. For example, if there was an individual who was censored during the fourth time period such that the third time period was the last complete time period of observation, his or her observed chain would look like the following:

$$e_i = (0 \quad 0 \quad 0 \quad \bullet \quad \bullet \quad \bullet),$$

where "$\bullet$" denotes a missing observation. Such an individual contributes some information to estimate the model—we know that he or she could only have a complete chain matching one of the last four in Table 5.1.

It is assumed for the purposes of this chapter that the missing data in the above example are ignorable in the sense that the individual's ultimate event time, though unobserved, is unrelated to the timing of the final (censored) observation on that individual. The conventional assumption of noninformative censoring (i.e., that censoring times are independent of event times conditional on the observed covariates) corresponds to the assumption of ignorable missingness in a general latent variable modeling framework. These models can be estimated using maximum likelihood under the assumption of MAR (Little & Rubin, 2002). The observed data likelihood for uncensored individuals with $T_i = t_i$ where $t_i \leq j_i \leq J$, is given by:

$$l_i = \Pr(T = t_i) \tag{5.26}$$
$$= \Pr(E_1 = 0, E_2 = 0,\ldots, E_{t_i-1} = 0, E_{t_i} = 1, E_{t_i+1} = 2,\ldots, E_{j_i} = 2).$$

We see above that the observed data likelihood can be written in terms of the likelihood of the observed chain which is, in essence, the joint probability of the event indicators at the observed values for each uncensored individual. The joint probability given in Equation 5.26 can be expressed as a product of conditional probabilities given by:

$$l_i = \Pr(E_1 = 0) \cdot \Pr(E_2 = 0 \mid E_1 = 0) \cdot \Pr(E_3 = 0 \mid E_2 = 0, E_1 = 0) \cdots$$
$$\Pr(E_{t_i-1} = 0 \mid E_{t_i-2} = 0,\ldots, E_1 = 0) \cdot \Pr(E_{t_i} = 1 \mid E_{t_i-1} = 0,\ldots, E_1 = 0) \cdot$$
$$\Pr(E_{t_i+1} = 2 \mid E_{t_i} = 1, E_{t_i-1} = 0,\ldots, E_1 = 0) \cdot \Pr(E_{t_i+2} = 2 \mid E_{t_i+1} = 2, \tag{5.27}$$
$$E_{t_i} = 1, E_{t_i-1} = 0,\ldots, E_1 = 0) \cdots$$
$$\Pr(E_{j_i} = 2 \mid E_{j_i-1} = 2,\ldots, E_{t_i+1} = 2, E_{t_i} = 1, E_{t_i-1} = 0,\ldots, E_1 = 0).$$

Since the model for the event history is a requisite first-order Markov chain, all the conditional probabilities given in Equation 5.27 reduce to transition probabilities, for example:

$$\Pr(E_{t_i+1} = 2 \mid E_{t_i} = 1, E_{t_i-1} = 0, \ldots, E_1 = 0) = \Pr(E_{t_i+1} = 2 \mid E_{t_i} = 1).$$

So the observed data likelihood further simplifies to:

$$l_i = \Pr(E_1 = 0) \cdot \Pr(E_2 = 0 \mid E_1 = 0) \cdots \Pr(E_{t_i-1} = 0 \mid E_{t_i-2} = 0) \cdot \quad (5.28)$$
$$\Pr(E_{t_i} = 1 \mid E_{t_i-1} = 0) \cdot \Pr(E_{t_i+1} = 2 \mid E_{t_i} = 1) \cdot$$
$$\Pr(E_{t_i+2} = 2 \mid E_{t_i+1} = 2) \cdots \Pr(E_{j_i} = 2 \mid E_{j_i-1} = 2).$$

Looking at the product pattern in Equation 5.28, the observed data likelihood can be described by a product of a marginal probability in the first time point, transition probabilities from a pre-event to pre-event state in time periods 2 through $t_i - 1$, the transition probability from a pre-event state in time period $t_i - 1$ to an event state in time period t_i, the transition probability from an event state in time period t_i to a post-event state in time period $t_i + 1$, and transition probabilities from a post-event to post-event state in time periods $t_i + 1$ through j_i. Thus, the likelihood of the observed event chain can be expressed in terms of the marginal probability in the first time period and the transition probabilities for all remaining time periods. That is:

$$l_i = \left(\Pr(E_1 = 0)\right) \cdot \left(\prod_{v=2}^{t_i-1} \Pr(E_v = 0 \mid E_{v-1} = 0)\right) \cdot \left(\Pr(E_{t_i} = 1 \mid E_{t_i-1} = 0)\right) \cdot \quad (5.29)$$

$$\left(\Pr(E_{t_i+1} = 2 \mid E_{t_i} = 1)\right) \cdot \left(\prod_{v=t_i+2}^{j_i} \Pr(E_v = 2 \mid E_{v-1} = 2)\right)$$

$$= (\pi_0) \cdot \left(\prod_{v=2}^{t_i-1} \tau_{0(v)|0(v-1)}\right) \cdot (\tau_{1(t_i)|0(t_i-1)}) \cdot (\tau_{2(t_i+1)|1(t_i)}) \cdot \left(\prod_{v=t_i+2}^{j_i} \tau_{2(v)|2(v-1)}\right)$$

$$= (\pi_0) \cdot \left(\prod_{v=2}^{t_i-1} \left(1 - \tau_{1(v)|0(v-1)}\right)\right) \cdot (\tau_{1(t_i)|0(t_i-1)})$$

$$= \left(\prod_{v=1}^{t_i-1} \left(1 - P_h(v)\right)\right) \cdot \left(P_h(t_i)\right).$$

The above likelihood holds for all individuals known to be in one of the first six chain patterns in Table 5.1, including those that go missing after the event occurrence but before the conclusion of the study. For right-censored individuals with $T_i > j_i$ and $j_i \leq J$, the observed data likelihood is given by:

$$l_i = \Pr(T > j_i) \qquad (5.30)$$

$$= \Pr(E_1 = 0, E_2 = 0, \ldots, E_{j_i} = 0)$$

$$= \left(\Pr(E_1 = 0)\right) \cdot \left(\prod_{v=2}^{j_i} \Pr(E_v = 0 \mid E_{v-1} = 0)\right)$$

$$= (\pi_0) \cdot \left(\prod_{v=2}^{j_i} \tau_{0(v)|0(v-1)}\right)$$

$$= (\pi_0) \cdot \left(\prod_{v=2}^{j_i} (1 - \tau_{1(v)|0(v-1)})\right)$$

$$= \left(\prod_{v=1}^{j_i} (1 - P_h(v))\right).$$

The above likelihood holds for individuals in the last chain pattern in Table 5.1 as well as all those in the first six chains who go missing *before* the event occurrence. It follows that the observed data likelihood for the sample is given by:

$$L = \prod_{i=1}^{n} \left[\left(P_h(t_i) \cdot \prod_{v=1}^{t_i-1} (1 - P_h(v)) \right)^{I(T_i \leq j_i)} \cdot \left(\prod_{v=1}^{j_i} (1 - P_h(v)) \right)^{I(T_i > j_i)} \right], \qquad (5.31)$$

which is identical to the likelihood we constructed in an earlier section. Note that we carry over our earlier assumption of $T_i \sim T$ to this likelihood construction. In the Markov chain setting this is referred to as a (population) *homogeneous* Markov chain meaning that the transition probabilities hold for all members of the population from which the sample was drawn.

The discrete-time survival model as a Markov chain model can be represented diagrammatically at shown in Figure 5.1. If we examine the figure in traditional path diagram fashion, we would interpret the paths between each of the adjacent E elements as regression paths. In fact, when we go to specify this model in software such as M*plus* (Muthén

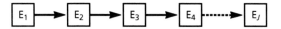

Figure 5.1   Path diagram of a discrete-time survival process as a Markov chain.

& Muthén, 1998–2006), we need to re-express the transition matrices in terms of multinomial logistic regressions.[5] It will then be the regression parameters rather than the actual probabilities that will be estimated in the maximum likelihood estimation procedure, but those parameter estimates are directly translatable into estimates for the transition probabilities of interest.

The general multinomial logistic regression for relating a categorical variable, C, with K categories, to a covariate, X, is given by:

$$\Pr(C = k \mid x) = \frac{\exp(\alpha_k + \beta_k x)}{\sum_{m=1}^{K} \exp(\alpha_m + \beta_m x)}. \tag{5.32}$$

Usually, the last category, K, is selected as the reference class, but in this case we will specify the first category as the reference with $\alpha_1 = 0$ and $\beta_1 = 0$. For the Markov chain without covariates, X is the preceding state variable. In this case, the preceding state variable would have three states (except for the two states of time period 1) that go into the regression model as two dummy variables with the first category ($E_{j-1} = 0$) as the reference group. We will see later how to incorporate observed covariates into the model. Thus, the probabilities for state variable E_j conditional on E_{j-1} in terms of a multinomial logistic regression is given by:

$$\Pr(E_{ji} = k \mid E_{(j-1)i}) = \frac{\exp\left(\alpha_{jk} + \beta_{jk1} \cdot I(E_{(j-1)i} = 1) + \beta_{jk2} \cdot I(E_{(j-1)i} = 2)\right)}{\sum_{m=0}^{2} \exp\left(\alpha_{jm} + \beta_{jm1} \cdot I(E_{(j-1)i} = 1) + \beta_{jm2} \cdot I(E_{(j-1)i} = 2)\right)}. \tag{5.33}$$

where $k \in \{0,1,2\}$, $\alpha_{j0} = 0$, and $\beta_{j01} = \beta_{j02} = 0$. Substituting the multinomial logistic regressions in place of the transition probabilities in the transition matrix gives (displayed by column because of space restrictions):

$$\mathbf{T}_{jj-1}^{\cdot1} = \begin{bmatrix} \dfrac{1}{1+\exp(\alpha_{j1})+\exp(\alpha_{j2})} \\[2ex] \dfrac{1}{1+\exp(\alpha_{j1}+\beta_{j11})+\exp(\alpha_{j2}+\beta_{j21})} \\[2ex] \dfrac{1}{1+\exp(\alpha_{j1}+\beta_{j12})+\exp(\alpha_{j2}+\beta_{j22})} \end{bmatrix} = \begin{bmatrix} \tau_{0(j)|0(j-1)} \\ 0 \\ 0 \end{bmatrix} = \begin{bmatrix} 1-P_h(j) \\ 0 \\ 0 \end{bmatrix}, \quad (5.34)$$

$$\mathbf{T}_{jj-1}^{\cdot2} = \begin{bmatrix} \dfrac{\exp(\alpha_{j1})}{1+\exp(\alpha_{j1})+\exp(\alpha_{j2})} \\[2ex] \dfrac{\exp(\alpha_{j1}+\beta_{j11})}{1+\exp(\alpha_{j1}+\beta_{j11})+\exp(\alpha_{j2}+\beta_{j21})} \\[2ex] \dfrac{\exp(\alpha_{j1}+\beta_{j12})}{1+\exp(\alpha_{j1}+\beta_{j12})+\exp(\alpha_{j2}+\beta_{j22})} \end{bmatrix} = \begin{bmatrix} \tau_{1(j)|0(j-1)} \\ 0 \\ 0 \end{bmatrix} = \begin{bmatrix} P_h(j) \\ 0 \\ 0 \end{bmatrix},$$

$$\mathbf{T}_{jj-1}^{\cdot3} = \begin{bmatrix} \dfrac{\exp(\alpha_{j2})}{1+\exp(\alpha_{j1})+\exp(\alpha_{j2})} \\[2ex] \dfrac{\exp(\alpha_{j2}+\beta_{j21})}{1+\exp(\alpha_{j1}+\beta_{j11})+\exp(\alpha_{j2}+\beta_{j21})} \\[2ex] \dfrac{\exp(\alpha_{j2}+\beta_{j22})}{1+\exp(\alpha_{j1}+\beta_{j12})+\exp(\alpha_{j2}+\beta_{j22})} \end{bmatrix} = \begin{bmatrix} 0 \\ 1 \\ 1 \end{bmatrix}.$$

The elements of the transition matrix above are a function of six regression parameters: α_{j1}, α_{j2}, β_{j11}, β_{j12}, β_{j21}, and β_{j22} (not including α_{j0}, β_{j01}, and β_{j02} that are already fixed at zero). As noted previously, without observed covariates there is only one degree of freedom available for parameter estimation for each transition matrix. The most direct way of achieving model identification is to fix five of the six regression parameters for each matrix. The key here is to find fixed values for five of the six parameters that will properly correspond to the fixed probabilities in the transition matrix, such as $\tau_{2(j)|2(j-1)} = 1$. Since we are using the logit link function to relate the event state in time period j to the event state in time period $j-1$, we can only approximate probabilities of 0 and 1. Take, for example the regression corresponding to $\tau_{2(j)|0(j-1)}$:

$$\tau_{2(j)|0(j-1)} = \frac{\exp(\alpha_{j2})}{1+\exp(\alpha_{j1})+\exp(\alpha_{j2})} = 0. \quad (5.35)$$

The term $\exp(\alpha_{j2})$ in the numerator can become very small when α_{j2} is very small (that is, a large and negative number) and since $\exp(\alpha_{j1})$ and

$\exp(\alpha_{j2})$ will always be greater than zero, the denominator will always be greater than 1. Suppose we choose a values for α_{j2} sufficiently small that, regardless of the value of α_{j1}, the quantity given above will approximate 0, say $\alpha_{j2} = -20$. Then:

$$\tau_{2(j)|0(j-1)} = \frac{\exp(-20)}{1+\exp(\alpha_{j1})+\exp(-20)} = \frac{2.06 \cdot 10^{-9}}{1+\exp(\alpha_{j1})+2.06 \cdot 10^{-9}} \approx 0.$$

If we fix the value of α_{j2} then we must allow the value of α_{j1} to be freely estimated since the only non-restricted elements of the transition matrix, $\tau_{0(j)|0(j-1)}$ and $\tau_{1(j)|0(j-1)}$, are functions of α_{j1} and α_{j2}. If we leave α_{j1} free to be estimated, then the remaining regression parameters must be fixed. Using similar reasoning as for α_{j2}, we need to choose values for β_{j21} and β_{j22} sufficiently large that $\tau_{2(j)|1(j-1)}$ and $\tau_{2(j)|2(j-1)}$ will approximate 1, say $\beta_{j21} = \beta_{j22} = 40$. And, β_{j11} and β_{j12} must be sufficiently small such that $\tau_{0(j)|1(j-1)}$, $\tau_{0(j)|2(j-1)}$, $\tau_{1(j)|1(j-1)}$, and $\tau_{1(j)|2(j-1)}$ will approximate 0, say $\beta_{j11} = \beta_{j12} = -10.^6$

Once estimates for the free parameters are obtained, the fixed values for α_{j2}, β_{j11}, β_{j12}, β_{j21}, and β_{j22}, along with the estimate for α_{j1}, can be substituted back into the transition matrix to obtain the estimated transition probabilities, mainly the estimates for $\tau_{1(j)|0(j-1)} = P_h(j)$. For the first time interval, the marginal probabilities can also be expressed through parameters in an unconditional logistic regression given by:

$$\Pr(E_1 = 0) = \frac{1}{1+\exp(\alpha_{11})} = 1 - P_h(1), \tag{5.36}$$

$$\Pr(E_1 = 1) = \frac{\exp(\alpha_{11})}{1+\exp(\alpha_{11})} = P_h(1).$$

Since α_{11} is the only parameter associated with E_1, it can be freely estimated. Notice that there is no α_{12} in the model although there is an implicit α_{10} fixed at zero. Furthermore, the regression for E_2 on E_1 only includes an indicator for $E_1 = 1$, so there are no β_{2k2} coefficients for $k = 0, 1, 2$.

OBSERVED INDICATORS OF EVENT STATES

Up until this point, we have dealt with event history data in the form of a J element vector of event states, $\mathbf{E}_i = (E_1, E_2, \ldots, E_J)$. Now consider an alternate form of discrete-time event data, especially common in prospective longitudinal studies, where event occurrence is recorded separately for each time period. In other words, for each time period there is an event indicator, U_j, where $U_j = 1$ if the event occurred in time period j and $U_j = 0$ otherwise. It is only by examining the whole string of U_j terms from $j = 1$ to $j = J$ that it is possible to determine whether $U_j = 0$ is indicating a pre-event state or a post-event state. This presupposes that event occurrence does not necessarily prohibit future observation of the individual, that is, that U_j can be observed for $j > T_i$. Let us consider three hypothetical cases. An individual who experienced the event in time period 3 would have the following **U** and **E** vectors:

$$\mathbf{u}_i = (0 \quad 0 \quad 1 \quad 0 \quad 0 \quad 0) \text{ and}$$
$$\mathbf{e}_i = (0 \quad 0 \quad 1 \quad 2 \quad 2 \quad 2).$$

An individual who did not experience the event during the entire observation period would have:

$$\mathbf{u}_i = (0 \quad 0 \quad 0 \quad 0 \quad 0 \quad 0) \text{ and}$$
$$\mathbf{e}_i = (0 \quad 0 \quad 0 \quad 0 \quad 0 \quad 0).$$

Finally, an individual who was censored during the fourth time period such that the third time period is the last complete time period of observation would have the following **U** and **E** vectors:

$$\mathbf{u}_i = (0 \quad 0 \quad 0 \quad \bullet \quad \bullet \quad \bullet) \text{ and}$$
$$\mathbf{e}_i = (0 \quad 0 \quad 0 \quad \bullet \quad \bullet \quad \bullet),$$

where "$\bullet$" denotes a missing observation.

Thinking of the U_j terms as indicators of the E_j elements, we can reframe those E_j as (partially) latent state (or class) variables whose values are determined by the observed event indicators, U_j, and the previous latent event state variable, E_{j-1}. Now the transitions are defined on the structural level of a latent variable model. Instead of a discrete-time Markov chain, we now have a discrete-time *latent* Markov chain. There are advantages to reformulating the model this way that will be discussed later in the chapter. Figure 5.2 displays the path diagram representation of this model.

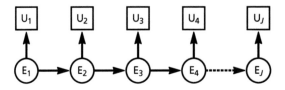

Figure 5.2 Path diagram of a discrete-time survival process as a latent Markov chain.

For the model depicted in Figure 5.2, the event states are still related to one another through a series of multinomial logistic regressions specified exactly as was done in the previous section. The additional part of the model that must be newly specified is the measurement model, relating the U_j terms to the corresponding E_j elements. For now, we will assume that each event indicator, U_j, is a perfect (i.e., without error) indicator of each E_j. That is:

$$\Pr(U_j = 0 \mid E_j = 0) = 0, \tag{5.37}$$

$$\Pr(U_j = 0 \mid E_j = 2) = 0, \text{ and}$$

$$\Pr(U_j = 1 \mid E_j = 1) = 1.$$

As with the conditional probabilities in the transition matrices, the probabilities given above must be re-specified by another series of logistic regressions, relating each U_j to the underlying E_j. Here we will again use a regression specification that matches the one used by M*plus* (Muthén & Muthén, 1998-2006) to facilitate implementation of these models in that software. The logistic regression relating U_j to E_j is given by:

$$\Pr(U_j = 1 \mid E_j = k) = \frac{1}{1 + \exp(\omega_{jk})}, \tag{5.38}$$

where $k \in \{0,1,2\}$.[7] In order to impose the restrictions on the regression parameters to match the restrictions on the conditional probabilities above, we must again settle for approximations of 0 and 1. Fixing $\omega_{j0} = \omega_{j2} = 20$ and $\omega_{j1} = -20$ yields

$$\Pr(U_j = 1 \mid E_j = 0) = \frac{1}{1 + \exp(\omega_{j0})} = \frac{1}{1 + \exp(20)} = \frac{1}{1 + 4.85 \cdot 10^8} \approx 0,$$

$$\Pr(U_j = 1 \mid E_j = 1) = \frac{1}{1 + \exp(\omega_{j1})} = \frac{1}{1 + \exp(-20)} = \frac{1}{1 + 2.06 \cdot 10^{-9}} \approx 1,$$

$$\Pr(U_j = 1 \mid E_j = 2) = \frac{1}{1 + \exp(\omega_{j2})} = \frac{1}{1 + \exp(20)} = \frac{1}{1 + 4.85 \cdot 10^8} \approx 0.$$

Since individuals in time period one can only occupy states 0 or 1, there is no ω_{12} in the model.

The observed data likelihood for an individual i is now given in terms of both U and E elements by:

$$l_i = \Pr(U_1 = u_{1i}, U_2 = u_{2i}, \ldots, U_{j_i} = u_{j_i})$$

$$= \sum_{w=1}^{j_i+1} \left(\Pr\left(U_1 = u_{1i}, U_2 = u_{2i}, \ldots, U_{j_i} = u_{j_i} \mid (E_1, E_2, \ldots, E_{j_i}) = \mathbf{e}_w \right) \cdot \Pr\left((E_1, E_2, \ldots, E_{j_i}) = \mathbf{e}_w\right) \right)$$

$$= \sum_{w=1}^{j_i+1} \left[\left(\prod_{v=1}^{j_i} \Pr(U_v = u_{vi} \mid (E_1, E_2, \ldots, E_{j_i}) = \mathbf{e}_w) \right) \cdot \Pr\left((E_1, E_2, \ldots, E_{j_i}) = \mathbf{e}_w\right) \right] \tag{5.39}$$

$$= \sum_{w=1}^{j_i+1} \left[\left(\prod_{v=1}^{j_i} \Pr(U_v = u_{vi} \mid E_v = e_{wv}) \right) \cdot \Pr(E_1) \cdot \prod_{v=2}^{j_i} \Pr(E_v = e_{wv} \mid E_{v-1} = e_{w,v-1}) \right],$$

where $\{\mathbf{e}_1, \mathbf{e}_2, \ldots, \mathbf{e}_{j_i+1}\}$ represents the set of all possible chains for $(E_1, E_2, \ldots, E_{j_i})$ and e_{wv} represents the value of E_v in chain w. Notice that in this formulation of the likelihood, we assume that the event indicators are independent of each other conditional on the underlying event state variables and that each event indicator only depends directly on the corresponding event state for that time period.

Event History Predictors

Including covariate predictors of event states across time is reasonably straightforward. Since we already have the probability distributions of the E_j event state variables specified as multinomial logistic regressions, we need only add the covariates as additional predictors in the regressions. However, given the restrictions we have imposed on the transition matrices, the only transition probabilities that may be influenced by covariates are $\tau_{1(j)|0(j-1)}$ and, as its complement, $\tau_{0(j)|0(j-1)}$. In other words, a covariate, X, may influence E_j only if $E_{j-1} = 0$. This restriction can be imposed by only allowing X to have an effect on $\Pr(E_j = 1 \mid E_{j-1})$ through an interaction term in the regression equation between the X and the indicator for E_{j-1} as shown below:

$$\Pr(E_{ji} = k \mid E_{(j-1)i}, x_i) =$$

$$\frac{\exp\left(\alpha_{jk} + \beta_{jk1} \cdot I(E_{(j-1)i} = 1) + \beta_{jk2} \cdot I(E_{(j-1)i} = 2) + \gamma_{jk} x_i \cdot I(E_{(j-1)i} = 0)\right)}{\sum_{m=0}^{2} \exp\left(\alpha_{jm} + \beta_{jm1} \cdot I(E_{(j-1)i} = 1) + \beta_{jm2} \cdot I(E_{(j-1)i} = 2) + \gamma_{jk} x_i \cdot I(E_{(j-1)i} = 0)\right)}. \tag{5.40}$$

In this case, $\gamma_{j0} = \gamma_{j2} = 0$ while γ_{j1} is freely estimated. The parameter γ_{j1} can be interpreted as the log hazard odds ratio for transitioning to an event state in time period j associated with a one unit increase in X among those in a pre-event state in time period $j - 1$.

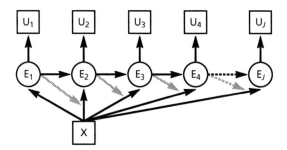

Figure 5.3 Path diagram of a discrete-time survival process as a latent Markov chain with a time-invariant covariate.

For the first event state, E_1, the effect of X is through the logistic regression as given by:

$$\Pr(E_1 = 1 \mid x_i) = \frac{\exp(\alpha_{11} + \gamma_{11}x_i)}{1 + \exp(\alpha_{11} + \gamma_{11}x_i)}. \qquad (5.41)$$

Notice that the coefficient on X, γ_{j1}, is indexed by j, which implies that the effect of X on $\Pr(E = 1)$ may differ across the time intervals $j = 1, \ldots, J$. In addition, a covariate X could also be time-varying. Of course, it is possible to have multiple time-varying and time-invariant covariates in a single model. The proportional hazard odds model, equivalent to assuming a time-invariant effect of X, can be obtained by imposing an equality restriction such that $\gamma_{j1} = \gamma_1$ for all j. Figure 5.3 displays the path diagram for the model with a covariate included. In the figure, the arrows pointing from each E_j to the path from X to E_{j+1} are used to represent the interaction terms in the multinomial regressions as given in Equation 5.39. (For more general discrete-time latent Markov chain models with time-invariant and time-varying covariates, see, e.g., Nylund, Muthén, Nishina, Bellmore, & Graham, 2006; Vermunt et al., 1999.)

Recidivism Example

In order to demonstrate how this model may be applied in a real data setting, we utilize a data set from a randomized field experiment originally reported by Rossi, Berk, and Lenihan (1980) that has been used extensively by Allison (1984, 1995) as a pedagogical example in a continuous-time survival analysis framework and also by Muthén and Masyn (2005) as an example in the discrete-time setting. In this study, 432 inmates released from Maryland state prisons were randomly assigned to either an intervention or control condition. The intervention consisted of financial assistance provided to the released inmates for the duration of the study period. Those in the control condition received no aid. The inmates were followed for one year after their release. The event of interest was re-arrest with an emphasis on the influence of a set of explanatory variables (including intervention status) on the likelihood of recidivism. The data available on each inmate is detailed to the week level (i.e., 52 observation intervals). However, for the illustrative purposes of this chapter, the data were recoded into 13 four-week intervals, referred to as "months," identical to the use of the data by Muthén and Masyn (2005). For this chapter, we will estimate the baseline hazard probabilities in the control group as well as the effect of financial aid on the hazard probability of re-arrest under the proportional hazard odds assumption for the first six months following release. Select portions of the M*plus* syntax can be found in the appendix.[8] The observed data consist of six binary event indicators, $U_1, \ldots, U_6$, where $U_j = 1$ if the first re-arrest occurred in month j and is equal to zero otherwise. Results in terms of the regression parameters are given in Table 5.2. Substituting the estimated parameter values back into the regression equations, we can obtain the estimated marginal probabilities for time period 1 and the estimated transition matrices for the control group (financial aid intervention indicator = 0) as

TABLE 5.2   Recidivism Model Results (LL = –233.91)

Parameter	Estimate	Standard Error	p-value
$\omega_{10}, \ldots, \omega_{60}$	20.00	fixed	—
$\omega_{11}, \ldots, \omega_{61}$	–20.00	fixed	—
$\omega_{22}, \ldots, \omega_{62}$	20.00	fixed	—
$\beta_{201}, \ldots, \beta_{601}$	0.00	fixed	—
$\beta_{302}, \ldots, \beta_{602}$	0.00	fixed	—
$\beta_{211}, \ldots, \beta_{611}$	–10.00	fixed	—
$\beta_{312}, \ldots, \beta_{612}$	–10.00	fixed	—
$\beta_{221}, \ldots, \beta_{621}$	40.00	fixed	—
$\beta_{322}, \ldots, \beta_{622}$	40.00	fixed	—
$\alpha_{10}, \ldots, \alpha_{60}$	0.00	fixed	—
$\alpha_{22}, \ldots, \alpha_{62}$	–20.00	fixed	—
α_{11}	–4.59	0.55	<0.001
α_{21}	–3.87	0.38	<0.001
α_{31}	–3.99	0.38	<0.001
α_{41}	–3.84	0.38	<0.001
α_{51}	–3.32	0.31	<0.001
α_{61}	–3.78	0.39	<0.001
γ_1 (Intervention)	–0.18	0.29	0.54

given below. Although the estimated effect of the financial aid intervention is small and statistically non-significant with an estimated hazard odds ratio (hOR) of 0.84, the estimated transition matrices for the intervention group are computed as well for the sake of completeness.

$$\hat{Pr}(E_1 = 0 \mid \text{control}) = 0.991, \qquad \hat{Pr}(E_1 = 0 \mid \text{intervention}) = 0.992,$$

$$\Pr(E_1 = 1 \mid \text{control}) = 0.009, \qquad \Pr(E_1 = 1 \mid \text{intervention}) = 0.008,$$

$$\hat{T}_{21(\text{control})} = \begin{bmatrix} 0.981 & 0.019 & 0.00 \\ 0.00 & 0.00 & 1.00 \end{bmatrix}, \quad \hat{T}_{21(\text{intervention})} = \begin{bmatrix} 0.984 & 0.016 & 0.00 \\ 0.00 & 0.00 & 1.00 \end{bmatrix},$$

$$\hat{T}_{32(\text{control})} = \begin{bmatrix} 0.983 & 0.017 & 0.00 \\ 0.00 & 0.00 & 1.00 \\ 0.00 & 0.00 & 1.00 \end{bmatrix}, \quad \hat{T}_{32(\text{intervention})} = \begin{bmatrix} 0.986 & 0.014 & 0.00 \\ 0.00 & 0.00 & 1.00 \\ 0.00 & 0.00 & 1.00 \end{bmatrix},$$

$$\hat{T}_{43(\text{control})} = \begin{bmatrix} 0.981 & 0.019 & 0.00 \\ 0.00 & 0.00 & 1.00 \\ 0.00 & 0.00 & 1.00 \end{bmatrix}, \quad \hat{T}_{43(\text{intervention})} = \begin{bmatrix} 0.984 & 0.016 & 0.00 \\ 0.00 & 0.00 & 1.00 \\ 0.00 & 0.00 & 1.00 \end{bmatrix},$$

$$\hat{T}_{54(\text{control})} = \begin{bmatrix} 0.968 & 0.032 & 0.00 \\ 0.00 & 0.00 & 1.00 \\ 0.00 & 0.00 & 1.00 \end{bmatrix}, \quad \hat{T}_{54(\text{intervention})} = \begin{bmatrix} 0.973 & 0.027 & 0.00 \\ 0.00 & 0.00 & 1.00 \\ 0.00 & 0.00 & 1.00 \end{bmatrix},$$

$$\hat{T}_{65(\text{control})} = \begin{bmatrix} 0.980 & 0.020 & 0.00 \\ 0.00 & 0.00 & 1.00 \\ 0.00 & 0.00 & 1.00 \end{bmatrix}, \quad \hat{T}_{65(\text{intervention})} = \begin{bmatrix} 0.983 & 0.017 & 0.00 \\ 0.00 & 0.00 & 1.00 \\ 0.00 & 0.00 & 1.00 \end{bmatrix}.$$

These results (log likelihood value, baseline hazard probabilities, and intervention effect) match exactly the results obtained using the latent class regression approach presented in Muthén and Masyn (2005). The results do not match the final analysis presented in previous papers because for this analysis illustration, only six time periods were used and none of the other measured covariates from the original study were included.

Measurement Error on the Event Indicators

The model specification described in the previous sections may seem needlessly complicated for a single, non-recurring event history analysis. However, approaching the discrete-time model in this way allows us to deal with the possibility of measurement error on the event indicators. Consider a simplified scenario where a sample of children, say age 10, none of whom have ever had a drink of alcohol prior to age 10, are asked at 12 yearly follow-ups if they had their first drink in the previous year (yes/no). If we assume they respond with total accuracy, then they will respond in the affirmative for one and only one year and that year will mark the age of onset for alcohol consumption. However, in questions such as the ones in this example, there is likely to be some error (e.g., a child reports having his or her first drink in the previous year at two different follow-ups). To understand the impact that such error in the determination of event status can have on successful estimation of the hazard probabilities and covariate effects, we first need to define the types of error that can be made. Borrowing from the medical and epidemiological literature, we define the *sensitivity* of an event indicator as the likelihood that the indicator will have a value of 1 given that an individual is in a "true" event state. That is:

$$\text{Sensitivity} = \Pr(U_j = 1 \mid E_j = 1). \tag{5.42}$$

Recall in the previous section, we fixed the sensitivity of the event indicators to 1 by fixing the ω_{j1} parameters to –20. We define the *specificity* of an event indicator as the likelihood that the indicator will have a value of 0 given that an individual is in either a pre-event or post-event state. That is:

$$\text{Specificity} = \Pr(U_j = 0 \mid E_j \neq 1). \tag{5.43}$$

In the previous section, we fixed the specificity of the event indicators to 1 by fixing the ω_{j0} parameters and ω_{j2} parameters to 20. Note that it would be possible to have unique specificities for each event indicator conditional on the pre-event or post-event state, but here it will be assumed that:

$$\Pr(U_j = 0 \mid E_j = 0) = \Pr(U_j = 0 \mid E_j = 2). \tag{5.44}$$

(For another example of the use of sensitivity and specificity in a latent class setting, see Rindskopf & Rindskopf, 1986.)

One can intuit the impact that less than perfect sensitivity or specificity might have on the estimated hazard probabilities. With sensitivity less than 1, some individuals in a true event state will not be identified as such and we would expect the hazard probabilities to be under-estimated. With specificity less that 1, some individuals in a true pre-event state will be identified as being in an event state and we would expect the hazard probabilities to be over-estimated. As is the case with any outcome measured with error, we would expect the effects of a covariate on the hazard odds in the presence of less than perfect sensitivity or specificity to be attenuated. For the purposes of this chapter, we assume that the measurement error is random at each time period and is independent of the error at other time periods.[9]

It is possible to directly compute the actual distortion in the hazard and survival probabilities in the case of complete data. Consider an example with only three time periods of measure. Suppose the hazard probability is equal to 0.05 in all three time periods. Suppose also that the sensitivity is equal to 0.80 and the specificity is equal to 0.90. Table 5.3 gives the total probabilities (relative frequencies) of each of the possible chains on the structural level. Based on the relative frequencies in Table 5.3 and the given sensitivity and specificity levels, we can compute the probabilities for each possible event indicator sequence over the three time periods. An example for computing the probability of observing $U = (0, 0, 0)$ is given below:

$$\Pr(U_1 = 0, U_2 = 0, U_3 = 0) = \left(\begin{array}{l} \Pr\!\left(U_1 = 0, U_2 = 0, U_3 = 0 \mid \mathbf{E} = (1,2,2)\right) \cdot \Pr\!\left(\mathbf{E} = (1,2,2)\right) + \\ \Pr\!\left(U_1 = 0, U_2 = 0, U_3 = 0 \mid \mathbf{E} = (0,1,2)\right) \cdot \Pr\!\left(\mathbf{E} = (0,1,2)\right) + \\ \Pr\!\left(U_1 = 0, U_2 = 0, U_3 = 0 \mid \mathbf{E} = (0,0,1)\right) \cdot \Pr\!\left(\mathbf{E} = (0,0,1)\right) + \\ \Pr\!\left(U_1 = 0, U_2 = 0, U_3 = 0 \mid \mathbf{E} = (0,0,0)\right) \cdot \Pr\!\left(\mathbf{E} = (0,0,0)\right) \end{array} \right)$$

$$= \left(\begin{array}{l} \Pr(U_1 = 0 \mid E_1 = 1) \cdot \Pr(U_2 = 0 \mid E_2 = 2) \cdot \Pr(U_3 = 0 \mid E_3 = 2) \cdot \Pr\!\left(\mathbf{E} = (1,2,2)\right) + \\ \Pr(U_1 = 0 \mid E_1 = 0) \cdot \Pr(U_2 = 0 \mid E_2 = 1) \cdot \Pr(U_3 = 0 \mid E_3 = 2) \cdot \Pr\!\left(\mathbf{E} = (0,1,2)\right) + \\ \Pr(U_1 = 0 \mid E_1 = 0) \cdot \Pr(U_2 = 0 \mid E_2 = 0) \cdot \Pr(U_3 = 0 \mid E_3 = 1) \cdot \Pr\!\left(\mathbf{E} = (0,0,1)\right) + \\ \Pr(U_1 = 0 \mid E_1 = 0) \cdot \Pr(U_2 = 0 \mid E_2 = 0) \cdot \Pr(U_3 = 0 \mid E_3 = 0) \cdot \Pr\!\left(\mathbf{E} = (0,0,0)\right) \end{array} \right)$$

$$= \left(\begin{array}{l} (0.20) \cdot (0.90) \cdot (0.90) \cdot (0.05) + \\ (0.90) \cdot (0.20) \cdot (0.90) \cdot (0.0475) + \\ (0.90) \cdot (0.90) \cdot (0.20) \cdot (0.045) + \\ (0.90) \cdot (0.90) \cdot (0.90) \cdot (0.857) \end{array} \right)$$

$$= 0.65.$$

Table 5.4 summarizes the relative frequencies for all of the possible event indicator sequences computed in a similar manner to the example above.

If a model were fit that assumed the event indicators functioned without error, then the first four indicator sequences (1–4) in Table 5.4 would all en-

TABLE 5.3   Expected Relative Frequencies of (Latent) Event State Chains for Constant $P_h(j) = 0.05$

Chain #	E_1	E_2	E_3	rf
1	1	2	2	0.050
2	0	1	2	0.048
3	0	0	1	0.045
4	0	0	0	0.857

TABLE 5.4   Expected Relative Frequencies of Event Indicator Sequences for Constant $P_h(j) = 0.05$, Sensitivity = 0.80, and Specificity = 0.90

Sequence #	U_1	U_2	U_3	rf
1	1	1	1	0.002
2	1	1	0	0.015
3	1	0	1	0.015
4	1	0	0	0.100
5	0	1	1	0.014
6	0	1	0	0.100
7	0	0	1	0.100
8	0	0	0	0.650

ter the likelihood as corresponding to the first state chain (1) in Table 5.3, equivalent to entering a true event state in the first time period. So the expected estimated probability for that chain is $0.002 + 0.015 + 0.015 + 0.10 = 0.132$—a notable overestimation of the true chain probability (and time period 1 hazard probability) of 0.050. The next two indicator sequences (5–6) in Table 5.4 would enter the likelihood as corresponding to the second state chain (2) in Table 5.3, equivalent to entering a true event state in the second time period, and the expected estimated probability is $0.014 + 0.10 = 0.114$—also an overestimation of the true chain probability (and time period 2 hazard probability) of 0.048. The next indicator sequence (7) in Table 5.4 would enter the likelihood as corresponding to the third state chain (3) in Table 5.3, equivalent to entering a true event state in the third time period, and the expected estimated probability is 0.100—another overestimation of the true chain probability (and time period 3 hazard probability) of 0.045. The final indicator sequence (8) in Table 5.4 would enter the likelihood as corresponding to never entering a true event state during the three time periods, i.e., state chain (4) in Table 5.3, and the expected estimated probability is 0.650. This corresponds to the expected estimate for $P_s(3)$ and is less than the true survival probability of 0.857.

Table 5.5 gives a summary of similar calculations for a population with a constant hazard probability of 0.05 across each of six time periods. Notice that with sensitivity and specificity values of 1.0, we obtain the population values as would be expected. Holding the sensitivity level at 1.0, a decrease in the specificity level from 1.0 to 0.9 and 0.8 leads to a remarkable level of distortion in the hazard probabilities—not only is there an upward bias in the hazard probabilities, that bias increases over the six time periods, distorting not only the size of the hazard probabilities but also the change in the hazard probabilities over time. And because of the relationship be-

TABLE 5.5 Expected Estimated Hazard Probabilities and Hazard Odds Ratio by Event Indicator Sensitivity and Specificity

Sensitivity Pr(U = 1|E = 1)	Specificity Pr(U = 0|E = 0), Pr(U = 0|E = 2)	Expected Estimated Hazard Probability Time Period						Expected Estimated Survival Probability $P_S(6)$	Expected Estimated Hazard Odds Ratio hOR
		1	2	3	4	5	6		
1.0	1.0	0.05	0.05	0.05	0.05	0.05	0.05	0.74	2.00
	0.9	0.11	0.12	0.13	0.15	0.17	0.21	0.38	1.37
	0.8	0.17	0.18	0.21	0.24	0.30	0.45	0.16	1.23
0.9	1.0	0.045	0.045	0.044	0.045	0.044	0.045	0.76	1.99
	0.9	0.11	0.12	0.13	0.14	0.17	0.20	0.39	1.32
	0.8	0.16	0.18	0.20	0.24	0.30	0.43	0.17	1.21
0.8	1.0	0.04	0.04	0.04	0.04	0.04	0.04	0.78	1.95
	0.9	0.11	0.11	0.13	0.14	0.16	0.19	0.40	1.28
	0.8	0.16	0.17	0.20	0.23	0.29	0.42	0.18	1.15

tween the hazard probabilities and the survival probabilities, the survival probability for the final time period is significantly under-estimated. Holding the specificity level at 1.0, a decrease in the sensitivity level from 1.0 to 0.9 and 0.8 leads to a downward bias in the hazard probability estimates. Of course, the total impact of sensitivity and specificity values less than 1.0 on the hazard probability estimates will depend, in part, on the size of the true hazard probabilities. This table illustrates that the impact on the (baseline) hazard probabilities of measurement error on event indicators can be quite different than the impact of unobserved heterogeneity (or unmeasured covariates) which always results in a downward bias in the baseline hazard.

The last column in Table 5.5 displays the impact of a range of sensitivity and specificity values on the hazard odds ratio assuming a "true" population with a binary covariate ($X = 0/1$) with a population prevalence of 0.5 and an effect of 0.693 on the logit scale (which translates to a hazard odds ratio (hOR) of 2.0). The baseline hazard probabilities ($X = 0$) for the population were a constant value of 0.05. We can see the under-estimation of the covariate effect that occurs. As with the baseline hazard probabilities, the total impact of sensitivity and specificity values less than 1.0 on the covariate effect estimates will depend on the size of the true covariate effect as well as the true baseline hazard probabilities. (For a more general discussion of uncorrelated and correlated measurement error in discrete-time Markov chain models, see, e.g., Bassi, Hagenaars, Croon, & Vermunt, 2000.)

As was discussed in the previous section, the discrete-time survival model without covariates and without restrictions on the hazard probabilities is a just-identified model. With event indicators, there are more degrees of freedom available (theoretically, $2^J - 1$); however, there are likely to be enough empty cells in the joint distribution of the event indicators to result in empirical non-identification when attempting to estimate the ω_j parameters. Consider the case where the U terms function without measurement error. In that situation, there are only $J+1$ observed patterns for the event indicators and that means there is not enough information to estimate ω_j parameters as well as the unique transition probabilities. Ultimately, this means that even if we believed there to be measurement error on the event indicators, it is unlikely we would be able to estimate any of the ω parameters, even when imposing constraints on model parameters such as measurement invariance (i.e., $\omega_{j0} = \omega_{k0}$, $\omega_{j1} = \omega_{k1}$, and $\omega_{j2} = \omega_{k2}$ for all $j, k = 1, \ldots, J$) and uniformity in the specificity of the event indicators for pre-event and post-event states (i.e, $\omega_{j0} = \omega_{j2}$ for all $j = 1, \ldots, J$). However, if we knew from a previous study or another source the approximate sensitivity and specificity of the event indicators, we could fix the ω parameters to values corresponding to those accuracy rates rather than fixing them at values corresponding to sensitivity and specificity of 1.[10] For example, if we knew the approximate specificity of the event indicator to be 0.80, we could fix the ω_{j0} parameters and ω_{j2} parameters to the value 1.386 (= logit(0.8)) in our estimation model. (For more information about identification of latent Markov models, see, e.g., Van de Pol & Langeheine, 1990.)

It is also possible to improve the chances of having an empirically identified model, and recovering the sensitivity and specificity of the event indicators, by including one or more predictors of event history in the model. To briefly explore this possibility, we conducted a simulation study, drawing 100 samples of size 1,000 from each of three populations. For each population, there was a single observed event indicator at each of six time periods. The sensitivity and specificity for all of the indicators were 0.90 (corresponding to population parameter values $\omega_0 = \omega_2 = 2.197$ and $\omega_1 = -2.197$). For each population, there was a time-invariant binary (0/1) predictor, evenly distributed across each population, with a time-invariant hazard odds ratio of 2.0 (corresponding to population parameter values $\gamma_{11} = \gamma_{21} = \ldots = \gamma_{61} = 0.693$). Each population had a constant baseline hazard probability—the hazard probability when the covariate was equal to zero—across the six time periods. This was the only feature that differed across the three populations. Population 1 had a baseline hazard probability of 0.05 (corresponding to population parameter values $\alpha_{11} = \alpha_{21} = \ldots = \alpha_{61} = -2.944$); Population 2 had a baseline hazard probability of 0.10 (corresponding to population parameter values $\alpha_{11} = \alpha_{21} = \ldots = \alpha_{61} = -2.197$); and Population 3 had a baseline hazard probability of 0.25 (corresponding to population parameter values $\alpha_{11} = \alpha_{21} = \ldots = \alpha_{61} = -1.099$). For each sample of 1,000 observations drawn from each population (100 draws or replications per population), a model was fit that estimated the ω_{jk} parameters under the assumption of measurement invariance and equal specificity for $E_j = 0$ and $E_j = 2$, the γ_{j1} parameters under the assumption of time-invariant effects of the covariate, and the α_{j1} parameters.

Table 5.6 summarizes the model results across the 100 replications for each of the three populations. The rows labeled "Population" give the values of the parameters in the population from which each of the 100 samples of $n = 1,000$ was drawn. The rows labeled "Avg. Est." give the average parameter estimate across the 100 estimated models. The rows labeled "Bias" give the difference between the average parameter estimate from the estimated models and the true population value and the "Relative Bias" is the estimated bias divided by the absolute value of the true population parameter value. The rows labeled "MSE" give the mean squared error which decomposes into a sum of the squared bias and variance of the estimates. The last rows, labeled "95% coverage," give the proportion of 95% confidence intervals for the estimate from the replication models that contained the true population parameter value. For both Populations

TABLE 5.6 Simulation Results for 3 Populations Based on 100 Replications of $n = 1000$

Parameter	ω_0, ω_2	ω_1	α_{11}	α_{21}	α_{31}	α_{41}	α_{51}	α_{61}	$\gamma_{.1}$
Population 1: Sensitivity = 0.90; Specificity = 0.90; Baseline Hazard Probability = 0.05; hOR = 2.0									
Population	2.197	-2.944	-2.944	-2.944	-2.944	-2.944	-2.944	-2.944	0.693
Avg. Est.	2.163	-7.153	-8.573	-3.922	-33.253	-3.498	-6.047	-2.304	1.265
Bias	-0.034	-4.956	-5.629	-0.978	-30.309	-0.554	-3.103	0.640	0.572
Relative Bias	-0.015	-2.256	-1.912	-0.332	-10.295	-0.188	-1.054	0.217	0.825
MSE	0.022	78.667	2184.134	21.971	86567.688	27.227	1030.000	30.725	38.420
95% coverage	0.920	0.240	0.850	0.860	0.860	0.900	0.870	0.900	0.890
Population 2: Sensitivity = 0.90; Specificity = 0.90; Baseline Hazard Probability = 0.10; hOR = 2.0									
Population	2.197	-2.197	-2.197	-2.197	-2.197	-2.197	-2.197	-2.197	0.693
Avg. Est.	2.203	-6.560	-2.207	-2.165	-2.179	-2.137	-2.094	-2.047	0.727
Bias	0.006	-4.363	-0.010	0.032	0.018	0.060	0.100	0.150	0.088
Relative Bias	0.003	-1.986	-0.005	0.015	0.008	0.027	0.046	0.068	0.127
MSE	0.005	59.909	0.058	0.063	0.103	0.164	0.187	0.354	0.036
95% coverage	0.970	0.420	0.940	0.940	0.930	0.950	0.950	0.970	0.940
Population 3: Sensitivity = 0.90; Specificity = 0.90; Baseline Hazard Probability = 0.25; hOR = 2.0									
Population	2.197	-2.197	-1.099	-1.099	-1.099	-1.099	-1.099	-1.099	0.693
Avg. Est.	2.190	-2.574	-1.118	-1.092	-1.101	-1.109	-1.092	-1.016	0.688
Bias	-0.007	-0.377	-0.019	0.007	-0.002	-0.010	0.007	0.083	-0.005
Relative Bias	-0.003	-0.172	-0.017	0.006	-0.002	-0.009	0.006	0.076	-0.007
MSE	0.003	3.607	0.016	0.024	0.044	0.093	0.188	0.276	0.016
95% coverage	0.940	0.920	0.960	0.960	0.960	0.950	0.970	0.990	0.960

1 and 2, the parameter ω_1, corresponding to the event indicator sensitivity, is poorly estimated with a large negative relative bias (which translates to an overestimation of the sensitivity), large MSE, and low coverage proportion. However, for Population 1, there is also extremely poor estimation of the baseline hazard probabilities and the covariate effect is overestimated by an average of more than 80%. Note that this stands in contrast to the attenuated covariate effect when measurement error in the event indicators is ignored. The poor performance of the model estimates over the Population 1 replications should not be too surprising when we considered that with a true baseline hazard probability of only 0.05, there is very little information about latent state changes from pre-event to event. With Population 2, the model performance, with the exception of the estimation of event indicator sensitivity, is notably improved over the replications from Population 1, with much smaller relative bias, smaller MSE, and actual coverage near the expect 0.95. For Population 3, with a baseline hazard of 0.25, even the estimation for the parameter corresponding to the item sensitivity is much improved and the relative bias for the covariate effect is less than 1%.

This limited simulation study demonstrates that the actual baseline hazard probability can influence the ability of the model that allows for measurement error on single event indicators with at least one covariate to recover the true population parameters. It appears that for rare events, a less than perfect item sensitivity is difficult to estimate correctly, but that as the baseline hazard probability increases, the likelihood of recovery of hazard probabilities and covariate effects improves. The effect of the baseline hazard probability shown here represents only one of a number of dimensions, including sample size, number of time periods, true covariate effect size, true item specificity and sensitivity, that could influence the quality, in terms of both accuracy and precision, of parameter estimates in these single event indicator models. In general, having the empirical identification of the model dependent upon a covariate is less than ideal, and that will be reflected in model performance. As with any latent variable model, if we want a stable measurement model for the event states, we need multiple event indicators for each time period so that the measurement model at each time period is independently identifiable.

Multiple Event Indicators

If there is more than one measure of event status at each time period, we can extend the model previously presented to include M event indicators at each time point j, U_{mj}. Figure 5.4 displays the path diagram for this extension. The measurement model for E is now defined by the set of event indicators, and the relationship between each of the U_{mj} terms and E_j is

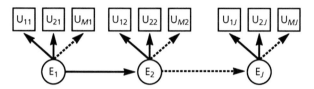

Figure 5.4   Path diagram of a discrete-time survival process as a latent Markov chain with multiple event indicators for each time period.

specified through a series of logistic regressions. The logistic regression relating U_{mj} to E_j is given by:

$$\Pr(U_{mj} = 1 \mid E_j = k) = \frac{1}{1 + \exp(\omega_{mjk})}. \qquad (5.45)$$

where $k \in \{0,1,2\}$. Essentially, the measurement models for the time periods are a set of latent class models (see, e.g., McCutcheon, 1987). As with a traditional latent class analysis, we assume that the event indicators at each time point j, $\mathbf{U}_j = (U_{1j}, U_{2j}, \ldots, U_{Mj})$, are independent of each other conditional on event status, in addition to assuming that the event indicators across time periods are independent of each other conditional on the underlying state variables and that each set of event indicators depend only on the corresponding event state for that time period. Under those assumptions, the observed data likelihood is given by:

$$l_i = \Pr(\mathbf{U}_1 = \mathbf{u}_{1i}, \mathbf{U}_2 = \mathbf{u}_{2i}, \ldots, \mathbf{U}_{j_i} = \mathbf{u}_{j_i})$$

$$= \sum_{w=1}^{j_i+1} \left(\begin{array}{l} \Pr\left(\mathbf{U}_1 = \mathbf{u}_{1i}, \mathbf{U}_2 = \mathbf{u}_{2i}, \ldots, \mathbf{U}_{j_i} = \mathbf{u}_{j_i} \mid (E_1, E_2, \ldots, E_{j_i}) = e_w\right) \cdot \\ \Pr\left((E_1, E_2, \ldots, E_{j_i}) = e_w\right) \end{array} \right) \qquad (5.46)$$

$$= \sum_{w=1}^{j_i+1} \left[\left(\prod_{v=1}^{j_i} \prod_{m=1}^{M} \Pr(U_{mv} = u_{mvi} \mid E_v = e_{wv}) \right) \cdot \Pr(E_1) \cdot \prod_{v=2}^{j_i} \Pr(E_v = e_{wv} \mid E_{v-1} = e_{w,v-1}) \right],$$

where, as before, $\{\mathbf{e}_1, \mathbf{e}_2, \ldots, \mathbf{e}_{j_i+1}\}$ represents the set of all possible chains for $(E_1, E_2, \ldots, E_{j_i})$ and e_{wv} represents the value of E_v in chain w.

With multiple event indicators at each time, model identification may not necessitate the imposition of measurement invariance and uniformity of indicator sensitivity and specificity for pre-event and post-event states as it does in the case with only one event indicator per time period. For example, with four event indicators per time period, it would be possible to estimate time- and indicator-specific ω parameters while only imposing constraints corresponding to equal specificities for $E_j = 0$ and $E_j = 2$. It becomes essential with these multiple event indicator models to consider not only the constraints that are necessary for identification, but also the constraints that are necessary for interpretation. It may be quite reasonable to allow for item-specific sensitivity and specificity values since the different event indicators may have different levels of precision in their measurement of event status. However, it may not be reasonable to allow time-specific sensitivity and specificity for one or more of the event indicators, that is, to allow measurement non-invariance of event states over time. In the presence of measurement non-invariance, it becomes more difficult to assert that the levels of E have the same *meaning* across time. And without that consistency of meaning (i.e., "true" pre-event, event, and post-event states), the validity of the constraints on the transition probabilities, and the interpretations of the unconstrained transition probabilities as relating to the hazard probabilities of an event history process, diminishes.

Multiple event indicators can come in various forms. In some cases, the indicators may represent responses to the same question asked at different points in time. Returning to our earlier scenario, suppose that rather than asking the sample of children, who never drank prior to age 10, whether or not they had had their first drink in the previous year (yes/no) at each yearly follow-up, the children are asked at each yearly follow-up how old they were when they had their first drink. In this situation, a child may report two or more different ages of first drink. Instead of averaging the re-ported ages or favoring one response over another, all the responses can be taken as indicators of the "true" event status at each age. Supposing that all the children are at the age of 10 when the study begins and none have had their first drink prior to age 9,[11] at intake they could report an age of 10 as the age of first drink or report that they had not yet had their first drink; at the first follow-up at the age 11, the children could report an age of 10 or 11 as the age of first drink or report that they had not yet had their first drink; at the age 12 follow-up, children could report an age of 10, 11, or 12 as the age of first drink or report that they had not yet had their first drink; and so on. Supposing a 6-year (or 6-wave) study with yearly assessments starting at age 10, let E_j be the event state at age j where $j = 10, \ldots, J$ and $J = 15$. Let U_{mj} be the indicator for age of first drinking equal to j based on the re-sponse given during the wave m where $m = 1, \ldots, M_j$ and $M_j = J - j + 1$. In this case, there are actually a different number of event indicators for each time period. For age $j = 10$, there are a possible $J - j + 1 = 15 - 10 + 1 = 6$ event indicators; for age $j = 15$, there is only one event indicator from the final wave of assessment. Consider the hypothetical response sequence for waves 1-6 given in the response column of Table 5.7. This response sequence pro-vides information on $U_{1,10}, \ldots, U_{6,10}; U_{2,11}, \ldots, U_{6,11}; U_{3,12}, \ldots, U_{6,12}; U_{4,13}, \ldots, U_{6,13}; U_{5,14}, U_{6,14};$ and $U_{6,15}$ as given in Table 5.7.

It would be important in this setting, as in any other, to carefully consid-er the constraints placed on the measurement models for the event states

TABLE 5.7 Hypothetical Question Response Sequence and Corresponding Event Indicator Values

Wave	Age	Response	Event Age					
			10	11	12	13	14	15
1	10	Never had a drink	$U_{1,10}=0$					
2	11	Never had a drink	$U_{2,10}=0$	$U_{2,11}=0$				
3	12	First drink at 12	$U_{3,10}=0$	$U_{3,11}=0$	$U_{3,12}=1$			
4	13	First drink at 11	$U_{4,10}=0$	$U_{4,11}=1$	$U_{4,12}=0$	$U_{4,13}=0$		
5	14	First drink at 12	$U_{5,10}=0$	$U_{5,11}=0$	$U_{5,12}=1$	$U_{5,13}=0$	$U_{5,14}=0$	
6	15	First drink at 13	$U_{6,10}=0$	$U_{6,11}=0$	$U_{6,12}=0$	$U_{6,13}=1$	$U_{6,14}=0$	$U_{6,15}=0$

across time. In this case, it might make sense to assume the same sensitivity and specificity for indicators with the same number of years between the age the response was given and the age to which the response corresponds. For example, $U_{3,10}$, the indicator based on the response at wave 3 (age 12) about event status at age 10, may have the same sensitivity and specificity as $U_{5,12}$, the indicator based on the response at wave 5 (age 14) about event status at age 12.

In others cases, multiple indicators may correspond to a set of measures administered during each time period that are intended to collectively ascertain event status. For example, consider the proposed latent class model for the diagnosis of myocardial infarction (MI) presented by Rindskopf and Rindskopf (1986). Their latent class variable had two levels—MI and no MI—and was measured by a set of four indicators: presence of a positive Q-wave, classical clinical history, flipped LDH, and high CPK-MB. This latent class model could be integrated into an event history analysis of age of first myocardial infarction. In this case, only those hospitalized during a given time period would have measures on these indicators. So one might add a fifth event indicator so that those not hospitalized in a given year were known with a specificity of 1.0 not to have experienced the event in that time period. Here it would probably be quite reasonable to impose measurement invariance on the event indicators across the time periods of observation.

SUMMARY

This chapter has introduced the principles of discrete-time survival analysis and demonstrated, in detail, how an event history model can be reformulated as a restricted discrete-time Markov chain model. The problems that can be caused by measurement error in event occurrence were discussed, and it was shown how a discrete-time latent Markov chain model could be specified to account for measurement error. The presentation here was limited to single, non-recurring event history processes with complete and right-censored data (with non-informative censoring) measured in discrete time periods of equal width. It was assumed that no individual could occupy an event state for more than one time period and that event occurrence could be represented by a single state. It was also assumed that there was neither unobserved heterogeneity nor unmeasured covariates. However, the modeling framework presented in this chapter can accommodate recurring events, competing risks, multiple spells, frailties or unobserved heterogeneity (including the long-term survivor model which could be specified as restricted mover-stayer Markov chain model), informative censoring, and clustered data. Furthermore, there is nothing in the framework that restricts event indicators to binary measures—event indicators could have multiple categories or even be continuous. Some of the same identification issues discussed earlier might still apply depending on the nature and number of the event indicators for each time period. The single necessity for the measurement model for event status is consistency across time so that the event states retain their meaning throughout the observation period. All of the models presented and the extensions mentioned above can be specified and estimated using full-information maximum likelihood enabled by some of the more advanced statistical modeling software packages such as M*plus* (Muthén & Muthén, 1998–2006).

As noted in the beginning of this chapter, there are many approaches to discrete-time survival analysis available to applied researchers. The great advantage of working in a Markov chain modeling framework is gained in situations where the determination of event occurrence is likely to be imperfect and subject to measurement error. These situations are common, even in prospective longitudinal studies, when researchers must rely on self-reports of event occurrence or when the event of interest itself is not directly observable. This approach offers a promising alternative to mitigate the significant distortions in estimation and inference that may occur when not accounting for or presuming an absence of measurement error in the event history process under study.

NOTES

1. Discrete-time survival analysis can also be applied to events that are themselves occurring on a discrete-time scale, such as grade retention.
2. Although beyond the scope of this chapter, it is possible to extend these models to a multilevel setting with individuals clustered in higher-level units. See, for example, Steele (2003).
3. Although we assume here that the time intervals are all of equal length, this assumption is not necessary for any of the models presented.
4. In the first time period, there are actually only two possible states—pre-event and event—as will be explained later in this section.
5. Log-linear models could also be used, but would only allow for the inclusion of categorical predictors of E (see, e.g., Vermunt, 1997).
6. Keep in mind that the values that we have chosen are somewhat arbitrary in that we are selecting values that will allow us to approximate the necessary fixed transition probabilities and that other values of similar magnitude and direction would work equally well.
7. Note that we follow the M*plus* specification for binary and ordered categorical variables where the ω parameters are referred to as *thresholds* and are equivalent to the additive inverses of the intercepts in a traditional binary logistic regression. For more information, see Muthén and Muthén (1998–2006).
8. Full input and output files are available from the author upon request.

9. This situation is quite different from the situation with unmeasured heterogeneity in the event history process when there would be additional correlation in the event states across time due to one or more unmeasured covariates, often referred to collectively as *frailty*. We will not deal with *frailties* in this chapter, but it is possible to extend the models presented here to account for possible unobserved heterogeneity in the form of a higher-order random effect or latent class variable. For more information on modeling unobserved heterogeneity, see, for example, Heckman and Singer (1984); Land et al. (2001); Masyn (2003); Muthén and Masyn (2005); Trussel and Richard (1985); Vaupel, Manton, and Stanton (1979); and Vermunt (1997, 2002).
10. This is analogous to fixing the reliability for a single factor indicator.
11. It is not a necessary assumption that all the subjects be in a pre-event state upon entry into the study. The timeline could extend back before the beginning of the study so that subjects' reports of behavior prior to the study could also be included in the model. For example, some children at age 10 may report having their first drink at age 8 or 9.

REFERENCES

Aalen, O., & Johansen, S. (1978). An empirical transition matrix for non-homogeneous Markov chains based on censored observations. *Scandinavian Journal of Statistics, 5,* 141–150.

Allison, P. (1982). Discrete-time methods for the analysis of event histories. *Sociological Methodology, 13,* 61–98.

Allison, P. (1984). *Event history analysis. Quantitative Applications in the Social Sciences, 46.* Thousand Oaks, CA: Sage.

Allison, P. (1995). *Survival analysis using the SAS system: A practical guide.* Cary, NC: SAS.

Andersen, P. (1988). Multistate models in survival analysis: A study of nephropathy and mortality in diabetes. *Statistics in Medicine, 7,* 661–670.

Bassi, F., Hagenaars, J., Croon, M., & Vermunt, J. (2000). Estimating true changes when categorical panel data are affected by uncorrelated and correlated classification errors: An application to unemployment data. *Sociological Methods and Research, 29,* 230–268.

Cox, D. (1972). Regression models and life-tables. *Journal of the Royal Statistical Society, 34,* 187–220.

Gaskell, G., Wright, D., & O'Muircheartaigh, C. (2000). Telescoping of landmark events: Implications for survey research. *Public Opinion Quarterly, 64,* 77–89.

Heckman, J., & Singer, B. (1984). Economic duration analysis. *Journal of Econometrics, 24,* 63–132.

Hedeker, D., Siddiqui, O., & Hu, F. (2000). Random-effects regression analysis of correlated grouped-time survival data. *Statistical Methods in Medical Research, 9,* 161–179.

Laird, N., & Oliver, D. (1981). Covariance analysis of censored survival data using log-linear analysis techniques. *Journal of the American Statistical Association, 76,* 231–240.

Land, K., Nagin, D., & McCall, P. (2001). Discrete-time hazard regression with hidden heterogeneity: The semiparametric mixed Poisson regression approach. *Sociological Methods and Research, 29,* 342–373.

Langeheine, R., & Van de Pol, F. (2002). Latent Markov models. In J. Hagenaars & McCutcheon (Eds.), *Applied latent class analysis* (pp. 304–344). Cambridge: Cambridge University Press.

Lindeboom, M., & Kerkhofs, M. (2000). Multistate models for clustered duration data: An application to workplace effects on individual sickness absenteeism. *The Review of Economics and Statistics, 82,* 668–684.

Little, R., & Rubin, D. (2002). *Statistical analysis with missing data* (2nd ed.). New York: Wiley.

Masyn, K. (2003). *Discrete-time survival mixture analysis for single and recurrent events using latent variables.* Unpublished doctoral dissertation, University of California, Los Angeles.

McCutcheon, A. (1987). *Latent class analysis.* Newbury Park, CA: Sage.

Muthén, B., & Masyn, K. (2005). Discrete-time survival mixture analysis. *Journal of Educational and Behavioral Statistics, 30,* 27–58.

Muthén, L., & Muthén, B. (1998-2006). *Mplus user's guide* (4th ed.). Los Angeles, CA: Muthén & Muthén.

Nylund, K. L., Muthén, B., Nishina, A., Bellmore, A., & Graham, S. (2006). *Stability and instability of peer victimization during middle school: Using latent transition analysis with covariates, distal outcomes, and modeling extensions.* Manuscript submitted for publication.

Prentice, R., & Gloeckler, L. (1978). Regression analysis of grouped survival data with application to breast cancer data. *Biometrics, 34,* 57–67.

Rindskopf, D., & Rindskopf, W. (1986). The value of latent class analysis in medical diagnosis. *Statistics in Medicine, 5,* 21–27.

Rossi, P., Berk, R., & Lenihan, K. (1980). *Money, work, and crime: Some experimental results.* New York: Academic Press.

Singer, J., & Willett, J. (1993). It's about time: Using discrete-time survival analysis to study duration and the timing of events. *Journal of Educational Statistics, 18,* 155–195.

Singer, J., & Willett, J. (2003). *Applied longitudinal data analysis: Modeling change and event occurrence.* New York: Oxford University Press.

Steele, F. (2003). A multilevel mixture model for event history data with long-term survivors: An application to an analysis for contraceptive sterilisation in Bangladesh. *Lifetime Data Analysis, 9,* 155–174.

Steele, F., Goldstein, H., & Browne, W. (2004). A general multilevel multistate competing risks model for event history data, with an application to a study of contraceptive use dynamics. *Statistical Modelling, 4,* 145–159.

Trussel, J., & Richards, T. (1985). Correcting for unmeasured heterogeneity in hazard modeling using the Heckman-Singer procedure. *Sociological Methodology,* 242–276.

Tuma, N., & Hannan, M. (1984). *Social dynamics: Models and methods.* New York: Academic Press.

Van de Pol, F., & Langeheine, R. (1990). Mixed Markov latent class models. *Sociological Methodology,* 213–247.

Vaupel, J., Manton, K., & Stallard, E. (1979). The impact of hetergeneity in individual frailty on the dynamics of mortality. *Demography, 16,* 439–454.

Vermunt, J. (1997). *Log-linear models for event histories.* Thousand Oaks, CA: Sage Publications, Inc.

Vermunt, J. (2002). A general latent class approach to unobserved heterogeneity in the analysis of event history data. In J. Hagenaars & A. McCutcheon (Eds.), *Applied latent class analysis* (pp. 383–407). Cambridge: Cambridge University Press.

Vermunt, J., Langeheine, R., & Bockenholt, U. (1999). Discrete-time discrete-state latent Markov models with time-constant and time-varying covariates. *Journal of Educational and Behavioral Statistics, 24,* 179–207.

APPENDIX

This appendix contains select M*plus* syntax for the recidivism example with the financial aid covariate under the proportional hazard odds assumption. Note that M*plus* treats the last class of a latent class variable as the reference class both when it is the outcome in a multinomial regression and when it is the predictor, reformulated as dummy variables. Classes are also labeled beginning with "1". Thus, in this syntax, to match the model specification given in the text with the pre-event state as the reference category, the measurement model for e1 is reversed so that e1 = 1 is the event state and e1 = 2 is the pre-event state. For e2–e6, ej = 1 is the post-event state, ej = 2 is the event state, and ej = 3 is the pre-event state.

```
VARIABLE:

Usevariables are u1-u6 finaid;
Categorical are u1-u6;
Classes are e1(2) e2(3) e3(3)
           e4(3) e5(3) e6(3);

MODEL:

%overall%
e2#1 on e1#1@40;
e2#2 on e1#1@-10;
e3#1 on e2#1@40 e2#2@40;
e3#2 on e2#1@-10 e2#2@-10;
e4#1 on e3#1@40 e3#2@40;
e4#2 on e3#1@-10 e3#2@-10;
e5#1 on e4#1@40 e4#2@40;
e5#2 on e4#1@-10 e4#2@-10;
e6#1 on e5#1@40 e5#2@40;
e6#2 on e5#1@-10 e5#2@-10;
```

```
[e2#1@-20 e2#2];
[e3#1@-20 e3#2];
[e4#1@-20 e4#2];
[e5#1@-20 e5#2];
[e6#1@-20 e6#2];
e1#1 on finaid (1);

Model e1:
%e1#1% !event
[u1$1@-20];
e2#2 on finaid@0;
%e1#2% !pre-event
[u1$1@20];
e2#2 on finaid (1);

Model e2:
%e2#1% !post-event
[u2$1@20];
e3#2 on finaid@0;
%e2#2% !event
[u2$1@-20];
e3#2 on finaid@0;
%e2#3% !pre-event
[u2$1@20];
e3#2 on finaid (1);

Model e3:
%e3#1% !post-event
[u3$1@20];
e4#2 on finaid@0;
%e3#2% !event
[u3$1@-20];
e4#2 on finaid@0;
%e3#3% !pre-event
[u3$1@20];
e4#2 on finaid (1);

Model e4:
%e4#1% !post-event
[u4$1@20];
e5#2 on finaid@0;
%e4#2% !event
[u4$1@-20];
e5#2 on finaid@0;
%e4#3% !pre-event
[u4$1@20];
e5#2 on finaid (1);
```

```
Model e5:
%e5#1% !post-event
[u5$1@20];
e6#2 on finaid@0;
%e5#2% !event
[u5$1@-20];
e6#2 on finaid@0;
%e5#3% !pre-event
[u5$1@20];
e6#2 on finaid (1);

Model e6:
%e6#1% !post-event
[u6$1@20];
%e6#2% !event
[u6$1@-20];
%e6#3% !pre-event
[u6$1@20];
```

PART II

MODELS FOR ASSESSMENT AND DIAGNOSIS

CHAPTER 6

EVIDENTIARY FOUNDATIONS OF MIXTURE ITEM RESPONSE THEORY MODELS[1]

Robert J. Mislevy
University of Maryland

Roy Levy
Arizona State University

Marc Kroopnick
Daisy Rutstein
University of Maryland

Methodological advances in the area of latent variable modeling allow for the specification and estimation of an array of psychometric models, many of which were developed and have natural interpretations from behavioral and trait-based psychological perspectives (Rupp & Mislevy, 2007). Recently, movements in cognitive psychology have started to offer new perspectives on human behavior and reasoning. The psychometric community is beginning to embrace these themes in task construction, assessment design, and statistical modeling (National Research Council, 2001). Regarding the latter, structured, mixture, and mixture structured models represent statistical approaches to pursue theoretically motivated quantitative and qualitative differences among subjects and tasks and accordingly offer the potential

Advances in Latent Variable Mixture Models, pages 149–175

to better align statistical models with domain-specific theory (de Boeck & Wilson, 2004; Mislevy & Verhelst, 1990; Rupp & Mislevy, 2007). We join the efforts to bridge substantive and methodological themes by drawing out the common evidentiary foundations on which they are based in the context of mixture modeling for assessment.

In what follows, we characterize a sequence of assessment modeling scenarios, focusing on the underlying evidentiary structure that has, in parallel, both substantive motivations and methodological manifestations. The goal is to sketch the development of test theory from naïve conceptions to mixtures of structured item response theory (IRT) models, from a perspective that integrates probability-based reasoning and evolving substantive foundations. In each case we discuss the substantive and psychological grounding of the model, its expression in mathematical terms, and Bayesian inference in the model framework. This progression establishes a consistent evidentiary-reasoning framework—a continuity in the kinds and tools of reasoning that accommodate test theory as it has developed to this point, and as it may evolve in the future.

THEORETICAL FRAMEWORK

Assessments as Evidentiary Arguments

An assessment is an argument structure for reasoning from what examinees do, produce, or say to constructs, knowledge, or skills more broadly conceived. Traditionally, the domain of psychometrics has circumscribed itself to the quantification of the assessment argument; a hallmark of modern psychometrics is the use of latent variable statistical models in this capacity. At its core, however, an assessment is an *evidentiary* argument. Like other evidentiary arguments, it may be well served by leveraging probability-based reasoning to build and carry out the argument (Schum, 1994). Viewing assessments from this perspective has far-reaching implications for task construction, assessment design, administration, and validation (e.g., Bachman, 2005). What's more, this perspective casts statistical models as tools that employ probability-based reasoning to structure the evidentiary argument for making, justifying, and qualifying inferences or decisions about examinees (Mislevy, 1994).

Drawing from the seminal work of Messick (1994), an evidentiary perspective views an assessment system as addressing—explicitly or implicitly—a series of questions (Mislevy, Steinberg, & Almond, 2003):

- What constructs, knowledge, skills, or other attributes should be assessed?

- What behaviors or otherwise observable phenomena should reveal those constructs?
- What situations or tasks should elicit those behaviors?

Relevant to the first question, a *claim* is a declarative statement about an examinee in terms of constructs broadly conceived. In order to gain information regarding the claims, examinees are presented with tasks or stimuli. In response to the tasks or stimuli, examinees produce work products that are evaluated or scored, resulting in *observable data* that serve as evidence for evaluating the claims.

Relations amongst the components of the assessment argument may be structured by narrative logic (Toulmin, 1958) and represented diagrammatically (Figure 6.1). Inference about a claim is based on data that constitute evidence once there is an established relation between the data and the desired inference (Schum, 1994). This relation is captured by the *warrant*, which is based on some *backing*. Inferences may be tempered by *alternative explanations* which themselves are evidenced by *rebuttal data*.

Probability-Based Reasoning

The possibility of alternative explanations has long been recognized in educational assessment contexts (Mislevy & Levy, 2007). A key implication of this acknowledgment is the importance of using probabilistic relationships in modeling (Samejima, 1983). Deterministic rules for inference, though powerful when applicable, are inappropriate in assessment as the desired inferences concern latent characteristics of examinees. Probabilistic relations offer greater flexibility for characterizing relationships between claims and observations and hence are suitable for reasoning under uncertainty.

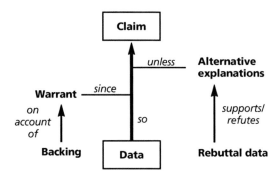

Figure 6.1   Structure of an evidentiary argument.

A properly structured statistical model overlays a substantive model for the situation with a model for our knowledge of the situation, so that we may characterize and communicate what we come to believe—as to both content and conviction—and why we believe it—as to our assumptions, our conjectures, our evidence, and the structure of our reasoning (Mislevy & Gitomer, 1996). In psychometric models, the defining variables are those that relate to the claims we would like to make and those that relate to the observations we need to make. By employing a probabilistic psychometric model, we implicitly employ an accompanying *frame of discernment* (Shafer, 1976). A frame of discernment specifies what we may become aware of and what distinctions we may make in using a model, in terms of the possible combinations of all the variables in that model. In psychometric models, this comes to understanding in what ways the model allows us to differentiate among examinees and among task performances in terms of the defining variables.

In probability-based reasoning, beliefs and uncertainty regarding variables are captured by probability distributions. Inference is conducted by incorporating evidence in the form of observations to update relevant probability distributions. The set of variables that capture the student proficiencies of interest comprise the *student model*; let Θ denote the full collection of student model variables across examinees. Similarly, let $\mathbf{B}$ denote the complete collection of parameters that characterize the psychometric properties of the observables and let $\mathbf{x}$ denote the full collection of those observables. Then, the conditional probabilities for the observations given the model parameters can be expressed as $P(\mathbf{x}|\Theta,\mathbf{B})$. The first step in probabilistic modeling is to construct the joint distribution $P(\Theta,\mathbf{B},\mathbf{x})$ in accordance with all substantive knowledge regarding the domain, examinees, tasks, and the data collection process. In the second step, the observed data are conditioned upon to arrive at the posterior distribution of the unknown quantities. Following Bayes' theorem, the posterior distribution for Θ and $\mathbf{B}$ given that $\mathbf{x}$ is observed to take the particular values $\mathbf{x}^*$ may be represented as

$$P(\Theta,\mathbf{B}\,|\,\mathbf{x}^*) \propto P(\Theta,\mathbf{B}) \times P(\mathbf{x}^*\,|\,\Theta,\mathbf{B}) \qquad (6.1)$$

In practice, the specification of multivariate probability distributions is simplified by independence and *conditional* independence assumptions regarding the observables. In considering a sequence of models, we will see how the conceptualization of Θ and $\mathbf{B}$ and associated conditional independence relationships in the probability model evolve in conjunction with an expanding theory-based narrative of the assessment.

The Assessment Triangle

Alignment among the statistical model, evidence from an assessment, and the domain specific theory can be represented by the *Assessment Triangle* (NRC, 2001). The elements of the triangle, namely cognition, observation, and interpretation, must not only make sense on their own, but must also be coordinated with one another when one constructs an assessment. Some model of cognition, or more broadly the character of knowledge in a domain, underlies every assessment. This conception may be very straightforward or quite complicated depending on the purpose of the assessment and/or the domain. When creating an assessment a test developer may use only subsets or broad principles of the applicable theory about knowledge, but in all cases this model shapes how the assessment is constructed.

In order to make proper inferences about a student's learning in a specific domain, tasks must be constructed to elicit observable evidence (the observation element of the triangle) consistent with the knowledge and cognitive processes that are part of the cognitive model, as well as with the purpose of the assessment. A statistical or psychometric model (the interpretation element) must be specified to interpret this observed evidence and support the corresponding inferences. Thus, there will be a strong and well defined connection between the theoretical model of cognition and the statistical model. Advances in educational measurement such as structured, mixture, and mixture structured models help to serve this purpose especially for complex assessment designs where there is a great need for flexible psychometric models.

Developing psychometric models depends heavily on structuring plausible conditional independence assumptions, particularly for modular or piecewise model construction (Pearl, 1988; Rupp 2002). Not only does the psychometric model help to mathematically define how domain elements relate in the cognitive model, it also incorporates conditional independence assumptions that are consistent with the cognitive model. For example, while exchangeability (de Finetti, 1964) has a mathematical definition, at its heart there is an assumption made about the cognitive model and which elements are taken to be distinguishable for a given modeling application and which are not. The latter can be framed mathematically in terms of exchangeability structures. Before we see responses to mathematics items from students in a class, for example, we may have no information that leads us to different beliefs about those students. As the cognitive model increases in complexity, elements may be indistinguishable only after accounting for some other factor; such elements are conditionally exchangeable. We may have reason to believe that students' solution strategies will affect their performance, so we would consider the students exchangeable only within groups using the same strategy. The more complex cognitive model can be linked to the psychometric (interpretation) model, in which (conditional) exchangeability assumptions show up as (conditional) independence assumptions. In pursuing increasingly complex psychometric models, parameters are not merely added to the statistical model; rather, a more complicated cognitive model is considered. The frame of discernment is expanded. The more complicated model allows for inferences about finer and more directed hypotheses that can be framed under the richer cognitive model.

Below we introduce an example assessment scenario to ground the discussion of the following models, which are treated in turn in the balance of this work: A total-score model, classical test theory, item response theory, structured item response theory, and mixtures of structured item response theory models. For each model under consideration, there is a corresponding narrative and a frame of discernment. In building from simple to complex narratives, the statistical models expand to meet the growing needs to address inferences regarding examinees and tasks. Specifically we will see the evolution of assumptions regarding the absence or presence of measurement error, differences (or the lack thereof) between tasks, and conceptions of proficiency. For all but the most basic models, textual, graphical, and mathematical expressions of the models are presented, which serve as (a) parallel representations of each model and (b) mechanisms for tracking differences between models.

Jointly construing the theoretical basis, statistical model, and data facilitates theoretical interpretations of a critique of the statistical model. Data-model fit assessment addresses the discrepancy between the observed data and the statistical model. Inadequate data-model fit is cause to proceed with caution (if at all) in making inferences based on the model. Furthermore, owing to the connections between the cognitive underpinnings and the statistical model, data-model fit assessment may be suggestive of the strengths and weaknesses of the theory that underlies the statistical model. It may, finally, reveal defects in the data-collection methods that need to be rectified in order to obtain better coherence among theory, model, and data. In what follows we do not discuss details for conducting data-model fit assessment; instead, attention will be granted to the ways in which data-model fit assessment may inform upon the cognitive underpinnings and the accompanying narrative.

Before turning to the models, we introduce an assessment scenario from the domain of spatial visualization that will serve as a running example. Examinees are presented with a collection of tasks that depict two right triangles; the second triangle is either a rotated version of the first or is both rotated and flipped. The examinee is instructed to determine if the second triangle is (a) the same as the first in the sense that it can be rotated to match up with the first, or (b) a mirror of the first in that it cannot be maneuvered around the plane to line up with the first (i.e., it would need

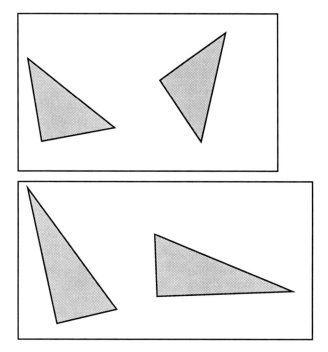

Figure 6.2   Examples of pairs of triangles in spatial rotation tasks.

to be flipped in addition to being rotated). For example, in Figure 6.2 the top pair of triangles are the same and the bottom pair of triangles are mirrors. In progressing through the psychometric models, returning to this example will highlight the features and limitations of the models as inferential machinery.

TOTAL SCORES

The most basic of models considered here is one in which each examinee's score is the count of observations of correct responses to tasks assumed to signify proficiency. Inferences regarding examinees are made in terms of the total scores where higher total scores indicate higher proficiency. Such models are not altogether inappropriate if certain assumptions are met. For example, if the implicit assumption that all the examinees take the same tasks is met, this simple model may adequately capture examinee proficiency.

In terms of probability-based reasoning and a psychological narrative, this model is best characterized in terms of what it is *not*. There is no notion of measurement error, no distinction between the observation and the inferential target, and hence no probabilistic reasoning for characterizing and synthesizing evidence. Furthermore, the tasks are presumed to be related to inferential target; this presumption, however, is not formalized in the model.

Turning to the substantive interpretation, the associated narrative is rather basic; examinees with higher scores have more proficiency. This story rests on the assumption that the scores are in fact related to construct they are alleged to measure. As there is no distinction between the observation and the inferential target, there is no distinction between the scores and the construct. Put differently, the scores fully operationalize the construct. Further, as it is not a probabilistic model, no statistical notions of data-model fit are available to critique the underlying substantive theory.

When the total score approach is applied to the spatial visualization assessment, examinees are presented a fixed set of tasks and are characterized by the number of tasks they correctly solve. Examinees with higher scores are interpreted as having more spatial visualization proficiency than their lower scoring counterparts—end of story.

CLASSICAL TEST THEORY

In classical test theory (CTT) approaches total scores are still employed, but the narrative introduces the key concept of measurement error, drawing a distinction between observed values and an unobserved inferential target. Multiple parallel tests x_j are all viewed as imperfect indicators of the same true score. Examinees differ with respect to their true scores, and for any particular examinee, the values on the x_j differ from the true score (and from each other) due to measurement error:

$$x_{ij} = \theta_i + e_{ij} \qquad (6.2)$$

where x_{ij} denotes the total score for examinee i on test j, θ_i is the true score for examinee i, and e_{ij} is an examinee- and test-specific error term.

Whereas before examinees differed in terms of their total scores, here the differences in true scores induce differences in observed scores, though the relationship between true and observed scores is clouded by measurement error. This expanded account of how the data arise and the additional dimension on which examinees may vary represent expansions in the narrative and the frame of discernment.

Historically, classical test theory addressed only the means, standard deviations, and correlations of true scores, observed scores, and errors; particular forms of distributions were not addressed. In order to illustrate probability-based reasoning and Bayesian inference, however, we will work with the parametric version of CTT. In this formulation, the true scores are typically assumed to be normally distributed:

$$\theta_i \sim N(\mu, \sigma_\theta^2) \tag{6.3}$$

and the error scores are assumed to be normally distributed with mean zero

$$e_{ij} \sim N(0, \sigma_e^2) \tag{6.4}$$

The full probability model is then:

$$P\left(\mathbf{x}, \mathbf{\Theta}, \mu, \sigma_\theta^2, \sigma_e^2\right) = P\left(\mathbf{x} \mid \mathbf{\Theta}, \sigma_e^2\right) \times P\left(\mathbf{\Theta} \mid \mu, \sigma_\theta^2\right) \times P(\mu) \times P\left(\sigma_\theta^2\right) \times P\left(\sigma_e^2\right) \tag{6.5}$$

$$= \prod_i \prod_j P\left(x_{ij} \mid \theta_i, \sigma_e^2\right) \times P\left(\theta_i \mid \mu, \sigma_\theta^2\right) \times P(\mu) \times$$

$$P\left(\sigma_\theta^2\right) \times P\left(\sigma_e^2\right),$$

which reflects independence assumptions (regarding μ, σ_θ^2, and σ_e^2) and conditional independence assumptions. More specifically, note that the distribution for each observable is conditional on the true score for the examinee and no one else. This, in conjunction with the assumption that the error scores are independent over examinees and tests, allows the factorization of the joint probability into the product over examinees and tests.

The factorization of the joint distribution of examinee variables $P(\mathbf{\Theta} \mid \mu, \sigma_\theta^2)$ into the product of univariate distributions $P(\theta_i \mid \mu, \sigma_\theta^2)$ over examinees reflects an independence assumption for examinees. The underlying narrative here is one of indifference regarding examinees. That is, *a priori* we have no theory about differences among examinees; beliefs about the next examinee to take the assessment are the same regardless of who it is. This theoretical stance may be expressed mathematically as exchangeability structures (de Finetti, 1964; Lindley & Novick, 1981). The implication for the probability model is that a common prior distribution ought to be assigned (Lindley & Smith, 1972). (If we know more about each examinee, in terms of covariates such as age or grade that we suspect may be related to true scores, we might instead posit a common prior among all examinees with the same covariates under a conditional exchangeability model.) In the current example, we specify the same prior distribution for all examinees (Equation 6.3). In this way, theoretical beliefs regarding the assessment have direct manifestations in the probability model.

Graphical models afford efficient representations for depicting joint probability distributions, including the conditional independence assump-

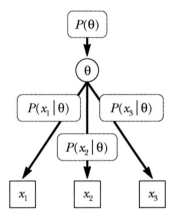

Figure 6.3 Graphical CTT model of examinee variables.

tions (Pearl, 1988). Figure 6.3 presents a graphical model for a CTT model of three parallel tests. We employ boxes for observed variables and circles for unobservable variables. The arrows, or directed edges, from θ to x_1, x_2, and x_3 convey that the test scores are probabilistically dependent on the unobservable true score. Accordingly, for each observable there is a conditional probability structure that depends on θ. The absence of any edges directly connecting the test scores indicates that they are conditionally independent given the variables on the paths between them, in this case θ. In this way, the pattern of the edges leading into x_1, x_2, and x_3 reflects the conditional independence assumptions that allow for the factorization in the first term in Equation 6.5.

The edge leading into θ has no source, hence θ is exogenous in the sense that it does not depend on any other variables at the *examinee* level. The last clause in the preceding sentence highlights that the graphical model in Figure 6.3 contains only examinee variables. The graph is written at the examinee level; the same structure is assumed to hold over all examinees.

Alternative graphical modeling frameworks make these points explicit. Figure 6.4 contains a graphical model in which all the parameters of the model are treated as variables and hence have nodes in the graph. Beginning on the left, nodes for μ and σ_θ^2 are depicted as exogenous and unknown. The edges leading from these nodes to a node for θ_i indicate that the distributions of the true scores $\theta_i,\ldots,\theta_N$ depend on μ and σ_θ^2. This replication of identical structures for θ_i over examinees is conveyed by placing the node for θ_i in a plate in which the index i ranges from $1,\ldots,N$, where N is the number of examinees. As discussed above, an exchangeability assumption regarding examinees implies the use of a common distribution, with the same higher-level parameters for all true scores. In the graphical

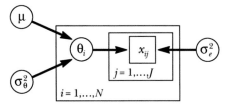

Figure 6.4   Graphical CTT model.

model, this is conveyed by having μ and σ_θ^2 lie *outside* the plate that represents the replication over examinees; that is, μ and σ_θ^2 do not vary over examinees.

The node for x_{ij} lies within the same plate and within a smaller plate for j, ranging from $1,...,J$, where J is the number of tests. This indicates that the stochastic structure for the x_{ij} variables is replicated over all subjects and all tests. Edges from θ_i and σ_e^2 to x_{ij} denote the dependence of the observed scores on the true scores and the error variance.

Though not pursued in the current work, graphical models structure the computations necessary to arrive at the posterior distribution (Lauritzen & Spiegelhalter, 1988; Pearl, 1988), which in the current case is:

$$P\left(\Theta,\mu,\sigma_\theta^2,\sigma_e^2 \mid \mathbf{x}^*\right) \propto \prod_i \prod_j P\left(x_{ij}^* \mid \theta_i, \sigma_e^2\right) \times P\left(\theta_i \mid \mu, \sigma_\theta^2\right) \times \qquad (6.6)$$

$$P(\mu) \times P\left(\sigma_\theta^2\right) \times P\left(\sigma_e^2\right)$$

Marginal posterior distributions for μ, σ_θ^2, and σ_e^2 may be interpreted as beliefs about population characteristics after having observed test scores, reasoning through the posited model. In addition, we may obtain the posterior distribution for any function of the parameters, such as the reliability $\rho = \sigma_\theta^2 / (\sigma_\theta^2 + \sigma_e^2)$.

At the level of each individual, inference about the true score for examinee i after having observed x_i is conducted in terms of the posterior distribution of θ_i. The posterior mean of θ_i is the expected value for any test score for examinee i and its standard deviation captures our uncertainty regarding the examinee's true score. The interpretation of θ is bound to the test form; examinees can be differentiated strictly in terms of their propensity to make correct responses to that test form. The narrative is simply that people differ with respect to their performance on this particular test form. The model works with a narrow frame of discernment; we permit and pursue differences among examinees in terms of their observed scores, which contain measurement error, and their unknown true scores, which are free from measurement error.

Returning to the example, under a CTT model higher scores on an assessment containing tasks like those in Figure 6.2 are still interpreted as having more spatial visualization proficiency. However, this interpretation is afforded because the observed total scores are dependent on the true scores. This distinction between the observed variable and a construct of interest tempers our inferences about examinees—specifically, it structurally admits alternative explanations of good performance despite low true ability and low performance despite high true ability due to measurement error—and facilitates basic characterizations of the assessment in this regard, such as the reliability of the set of spatial visualization tasks.

As always, model-based inferences are conditional on the suitability of the model. Data-model fit assessment may take on a number of forms, such as evaluating the reliability, characterizing deviations from the conditional independence assumptions, and so forth. Substantive interpretations of inadequate data-model fit may call into question the assumption of a single underlying dimension; in the context of the example, it may suggest that spatial visualization is multidimensional and that a single true score may not be adequate. Accordingly, the CTT narrative of a single proficiency along which examinees are characterized may need to be revisited, and the probability framework provides tools to help explore this possibility. Testing the equality of means of randomly-equivalent samples on putatively parallel forms, for example, helps testing companies maintain the comparability of their examinations.

ITEM RESPONSE THEORY

Model Development

The CTT narrative regarding observations from tasks is limited in that it is framed at the level of test scores that are assumed to be parallel. Tasks and task-level patterns of response are not part of the CTT frame of discernment. Differences on observed scores are not explained, beyond the narrative frame of examinees' having different expected scores on the test as a whole and variations of observed scores attributable to random measurement error. IRT relaxes the parallelism assumption by shifting the unit of analysis from a test comprised of multiple items or tasks to the tasks individually. That is, the frame of discernment for IRT extends the narrative space to responses to and patterns among responses to particular, individuated tasks. In CTT, the observable variables x refer to observed scores at the level of *tests*, while in IRT the observable variables x refer to observed responses at the level of *items*.

There is then the corresponding probability model that comports with this extended narrative frame. Popular IRT models assume multiple, not necessarily parallel observable (task) responses x_j that may differ, but all depend on a single latent variable θ. For examinee i,

$$P(x_{i1},\ldots,x_{iJ} \mid \theta_i,\boldsymbol{\beta}_1,\ldots,\boldsymbol{\beta}_J) = \prod_j P(x_{ij} \mid \theta_i,\boldsymbol{\beta}_j) \qquad (6.7)$$

where $\boldsymbol{\beta}_j$ is a possibly vector-valued parameter of task j. Equation 6.7 reflects conditional independence assumptions in the model; given the value of θ_i and $\boldsymbol{\beta}_j$, the responses x_{ij} are independent of all other variables in the model.

Here x_{ij} denotes the scored response from examinee i to task j, whereas in CTT models, it denotes the score from examinee i to test j. This difference underscores that (a) CTT was developed by treating an assessment as a fixed collection of tasks, rather than at the task level, and (b) viewing principles of CTT at the task level reveals the restrictive nature of the assumptions relative to the expanded frame of discernment in IRT.

By modeling at the task level, IRT affords the power to model more complex assessment scenarios. In CTT, all examinees were assumed to take the same tasks that constitute a test form. IRT permits administration of different subsets of tasks to different examinees, as in matrix sampling schemes (Lord, 1962). Similarly, IRT permits test assembly that targets levels of proficiency or specific test information functions (Lord, 1980) and adaptive task selection (Wainer, 2000). These practical advantages of IRT are possible because the model affords the necessary evidence to address the desired inferences under these scenarios.

Probability-based inference under IRT is a natural elaboration of probability based inference under CTT. Figure 6.5 depicts a graphical model for IRT. Following Equation 6.7, an observable response to task j from examinee i is dependent on the examinee's latent variable θ_i and the task's parameters $\boldsymbol{\beta}_j$. Distributions for examinee abilities and task parameters are governed by possibly vector-valued parameters η and τ, respectively.

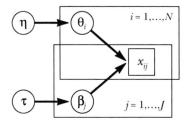

Figure 6.5   Graphical IRT model.

This graphical model corresponds to the probability model:

$$P(\mathbf{x}, \Theta, \mathbf{B}, \eta, \tau) = \prod_i \prod_j P(x_{ij} \mid \theta_i, \beta_j) \times P(\theta_i \mid \eta) \times P(\beta_j \mid \tau) \times P(\eta) \times P(\tau) \quad (6.8)$$

Figure 6.5 and Equation 6.8 indicate that the examinee parameters are assumed conditionally independent given η. As before, an exchangeability assumption regarding examinees implies the use of a common prior, which allows the factorization of the distribution of Θ in Equation 6.8. In Figure 6.5, this manifests itself by having η outside the plate over examinees.

The specification of the task parameters parallels this line of reasoning. In the IRT model presented here, task parameters are assumed conditionally independent given τ. Accordingly, the node for τ lies outside the plate over tasks in Figure 6.5 and the distribution for $\mathbf{B}$ is factored into the product of distributions of β_j over j in Equation 6.8. The underlying narrative here is absent any *substantive* specifications of differences among the tasks. Although tasks are permitted to vary in their *psychometric* properties (e.g., difficulty), no *a priori* theory regarding why such variation occurs is present.

Posterior inference is given by:

$$P(\Theta, \mathbf{B}, \eta, \tau \mid \mathbf{x}^*) \propto \prod_i \prod_j P(x_{ij}^* \mid \theta_i, \beta_j) \times P(\theta_i \mid \eta) \times P(\beta_j \mid \tau) \times P(\eta) \times P(\tau). \quad (6.9)$$

For examinees, the posterior distribution of θ_i represents posterior beliefs about ability. For tasks, the posterior distribution of β_j represents posterior beliefs about task parameters.

Example: The Rasch Model

The Rasch model for dichotomously scored task responses (in which an incorrect response is coded 0 and a correct response is coded 1) specifies a single task parameter $\beta_j = \beta_j$ and specifies the probability of a correct task response via a logistic function:

$$P(x_{ij} = 1 \mid \theta_i, \beta_j) = \frac{\exp(\theta_i - \beta_j)}{1 + \exp(\theta_i - \beta_j)} \quad (6.10)$$

The model locates examinees and tasks along a latent continuum in terms of the values of θ and β, respectively (Figure 6.6). Examinees with higher values of θ are interpreted as having more ability. In CTT, the interpretation of θ was restricted to the particular set of tasks that make up the test form. This is not the case here in IRT, in which θ is interpreted as

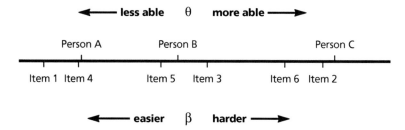

Figure 6.6   Latent continuum from the Rasch model.

ability independent of observed scores. Tasks with higher values of β are more difficult.

As was the case in CTT, θ_i is interpreted as a propensity to make correct responses, and examinees are differentiated in terms of their propensities. The incorporation of task parameters marks the key departure from CTT; IRT models differentiate tasks as well as examinees. In this expanded frame of discernment, our narrative includes the possibility of tasks varying in their difficulty, represented in the psychometric model via task-specific parameters β_j. In the Rasch model in particular, tasks differ in terms of their difficulty along a single dimension. Though more complex than that for CTT, the narrative here is somewhat basic in that the tasks are assumed to have the same ordering for all examinees and there is no expressed connection between task difficulty and content. The model locates examinees and tasks in such a way that we may make substantive interpretations regarding examinees having more or less ability and tasks being more or less difficult. However, there is no mechanism in the model for explaining how or why those locations came to be.

An IRT analysis of the spatial visualization assessment now permits distinctions among the tasks as well as examinees (Figure 6.6) in terms of the latent spatial visualization proficiency. Having item-specific parameters allows for a targeted test construction (e.g., if we wanted to construct a difficult spatial visualization test) either in advance or dynamically (via adaptive testing).

For example, Person C is located toward the upper end of the continuum, indicating high ability. Items 2 and 6 are also located toward the upper end of the continuum, indicating they are more difficult than the other items; Person C would have about a 50% chance of answering each correctly. Items 1 and 4 are very easy for Person C, but more in the 50% range for the less proficient Person A. Data-model fit assessment may include a variety of aspects (global model fit, item fit, differential item functioning, dimensionality, etc.), all of which have implications for the underlying narrative about the assessment and examinees. Even surface-level investigations of the results of fitting the statistical model can inform upon the narrative. A key assumption at issue in tests of the fit of the Rasch model is the invariant ordering of difficulty across demographic groups, score levels, time points, and so forth. Mixture models discussed in a following section are one way of extending the narrative space further to accommodate such patterns.

STRUCTURED ITEM RESPONSE THEORY

Model Development

The "cognitive revolution" of the 1960s and 1970s, exemplified by Newell and Simon's (1972) *Human Information Processing*, called attention to the nature of knowledge, and the ways that people acquire and use it. How do people represent the information in a situation? What operations and strategies do they use to solve problems? What aspects of problems make them difficult, or call for various knowledge or processes? Viewing assessment from this perspective, Snow and Lohman (1989) pointed out in the Third Edition of *Educational Measurement* that "the evidence from cognitive psychology suggests that test performances are comprised of complex assemblies of component information-processing actions that are adapted to task requirements during performance" (p. 317).

Basic IRT models permit differences among tasks but yield no information as to the underlying reasons for such differences. However, many domains have theoretical hypotheses regarding the component processes involved in working through tasks. The implication for assessment is that the psychometric properties of a task (e.g., difficulty) may be thought of as dependent on features of the task, by virtue of the knowledge or processes they evoke on the part of the examinees who attempt to solve them (Rupp & Mislevy, 2007).

The narrative of such an assessment context is now much richer theoretically. Domain-specific substantive knowledge is available to motivate *a priori* hypotheses regarding tasks in terms of how examinees solve them and hence the resulting psychometric properties. What is then needed is a statistical model that can support probability-based reasoning in this further-extended narrative space. As we have seen, the IRT model in Figure 6.5 and Equation 6.8 is insufficient. Structured IRT (de Boeck & Wilson, 2004) extends the IRT framework by modeling the task parameters that define the conditional distribution of the observable responses as dependent on the known substantively relevant properties of the task.

Figure 6.7 contains the graphical model for a structured IRT model where q_j is a vector of M known elements expressing the extent of the presence of M substantive features that are relevant to psychometric properties

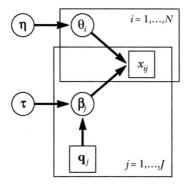

Figure 6.7   Graphical structured IRT model.

of tasks for task j and τ is a vector with elements that reflect, quantitatively, the influences of the task features on the psychometric properties. Of chief importance is the inclusion of the task features *inside* the plate that signifies replication over tasks, which indicates that the psychometric properties of each task depend on the features of the task. Letting $\mathbf{Q}$ denote the collection of $\mathbf{q}_j$ over tasks, the corresponding probability model is now:

$$P(\mathbf{x},\Theta,\mathbf{B},\boldsymbol{\eta},\tau,\mathbf{Q}) = \prod_i \prod_j P(x_{ij} \mid \theta_i, \boldsymbol{\beta}_j) \times P(\theta_i \mid \boldsymbol{\eta}) \times P(\boldsymbol{\beta}_j \mid \mathbf{q}_j, \tau) \times \quad (6.11)$$

$$P(\boldsymbol{\eta}) \times P(\tau),$$

which makes explicit that the task parameters are conditional on the task features. The dependence of $\boldsymbol{\beta}_j$ on $\mathbf{q}_j$ reflects the additional information needed to render the tasks conditionally exchangeable. Whereas previously the tasks were thought to exchangeable—and modeled as independent given τ (Equation 6.8)—we now consider tasks to vary in accordance with their properties and they therefore are exchangeable only after conditioning on task features as well. The factorization of the joint distribution of task parameters into the product of the task-specific distributions as conditional on τ and $\mathbf{q}_j$ reflects (a) a belief that the *psychometric* properties of the tasks depend on the *substantive* properties of the tasks, and (b) the lack of any other belief regarding further influences on the psychometric properties of the tasks.

The posterior distribution that forms the basis of inference is:

$$P(\Theta,\mathbf{B},\boldsymbol{\eta},\tau \mid \mathbf{x}^*,\mathbf{Q}) \propto \prod_i \prod_j P(x_{ij}^* \mid \theta_i, \boldsymbol{\beta}_j) \times P(\theta_i \mid \boldsymbol{\eta}) \times P(\boldsymbol{\beta}_j \mid \mathbf{q}_j, \tau) \times \quad (6.12)$$

$$P(\boldsymbol{\eta}) \times P(\tau).$$

Marginal posterior distributions for the $\boldsymbol{\beta}_j$ still reflect updated beliefs regarding psychometric properties of the tasks, but now we have a probability-model connection to substantive theory about *why* certain tasks exhibit these psychometric properties based on the task features. More specifically, the posterior distribution for τ constitutes updated beliefs regarding the influences of task properties on psychometric properties.

For each examinee, the posterior distribution of θ_i again represents posterior beliefs about ability. But in addition to the test-centered and empirical "propensity to make correct responses" interpretation of ability we now have a theory-based interpretation couched in terms of task properties.

Example: The Linear Logistic Test Model

The linear logistic test model (LLTM; Fischer, 1973) decomposes the task difficulty parameter in the Rasch model into a weighted sum of components:

$$\beta_j = \sum_{m=1}^{M} q_{jm}\tau_m = \mathbf{q}'_j\tau \tag{6.13}$$

where $\mathbf{q}_j$ and τ are vectors of length M, the number of task features relevant to task difficulty.

As in simpler IRT models, θ is interpreted as an ability that leads to a propensity to produce correct responses and examinees may be differentiated along these grounds. The surface level interpretation of β remains the same as in the Rasch model: higher values correspond to more difficult tasks. However, by modeling β, a more complex interpretation emerges in terms of the task features.

To illustrate, we return to the example the spatial visualization assessment from the perspective of a structured IRT model. Mislevy, Wingersky, Irvine, and Dann (1991) modeled spatial visualization tasks in which the key task feature is the degree of rotation necessary to line up the geometric figures. Under this hypothesis, correctly solving for the top pair of triangles in Figure 6.2 requires less rotation and is therefore easier than solving the bottom pair of triangles.

Figure 6.8 depicts hypothetical results from such a model, where values of β—which, as before, are interpreted as task difficulty—are linked to the amount of mental rotation for the task. By positing a formal structure for β, the model explicitly incorporates a substantive hypothesis about how it came to be that tasks differ in their difficulty, in this case the differences in task difficulty are *explained* by differences in the amount of mental rotation required to solve them.

The frame of discernment of the LLTM encompasses that of the Rasch model; the model permits differentiation amongst examinees in terms of

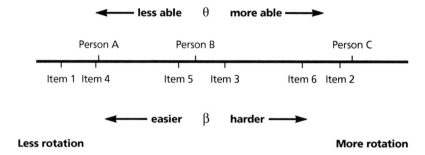

Figure 6.8   Latent continuum from the LLTM.

θ and amongst tasks in terms of β. However, it is extended in terms of the values of the substantively connected τ elements, and correspondingly the narrative for the LLTM is richer than that of the Rasch model. No longer are tasks considered exchangeable. Rather, we have a substantive theory for why tasks might differ. With regard to the mental rotation test, we are no longer *a priori* indifferent with respect to the tasks. Instead, we have a theory-based belief that ties task difficulty to the angle of rotation. This assumption manifests itself in the probability model by the additional conditioning on task features in specifying the distributions of task difficulty parameters. The resulting change in interpreting task difficulty induces a parallel change in interpreting ability, which is now viewed in terms of the processes involved in the successfully navigating the challenges posed by the varying features of the tasks. For the spatial visualization tasks, examinees with higher ability are inferred to be better at mentally rotating objects, and the psychometric model is explicitly and formally connected to an extensive research literature on mental rotation.

Incorporating the narrative for task difficulty via the model in Equation 6.13 allows for a direct evaluation of the adequacy of that narrative. Magnitudes of the elements of τ capture the associations between the task features and task difficulty and therefore direct interpretations for the relevance of the task features. In the case of the spatial visualization tasks, the narrative states that those that require more rotation should be more difficult. Investigating τ allows an overall assessment of this hypothesis. A value near zero would indicate that, in contrast to the underlying theory, the required degree of rotation is not a principal aspect of the task in terms of its difficulty. Conversely, assuming an appropriate coding scheme, a positive value of τ would indicate that the degree of rotation is a key feature of tasks. Turning to the individual tasks, we might then investigate if certain tasks do not fit this pattern, either because they require (a) a large amount of rotation yet seem to be easy, or (b) a small amount of rotation yet seem to be difficult.

Such findings would call into question the breadth of the influence of mental rotation and hence, the completeness of the narrative.

MIXTURE STRUCTURED ITEM RESPONSE THEORY

Model Development

The total score, CTT, IRT, and structured IRT models all assume the tasks behave in the same way for all examinees. For each task, a single set of parameters β_j is posited and employed in modeling the task responses for all examinees. In the Rasch and LLTM models, a single difficulty parameter β_j is estimated and all the tasks' difficulty parameters are located on a single dimension along with a single ability parameter for each examinee (Figures 6.6 and 6.8).

Such dimensionality assumptions may be questioned. For example, differential item functioning (DIF) may be viewed as multidimensionality (Ackerman, 1992), which suggests that when DIF is exhibited a single set of parameters for a task is insufficient. More substantively, research into the domain may suggest that tasks can function differently for populations of examinees because multiple solution strategies may be adopted (e.g., Tatsuoka, Linn, Tatsuoka, & Yamamoto, 1988). Furthermore, the features and properties that make a task difficult may vary depending on the adopted strategy. Tasks with certain features may be very difficult under one solution strategy but considerably easier under another strategy.

For example, in spatial visualization tasks one strategy involves rotating the object where, as discussed above, the amount of rotation required contributes to task difficulty. An alternative strategy approaches the task by analytically evaluating the side clockwise adjacent to the right angle in both triangles. If on one triangle this is the longer side but on the other triangle it is the shorter side, the triangles are mirror images. If this side is either the shorter side of both triangles or the longer side of both triangles, they are the same. Under such a strategy, no rotation is necessary, so the angle that the second triangle is rotated away from the first should not influence task difficulty. Rather, the comparability of the two non-hypotenuse sides ought to be a determining factor. The closer the triangles are to being isosceles, the more difficult to determine if the clockwise adjacent side is the shorter or longer side (see Mislevy et al., 1991, for details). To illustrate, reconsider the pairs of triangles in Figure 6.2. It was argued that under the rotational strategy solving for the top pair of triangles would be easier than solving for the bottom pair. Under the analytic strategy the reverse is the case. It is much easier to evaluate the sides clockwise adjacent to the right angle in the bottom pair of triangles—and see that they are different—than it is for the top pair.

The psychological narrative and frame of discernment is now qualitatively expanded. Examinees differ not only in ability, but in the ways they approach the tasks. Ability is now formulated *with respect to* a particular strategy; examinees may be quite proficient using one strategy but not the other. This multidimensionality is similarly projected onto the view of tasks as well; psychometric properties are formulated *with respect to* a particular strategy.

Likewise, the probability model is expanded so that examinee and task parameters are formulated with respect to multiple, latent groups. More specifically, examinees are hypothesized to belong to one of K latent groups, corresponding to strategy. Let $\boldsymbol{\varphi}_i = (\phi_{i1},\dots,\phi_{iK})$ be an examinee-specific K-dimensional vector where $\phi_{ik} = 1$ if examinee i is a member of group k (i.e., employs strategy k) and 0 otherwise. Let θ_{ik} be the ability of examinee i under strategy k; parameters governing the ability distribution under strategy k are contained in $\boldsymbol{\eta}_k$. Turning to the tasks, let $\boldsymbol{\beta}_{jk}$ be the parameters of psychometric properties of task j under strategy k. Let $\mathbf{q}_{jk} = (q_{jk1},\dots,q_{jkM_k})$ be the vector of M_k known features of task j relevant to strategy k. Finally, let $\boldsymbol{\tau}_k$ be the strategy-specific vector of unknown parameters that govern the dependence of $\boldsymbol{\beta}_{jk}$ on $\mathbf{q}_{jk}$.

Figure 6.9 contains the graphical model for a mixture structured IRT model. The key difference between the graphical model for structured IRT (Figure 6.7) is the addition of a plate over k, which renders the variables in the plate to be strategy-specific. In addition, the node for $\boldsymbol{\varphi}_i$ is introduced to capture examinee group membership.

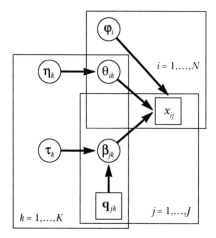

Figure 6.9 Graphical mixture structured IRT model.

The corresponding probability model is:

$$P(\mathbf{x},\mathbf{Q},\boldsymbol{\varphi},\mathbf{B},\boldsymbol{\eta},\boldsymbol{\tau},\mathbf{Q}) = \prod_i \prod_j \prod_{k \ni \phi_{ik}=1} P\left(x_{ij} \mid \theta_{ik},\beta_{jk},\varphi_i\right) \times P\left(\theta_{ik} \mid \eta_k\right) \times P\left(\varphi_i\right) \times \quad (6.14)$$

$$P\left(\beta_{jk} \mid \mathbf{q}_{jk},\tau_k\right) \times P\left(\eta_k\right) \times P\left(\tau_k\right),$$

where Θ, $\mathbf{B}$, η, τ, $\mathbf{Q}$, and φ are the full collections of the corresponding parameters. The prevalence of the subscript for latent groups (k) dovetails with the inclusion of the parameter laden plate for k in the graph (Figure 6.9) and makes explicit the manifestation of the more complex narrative.

Posterior inference is given by:

$$P\left(\Theta,\boldsymbol{\varphi},\mathbf{B},\boldsymbol{\eta},\boldsymbol{\tau} \mid \mathbf{x}^*,\mathbf{Q}\right) \propto \prod_i \prod_j \prod_{k \ni \phi_{ik}=1} P\left(x_{ij}^* \mid \theta_{ik},\beta_{jk},\varphi_i\right) \times P\left(\theta_{ik} \mid \eta_k\right) \times P\left(\varphi_i\right) \times (6.15)$$

$$P\left(\beta_{jk} \mid \mathbf{q}_{jk},\tau_k\right) \times P\left(\eta_k\right) \times P\left(\tau_k\right).$$

As in structured IRT, inferences regarding psychometric properties of tasks are interpreted via the influences of the task features. However, here in the mixture case, posterior distributions for τ_k characterize group-specific influences of group-relevant task features. The results are group-specific psychometric parameters β_{jk} for each task. For each examinee, the marginal posterior distributions for $\theta_{i1},\dots,\theta_{iK}$ summarize beliefs about the abilities of each examinee with respect to each of the K strategies. The posterior distribution for φ_i (i.e., $\phi_{i1},\dots,\phi_{iK}$) summarizes beliefs about examinee i's group membership regarding which strategy he/she used throughout the test, based on his/her pattern of responses.

Example: The Mixture Linear Logistic Test Model

Consider the situation in which the K groups correspond to K different strategies and task difficulty under each strategy depends on features of the tasks relevant to the strategy. A LLTM is formulated *within* each strategy. Let q_{jkm} denote the mth feature of task j relevant under strategy k. The difficulty of task j under strategy k is:

$$\beta_{jk} = \sum_{m=1}^{M_k} q_{jkm}\tau_{km} \quad (6.16)$$

Previously, the components of the model (β, q, τ) were modeled at the task level and hence indexed by the subscript j in Equation 6.13. Here, the components are modeled at the level of the task for each class (strategy) and hence subscripted by j (for tasks) and k (for classes).

The probability of a correct response is now a latent mixture of LLTM models:

$$P\left(x_{ij} \mid \boldsymbol{\theta}_i, \boldsymbol{\phi}_i, \boldsymbol{\beta}_j\right) = \prod_{k=1}^{K} \left[\frac{\exp(\theta_{ik} - \beta_{jk})}{1 + \exp(\theta_{ik} - \beta_{jk})} \right]^{\phi_k}, \tag{6.17}$$

where $\boldsymbol{\theta}_i = (\theta_{i1}, \ldots, \theta_{iK})$ and $\boldsymbol{\beta}_j = (\beta_{j1}, \ldots, \beta_{jK})$.

For the mental rotation example, Mislevy et al. (1991) fit mixture LLTM models to data from spatial visualization tasks in which latent classes are associated with strategy use. Figure 6.10 depicts hypothetical results for two dimensions corresponding to the two strategies discussed above for approaching spatial visualization tasks. The model locates tasks in terms of relative difficulty along each dimension. Drawing from the within-group LLTM structure, there are substantive explanations regarding what makes tasks easier or harder under each strategy: the amount of rotation and the acuteness of the angle. Similarly, the model locates examinees in terms of ability along each dimension. Again, we have a theoretical interpretation of ability for each strategy. By linking task difficulty to task features relevant to each strategy the examinee abilities take on interpretations in terms of the different processes involved in following the strategies, that is, mentally

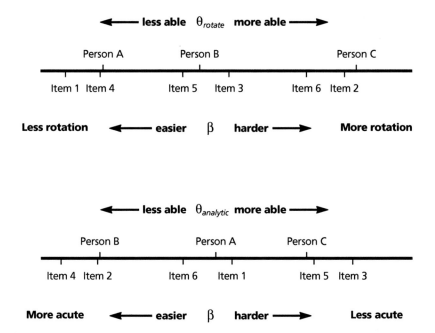

Figure 6.10 Latent continua from the mixture LLTM.

rotating the objects or analytically evaluating the sides clockwise adjacent to the right angle.

Neither tasks nor examinees need be comparably located under the different strategies. In Figure 6.10 task 2 is difficult (relative to the other tasks) for examinees attempting to rotate the figure but relatively easy for examinees analytically approaching the task. Examinee B is more proficient than examinee A in terms of the rotation strategy; their relative order is reversed for the analytic strategy. Although which strategy a particular examinee used is not observed directly, posterior probabilities for ϕ_i summarize the *a posteriori* information we have regarding the strategy examinee i employed. The probability favors the rotational strategy if items with less rotation were more frequently answered correctly, and the analytic strategy if items with sharper angles were more frequently answered correctly regardless of their degree of rotation.

The narrative at play here is a more complex view of the domain in which one of multiple strategies may be employed when approaching tasks. The use of LLTM models within groups incorporates a domain-based structure specialized to the group-relevant task features. The result is that tasks may be differentially difficult for different groups based on substantive theories about the domain regarding which aspects of the tasks pose challenges for the different groups. Theory-based approaches to modeling such situations leverage these differences to form more refined inferences regarding examinees. By creating assessments that employ tasks with differential difficulty under the alternative strategies, inferences regarding group membership and proficiency may be obtained from the task responses.

Again, data-model fit assessment has implications for the narrative. As in structured IRT models, evaluation of the parameters τ informs upon the hypotheses regarding the relevance of the task properties, only now the evaluation may be done with respect to each strategy separately. On a different note, we may investigate situations in which the posterior inference regarding examinees in terms of their strategy use or proficiencies is difficult, as that may be further suggestive of a need to expand our narrative, such as to a situation in which we consider that examinees may switch strategies from one task to another, or even within solutions to a given task (Kyllonen, Lohman, & Snow, 1984).

DISCUSSION

This chapter has traced a sequence of statistical models used in psychometrics from rudimentary total score models to complex IRT models. This sequence tracks not only increasingly complex mathematical models for assessment, but the dual development of increasingly intricate psychological narratives regarding subjects, tasks, and the processes invoked by subjects in approaching those tasks. In building to a theory in which

- an examinee may employ one of possibly many strategies to solve tasks and may be differentially proficient with respect to the skills employed under each strategy, and
- tasks may be differentially difficult under the alternative strategies, owing to the alignment of the task properties with theories about what makes tasks difficult under the different strategies.

The psychometric model is likewise built up to be one in which

- group membership and group-specific ability parameters are estimated for each examinee, and
- group-specific difficulty parameters are estimated for each task, as well as group-specific component-wise influences of task features.

This presentation illustrates the joint evolution of psychological narratives and measurement models. Increases in the complexity of the psychological narrative guide both the increase in the complexity in the statistical model and the changes in the interpretation of the parameters in the model. Probability-based reasoning—specifically Bayesian inference—provides a coherent framework for structuring inference at all stages of development. We note in particular that mixture models are stories as much as they are statistical models—the model follows the narrative and only supports inferences to the extent that we have a rich enough frame of discernment in the probability model to support an evidentiary argument. Judicious choices for task administration can aid in estimating strategy use, ability, and psychometric properties relative to strategy. These choices are motivated by a theory-based understanding of the domain and the cognitive processes and skills examinees invoke in working through tasks, made explicit in the model by structuring the psychometric properties in terms of task features.

REFERENCES

Ackerman, T. A. (1992). A didactic explanation of item bias, item impact, and item validity from a multidimensional perspective. *Journal of Educational Measurement, 29*, 67–91.

Bachman, L. F. (2005). Building and supporting a case for test use. *Language Assessment Quarterly, 2*, 1–34.

de Boeck, P., & Wilson, M. (Eds.) (2004). *Explanatory item response models: A generalized linear and nonlinear approach.* New York: Springer.

de Finetti, B. (1964). Foresight: Its logical laws, its subjective sources. In H. E. Kyburg & H. E. Smokler (Eds.), *Studies in subjective probability* (pp. 93–158). New York: Wiley.

Fischer, G. H. (1973). The linear logistic test model as an instrument in educational research. *Acta Psychologica, 37*, 359–374.

Kyllonen, P. C., Lohman, D. F., & Snow, R. E. (1984). Effects of aptitudes, strategy training, and task facets on spatial task performance. *Journal of Educational Psychology, 76*, 130–145.

Lauritzen, S. L., & Spiegelhalter, D. J. (1988). Local computations with probabilities on graphical structures and their application to expert systems (with discussion). *Journal of the Royal Statistical Society, Series B, 50*, 157–224.

Lindley, D. V., & Novick, M. R. (1981). The role of exchangeability in inference. *The Annals of Statistics, 9*, 45–58.

Lindley, D. V., & Smith, A. F. M. (1972). Bayes estimates for the linear model. *Journal of the Royal Statistical Society, Series B, 34*, 1–42.

Lord, F. M. (1962). Estimating norms by item sampling. *Educational and Psychological Measurement, 22*, 259–267.

Lord, F. M. (1980). *Applications of item response theory to practical testing problems.* Hillsdale, NJ: Erlbaum.

Messick, S. (1994). The interplay of evidence and consequences in the validation of performance assessments. *Educational Researcher, 23*, 13–23.

Mislevy, R. J. (1994). Evidence and inference in educational assessment. *Psychometrika, 59*, 439–483.

Mislevy, R. J., & Gitomer, D. H. (1996). The role of probability-based inference in an intelligent tutoring system. *User-Modeling and User-Adapted Interaction, 5*, 253–282.

Mislevy, R. J., & Levy, R. (2007). Bayesian psychometric modeling from an evidence-centered design perspective. In C. R. Rao & S. Sinharay (Eds.), *Handbook of statistics, Volume 26*, (pp. 839–865). North-Holland: Elsevier.

Mislevy, R. J., Steinberg, L. S., & Almond, R. G. (2003). On the structure of educational assessments. *Measurement: Interdisciplinary Research and Perspectives, 1*, 3–67.

Mislevy, R. J., & Verhelst, N. (1990). Modeling item responses when different subjects employ different solution strategies. *Psychometrika, 55*, 195–215.

Mislevy, R. J., Wingersky, M. S., Irvine, S. H., & Dann, P. L. (1991). Resolving mixtures of strategies in spatial visualization tasks. *British Journal of Mathematical and Statistical Psychology, 44*, 265–288.

National Research Council (2001). In J. Pellegrino, N. Chudowsky, & R. Glaser (Eds.). *Knowing what students know: The science and design of educational assessment.* Committee on the Foundations of AssessmentWashington, DC: National Academy Press.

Newell, A., & Simon, H.A. (1972). *Human problem solving.* Englewood Cliffs, NJ: Prentice-Hall.

Pearl, J. (1988). *Probabilistic reasoning in intelligent systems: Networks of plausible inference.* San Mateo, CA: Kaufmann.

Rupp, A. A. (2002). Feature selection for choosing and assembling measurement models: A building-block-based organization. *International Journal of Testing, 2*, 311–360.

Rupp, A. A., & Mislevy, R. J. (2007). Cognitive foundations of structured item response models. In J. P. Leighton & M. J. Gierl (Eds.), *Cognitive diagnostic assessment: Theories and applications* (pp. 205–241). Cambridge: Cambridge University Press.

Samejima, F. (1983). Some methods and approaches of estimating the operating characteristics of discrete item responses. In H. Wainer & S. Messick (Eds.), *Principals (sic) of modern psychological measurement* (pp. 154–182). Hillsdale, NJ: Erlbaum.

Schum, D. A. (1994). *The evidential foundations of probabilistic reasoning.* New York: Wiley.

Shafer, G. (1976). *A mathematical theory of evidence.* Princeton, NJ: Princeton University Press.

Snow, R. E., & Lohman, D. F. (1989). Implications of cognitive psychology for educational measurement. In R. L. Linn (Ed.), *Educational measurement* (3rd ed., 263–331). New York: American Council on Education/Macmillan.

Tatsuoka, K. K., Linn, R. L., Tatsuoka, M. M., & Yamamoto, K. (1988). Differential item functioning resulting from the use of different solution strategies. *Journal of Educational Measurement, 25,* 301–319.

Toulmin, S. E. (1958). *The uses of argument.* Cambridge: Cambridge University Press.

Wainer, H. (2000). *Computerized adaptive testing: A primer* (2nd ed.). Mahwah, NJ: Erlbaum.

NOTE

1. This work was supported by a research contract with Cisco Systems, Inc. We are grateful to John Behrens and Sarah Demark for conversations on the topics discussed herein.

CHAPTER 7

EXAMINING DIFFERENTIAL ITEM FUNCTIONING FROM A LATENT MIXTURE PERSPECTIVE

Karen M. Samuelsen
University of Georgia

The chapter by Mislevy, Levy, Kroopnick, and Rutstein (2008, this volume) discusses the narratives and frames of discernment related to a series of increasingly complex statistical models. In doing so they note, and I agree, that "mixture models are stories as much as they are statistical models." The story that I wish to tell involves differential item functioning (DIF). I believe that it is possible to support a more complex narrative regarding DIF than is currently considered by utilizing a mixture model that examines both quantitative and qualitative differences among examinees. By doing so we may be able to align our statistical model with substantive theories regarding the causes of the differential functioning.

In what follows I contrast the current conception of DIF, based on manifest group differences, with one based on latent differences. The goal is to highlight the need for a latent approach to DIF because a) the accepted paradigm is so limited and the ramifications of using it so severe, and b) a latent DIF paradigm fits with our understanding of students and the purposes of educational testing.

Advances in Latent Variable Mixture Models, pages 177–197
Copyright © 2008 by Information Age Publishing
All rights of reproduction in any form reserved.

THEORETICAL BACKGROUND

Differential item functioning occurs "when examinees from different groups have differing probabilities or likelihoods of success on an item, after they have been matched on the ability of interest" (Clauser & Mazor, 1998, p. 31). The presence of DIF means that scores from different groups are not comparable—a fact that compromises our ability to make valid inferences regarding student achievement vis-à-vis a construct of interest. Differential item functioning also signals multidimensionality due to the presence of nuisance dimensions (Ackerman, 1992); this calls into question the inferences drawn through the unidimensional models most often used in applied assessment scenarios. Finally, at a more fundamental level, the presence of DIF raises issues regarding fairness and equity in testing.

Because DIF does have such serious consequences, it has generated extensive research. This research has focused largely on psychometric concerns such as the appropriateness of the matching criterion, the question of whether the item of interest should be included in that matching criterion, and which procedures work best under a variety of conditions (see Clauser & Mazor, 1998, for an overview). While these issues are important, they rest on the underlying notion that the current manifest paradigm for DIF is correct. The current chapter joins recent studies (Bandalos, Cohen, & Cho, 2006; Cohen & Bolt, 2005; DeAyala, Kim, Stapleton, & Dayton, 2002) in challenging this assumption and positing a mixture model conception for DIF as an alternative.

The accepted paradigm for DIF rests on a relatively strong assumption: all members of a manifest group utilize the same strategies or problem solving techniques, and have similar backgrounds in relation to the content of an item. Therefore, though the probability of responding correctly to an item is contingent on examinee ability, all members of a manifest group see that item in the same manner. One implication of this model is that items with DIF against males (as an example) disadvantage *all* males. This means that removing those differentially functioning items would raise the scores of *all* males. This model further implies that the root causes of that DIF can be identified by finding covariates related to gender. The final implication is that items that do not function differentially with regard to some "socially identifiable groups" (DeAyala et al., 2002, p. 274) do not have DIF.

A competing paradigm for DIF assumes that there are qualitative differences in the manner in which examinees respond to test items and that these differences stem from latent, rather than manifest, group membership. Using the example of Mislevy et al. (2008, this volume), both male and female examinees faced with mental rotation tasks may employ either a mental rotation or an analytic strategy, meaning that there are two latent classes of examinees. This model implies that the items with DIF against one latent class may adversely affect members of both manifest groups. Furthermore, removing these items may or may not impact test score averages, depending on the proportions of the manifest groups within the latent classes. There exist theoretical and empirical reasons to favor this DIF paradigm over the model currently employed. These will be delineated in the following paragraphs.

Theoretical Evidence

It has been stated that "traditional DIF analyses are based on the *de facto* assumption that individuals within a manifest group are more similar to one another than they are to members of the other manifest group" (DeAyala et al., 2002, p. 247). In reality, although genders, racial groups, and ethnic groups are easily identified, they often do not represent homogeneous populations. One example showing this variability within groups is the Hispanic population in the United States. According to the U.S. Census Bureau (1993) persons of Hispanic origin may be from Mexico, Puerto Rico, Cuba, Central or South American, or some other origin, and they may be of any race. Given this diversity in place of origin and race, it seems obvious that a classification of Hispanic will yield a heterogeneous group. The same can be said for classifications based on other ethnicities, race, or gender. Given this lack of homogeneity, when items demonstrate DIF with regard to a manifest group, a portion of the subjects should not be expected to respond like other members of their group.

In addition to the lack of homogeneity within these groups, there is also the possibility that the groups being examined are not really the manifest groups affected. Hu and Dorans (1989) demonstrated a flaw in DIF analyses that concentrated on the marginal distributions and posited that it is necessary to consider interactions in DIF analyses. They found that the removal of an item favoring females resulted in slightly lower scores for females and slightly higher scores for males. This was to be expected. What surprised the researchers was that the scores of both Hispanics and Asian-Americans were raised more than the scores of males, meaning that females *in those groups* actually received an advantage by the removal of the item. It is also possible that the manifest groups often examined are not really the ones of interest. Other manifest grouping variables such as socioeconomic status, type of school (home, private, public), and school size are potentially interesting and informative in terms of DIF. These may also represent more homogeneous subpopulations.

Another reason, and perhaps the most compelling one, not to use manifest groups for DIF is they are not directly related to the issues of learning that educators care about. Researchers have long argued that manifest groups defined by characteristics like gender and ethnicity are really proxies for something else. Dorans and Holland (1993) wrote:

> It could be argued...that these intact ethnic groups are merely surrogates for an educational disadvantage attribute that should be used in focal group definition. In fact, within any of these groups, there is probably a considerable degree of variability with respect to educational advantage or disadvantage. Perhaps we should be focusing our group definition efforts toward defining and measuring educational advantage or disadvantage directly. (p. 65)

Besides being consistent with a view of DIF stemming from multidimensionality, this latent conceptualization maximizes the differences between the classes being studied and thereby helps clarify which items function differentially. This can provide insights into the cause of the DIF. Kelderman and Macready (1990) asserted,

> The use of latent grouping variables...allows for the assessment of DIF without tying that DIF to any specific variable or set of variables. Thus, it may be possible following the investigation of DIF to make a more definitive statement regarding its presence. (p. 309)

Empirical Evidence

Cohen and Bolt (2005) provided empirical evidence that a manifest groups approach to DIF is problematic. They estimated item parameters using a likelihood ratio test for DIF and found five of their 32 test items to have DIF with respect to gender. The resultant item parameters were then used in a mixture three-parameter logistic (3-PL) model allowing examinees to be in latent groups regardless of their gender. The mixing proportions, latent class ability distributions, and class membership for individual examinees were then estimated. Though the results yielded mixing proportions that approximated the percentages of males and females in the population, closer examination showed "substantial cross-over occurred in classification of males and females into the latent class opposite to their gender" (Cohen & Bolt, 2005, p. 139), meaning that items with DIF against one manifest group did not function differentially against all members of that group. This study found covariates that showed no differences with regard to the manifest groups, but differed with respect to the latent classes. Alternately, covariates that showed differences between the manifest groups sometimes revealed no such differences between the latent classes.

DeAyala et al. (2002) examined test items, which included questions containing traditional vocabulary and urban slang, using a standard manifest DIF procedure, latent class analysis, and DIF analyses conducted within and across latent classes. The authors found examinees within latent classes responded more similarly to test items than examinees within manifest groups. Additionally they found that black examinees in one latent class were disadvantaged by some test items, while black examinees in the other class were not, indicating that it would be improper to say that a manifest group of students was adversely affected by the presence of those items. Finally, though not a focus of their study, the quantity of items identified as having DIF using latent class analyses was much greater than one would generally expect with traditional analyses. This lends credence to the notion that a latent approach may provide more information, making statements about the causes of the DIF more likely.

Ramifications of a Manifest Approach to DIF

There are several ramifications of using manifest grouping variables as surrogates for latent attributes. One possibility is that we miss items that are functioning differentially based on this latent attribute but not based on the manifest grouping variable. Samuelsen (2005) examined this issue in a simulation study in which data were simulated for a fixed length test of 20 items. Five levels of overlap between manifest groups and the latent classes were used to judge the impact of that variable on the power to correctly identify items with DIF. In that study, as the amount of overlap decreased the membership of each latent class became more of a mixture of the manifest groups. That is, an overlap of 100% between latent class and gender would mean one class was entirely made up of males and the other females. On the other end of the spectrum, with overlap of 60%, both males and females would be well represented in each of the latent classes, making it increasingly difficult to see differences between those classes. Five other variables were also manipulated in that study: a) sample size, b) manifest proportions, c) number of items exhibiting DIF, d) effect size of the DIF, and e) ability distributions within the latent classes.

Figure 7.1 shows the correct number of identifications from Samuelsen (2005) as a function of the percent overlap, effect size, and differences in the ability distributions. Each data point in this graph represents the average for the items with DIF under a particular set of conditions. The downward slopes of the curves in Figure 7.1 show the impact of the decreasing overlap of latent and manifest groups on power. Using the standard set by Cohen (1988), that power is considered to be sufficient when it is above 0.80, it is apparent that lack of overlap caused problems. When the magnitude of the differential functioning was small (i.e., the difference between the difficulty parameters for the two latent classes was 0.40), there was not sufficient power to see DIF when *any* overlap existed despite the relatively

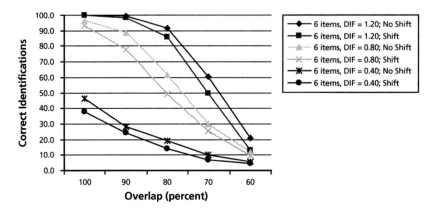

Figure 7.1 Correct identifications for a 50/50 manifest split with 2,000 examinees ($\alpha = 0.05$).

large sample size (2,000 examinees). As the magnitude of the DIF got larger there was power to see it even when there was some overlap. However, even in the most advantageous situation with regard to power—large DIF, a 50/50 manifest split, and 2,000 examinees—sufficient power existed only down to an overlap of 70%. Figure 7.1 also shows that the lack of power is exacerbated by differences in the ability distributions of the latent classes as indicated by the pairs of curves labeled shift (meaning there were differences in the means of the ability distributions) and no shift. Other findings of interest from the Samuelsen (2005) study were the negative impacts on power of decreases in sample size, and increases in the contamination of the matching criterion by items with DIF.

One implication of that simulation study is that the sample sizes typically used in manifest DIF analyses appear to be too small. At Educational Testing Service (ETS) total sample sizes as low as 500 are acceptable during some parts of the test construction process. Based on the research by Samuelsen (2005) it appears that when the sample size is that small, one will only see DIF if the overlap between the latent class and manifest groups is greater than 80% and the magnitude of the DIF is large. From this one could infer that the relatively small number of items identified using a manifest DIF procedure are an uninformative subset of the items functioning differentially from a latent perspective. That means they can provide only limited information regarding the true nature of the DIF, whereas a latent class DIF analysis could yield many more insights into why items functioned differentially.

Another possibility when items have DIF at a latent level is that we identify items as having DIF based on differences in response probabilities for a relatively small number of examinees. This scenario is depicted in Figure

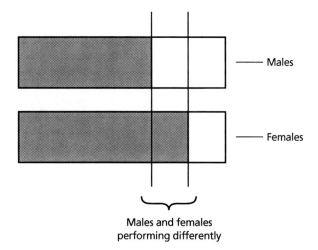

Males

Females

Males and females
performing differently

Figure 7.2 Mapping manifest distinctions onto a latent class analysis.

7.2. In this case, all of the males in the first latent class, shown by the gray portion of the top box, and a large portion of the females in that class should perform similarly on test items. Females in the second class, shown by the white portion of the bottom box, and a portion of the males in that class will also perform similarly. That leaves only the remaining males in the second class and the remaining females in the first class who will respond to the test items differently. This may explain a) the lack of consistency of DIF detection methods in identifying DIF items across test administrations (Skaggs & Lissitz, 1992), and b) differences between empirical evidence and subjective evaluations of DIF.

The fact that the manifest DIF detected by traditional strategies may be an artifact of differences among relatively small numbers of examinees calls the appropriateness of those procedures into question. Do we really care if 20% of males and females respond differently to items if the remaining 80% respond in a similar fashion? The answer to that question may be context dependent, and its debate is beyond the scope of this research. However, providing a mechanism that highlights the magnitude of the latent differences between manifest groups is one of the strengths of the latent strategy described in this chapter.

A third possibility for items that do exhibit DIF is that the true magnitude of the differential functioning may be obscured due to the lack of overlap between the manifest groups and the latent classes. This has consequences for testing companies because they treat this "observed DIF" as though it were truth and, in the case of ETS, use the magnitude of the DIF in classifying items into three categories that are used in the selection of items for operational tests (Zieky, 1993). In that system, items in category

TABLE 7.1 Amount of Overlap Necessary to Ensure Classification as a B or C (in the ETS classification system) as a Function of the Magnitude of the Differential Functioning

B Classification		C Classification	
Magnitude of DIF	Overlap (percent)	Magnitude of DIF	Overlap (percent)
1.20	70	1.20	80
0.80	80	0.80	90
0.40	100	0.40	Never classified

A are those with "negligible or nonsignificant DIF" (Zieky, 1993, p. 342). Category B includes items with slight to moderate DIF that may be used on test forms with the caveat that items with smaller absolute values of DIF are preferred over those with larger values. Items in category C are generally not used for operational tests as those contain moderate to large amounts of DIF. Examining Table 7.1 and applying the ETS classification strategy, we see that as the amount of overlap gets smaller it becomes increasingly more difficult to classify an item that is truly bad as having enough DIF to ensure it does not appear on an operational assessment. As shown in Table 7.1, with overlap less than 80% even items with a large amount of DIF would escape a "C Classification."

A final ramification of using a manifest, rather than latent, approach to DIF detection is that it is difficult to determine the source of that DIF. Traditionally, investigations into the cause of DIF have mainly relied on statistical analyses followed by reviews by experts examining the content for obvious causes of DIF or searching for patterns that might suggest the identity of a nuisance dimension underlying it. Many agree these methodologies have had limited success in clearly defining why items function differentially (Camilli & Shepard, 1994; Gierl, Bisanz, Bisanz, Boughton & Khaliq, 2001; O'Neill & McPeek, 1993; Roussos & Stout, 1996). In a classic paper, Bond (1993) described how he and a student arrived at explanations for why certain items functioned differentially only to realize that they had focused on the wrong items. When they attended to the items that actually did have DIF the explanations for that differential function were in direct opposition to their original theories. Perhaps the most succinct commentary on the inadequacy of our current methodologies came in the 1999 Standards for Educational and Psychological Testing.

Although DIF procedures may hold some promise for improving test quality, there has been little progress in identifying the causes or substantive themes that characterize items exhibiting DIF. That is, once items on a test have been statistically identified as functioning differently from one examinee group to another, it has been difficult to specify the reasons for the differential performance or to identify the common deficiency among the identified items. (p. 78)

Using a latent class approach would help explain why the differential function is occurring in two ways. First, since all items functioning differentially would be identified, along with a truer indication of the magnitude of the DIF, there is more information available to the researcher. Current strategies may only identify a subset of the items functioning differentially and underestimate the magnitude of the DIF, making it more difficult to isolate the cause of the differential functioning. Second, a latent strategy would allow researchers to incorporate covariates as predictors of latent class, rather than manifest group, membership. Bandalos et al. (2006), for example, illustrated the inclusion of both categorical and continuous covariates as a means of understanding substantive differences among latent classes in an investigation of data from the 2003 ninth-grade Mathematics Test of the Florida Comprehensive Assessment Test.

Despite the above issues regarding the use of manifest grouping variables, they are still commonly used in DIF analyses. According to DeAyala et al. (2002) that is because, "The selection of manifest grouping variables is based on political not psychometric considerations" (p. 274). These political concerns may stem from litigation dating back to the 1980s, with the Golden Rule Settlement, which resulted in the courts finding that test makers would be at fault if they knowingly used a test that disadvantaged minority students. However, even though these lawsuits and findings must be taken seriously, a case can be made that using a latent class approach can both meet psychometric demands and satisfy these political realities. From a psychometric point of view, a latent class approach, in which group differences are maximized, allows researchers to accurately capture the presence and magnitude of the differential functioning. At the same time it is possible to map the manifest groups onto the latent classes to satisfy those who require that connection. The question that remains is how to structure a DIF analysis that has latent classes with manifest groups mapped onto them.

USING THE MIXED RASCH (1960) MODEL TO DETECT DIF

One approach to providing a solution to the problems plaguing the current DIF strategies is to utilize a mixed Rasch model (Rost, 1990). The main thrust of this approach is that the Rasch model can be used to describe "the response behavior of all persons within a latent class, but that different sets of item parameters hold for the different latent classes" (Rost, 1990,

p. 271). That is, two or more sub-populations of individuals can be identified that are "Rasch scalable" (p. 271).

Because item response theory (IRT) and latent class analysis are mixed within this approach, parameters from each need to be included. These parameters are ability parameters under the condition that person n belongs to latent class g (θ_{ng}), difficulty parameters for each item i that are also conditional upon latent class membership (b_{ig}), and latent class proportions (π_g) indicating the fraction of examinees in each of the latent classes. In latent class analysis it is assumed that the observed responses are independent within latent classes. Therefore, the probability of a correct response by person n to item i can be expressed as a weighted sum of conditional probabilities. That can be given by Equation 7.1.

$$p_{ni} = \sum_g \pi_g \frac{\exp(\theta_{ng} - b_{ig})}{1 + \exp(\theta_{ng} - b_{ig})} \tag{7.1}$$

This is an interesting formulation in that the probability of a positive response to an item is a weighted sum of the conditional probabilities. Therefore, there is not an assumption that an individual belongs to a certain latent class and that only the parameters associated with that class should be applied. Instead the probabilities associated with membership in each class are applied to each person. Constraints can be placed on this model in terms of the item difficulties within classes summing to zero. In addition to solving the indeterminacy issue, these constraints have the effect of putting both sets of item parameters on the same scale in the sense that if there is no DIF they are the same within estimation error; conversely, if there is DIF, the items parameters will be centered around zero in both groups making the DIF average to zero. In order to make the item parameters center around zero, the item difficulties can be estimated for the first $J-1$ items (where J is the total number of items) and the item difficulty for the Jth item can be defined as the negative sum of the other items within a given class.

Rost's mixed Rasch model is one of several approaches that could be employed for this purpose. Among these are the IRT model for different strategies (Mislevy & Verhelst, 1990), and the loglinear models of Kelderman and Macready (1990). Mislevy and Verhelst (1990) posited that standard IRT models are not satisfactory when examinees employ different strategies for solving problems. Though this model is similar in some respects to the mixed Rasch model, it is quite different in that "substantive theory associates the observable features of items with the probability of success for members of each strategy class" (Mislevy & Verhelst, 1990, p. 198). In DIF research that is exploratory in nature, with no substantive theory regarding item features, Mislevy and Verhelst's model would be inappropriate. The use of the mixed Rasch strategy to investigate DIF corresponds to one of the cases of the loglinear models of Kelderman and Macready (1990). One of their models included terms for the interactions between the latent variable and the items. Comparing this model with a null model is equivalent to testing all of the items for DIF. For this chapter the mixed Rasch model was highlighted rather than the analogous loglinear model because it is rooted in IRT. Because this is the case, DIF is a function of the differences between the item difficulties for the latent classes. For those accustomed to IRT parameters, this should directly yield a much more intuitive result regarding the magnitude of the DIF. In addition, as Kelderman and Macready acknowledged, parameter estimation in their models may be difficult when there are large numbers of variables as there would be on educational tests.

Likewise, more complex IRT models could also be employed for the detection of latent DIF. Certainly a 2-PL model could be employed for multiple-choice items; however, interpretations of differences between latent groups with regard to the item parameters become more difficult. A 3-PL model might prove even more problematic given the inherent difficulty in estimating the pseudo-guessing parameter. Latent class DIF studies could also incorporate differential test speededness into the model. Students in different latent classes may have different patterns of missingness, some due to not reaching items, others due to judiciously skipping high difficulty items to spend the limited time on other items. To account for this a model like Yamamoto and Everson's (1996) adaptation of the hybrid model should be incorporated into the mixed Rasch model. That way some of a respondent's answers could be based on the ability and latent class, and for the remaining items, where random guessing occurred, a multinomial model would hold.

Given that the sources of item difficulty differ widely from item to item (Whitely & Schneider, 1981), another possible adaptation would be to model the elemental components within items rather than looking at the items as a whole. This sort of decomposition has been done for verbal items (Janssen & DeBoeck, 1997; Sheehan & Mislevy, 1990), mathematical problems (Embretson, 1995; Fischer, 1973), and nonverbal items (Embretson, 1998; Green & Smith, 1987). One way to model item difficulty using elemental components is to replace the item difficulty term in the Rasch model with the sum of the products of the scored features of the items and the weights of those features, plus a constant. Using Embretson's (1998) model of abstract reasoning as an example, one could have five scored variables (number of rules, abstract correspondence, distortion, fusion, and overlay), and each of those variables would have a weight associated with it. For an item requiring three rules be applied to arrive at a correct answer, the item difficulty would simply be three times the weight for the number of rules variable plus a constant. It should be noted that using some sort of elemental components approach would provide researchers with more information regarding the underlying cause of DIF; however, this is not a *post hoc* strategy like many others. Items used on an assessment would need to be 'model-able' using a set of elemental components, and would therefore need to be chosen for the test with that in mind.

A FOUR STEP APPROACH FOR LATENT DIF

In contrast to a manifest groups approach, where examinees are split based on some physical attribute and the probabilities of success for examinees of similar ability are compared (generally by examining item characteristics curves or using a contingency table), a latent approach to DIF (even a relatively simple one like using the mixed Rasch model) is much more complicated. Below, I define a four step approach for examining differential item functioning using a latent class perspective. Those steps are discussed along with some examples from an analysis of data from Hispanic and Asian students. The data used in that analysis were a subset of responses for 1,016 students on Form A of an English language proficiency test in reading for grade cohort 3–5 (see Samuelsen, 2005, for a detailed discussion of these data from the English Language Development Assessment).

Step 1: Choose the Number of Latent Classes

An important first step in the analysis of items for DIF using the approach under consideration is to assess which latent class model(s) to use (1-class, 2-class, etc.). This can be done in several ways. One possible method is to use the model that best fits the data. With this empirical approach, for each model one asks whether it is a reasonable approximation to the observed data. The model that fits best and yields classes of meaningful size should be retained. This method, though intuitively appealing, may yield results that are not easily interpretable. For example, if a 3-class model resulted it might be difficult to think about DIF because we are accustomed to thinking of items adversely affecting one group or another. In this situation we would have to decide what it meant when an item showed DIF between two latent classes but not between either of those and the third. Alternately, one could choose a latent class model based on substantive grounds. For example, if an educational researcher believed that students utilized one of two strategies in solving problems but did not know which students used which strategy, a 2-class model might be appropriate. Finally, one could decide to have the same number of latent classes as manifest groups. In the case of gender DIF, as an example, a 2-class model would be used. While this method limits the information the researcher can gain from uncovering the number of latent classes empirically, it makes mapping the manifest groups onto the latent classes very simple, thereby making the results much more interpretable.

One concern in using a mixed Rasch model, or any latent class model, is that latent class membership, and the identity of those classes, is unknown. Therefore, data that are missing can play a part in determining membership in the classes. In educational assessment it is possible that students either skip questions or make random guesses, especially on items at the end of a test. Not answering questions at the end of the test may be linked to strategy usage in that one strategy may be more time consuming than another. If so, the skipping may provide more information about latent class membership. On the other hand, skipping or guessing may have something to do with "testwiseness." In that case some students using both strategies may exhibit that behavior, meaning that a third (or fourth) latent class might emerge.

Step 2: Decide Whether a Latent Class Analysis Is Necessary

The next step in the procedure is really a decision node. Once the percentage of people in each manifest group within the latent classes has been estimated, a determination can be made regarding the possibility of using the manifest groups as proxies for the latent groups. While I have argued for a latent approach, I recognize that the complexity of executing and interpreting the results from such a procedure must be worth the effort. For that reason, and because there are political reasons to utilize a manifest approach, I would advocate using manifest groups when there is sufficient overlap between the manifest groups and the latent classes. The question is, what is sufficient overlap? Most would agree that if there was 99% overlap between latent class and manifest groups it would be appropriate to use a manifest interpretation of DIF. The argument might grow more heated regarding the appropriateness of using the manifest groups if there was only 70% overlap, meaning 30% of the people in the one manifest group behaved like those in the other manifest group. Finally, most would agree that if the one latent class consisted of 80% of the females and 70% of males, gender would not be a particularly useful grouping variable and any DIF found using gender would be suspect. Though this chapter will not impose a decision about the cut-off for when that overlap is large enough, it is important to note that this decision can be made regarding when a latent class DIF approach is necessary, or conversely, when taking the simpler manifest groups approach is appropriate.

Step 3: Identify the Latent Attribute Responsible for the Classes

The third step in a latent class procedure is to examine the data from the latent class analysis for clues as to why there are items functioning differentially. This can be done by considering information such as the following:

1. Mean abilities within the latent class;
2. Differences among the classes on theoretically pertinent covariates (e.g., age);
3. Magnitudes of the differences in item difficulties among the latent classes;
4. Patterns of item difficulties within classes.

One would expect the results of these analyses, together with an understanding of both the examinees and the test, to yield some clues as to why there was DIF.

It is possible to consider the mean abilities at two different levels, first at the level of the latent classes and then at the level of the manifest groups within the latent classes. These two levels should provide separate but complementary pieces of information. Considering the data at the level of the latent classes, it is possible to see whether examinees in one latent class tend to be more able than those in the other class. From this we know that if latent class membership is predicated on strategy usage (as an example), the strategy used by the students in the second latent class is much less effective than the one used by the students in the first class. Information regarding the abilities of the manifest groups within the latent classes may be particularly valuable when an interaction between group and class shows that strategy usage (again, as an example) is more effective for students with certain characteristics. This is particularly meaningful if an intervention is being proposed to assist students in using the more effective strategy.

Differences among latent classes on theoretically pertinent covariates may also be meaningful in terms of identifying the secondary dimension(s) responsible for DIF. Cohen and Bolt's (2005) mixture model DIF study found that, while there were no differences in age between males and females in their sample, their latent classes did show some differences with respect to age. In domains where developmental theories indicate that stage mastery may be linked to age, this sort of information may be quite telling. Even in domains for which no such theories exist, the presence of age differences between latent classes could provide information regarding the sorts of cognitive or educational experiences of the students in the classes.

Comparing the differences in the item difficulties between latent classes to the characteristics of the items may provide information regarding the identity of those classes. Content matter, linguistic, and cognitive experts (among others) could categorize items based on distinctions that are apparent to them. For example, items could be classified using the following:

- Bloom's taxonomy (Anderson & Krathwohl, 2001; Bloom, Englehart, Furst, Hill, & Krathwohl, 1956) to examine the levels of cognitive thinking involved;
- General distinctions provided by test publishers as to domain or standard of interest;
- Specific features regarding the stimulus material or response option (e.g., short passages, graphic or verbal response);
- Linguistic features of the items including the structure of the sentences, presence of cognates, etc.

Note that these classifications are meant to be a representative sample rather than an exhaustive list; experts would undoubtedly be able to provide many more meaningful ways to categorize items. The sort of analysis of item features discussed here may not, on its own, provide sufficient evidence of why multiple latent classes exist and what secondary dimension(s) are causal. However, it may prove invaluable in concert with other pieces of information.

Figure 7.3 shows an example of an English language proficiency test in which a pattern exists for the item difficulties; for the first latent class the first third of the items tend to be easier and last third harder than for the second class. One could hypothesize the reason for this is that the initial

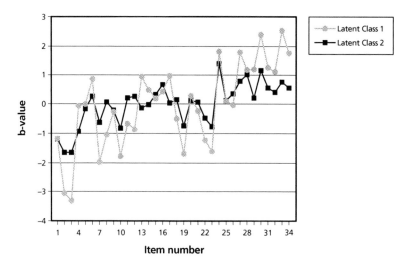

Figure 7.3 Item difficulties as a function of latent class.

items on this test dealt with smaller amounts of concrete information while the final items asked students to consider longer, more complex stimulus materials. Therefore, students who tended to memorize factual knowledge would do very well on the first group of items; however, they would perform poorly on the later items.

Based on the patterns of item difficulties for the two latent classes one could suggest several explanations. For example, it is possible that the two classes are related to the type of reading instruction employed in the students' classrooms. English language learners taught using a top-down, concept-driven approach (Weaver, 1994) would receive instruction through literacy activities, going from concepts to words. Students taught more traditionally, in a bottom-up sequence (Weaver, 1994) would learn through phonics and word recognition. We would expect students taught using the latter approach to find items dealing with reasoning to be much more difficult and items requiring word recognition easier than students taught using the former approach. Alternatively, membership in a latent class could have to do with the cognitive style of the student rather than the classroom. Some students may feel more comfortable learning English by memorizing words, while others might read books, newspapers and magazines. We would expect learners who memorize to find the questions on the first part of the test, requiring recall, to be extremely easy. Alternately, we would expect those same examinees to have trouble with the later items dealing with reading comprehension. Again, this is not meant to be a comprehensive list of potential explanations for the patterns of item difficulties shown. Instead, these possible explanations serve two purposes. First, they model the types of explanations experts might posit in response to these patterns, and second, they provide examples that can be carried further in the next step of this process.

Step 4: Use Covariates Linked to Latent Class Membership

The final step in this process is to gain further evidence to support the hypotheses generated regarding the classes using covariates to predict latent class membership. The choice of these covariates may stem directly from Step 3 of this process in a confirmatory manner, or may be more exploratory if Step 3 yields few clues as to why examinees perform differently on certain items. Continuing with the previous example, if the cognitive style of the student was to be investigated, one covariate of interest might be whether or not the English language learner was born in the United States. One would expect students born outside of the U.S. to be more likely to learn to read English by memorizing words in an attempt to catch up with their peers. Another possible covariate could deal with the type of instruction the student received in school. Students in dual language programs, which contain students who speak English learning Spanish (as an example) and Spanish speaking students learning English, might be more likely to learn their second language through literacy activities and not memorization.

Having articulated a four-step approach above, I should emphasize that it is not meant to be etched in stone. Instead, I would consider it a temporary scaffolding on which to stand as we build a latent approach that:

- Rests on firm psychometric grounds;
- Can be executed within education agencies and testing companies;
- Yields results that are accessible to a variety of stakeholders;
- Satisfies the political realities regarding maintaining manifest distinctions in DIF analyses.

These requirements are discussed in more depth in the following summary section.

SUMMARY

Strategies for the detection of DIF have evolved over the past several decades; however, most have had one inherent flaw—using manifest groups as the basis from which to make comparisons. This chapter has detailed a latent class strategy for DIF detection that retains the manifest groups often considered, but interweaves those within a latent framework. This alternative paradigm for DIF has some clear strengths and weaknesses. Its major strength is that a latent class, as opposed to a manifest group, approach to DIF conceptualizes the problem appropriately. The pithy comment by Skaggs and Lissitz (1992), that "Black is not a cognitively meaningful dimension and not even a well-defined one for that matter" (p. 239) highlights the difficulties with the manifest approaches currently employed by most researchers. Those authors sum up the ramifications of these approaches: "These characteristics are politically important and convenient for researchers, but they do not advance understanding of differential item performance" (p. 239). An argument can also be made that a latent approach maximizes the differences between groups, meaning that approach would be a better choice from a statistical standpoint as well as a substantive one. For these reasons many researchers argue that DIF analyses should be focused on latent attributes because they can provide more information, thereby making it possible to identify and interpret the reasons behind the differential item functioning. The fact that a new paradigm tells a better story is not necessarily reason enough to adopt it. Occam's razor argues that one should favor parsimony in the explanation of any phenomenon as any assumptions that are made introduce error, making a theory with those assumptions less desirable than one without them. It is that parsimony that one gains using a latent mixture approach to DIF as it rests on fewer, and weaker, assumptions.

One notable expense for these positive aspects of a latent DIF approach is that it is more complicated to execute. As this chapter detailed, a multiple-step strategy must be followed that starts with the definition of the model and ends with the utilization of covariates to help in the identification of the latent classes. Not only is this process lengthier than typical manifest approaches, it is also more difficult in that it requires many judgments along the way. Contrast this with the often used Mantel-Haenszel procedure (Holland & Thayer, 1988) which can be carried out in SPSS using Crosstabs. The former approach clearly requires a great deal more psychometric proficiency than the latter, which is problematic because there is currently a lack of expertise in that area to meet the needs of testing companies, and local, state and federal education agencies. Another problem with a latent approach is in the interpretation of the results. Unlike manifest approaches, where the groups are clearly defined and the results are explicable to all stakeholders, latent mixture strategies have the inherent difficulty of dealing with undefined groups. Test manufacturers, and state and local education agencies will be resistant because they will have problems explaining these sorts of analyses to stakeholders who might have troubling grasping the idea of latent constructs. Those concerns are real and have merit. Likewise, the apprehension test makers feel regarding possible litigation is valid. According to Phillips (2000), legal challenges to the psychometric quality of a high stakes test are almost inevitable:

> ...even when a state has worked hard to follow psychometric standards, a graduation test may be a visible and accessible target for those whose political and social beliefs lead to different conclusions about appropriate use. One important lesson from this lawsuit is that state testing programs must not only follow legal and professional standards but must also create detailed documentation of those efforts and be prepared to defend all their testing programs in court. (p. 382)

By weighing the appropriateness of a latent approach to DIF against the realities of the needs and concerns of state or local education agencies and testing companies, individual researchers can decide whether the procedure delineated in this chapter is worth the effort. I would argue, in fact, that there should be a role for latent analysis in any study of DIF even if that is simply to gain a better understanding of the manifest analysis that is going to be performed. This can come by simply knowing the percentages of examinees from the manifest groups within the latent classes so that we can be certain that the DIF found does not result from a relatively small number of examinees within the manifest group. Or, it might be interesting to see if the same latent classes result when different pairs of manifest groups are included in analyses. That is, would the items identified as having latent DIF be the same in an analysis with whites and Hispanics mapped onto the classes as in a parallel analysis of whites and Asians? If so, more information would be gained with each successive pair of manifest groups tested. In this way a latent approach can simply enhance the more typical approaches. Whether one uses a fully latent approach or a procedure that uses the latent class information to inform an existing manifest approach, the important thing is that we will be basing individual differences in human behavior on potentially meaningful dimensions rather than solely on externally accessible but likely fallible proxy characteristics. Once that happens, we gain the possibility of actually explaining why items function differentially—an option that does not readily present itself using manifest approaches to DIF.

REFERENCES

Ackerman, T. A. (1992). A didactic explanation of item bias, item impact, and item validity from a multidimensional perspective. *Journal of Educational Measurement, 29,* 67–91.

Anderson, L. W., & Krathwohl, D. (Eds.) (2001). *A taxonomy for learning, teaching, and assessing: A revision of Bloom's taxonomy of educational objectives.* New York: Longman.

Bandalos, D. L., Cohen, A. S., & Cho, S. (2006). *Using factor mixture models to identify differentially functioning test items.* Paper presented at the annual meeting of the American Educational Research Association, San Francisco, CA.

Bloom, B., Englehart, M., Furst, E., Hill, W., & Krathwohl, D. (1956). *Taxonomy of educational objectives: The classification of educational goals. Handbook I: Cognitive domain.* New York: Longmans, Green.

Bond, L. (1993). Comments on the O'Neill & McPeek paper. In P. W. Holland & H. Wainer (Eds.), *Differential item functioning.* Hillsdale, NJ: Erlbaum.

Camilli, G., & Shepard, L. (1994). *Methods for identifying biased test items.* Newbury Park, CA: Sage.

Clauser, B. E., & Mazor, K. M. (1998). Using statistical procedures to identify differentially functioning test items. Instructional Module for the National Council on Measurement in Education, Spring 1998.

Cohen, A. S., & Bolt, D. M. (2005). A mixture model analysis of differential item functioning. *Journal of Educational Measurement, 42,* 133–148.

Cohen, J. (1988). *Statistical power analysis for the behavioral sciences* (2nd ed.). Hillsdale, NJ: Erlbaum.

DeAyala, R. J., Kim, S.-H., Stapleton, L. M., & Dayton, C. M. (2002). Differential item functioning: A mixture distribution conceptualization. *International Journal of Testing, 2,* 243–276.

Dorans, N. J., & Holland, P. W. (1993). DIF detection and description: Mantel-Haenszel and standardization. In P. W. Holland & H. Wainer (Eds.), *Differential item functioning.* Hillsdale, NJ: Erlbaum.

Embretson, S. E. (1995). A measurement model for linking individual change to processes and knowledge: Application to mathematical learning. *Journal of Educational Measurement, 32,* 277–294.

Embretson, S. E. (1998). A cognitive design system approach to generating valid tests: Application to abstract reasoning. *Psychological Methods, 3,* 300–326.

Fischer, G. H. (1973). Linear logistic test model as an instrument in educational research. *Acta Psychologica, 37,* 359–374.

Gierl, M. J., Bisanz, J., Bisanz, G., Boughton, K., & Khaliq, S. (2001). Illustration the utility of differential bundle functioning analyses to identify and interpret group differences on achievement tests. *Educational Measurement: Issues and Practice, 20,* 26–36.

Green K. E., & Smith, R. M. (1987). A comparison of two methods of decomposing item difficulties. *Journal of Educational Statistics, 12,* 369–381.

Holland, P. W., & Thayer, D. T. (1988). Differential item performance and the Mantel-Haenszel procedure. In H. Wainer & H. I. Braun (Eds.), *Test validity.* Hillsdale, NJ: Erlbaum.

Hu, P. G., & Dorans, N. J. (1989). *The effect of deleting differentially functioning items on equating functions and reported score distributions.* Princeton, NJ: Educational Testing Service.

Janssen, R., & DeBoeck, P. (1997). Psychometric modeling of componentially designed synonym tasks. *Applied Psychological Measurement, 21,* 37–50.

Kelderman, H., & Macready, G. B. (1990). The use of loglinear models for assessing differential item functioning across manifest and latent examinee groups. *Journal of Educational Measurement, 27,* 307–327.

Mislevy, R. J., Levy, R., Kroopnick, M., & Rutstein, D. (2008). Evidentiary foundations of mixture item response theory models. In G. R. Hancock & K. M. Samuelsen (Eds.), *Advances in latent variable mixture models.* Charlotte, NC: Information Age Publishing.

Mislevy, R. J., & Verhelst, N. (1990). Modeling item responses when different subjects employ different solution strategies. *Psychometrika, 55,* 195–215.

O'Neill, K. A., & McPeek, W. M. (1993). Item and test characteristics that are associated with differential item functioning. In P. W. Holland & H. Wainer (Eds.), *Differential item functioning.* Hillsdale, NJ: Erlbaum.

Phillips, S. E. (2000). GI Forum v. Texas Education Agency: Psychometric Evidence. *Applied Measurement in Education, 13,* 343–385.

Rasch, G. (1960). *Probabilistic models for some intelligence and attainment tests.* Copenhagen: Denmarks Paedagogiske Institut. (Republished in 1980 by the University of Chicago Press, Chicago).

Rost, J. (1990). Rasch models in latent classes: An integration of two approaches to item analysis. *Applied Psychological Measurement, 14,* 271–282.

Roussos, L. A., & Stout, W. F. (1996). A multidimensionality-based DIF analysis paradigm. *Applied Psychological Measurement, 20,* 355–371.

Samuelsen, K. M. (2005). *Examining Differential Item Functioning from a Latent Class Perspective.* Unpublished PhD dissertation, University of Maryland, College Park.

Sheehan, K. M., & Mislevy, R. J. (1990). Integrating cognitive and psychometric models in a measure of document literacy. *Journal of Educational Measurement, 27,* 255–272.

Skaggs, G., & Lissitz, R. W. (1992). The consistency of detecting item bias across different test administrations: Implications of another failure. *Journal of Educational Measurement, 29,* 227–242.

Standards for Educational and Psychological Testing (1999). Washington, DC: American Educational Research Association, American Psychological Association, & National Council on Measurement in Education.

U.S. Census Bureau (1993). *The Hispanic Population in the United States: March 1993, Current Population Reports, Population Characteristics, Series P20-475.* From the website: http://www.census.gov/population/www/socdemo/hispanic/hispdef.html

Weaver, C. (1994). *Reading process and practice: From sociolinguistics to whole language* (2nd ed.). Portsmouth, NH: Heinemann.

Whitely, S. E., & Schneider, L. M. (1981). Information structures on geometric analogies: A test theory approach. *Applied Psychological Measurement, 5,* 383–397.

Yamamoto, K., & Everson, H. (1996). Modeling the effect of test length and test time on parameter estimation using the HYBRID model. In J. Rost & R. Langeheine (Eds.), *Applications of Latent Trait and Latent Class Models in the Social Sciences* (http://www.ipn.uni-kiel.de/aktuell/buecher/rostbuch/inhalt.htm).

Zieky, M. (1993). Practical questions in the use of DIF statistics in test development. In P. W. Holland & H. Wainer (Eds.), *Differential item functioning.* Hillsdale, NJ: Erlbaum.

CHAPTER 8

MIXTURE MODELS IN A DEVELOPMENTAL CONTEXT

Karen Draney and Mark Wilson
University of California, Berkeley

Judith Glück and Christiane Spiel
Institut für Psychologie der Universität Wien

Mixture item response theory (IRT) models are based on the assumption that the population being measured is composed of two or more latent subpopulations, each of which responds to a set of tasks in predictably different ways. Within each subpopulation, a latent trait model holds for the entire set of tasks; however, between the subpopulations, there are differences that cannot be described within the constraints of the latent trait model used for a given subpopulation.

One of the most general mixture IRT models is the mixed Rasch model (Rost, 1990). This model assumes that the population in question is made up of H subpopulations, and that a Rasch model holds within each subpopulation. There is no necessary relation among the various Rasch models; the ordering of the items in terms of their difficulty can be entirely different for each subpopulation. This model is exploratory in the sense that it simply divides the population into the "best" (i.e., most different) set of subpopulations. The user must then determine what is interesting about the differences among subpopulations.

Advances in Latent Variable Mixture Models, pages 199–216

Other mixture item response models are more confirmatory in nature. One example is given by Mislevy and Verhelst (1990). This model is an extension of the Linear Logistic Test Model (LLTM; Fischer, 1983). It posits a particular structure for item difficulty parameters within each subpopulation, based on characteristics of the tasks. A different LLTM may hold for each subpopulation, if each set of persons responds differently to the task characteristics, or to a different set of task characteristics. Such a model may even include a subpopulation of random guessers, whose probability of correctly answering multiple-choice items is a simple function of the number of choices. This model is a special case of Rost's mixed Rasch model described above.

The *saltus* model (*saltus* is Latin for "leap") (Draney, 1996; Wilson, 1989) is another type of confirmatory mixture IRT model. It was originally designed for the investigation of developmental stages. This model is a special case of both of the preceding models, with linear restrictions on the relations among sets of item difficulties for the different subpopulations. This model was developed as a method for detecting and analyzing discontinuities in performance that are hypothesized to occur as a result of rapidly occurring person growth (e.g., Fischer, Pipp, & Bullock, 1984). Such discontinuities are often theorized to occur as the result of progression through developmental stages or levels. Thus, the model is built upon the assumption that the subpopulations are ordered in some way (as are developmental stages in children), and that groups of items become predictably easier (or perhaps more difficult) for subpopulations further along the developmental continuum.

One of the most influential developmental theories was posited by Jean Piaget (e.g., Piaget, 1950; Inhelder & Piaget, 1958). The work of Piaget describes the cognitive developmental stages through which children progress as they grow. In particular, school-age children progress from the *preoperational* stage, through the *concrete operational* stage, to the *formal operational* stage. In the preoperational stage, children are able for the first time to produce mental representations of objects and events, but unable to consistently perform logical mental operations with these representations. In the concrete operational stage, children are able to perform logical operations, but only on representations of concrete objects. In the formal operational stage, which starts to occur around the beginning of adolescence, children are able to perform abstract operations on abstractions as well as concrete objects. According to Piaget, progress from stage to stage is characterized by more than simple linear growth in reasoning ability. The transition from one stage to another involves a major reorganization of the thinking processes used by children to solve various sorts of problems.

Theories with similar structure, but perhaps different substantive focus, are described by the many neo-Piagetian researchers, and by other educational and psychological researchers who use stage-based theories. For example, Siegler (1981) used the work of Piaget to develop sets of items regarding which side of a balance scale would go down, when one placed different combinations of weights and distances from the fulcrum on the two sides of the balance scale. These sets of items changed predictably in difficulty for different age groups of children, as the children progressed through Piagetian-based stages. Some groups of items became easier and some more difficult, while others remained the same. The developmental stages of the children thus resulted in relative shifts in the probability that certain groups of items would be answered correctly. The saltus model is suitable for use with such sets of items (see Wilson, 1989; and Draney, 1996). A more general mixture IRT model, such as the mixed Rasch model, would require the estimation of a difficulty parameter for each item within each developmental stage (if the items are dichotomous); the saltus model can accommodate many developmental theories by estimating one difficulty for each item, plus a small number of additional parameters to describe the changes associated with developmental stage.

Although Piagetian theory has been somewhat controversial of late (e.g., Lourenço & Machado, 1996), there is still a strong interest in stage-like development in a number of areas, including moral and ethical reasoning (e.g., Dawson, 2002; Kohlberg & Candee, 1984), evaluative reasoning (e.g., Armon, 1984; Dawson-Tunik 2004), adult development (e.g., Commons, Trudeau, Stein, Richards, & Krause, 1998; Fischer, Hand, & Russel, 1984), and cognitive development (e.g., Bond, 1995a, 1995b; Bond & Bunting, 1995; Demetriou & Efklides 1989, 1994; van Hiele, 1986).

Researchers in the Piagetian tradition are using increasingly complex statistical and psychometric models to analyze their data. For example, Béland and Mislevy (1996) analyzed proportional reasoning tasks using Bayesian inference networks. Noelting, Coudé, and Rousseau (1995) discussed the advantages of Rasch scaling for the understanding of Piagetian tasks. And Bond (1995a; 1995b) discussed the implications of Rasch-family models for Piagetian theory and philosophy. In addition, psychometric researchers have begun wrestling with the problem of developing and applying models with sufficient complexity to address specific substantive issues. For example, the three-parameter model has been used diagnostically by researchers such as Yen (1985), who described patterns of problematic item fit that are sometimes observed when analyzing complex data. She asserted that these may be indicators for increasing item complexity, which could potentially be indicative of a set of items that represent more than one developmental stage.

The current chapter will discuss the basic structure and parameterization of the saltus model, and then give an example of its use, comparing it with a prior analysis conducted by the authors who collected the original set of data, in which a more exploratory mixture model was fitted. The benefits of the saltus model, including the ability to quantify the magnitude of group membership effects on specific collections of items, will be examined, and the fit of the two models compared.

THE SALTUS MODEL

The saltus model is based on the assumption that there are H developmental stages in the population of interest. A different set of items represents each one of these stages, such that only persons at or above a stage are fully equipped to answer the items associated with that stage correctly. The saltus model assumes that all persons in stage h answer all items in a manner consistent with membership in that stage. However, persons within a stage may differ in proficiency. In a Piagetian context, this means that a child in, say, the concrete operational stage is always in that stage, and answers all items accordingly. The child does not show formal operational development for some items and concrete operational development for others. However, some concrete operational children may be more proficient at answering items than are other concrete operational children.

To describe the model, suppose that, as in the partial credit model (Masters, 1982), the random variable X_{ni} indicates the nth person's response to item i. Items have $J_i + 1$ possible response alternatives indexed $j = 0,1,\ldots,J_i$. The difference in difficulty between any two consecutive item levels is referred to as a step, as in Masters' representation of the model. The parameter indicating step j for item i will be indicated by β_{ij}; the vector of all β_{ij} by β.

In the saltus model, a person is characterized by a proficiency parameter θ_n and an indicator vector for stage membership ϕ_n. If there are H potential stages, $\phi_n = (\phi_{n1},\ldots,\phi_{nH})$, where ϕ_{nh} takes the value of 1 if person n is in stage h and 0 if not. Only one of the ϕ_{nh} is theoretically nonzero. As with θ_n, values of ϕ_n are not observable.

Just as persons are associated with one and only one stage, items are associated with one and only one stage. Unlike person stage membership, however, which is unknown and must be estimated, item stage is known *a priori*, based on the theory that was used to produce the items. It will be useful to denote item stage membership by the indicator vector b_i. As with ϕ_n, $b_i = (b_{i1},\ldots,b_{iH})$, where b_{ik} takes the value of 1 if item i belongs to item stage k, and 0 otherwise. The set of all b_i across all items is denoted by b.

The equation:

$$P\left(X_{nij} = j \mid \theta_n, \phi_{nh} = 1, \beta_i, \tau_{hk}\right) = \frac{\exp \sum_{s=0}^{j}\left(\theta_n - \beta_{is} + \tau_{hk}\right)}{\sum_{t=0}^{J_i}\exp \sum_{s=0}^{t}\left(\theta_n - \beta_{is} + \tau_{hk}\right)}, \tag{8.1}$$

indicates the probability of response j to item i. The saltus parameter τ_{hk} describes the additive effect—positive or negative—for people in stage h on the item parameters of all items in stage k. In a developmental context, this often takes the form of an increase in probability of success as the person achieves the stage at which an item is located, indicated by $\tau_{hk} > 0$ when $h \geq k$ (although this need not be the case). The saltus parameters can be represented together as an $H \times H$ matrix $\mathbf{T}$.

The probability that an examinee with stage membership parameter ϕ_n and proficiency θ_n will respond in category j to item i is given by:

$$P\left(X_{nij} = j | \theta_n, \phi_n, \beta_i, \mathbf{b}_i, \mathbf{T}\right) = \prod_h \prod_k P(X_{nij} = j | \theta_n, \phi_{nh} = 1, \beta_i, \tau_{hk})^{\phi_{nh} b_{ik}} \quad (8.2)$$

Assuming conditional independence, the modeled probability of a response vector is:

$$P\left(\mathbf{X}_n = \mathbf{x}_n | \theta_n, \phi_n, \beta_i, \mathbf{b}_i, \mathbf{T}\right) = \prod_h \prod_k \prod_i P(X_{nij} = x_{ij} | \theta_n, \phi_{nh} = 1, \beta_i, \tau_{hk})^{\phi_{nh} b_{ik}} \quad (8.3)$$

The model requires a number of constraints on the parameters. For item step parameters, we use two traditional constraints: first, $\beta_{i0} = 0$ for every item, and second, the sum of all the β_{ij} is set equal to zero. Some constraints are also necessary on the saltus parameters. The set of constraints we have chosen is the same as that used by Mislevy and Wilson (1996), and will allow us to interpret the saltus parameters as changes relative to the first (lowest) developmental stage. Two sets of constraints are used. First $\tau_{h1} = 0$; thus, the difficulty of the first stage of items is held constant for all person groups; changes in the difficulty of items representing higher stages are interpreted with respect to this first stage of items for all person stages. Also $\tau_{1k} = 0$; thus, items as seen by person stages higher than 1 will be interpreted relative to the difficulty of the items as seen by persons in the lowest developmental stage.

As in Mislevy and Wilson (1996), the EM algorithm (Dempster, Laird, & Rubin, 1977) is used to estimate the structural parameters for the model. Empirical Bayes estimation is then used to obtain estimates of the probabilities of stage membership for each subject, as well as proficiency estimates given membership in each stage. A person is classified into the stage for which that person's probability of membership is highest; however, it is possible to investigate the confidence with which we classify persons with various sorts of response patterns into that stage. Software for this purpose was developed by Draney (in press).

THE DEDUCTIVE REASONING TEST

Theoretical Background and Exploratory Data Analysis

The Competence Profile Test of Deductive Reasoning—Verbal (DRV; Spiel, Glück, & Gößler, 2001, 2004; Spiel & Glück, in press) was developed to assess competence profile and competence level in deductive reasoning in the course of the transition from the concrete-operational stage to the formal-operational stage as proposed by Piaget (1971). The test makes use of the four main types of syllogistic inference. Each item consists of a given premise ("if A, then B"), and a conclusion. The task is to evaluate a conclusion, assuming the premise as given. The four types of inferences are: Modus ponens (A, therefore B), Negation of Antecedent (Not A, therefore B or not B), Affirmation of Consequent (B, therefore A or not A), and Modus tollens (Not B, therefore not A). Table 8.1 gives examples of the four inference types. Modus ponens (MP) and modus tollens (MT) are biconditional conclusions, that is, the response to the respective items is either "yes" or "no." For negation of antecedent (NA) and affirmation of consequent (AC), however, the correct solution is "perhaps", as the premise does not allow for deciding whether these conclusions are correct. However, they provoke the choice of a biconditional, but logically incorrect conclusion ("no" for NA, "yes" for AC), which is why they are often called logical fallacies. Research has shown that individuals at the concrete operational stage treat all four inferences as biconditional (e.g., Evans, Newstead, & Byrne, 1993; Janveau-Brennan & Markovits, 1999). While solution probability for these fallacies increases with progress in cognitive development, performance on MT items and, in some cases, also on MP items decreases. This is interpret-

TABLE 8.1 Example Items from the DRV

Premise: *If Klaus is ill, he is lying in his bed.* (Concrete content, no negation)

Type of Inference	Item Text	Correct Solution
Modus Ponens (MP): A → B.	Tom is ill. Is Tom lying in his bed?	yes
Negation of Antecedent (NA): Not A → B or not B.	Tom is not ill. Is Tom lying in his bed?	perhaps (incorrect biconditional solution: no)
Affirmation of Consequent (AC): B → A or not A.	Tom is lying in his bed. Is Tom ill?	perhaps (incorrect biconditional solution: yes)
Modus Tollens (MT): Not B → not A.	Tom is not lying in his bed. Is Tom ill?	no

ed as developmental progress because individuals who have noticed the uncertainty of the fallacies tend to overgeneralize (e.g., Byrnes & Overton, 1986; Markovits, Fleury, Quinn, & Venet, 1998).

The DRV consists of 24 single items (6 different premises × 4 types of inference). The six premises were constructed based on the literature on moderator variables of syllogistic reasoning. Studies have consistently shown that concrete items are easier to solve than abstract and counterfactual items (e.g., Overton, 1985), while empirical evidence concerning differences between abstract and counterfactual items is mixed. In addition, empirical investigations show systematic increases in task difficulty when negations were used in the antecedents (e.g., Roberge & Mason, 1978). Therefore, the DRV (Spiel et al., 2001, 2004; Spiel & Glück, in press) systematically varied three item characteristics in a 4 × 3 × 2 design (see Table 8.1):

- Type of inference: Modus Ponens, Modus Tollens, Negation of Antecedent, Affirmation of Consequent;
- Content of the conditional: Concrete (premise example: "If Tom is ill, he is lying in his bed"), Abstract ("if Y belongs to group F, Y has attitude g"), Counterfactual ("if it is evening, the sun rises");
- Mode of presentation of the antecedent: with and without negation.

Previous analyses were conducted using an exploratory approach—the general mixed Rasch model. Based on the literature, we expected to identify at least four latent classes corresponding to distinct developmental stages: concrete-operational (high solution probabilities for the biconditionals, low solution probabilities for the fallacies); formal-operational (high solution probabilities for all items); and two intermediate stages with markedly higher solution probabilities for the fallacies than in the concrete-operational stage but differences depending on item content (for details see Spiel et al., 2004). Data analyses were based on a sample of 418 students in grades 7 through 12. The exploratory analysis produced a best-fitting model containing three latent classes, which were given the following names and descriptions:

- Concrete-operational (36% of participants; mean probability of class membership: 0.96): Tend to correctly solve MP and MT items, and no others.
- Intermediate (32%; mean probability of class membership: 0.93): Tend to correctly solve concrete-level fallacy items (i.e., NA and AC), but have difficulty with concrete MP and MT items. The pattern for abstract and counterfactual items is the same as in the concrete-operational class.

- Advanced intermediate (32%; mean probability of class membership: 0.95): Performed better in the fallacies than in the biconditionals for all items, independent of content.

The results are illustrated in Figure 8.1. There were too few formal-operational individuals, who tend to correctly solve most items, present in the sample to reliably estimate the relevant parameters. Therefore, this group was postulated theoretically, but has not yet been empirically identified.

The Saltus Analysis

When applying the saltus model to a set of items, it is necessary to determine which items are representative of which stages. Ideally, for each stage it should be the case that persons are first fully capable of answering those items correctly (or at their highest level of correctness) when entering that stage. It is, of course, possible for persons at lower developmental stages to perform the item correctly; however, this usually occurs because of guessing or a poorly developed strategy that happens to produce the correct answer in some cases. Similarly, it is possible for persons at higher developmental stages to miss items at or below their developmental stage—due to the usual causes such as carelessness, wrong choice of strategy, and so on. A prototypical example of this is given in the Juice Mixtures Data, as analyzed by Draney and Wilson (2007). Each of the three stages described by Noelting

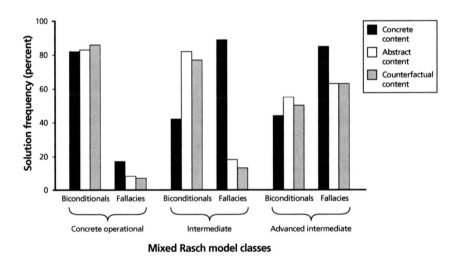

Figure 8.1 Results of prior mixed Rasch model analysis (Spiel, Glück, & Gößler, 2001, 2004).

(1980a, 1980b) is characterized by a set of skills that children acquire at that stage, and he has developed items representing each of those sets of skills.

In some cases the relation between item performance and stage membership is not so clear. This can happen for a number of reasons. One example is that persons answer certain item types correctly because they are disregarding part of the information available, information which actually makes the item more difficult. This is the case in children (and some adults) who tend to treat all syllogisms as biconditional because they do not understand that "if A then B" does not mean "if B then A". Once children understand this, they have a higher probability to solve the fallacies, but as was described above, for some time they tend to make more errors in the biconditional syllogisms (e.g., Byrnes & Overton, 1986; Markovits, Freury, Quinn, & Venet, 1998). A similar example concerning balance scale tasks was given by Siegler (1981).

Another difficulty that occurs when working with developmental theorists is that it is not always possible to develop a single group of items associated with each developmental stage. Instead, as in this case, there are several aspects (in this case type of inference, content, negation) which are fully crossed to form a set of items, for which it is then possible to predict the performance of each of the developmental stages. In such a case, it is more difficult to associate a set of items with each person group. We were not able to identify one class of items to be associated with each of four developmental groups, to attempt to replicate the results of the mixed Rasch analysis. However, we were able to propose two other saltus analyses: a two-group and a three-group analysis, as follow. Analysis 1 is a two-level analysis, in which the concrete person group is represented by all MP/MT items, and the formal person group is represented by all Fallacy items. Analysis 2 is a three-level analysis, in which the concrete person group is again represented by the MP/MT items, the intermediate person group is represented by the Concrete Fallacy items, and the formal person group is represented by Abstract and Counterfactual Fallacy items.

Saltus Results: Analysis 1

In this first analysis, the proportion of persons in the concrete group is estimated to be approximately 43%, and in the formal group 57%. Item difficulties ranged from –3.15 to –0.85 for the MP/MT items, and from 0.17 to 3.52 for the Fallacy items. This is as expected given that the MP/MT items are quite a bit easier than the Fallacy items, and the easiest Fallacy item is more difficult than the hardest of the MP/MT items. In addition, the estimated τ parameter was 4.28, suggesting that the formal group of persons has a substantial advantage over the concrete when performing the Fallacy items.

The estimated mean proficiency for the concrete group was –0.39 (with a standard deviation of 0.41), and for the formal group was –1.62 (with a standard deviation of 1.05). Thus, as was expected from the literature, although the formal group of persons has a substantial advantage on the Fallacy items, their performance on the MP/MT items was actually less good on average than that of the concrete group.

An examination of individual response patterns can shed light on such an analysis. Some illustrative response strings for the two groups, along with their classification probabilities, and proficiency estimates given membership in each group, are shown in Table 8.2. In this table, Persons A and B are most typical of persons assigned to the concrete group – persons who do well on the MP/MT items, and poorly on the Fallacy items. Persons similar to Person G, who do well on both groups of items, are most typical of persons assigned to the formal group. As persons C and D show, the tendency to begin to do well on some of the Fallacy items, especially on the more difficult items, is associated with an increasing probability of being in the formal group.

Persons like H, who do poorly on the MP/MT items, and well on the Fallacy items, are also not uncommon, and are also assigned to the formal group. Finally, persons who do poorly on both sets of items, such as persons E and F, are most likely to be in the formal group.

Examination of the score frequencies on both classes of items by classification group reveals that no one who scored over 5 on the Fallacy items was classified into the concrete group; most scored 0, 1, or 2. No one who scored under 6 on the MP/MT items was classified into the concrete group; most scored 9 or above. The persons who scored similarly (either low or high) on both sets of items were classified into the formal group. This helps to account for higher variance and lower mean of this group.

TABLE 8.2 Example Person Response Strings and Classifications for Analysis 1

Person	Responses MP/MT	Responses Fallacy	P(concrete)	P(formal)
A	111101111111	000000000000	1.00	.00
B	111011101100	110000000000	.98	.02
C	011011110100	100100000000	.86	.14
D	101111111011	111001001000	.36	.64
E	100000101111	101010000000	.08	.92
F	000010001100	100000000000	.01	.99
G	111111101100	111101111110	.00	1.00
H	000000000000	111111111000	.00	1.00

Thus, it does appear that more than one developmental level of subject has been classified into the formal group by this two-level analysis. There are persons who simply do poorly on all items (either students who are not yet developmentally capable of understanding the task, or perhaps students who are not paying particular attention); there are persons who, as Glück and Spiel (2007) describe, have begun to answer the Fallacy items correctly, but now are making errors on the MP/MT items; and there are those who are capable of correctly solving both types of items. This would indicate the need for a more sophisticated model. Thus, we fit a three-class model in Analysis 2, to see if this would accommodate such an effect.

Saltus Results: Analysis 2

Item difficulties in this analysis are similar to those in Analysis 1. Other results are shown in Table 8.3. It can be seen that several of the patterns from the first analysis hold in this second analysis. For example, the intermediate and formal groups have substantial advantages over the concrete group in answering the higher-level items (although the standard error for τ_{32} is large enough that this parameter is not statistically different from zero). In addition, the group means are ordered in the opposite way from which one might expect—the higher the group, the lower the overall mean proficiency. This shows that overall scores are often (in cases where the Rasch model does not hold across the whole set of items) less informative than score profiles across homogeneous groups of items. A profile contrasting the different types of inferences would show that participants' scores in the fallacy items increase whereas their scores in the biconditional items decrease. Overall, the largest proportion of persons (approximately half the sample) was classified into the intermediate group; 30% into the concrete group, and 20% into the formal.

The substantive interpretation here is more complex. Examination of individual response patterns shown in Table 8.4, as well as score cross-tabu-

TABLE 8.3   Parameter Estimates for Analysis 2

(a) Saltus parameters	Item class 1	Item class 2	Item class 3
Person group 1	—	—	—
Person group 2	—	4.88 (0.82)	7.84 (0.26)
Person group 3	—	3.31 (5.65)	7.20 (0.69)
(b) Person parameters	Group 1	Group 2	Group 3
Mean	−0.29	−1.65	−2.75
Standard Deviation	0.78	0.83	1.61
Proportion	0.31	0.51	0.18

TABLE 8.4 Example Person Response Strings and Classifications for Analysis 2

| | | Responses | | | | |
| | | Concrete | Abstract/ Counterfactual | | | |
Person	MP/MT	Fallacy	Fallacy	P(group 1)	P(group 2)	P(group 3)
A	111111110000	0000	00000000	.99	.01	.00
B	100111111011	0000	00001000	.99	.01	.00
C	110010111000	0000	00000001	.43	.57	.00
D	111111100000	0000	00000101	.29	.71	.00
E	111011101100	1100	00000000	.10	.90	.00
F	110100001111	0010	00100000	.08	.92	.00
G	101010111111	1111	10101001	.00	.99	.01
H	110111111111	1111	11000000	.01	.99	.00
I	111110001111	0111	11000010	.00	1.00	.00
J	000011011111	1111	00000000	.00	1.00	.00
K	111010101111	1111	10101111	.00	.50	.50
L	100010001111	1110	10110101	.00	.28	.72
M	111111101111	1111	11111111	.00	.04	.96
N	101010101011	1111	11111111	.00	.00	1.00
O	000000000000	1111	11111111	.00	.00	1.00
P	000000001000	0001	10011111	.00	.00	1.00
Q	000000000100	1010	11100001	.00	.00	1.00

lation by group classification, shows that the concrete group contains persons who scored low on both class 2 items (concrete fallacies) and class 3 items (abstract and counterfactual fallacies) and high on class 1 items (all biconditional syllogisms). This is just as in Analysis 1—such persons scored 6 or above on the class 1 items, and 4 or below on the class 3 items (the majority scored below 2); in addition, none correctly answered all 4 class 2 items, and most got one or less of these items correct. Persons A and B in Table 8.4 are examples of concrete group members.

The intermediate is a mixed group. Persons such as G, H, and I are one type in this group; they have answered most of the class 1 and class 2 items correctly, and few of the class 3 items. Persons C and D, although they still have some probability of being in the concrete, are most likely also in this group. In addition to responding correctly to the majority of the class 1 items, they have answered one or two of the most difficult class 3 items correctly, although they have answered none of the class 2 items correctly. Person J, while missing a significant number of the class 1 items and all of the class 3 items, has answered all of the class 2 items correctly, and is classified solidly in this group. Persons E and F are less intuitively obvious; although their probabilities clearly place them in the intermediate group, they look at first glance much like Persons C and D. Person E missed half of the class 2 items and several of the class 1 items, and thus could still be in the concrete group, but is most likely in the intermediate group; person F missed almost half of the class 1 items and most of the class 2 items, but perhaps because this person correctly answered one of the class 3 items, is still most likely to be in the intermediate group.

Persons who scored high on class 3 items (regardless of other scores) were in the formal group. Persons such as M—who answered nearly all the items correctly—typify what we would expect to see in this group. However, when examining the score distributions for persons with high scores on class 3 items, one tended in most cases to find the full range of possible scores on class 1 items (i.e., among persons who got more than 50% of the class 3 items correct, there were persons who had scores of 0 or 1 on the class 1 items). Hence, we see persons like O and P, who have missed many of the other items (especially those in class 1) but correctly answered more than half of the class 3 items, as well as persons like K, L, and N, who did well on class 2 and class 3 items, but missed significant numbers of the class 1 items. Finally, we see persons like Q, who has done uniformly poorly on all item types. This might account for the large standard error accompanying the advantage assigned to this group when taking class 2 items—some persons in this group did quite well on these items, while some did poorly.

Comparisons of the two models fit in Analyses 1 and 2, and to the one-group Rasch model (which was fit for comparison purposes only), are shown in Table 8.5. Comparisons across models with differing numbers of latent groups cannot be done using likelihood ratio tests, because of boundary problems (Böhning, 2000). Model comparisons are thus based on Akaike's information criterion (AIC; Akaike, 1974). In this table, it can be seen that the three-group saltus model does fit better than both the two-group saltus and the Rasch model, and thus is the preferred model of the three. Similar results were found in the exploratory analysis.

TABLE 8.5 AIC for One-, Two-, and Three-Class Models

Model	−2*log	# parameters	AIC
Rasch	11,456.12	25	11,506.12
2-class saltus	10,190.06	29	10,248.06
3-class saltus	9,751.21	35	9,820.21

DISCUSSION

The application of the more confirmatory saltus model to the deductive reasoning data, and the comparison of this set of analyses to the more exploratory mixed Rasch model, show a number of things. For example, positive saltus parameters show that persons at higher developmental levels did have a substantial advantage when performing the various types of fallacy items, and that the fallacy items decreased substantially in their difficulty as one attained the higher developmental groups, when compared to the performance of the concrete group. However, group means ordered such that the higher the developmental group, the lower the overall proficiency, indicates that the performance of the higher groups on the items associated with a lower developmental level (the MP/MT items) showed a reversal, and this reversal persisted at the highest developmental level. Indeed, consistent with theoretical assumptions as well as with the exploratory analysis, it was relatively unusual for persons classified at the higher developmental levels to achieve a perfect score on the lower level items.

Second, we see that while there are clearly latent groups of persons, with clear differences in their patterns of performance (as was also shown in the exploratory analysis), the relation between groups of persons and classes of items is more complex than can easily be shown by associating one class of items with each developmental group, and expecting better performance on that class of item by the group in question. The fact that the higher developmental groups tended to contain greatly varying subtypes of response patterns suggests that there are more than three differing groups. While there are groups that do successively better on more complex items, there are also groups that show interesting reversals in performance on particular sets. In some cases, this is predicted by theory (e.g., that intermediate-level persons would do poorly on the MP/MT items on which the concrete persons, assumed to be in a lower developmental level, do well). However, there are also persons who do well only on those items predicted to be the most difficult, and poorly on all other items. Finally, there are doubtless groups of persons who are simply guessing at random, or otherwise not paying close attention to the task.

It would thus be useful to fit a model which, for example, allowed estimation of the effect of the various aspects of the items (form, negation, complexity) on the performance of the various groups. This might allow us to investigate particularly troublesome effects, such as the tendency of persons who score uniformly poorly across all item types to be classified into the highest group, when this is quite counter-intuitive. It is also possible that various types of individual item and person fit analysis might prove useful in further understanding the causes of seemingly anomalous outcomes (e.g., helping us to detect persons who are likely to be random guessers, or using unusual solution strategies). For example, von Davier and Molenaar (2003) presented person fit statistics that can be used with latent class and discrete mixture Rasch models.

In addition, it may be helpful to develop a series of additional models to fit, and to compare to the results of the current model. For example, it might be useful to develop a saltus-like model with variable item slopes, as models with equal slopes for all items are often too restrictive to fit well. In addition, it might be the case that models which included saltus parameters indexed by individual item or step within item, rather than simply associating saltus parameters with items as a whole, and estimating a single parameter across all items within an item class, might yield interesting differences by item and/or step.

Von Davier and Rost (1995) discussed the estimation of mixed Rasch models, including models for polytomous data, with and without constraints using conditional maximum likelihood methods. These model are all members of the class of finite mixture distribution models (e.g., Everitt & Hand, 1981; Titterington, Smith, & Makov, 1985); the investigation of various such models could prove quite useful in understanding the subtleties of data such as the deductive reasoning data. Perhaps the most general of such models to have been discussed in an educational context is the Mixture Multidimensional Random Coefficients Multinomial Logit (M^2RCML) model described by Pirolli and Wilson (1998). There is currently no available software which has been programmed to estimate parameters for such a general class of models.

One promising method for such parameter estimation, however, is through their expression as generalized nonlinear mixed models. Statistical software packages are being developed which can estimate a wide variety of such models. An example of how this could be done using SAS was given by Fieuws, Spiessens, and Draney (2004); other software packages, such as GLLAMM (see Rabe-Hesketh & Skrondal, 2005) could also be used. In general, systematic comparison of various methodological approaches is recommended (see, e.g., Glück & Spiel, 1997, 2007).

In sum, the saltus model has shown potential for aiding researchers, especially in the fields of cognitive science and Piagetian or neo-Piagetian theory, as do other extended models able to reflect the complexities of polytomous data and latent classes. However, theories concerning the development of competence do not always indicate simple linear increases in performance. In such cases, one needs to combine complex item response models with careful item construction as in the DRV. Other promising applications should follow as researchers in psychometrics continue their collaboration with educational and psychological researchers.

REFERENCES

Akaike, H. (1974). A new look at the statistical model identification. *IEEE Transactions on Automatic Control, 19,* 716–723.

Armon, C. (1984). *Ideals of the good life: A longitudinal/cross-sectional study of evaluative reasoning in children and adults.* Unpublished doctoral dissertation, Harvard University, Boston.

Béland, A., & Mislevy, R. J. (1996). Probability-based inference in a domain of proportional reasoning tasks. *Journal of Educational Measurement, 33,* 3–27.

Böhning, D. (2000). Computer-assisted analysis of mixtures and applications: Meta-analysis, disease mapping and others. *Monographs on Statistics and Applied Probability, 81.* Boca Raton, FL: Chapman & Hall/CRC.

Bond, T. G. (1995a). Piaget and Measurement I: The twain really do meet. *Archives de Psychologie, 63,* 71–87.

Bond, T. G. (1995b). Piaget and Measurement II: Empirical validation of the Piagetian model. *Archives de Psychologie, 63,* 155–185.

Bond, T. G., & Bunting, E. M. (1995). Piaget and Measurement III: Reassessing the *methode clinique. Archives de Psychologie, 63,* 231–255.

Byrnes, J. P., & Overton, W. F. (1986). Reasoning about certainty and uncertainty in concrete, causal, and propositional contexts. *Developmental Psychology, 22,* 793–799.

Commons, M. L., Trudeau, E. J., Stein, S. A., Richards, F. A., & Krause, S. R. (1998). Hierarchical complexity of tasks shows the existence of developmental stages. *Developmental Review, 18,* 237–278.

Dawson, T. (2002). New tools, new insights. Kohlberg's moral judgment stages revisited. *International Journal of Behavior Development, 26,* 154–166.

Dawson-Tunik, T. L. (2004). "A good education is…" The development of evaluative thought across the life-span. *Genetic, Social, and General Psychology Monographs, 130,* 4–112.

Demetriou, A., & Efklides, A. (1989). The person's conception of the structures of developing intellect: Early adolescence to middle age. *Genetic, Social, and General Psychology Monographs, 115,* 371–423.

Demetriou, A., & Efklides, A. (1994). Structure, development, and dynamics of mind: A meta-Piagetian theory. In A. Demetriou & A. Efklides (Eds.), *Intelligence, mind, and reasoning: Structure and development. Advances in psychology.* Amsterdam: North-Holland/Elsevier Science.

Dempster, A. P., Laird, N. M., & Rubin, D. B. (1977). Maximum likelihood from incomplete data via the EM algorithm. *Journal of the Royal Statistical Society, Series B, 39,* 1–38.

Draney, K. (1996). The polytomous Saltus model: A mixture model approach to the diagnosis of developmental differences. Unpublished doctoral dissertation, University of California, Berkeley.

Draney, K. (in press). The saltus model applied to proportional reasoning data. *Journal of Applied Measurement.*

Draney, K., & Wilson, M (2007). Application of the Saltus model to stage-like data: Some applications and current developments. In M. von Davier & C. H.

Carstensen (Eds.), *Multivariate and mixture distribution Rasch models—Extensions and applications.* New York: Springer.

Evans, J. S. B. T., Newstead, S. E., & Byrne, R. M. J. (1993). *Human reasoning: The psychology of deduction.* Mahwah, NJ: Erlbaum.

Everitt, B. S., & Hand, D. J. (1981). Finite mixture distributions. New York: Chapman and Hall.

Fieuws, S., Spiessens, B., & Draney, K. (2004). Mixture models. In P. De Boeck & M. Wilson (Eds.), *Explanatory item response models: A generalized linear and nonlinear approach.* New York: Springer.

Fischer, G. (1983). Logistic latent trait models with linear constraints. *Psychometrika, 48,* 3–26.

Fischer, K. W., Hand, H. H., & Russel, S. (1984). The development of abstractions in adolescence and adulthood. In M. L. Commons, F. A. Richards, & C. Armon (Eds.), *Beyond formal operations: Late adolescent and adult cognitive development* (pp. 43–73). New York: Praeger.

Fischer, K. W., Pipp, S. L., & Bullock, D. (1984). Detecting discontinuities in development: Methods and measurement. In R. N. Emde & R. Harmon (Eds.), *Continuities and discontinuities in development.* Norwood, NJ: Ablex.

Glück, J., & Spiel, C. (1997). Item response models for repeated measures designs: Application and limitations of four different approaches. *Methods of Psychological Research—Online, 2 [Online Journal]; http://www.mpr-online.de.*

Glück, J., & Spiel, C. (2007). Using item response models to analyze change: Advantages and limitations. In M. von Davier & C. H. Carstensen (Eds.), *Multivariate and mixture distribution Rasch models—Extensions and applications.* New York: Springer.

Inhelder, B., & Piaget, J. (1958). *The growth of logical thinking from childhood to adolescence.* New York: Basic.

Janveau-Brennan, G., & Markovits, H. (1999). The development of reasoning with causal conditionals. *Developmental Psychology, 35,* 904–911.

Kohlberg, L., & Candee, D. (1984). The six stages of justice development. In L. Kohlberg (Ed.), The psychology of moral development: The nature and validity of moral stages (Vol. 2, pp. 621–683). San Francisco: Jossey-Bass.

Lourenço, O., & Machado, A. (1996). In defense of Piaget's theory: A reply to 10 common criticisms. *Psychological Review, 103,* 143–164.

Markovits, H., Fleury, M.-L., Quinn, S., & Venet, M. (1998). The development of conditional reasoning and the structure of semantic memory. *Child Development, 69,* 742–755.

Masters, G. N. (1982). A Rasch model for partial credit scoring. *Psychometrika, 47,* 149-174.

Mislevy, R. J., & Verhelst, N. (1990). Modeling item responses when different subjects employ different solution strategies. *Psychometrika, 55,* 195–215.

Mislevy, R. J., & Wilson, M. (1996). Marginal maximum likelihood estimation for a psychometric model of discontinuous development. *Psychometrika, 61,* 41–71

Noelting, G. (1980a). The development of proportional reasoning and the ratio concept—part I: Differentiation of stages. *Educational Studies in Mathematics, 11,* 217–253.

Noelting, G. (1980b). The development of proportional reasoning and the ratio concept—part II: Problem-structure at successive stages; problem-solving strategies and the mechanism of adaptive restructuring. *Educational Studies in Mathematics, 11,* 331–363.

Noelting, G., Coudé, G., & Rousseau, J. P. (1995, June). *Rasch analysis applied to multiple-domain tasks.* Paper presented at the twenty-fifth annual symposium of the Jean Piaget Society, Berkeley, CA.

Overton, W. F. (1985). Scientific methodologies and the competence-moderator-performance issue. In E. D. Neimark, R. de Lisi, & J. L. Newman (Eds.), *Moderators of competence* (pp. 15–41). Hillsdale: Erlbaum.

Piaget, J. (1950). *The Psychology of Intelligence.* (M. Piercy, Trans.) London: Lowe & Brydone. (Original work published 1947).

Piaget, J. (1971). *Biology and knowledge.* Chicago: University of Chicago Press.

Pirolli, P., & Wilson, M. (1998). A theory of the measurement of knowledge content, access, and learning. *Psychological Review, 105,* 58–82.

Rabe-Hesketh, S., & Skrondal, A. (2005). *Multilevel and longitudinal modeling using Stata.* College Station, TX: Stata Press.

Roberge, J. J., & Mason, E. J. (1978). Effects of negation on adolescents' class and conditional reasoning abilities. *The Journal of General Psychology, 98,* 187–195.

Rost, J. (1990). Rasch models in latent class analysis: An integration of two approaches to item analysis. *Applied Psychological Measurement, 14,* 271–282.

Siegler, R. S. (1981). Developmental sequences within and between concepts. *Monograph of the Society for Research in Child Development, 46*(1, Serial No. 189).

Spiel, C., Glück, J. & Gößler, H. (2001). Stability and change of unidimensionality: The sample case of deductive reasoning. *Adolescent Research, 16,* 150–168.

Spiel, C., Glück, J., & Gößler, M. (2004). Messung von Leistungsprofil und Leistungshöhe im schlussfolgernden Denken im SDV—Die Integration von Piagets Entwicklungskonzept und Item-Response Modellen. *Diagnostica, 50,* 145–152.

Spiel, C., & Glück, J. (in press). A model based test of competence profile and competence level in deductive reasoning. In J. Hartig, E. Klieme, & D. Leutner (Eds.), *Assessment of competencies in educational contexts: State of the art and future prospects.* Göttingen: Hogrefe.

Titterington, D. M., Smith, A. F. M., & Makov, U. E. (1985). *Statistical analysis of finite mixture distributions.* New York: Wiley.

van Hiele, P. M. (1986). *Structure and insight: A theory of mathematics education.* Orlando, FL: Academic Press.

von Davier, M., & Molenaar, I. W. (2003). *A person-fit index for polytomous Rasch models, latent class models, and their mixture generalizations.* Psychometrika, *68,* 213–228.

von Davier, M., & Rost, J. (1995). Polytomous mixed Rasch models. In Fischer, G. H., Molenaar, I. W. (Eds.), *Rasch models—Foundations, recent developments, and applications.* New York: Springer.

Wilson, M. (1989). Saltus: A psychometric model of discontinuity in cognitive development. *Psychological Bulletin, 105,* 276–289.

Yen, W. (1985). Increasing item complexity: A possible cause of scale shrinkage for unidimensional Item Response Theory. *Psychometrika, 50,* 399–410.

CHAPTER 9

APPLICATIONS OF STOCHASTIC ANALYSES FOR COLLABORATIVE LEARNING AND COGNITIVE ASSESSMENT[1]

Amy Soller
Institute for Defense Analyses, Alexandria, Virginia

Ron Stevens
University of California, Los Angeles

The growing trend in interdisciplinary graduate programs appropriately breeds small developing communities of researchers that close the gaps between mainstream fields such as artificial intelligence, statistics, engineering, cognitive science, and psychology. The result is twofold and realizes both advantages and disadvantages. While we may discover new applications of existing algorithms and methods, we may also uncover similarities among the algorithms and methods that cross discipline boundaries and realize that some effort has been wasted in reinventing the wheel. As an alumnus of an interdisciplinary graduate program in applied artificial intelligence, the first author notes that she is often struck by the distance be-

Advances in Latent Variable Mixture Models, pages 217–253
Copyright © 2008 by Information Age Publishing
217

tween communities that concurrently develop and apply identical methods to solve entirely different problems.

In this chapter, we explore statistical and artificial intelligence perspectives on the field of stochastic sequence analysis. This field is particularly susceptible to the cross-discipline effect because of the wide array of analytical possibilities for application. Examples throughout this chapter, from fields as diverse as defense analysis, cognitive science, and instruction, demonstrate the variety of applications that benefit from such stochastic analysis methods and models.

We begin with an introduction to probabilistic sequential class analysis aimed at addressing the terminological inconsistencies among the applied artificial intelligence, statistics, and educational psychology communities. This introduction helps explain why, for example, the literature in the applied artificial intelligence and biology communities on Hidden Markov Models is largely separate from the comparable body of literature in the sociological and psychological measurement and statistics communities on Latent Markov Models (Visser, Maartje, Raijmakers, & Molenaar, 2002).

The second part of this chapter illustrates two applications of the methods described in the first part. The first application, EPSILON (Encouraging Positive Social Interaction while Learning ON-Line), employs a combination of Latent Mixed Markov Modeling and Multidimensional Scaling for modeling, analyzing, and supporting the process of online student knowledge sharing. These analysis techniques are used to train a system to dynamically recognize (a) when students are having trouble learning the new concepts they share with each other, and (b) why they are having trouble. In the second application, IMMEX (Interactive Multi-Media EXercises) Collaborative, a combination of iterative nonlinear machine learning algorithms is applied to identify latent classes of student problem-solving strategies. The approach is used to predict students' future behaviors within a scientific inquiry environment and provide targeted non-intrusive facilitation. The final section in this chapter summarizes these analysis techniques and discusses how they might benefit other interdisciplinary areas.

INTRODUCTION TO APPLIED PROBABILISTIC CLASS ANALYSES

This section introduces the analysis methods and terminology that will be used in the remainder of this chapter. The two artificial intelligence models discussed in this section and the next provide the foundation for the cognitive assessment and collaborative learning applications to follow later. The goal in this chapter is not to provide a comprehensive overview of probabilistic class analysis methods, but rather to provide examples of the sorts of problems that seem to be amenable to latent class analysis, but for which more advanced methods such as Neural Networks or Hidden Markov Models might provide a new perspective. This section begins with a simple example that lends itself to Latent Class Analysis, and moves quickly into a discussion of more advanced statistical methods.

Latent Class Analysis has successfully been used to identify unobserved variables that explain the covariation (or non-independence) within a known set of observed variables. The unobserved variable is termed *latent* because it is presumably unknown even though it might be hypothesized (McCutcheon, 1987). The result of applying this method should be a model in which the latent classes render the observed variables to be locally independent of each other.

The practical application of this method can be explained through a simple notional example from the area of defense analysis. Suppose our dataset describes blue (friendly force) team reports of red (enemy force) team activities. Each blue report would contain observed variables such as activity type (e.g., weapon detonation, weapon emplacement, or movement of weapon components), activity time (e.g., early morning in June, late afternoon on Saturday), and location. Blue team reporting may also include observables that constrain the scope of the red team's available tactics such as their disposition (e.g., strength of force, training, morale), equipment, weapons, terrain, and weather conditions.

We would see covariation among these observed variables and thus hypothesize that an unknown variable such as red team strategy type (e.g., strategy of attrition or limited aims) explains why they chose a particular course of action and avoided an alternative. For example, an early morning explosion-based attack on the periphery of a small village may indicate a red team strategy that is ignorant of the ability of blue team radars to detect unusual activity in such areas with little or no "clutter". Late afternoon rush hour activities in large cities involving the movement of weapons and components may be more representative of red team strategies that take advantage of the populous urban warfare terrain. Confirmatory Latent Class Analysis in this case offers the possibility that an unknown but hypothesized latent variable (such as red team strategy type) can explain the relations among the observed variables to the level of chance covariation (McCutcheon, 1987).

Latent Class Analysis uses observed data to estimate model parameters. The parameters are determined iteratively, commonly using an expectation maximization (EM) variant (e.g., Baum, 1972; Baum, Petrie, Soules, & Weiss, 1970). They describe the likelihoods of the latent classes and the conditional response probabilities for the manifest variables within each latent class. For example, a conditional response probability parameter might describe the likelihood that the enemy who is employing a particular urban warfare strategy will emplace a weapon in the early morning at a particular location.

In the field of Artificial Intelligence, an array of nonlinear classification methods termed *unsupervised machine learning algorithms* offers approaches similar to Latent Class Analysis. The term *unsupervised* suggests that only the inputs to the model are given, and the goal is to discover (or *learn*, hence *machine learning*) the output distribution. *Supervised* methods assume that the conditional output distribution is also given, and the goal is to find an optimal mapping between the input and output.

For Neural Network analysis, algorithms are available in both the supervised and unsupervised forms. From one perspective, models developed using Neural Network analysis are less constrained than those developed using variants of Latent Class Analysis because the latent class probabilities and conditional response probabilities do not need to be known or estimated. Instead, the class membership of each observed sample feature vector is estimated based on a learned, weighted transformation function. In its simplest form, the neural network is a nonlinear transformation function that maps a set of weighted input variables onto a number of latent classes. The weights on the input variables are estimated by incrementally adjusting them while minimizing the total sum-squared or mean-squared error. The estimation algorithm is typically a gradient descent derivative such as back-propagation (Looney, 1997). The uniqueness of the method comes from its genesis in an early neurocognitive model of the human brain in which neurons in the brain either excite and fire (emit a 1) or do not fire (emit a 0) (McCulloch & Pitts, 1943). As such, the weighted sum of observed variables in a neural network is subject to a threshold function that filters the input and outputs a positive (1) or negative (0 or -1) response for each latent class. Continuing with this metaphor, because the threshold function activates the neural network nodes that represent the latent classes, it is commonly termed an *activation* function. This activation function may take many forms, the most common of which is a sigmoid as shown in Figure 9.1. The sum, s, in the sigmoid activation function is given by a weighted sum of input (observed) variables where b represents the bias (axis of symmetry for s) and α represents the growth rate (steepness of the curve).

Neural Networks have been used in cognitive and educational psychology applications to model student problem-solving strategies (Stevens, Ikeda, Casillas, Palacio-Cayetano, & Clyman, 1999) and the effectiveness of distributed collaborative interaction (Goodman, Linton, Gaimari, Hitzeman, Ross, & Zarrella, 2005). The input to the neural network in these cases consists of student activity (e.g., problem-solving actions, errors) or factors related to their conversation (e.g., type of speech act, presence of keywords or certain punctuation marks). One application of Neural Networks com-

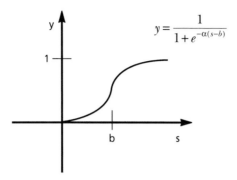

Figure 9.1   Sigmoid activation function.

bined with Hidden Markov Models (described in the next section) is presented later in this chapter.

Latent Class Analysis and Neural Network algorithms model systems of variables that remain constant over time and may not be appropriate for classes of problems whose variables describe processes that dynamically change. To illustrate, we revisit our earlier notional example of blue (friendly force) team responses to red (enemy force) team activities. Suppose we became aware that the red team was constantly changing its strategies to accommodate changing conditions and to counteract blue team defensive strategies. Activities that the blue team may have easily detected and thwarted might subsequently become very difficult to ascertain. Such change in behavior over time is modeled through the use of longitudinal stochastic models.

The maturity of efficient maximum likelihood estimation algorithms enabled the development of effective longitudinal stochastic models (such as Hidden Markov Models, described in the next section) that model and predict change over time. These models found some of their first applications in modeling learning and human behavior. For example, numerous applications of item response theory have successfully been shown to probabilistically relate students' individual characteristics to their responses to specific test items (De Boeck & Wilson, 2004). Soller, Martínez-Monés, Jermann, and Muehlenbrock (2005) reviewed a number of systems that apply artificial intelligence methodologies to support collaborative distance learning; however, the open issues, questions, and application possibilities still outnumber the research conducted thus far. The next section provides some technical background for the longitudinal stochastic latent class model that will be further developed through applications in the remainder of this chapter.

MODELING STOCHASTIC CHANGE OVER TIME

A Markov Chain is a useful tool for describing the way that samples taken at consecutive time intervals follow a representative path. A Mixed Markov Model is a mixture of a finite number of Markov chains. Mixed Markov models are thus restrictive in that each sample must be a member of one of the prescribed paths. The result of a Mixed Markov analysis might describe the probability that a vector of samples taken from one subject is a member of a particular Markov chain describing that subject's behavior. For example, Langeheine and van der Pol (2002) described the utility of Mixed Markov Model analysis in modeling the rate of change of life satisfaction for a population across several years. The subjects fell into representative groups that were either satisfied or unsatisfied with their lives and continued to generally feel the same over time, or they fell into groups that changed from feeling generally unsatisfied to gaining some satisfaction or vice versa. The Mixed Markov Model described the likelihood that each subject was a member of each group (chain) and exhibited its corresponding behavior.

Mixed Markov models require that each sample be a member of one of the prescribed paths described by the transition probabilities. Such limitations can be over-restrictive in longitudinal data analyses because individuals may change over time, and such models do not allow individuals to move between latent classes over time (Vermunt, 2007). The Latent Transition (or Hidden) Markov Model lessens the restrictions of Mixed Markov Models by allowing latent transitions, and the Latent Mixed Markov Model provides for a mixture of Markov chains with latent transitions. Thus, the response probabilities and transition probabilities for the Markov chains in the model can change over time. In this way, we are able to model the way that the rate of change for each subject also changes over time as different temporal variables impact the way in which subjects respond to stimuli.

The next section presents a brief introduction to Hidden Markov Modeling to provide background and context for the applications described in the second half of this chapter; a more complete formalization can be found in Rabiner (1989).

Hidden Markov Modeling

In the remainder of this chapter, Latent Transition and Latent Mixed Markov Models will be referred to as Hidden Markov Models (HMMs). The term *hidden* refers to the unobservable (latent) doubly stochastic process described by the latent transitions and the stochastic distribution of observations at each state. For example, observations might be classifications of different student problem-solving strategies with state transitions describing the likelihoods of transitioning from one general problem-solving strategy to another (e.g., on the next problem set, or during the next term). In a collaborative distance learning environment, observations might be sequences of online chat between students, and state transitions might describe the communicative roles of students (e.g., facilitator, critic, peer tutor) or the effectiveness of the information sharing and knowledge construction.

HMMs can be used to perform three fundamental types of analyses:

1. Estimating a model that best characterizes a set of observations;
2. Explaining sequences of observations, events, or behaviors in terms of latent class membership;
3. Predicting the likelihood of future observations, events, or behaviors.

The model estimation (1) is generally done first because the HMM that is the output of this step is subsequently used to perform analyses (2) and (3). The Baum-Welch or EM algorithms (Baum, 1972; Baum et al., 1970) are commonly used for parameter estimation (1) and prediction (3), and the Viterbi (1967) algorithm is commonly used for revealing the most likely sequence of latent classes transited by a given observation sequence (2).

We begin by introducing the HMM terminology and notation. An HMM is specified by the set of parameters that describe the model's prior probabilities, state transition probabilities, and observation symbol probabilities. At any given time (t_1, t_2, etc.) the model is understood to be in one of N states: $\{S_1, S_2, \ldots, S_N\}$. The variable q_t denotes the state at time t, and the sequence of states traversed by the model is denoted by $Q = q_1, q_2, \ldots, q_T$.

The matrix of prior probabilities (π) describes the unconditional likelihood of each state before beginning the iterative process of parameter estimation known as HMM *training*. The prior probabilities of each state, q_i, are given by the initial state distribution, $\pi = \Pr[q_1 = S_i]$.

The *transition probabilities* describe the likelihoods of transiting from state i to state j, that is, $\Pr(q_j | q_i)$. These values are stored in matrix $\mathbf{A} = \{a_{ij}\}$, where

$$a_{ij} = \Pr[q_t = S_j | q_{t-1} = S_i]. \tag{9.1}$$

The equation above states that the transition matrix describes the probabilities of the states q_t in the model, given that the previous state was q_{t-1} (see Figure 9.2). The way in which the HMM stochastically transits through states over time enables it to model dynamic temporal processes such as communication patterns or the shifting of problem-solving strategies over time.

The last set of parameters describes $\mathbf{B}$, the matrix of observation symbol probabilities for each state. Let O define an observation sequence, for example, a patient's changing mood over several months: $O = \{$Anxious, Distressed, Sad, Scared, Relieved$\}$. The observation symbol probability dis-

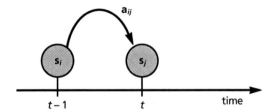

Figure 9.2 Illustration of notation for one HMM state transition.

tribution describes the probabilities of each of the observation symbols, $O = O_1, O_2, \ldots, O_T$ for each of the states at each time t. The *observation symbol probability distribution* in state j is given by $\mathbf{B} = \{b_j(o_t)\}$, where

$$b_j(o_t) = \Pr[o_t = O_t \mid q_t = S_j]; \tag{9.2}$$

O describes the set of all possible observation symbols. In the first application described later the observation symbols are given by online chat communication and problem-solving actions, and in the second application the observation symbols are given by the output of a Neural Network that describes student problem-solving strategies. Figure 9.3 illustrates an HMM for the notional defense analysis example that was described previously. Note how the temporal nature of the model accounts for how the unknown red team strategy might shift over time as soldiers are trained in different areas and as conditions change.

Formally, if we let $\pi = \{\pi_i\}$ describe the initial state distribution, where $\pi_i = \Pr[q_1 = S_i]$, then an HMM (λ) can be fully described as:

$$\lambda = (\mathbf{A}, \mathbf{B}, \pi), \tag{9.3}$$

where $\mathbf{A} = \{a_{ij}\}$ is the state transition matrix for the HMM, and $\mathbf{B} = \{b_j(o_t)\}$ is the observation symbol probability distribution for each state j.

The Baum-Welch algorithm (Baum, 1972) is the EM algorithm for computing (learning) the maximum likelihood estimate of the HMM parameters given samples of observation vectors. The E step of the algorithm provides the update rules for estimating the parameters in **A** (state probability distribution), and the M step describes the expected likelihood that the system will be in a given state and emit a particular observation in **B** (observation probability distribution). An explanatory presentation of the full derivation of the Baum-Welch algorithm can be found in (Bilmes, 1998). Although the algorithm is not guaranteed to converge at the optimal solution (global maximum), it has been found to produce good results in practice based on local maxima (Rabiner, 1989).

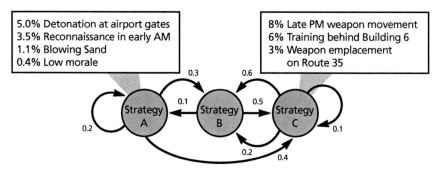

Figure 9.3   Example depiction of HMM for notional defense analysis example.

After an HMM is estimated from a set of observations, it can be used to explain sequences of observations, events, or behaviors in terms of latent class membership, or it can be used to predict the likelihood of future observations, events, or behaviors. Because examples of both types of analysis are given later, we provide some technical background here for both algorithms. The reader who is more application-oriented may skip to the next section without loss of continuity.

Given an HMM, the Viterbi algorithm (1967) finds the most likely latent class (state) sequence for a given sequence of observations; this is the problem of finding the maximum $\Pr(Q \mid O, \lambda)$. For a given observation sequence, we describe the probability of the most likely state sequence at any time, t, as follows:

$$\delta_t(i) = \max_{q_1, q_2, \dots, q_{t-1}} \Pr[q_1, q_2, \dots, q_t = i, O_1, O_2, \dots, O_t \mid \lambda]. \qquad (9.4)$$

To identify the state sequence that produces the maximum likelihood result for the entire observation sequence, the algorithm saves the argument that produces the best result at each time and state for $\delta_{t+1}(j)$:

$$\delta_{t+1}(j) = [\max_i \delta_t(i) a_{ij}] \cdot b_j(O_{t+1}). \qquad (9.5)$$

Observation sequences that begin the same but diverge over time may produce very different state sequences because, as observations accumulate, the HMM recalculates the most likely state sequence. Thus, it is not always possible to know what state the HMM is in (it is *hidden*).

The forward-backward procedure is used to estimate the likelihood of an observation sequence, given an HMM (Rabiner, 1989). This likelihood is denoted $\Pr(O \mid \lambda)$. Let $\alpha_t(i) = \Pr(O_1, O_2, \dots, O_t, q_t = S_i \mid \lambda)$. The variable $\alpha_t(i)$ is called the forward variable, and describes the probability of a partial observation sequence (up until time t), given model λ. In the first step, we initialize $\alpha_t(i):\alpha_1(i)=\pi_i b_i(O_1)$. This initializes the forward variable as the joint probability of state S_i and the initial observation O_1. The second step (induction) is given by the following equation, in which N denotes the number of states in the HMM:

$$\alpha_{t+1}(j)=\left[\sum_{i=1}^{N}\alpha_t(i)a_{ij}\right]b_j(O_{t+1}).\qquad(9.6)$$

The sum,

$$\sum_{i=1}^{N}\alpha_t(i)a_{ij},$$

describes the probability of the joint event in which $O_1,O_2,\ldots,O_t$ are observed, the state at time t is S_i, and the state S_j is reached at time $t+1$. In other words, it is the probability of being in state S_j at time $t+1$, accounting for all the accompanying previous partial observations. Then $\alpha_{t+1}(j)$ can be determined by multiplying this value by $b_j(O_{t+1})$.

The final estimated value of $\Pr(O \mid \lambda)$ is then given by summing over the terminal values:

$$\Pr(O\mid\lambda)=\sum_{i=1}^{N}\alpha_T(i).\qquad(9.7)$$

This completes our technical discussion of stochastic temporal class analysis methods. Additional introductory information on similar types of methods can be found in Rabiner (1989), Looney (1997), McCutcheon (1987), and Bilmes (1998). The next section discusses applications of these methods to the areas of collaborative learning and longitudinal cognitive assessment.

APPLICATIONS OF PROBABILISTIC SEQUENTIAL CLASS ANALYSIS TO EDUCATIONAL ASSESSMENT

Applications of probabilistic class analysis to psychology and education are copious in the literature with references reaching back as early as the 1950s (Miller, 1952). Examples include Greeno's (1967) Markov chain models of paired-associate learning (also see Greeno & Steiner, 1964), Kintsch and Morris' (1965) Markovian models of recall and recognition, Brainerd's (1979) models of conservation learning, and Wickens' (1982) stochastic models of short and long-term memory. This section describes two different applications in which longitudinal stochastic class analysis methods are used to assist an instructor or online coach in assessing and mediating online student interaction with the aim of improving the quality of students' distance learning experiences.

The first application, EPSILON, applied a combination of Hidden Markov Modeling and Multidimensional Scaling for modeling, analyzing, and supporting the process of online student knowledge sharing. These analysis techniques were used to train a system to dynamically recognize (a) when students are having trouble learning the new concepts they share with each other, and (b) why they are having trouble.

EPSILON

The EPSILON (Encouraging Positive Social Interaction while Learning ON-Line) project was motivated by the rapid advance of networked collaborative and distance learning technology which has enabled universities and corporations to reach across time and space barriers to educate learners. While this technology has removed many of the traditional constraints surrounding when, how, and what can be learned, the quality of distance learning still falls behind the standards set by structured face-to-face learning. The nature of the communication medium itself is partly responsible because supporting and mediating large numbers of online collaborative learning teams would require online instructors to spend an extraordinary amount of time in reviewing chat, email, and newsgroup discussions. The EPSILON effort aimed to demonstrate how a computer might assist an online instructor in assessing the effectiveness of students' collaborative learning interaction. The prerequisite for this effort involved identifying and understanding the processes involved in distributed collaboration and determining the support needed to facilitate and enhance these processes (Soller & Lesgold, 2007). For the remainder of this section, we focus on just one of these processes—the process of information sharing.

From a theoretical standpoint, a group's ability to share, understand, and construct new knowledge is an important predictor of the value of the distributed collaborative learning experience. The effectiveness of knowledge construction depends on the participants' evolving knowledge bases and the group's ability to share and assimilate the bits of knowledge necessary to construct new knowledge. As information is shared and assimilated into the group thinking process, group members evolve and develop a common understanding. From an intuitive standpoint, the knowledge that group members bring to bear on the problem, and how this knowledge is shared, understood, and further developed (or not) ultimately shapes both the process and the product of the collaboration. This section shows how some of the procedures described in the first part of this chapter can be applied to analyze the process of knowledge sharing during collaborative distance learning activities.

Experimental Design

The study (Soller, 2004) was designed in the style of traditional *Hidden Profile* studies in social psychology (Lavery, Franz, Winquist, & Larson, 1999; Mennecke, 1997; Stasser, 1999), which are specifically oriented to evaluate the effect of information sharing on group performance. Hidden Profile studies require that the knowledge needed to perform the task be divided among group members, such that each member's knowledge is incomplete before the group session begins. The group task is designed such that it cannot be successfully completed until all members share their unique knowledge. Group performance is typically measured by counting the number of individual knowledge elements that surface during group discussion and evaluating the group's solution, which is dependent on these elements. Although some studies do suggest that the quality and quantity of unique information shared by group members is a significant predictor of the quality of the group decision (Hollingshead, 1996; Winquist & Larson, 1998), other studies have historically and consistently shown that group members are not likely to discover their teammates' hidden profiles (Lavery et al., 1999; Stasser, 1999). Group members tend to focus on information that they share in common and tend not to share and discuss information they uniquely possess. The study described in this section aimed to identify the various ways that group members may effectively share information with each other, and the various ways that they may experience knowledge-sharing breakdowns. The results of this analysis could serve to inform and advise an instructor in selecting an appropriate facilitation strategy.

Twelve groups of three participants each participated in the study; however, the sample size was related less to the number of participants than to the amount of conversation about unique knowledge elements. All of the subjects (except for two technical staff members from a participating Federally Funded Research and Development Center) were undergraduates or first-year graduate students majoring in the physical sciences or engineering, and most were not experienced in the domain of Object-Oriented Analysis and Design (OOA&D). Each group was asked to solve one problem using a collaborative graphical OOA&D workspace while communicating through a structured chat interface. The chat interface contained sets of *sentence openers* (e.g., "I think," "I agree because") organized in intuitive categories (such as Inform, Request, or Acknowledge) that the students used to indicate (to the system) the general intentions underlying their chat contributions. After a brief training and practice period, the students were assigned to separate rooms, given *individual knowledge elements* (described next), and a pre-test was administered. More detailed information about the tool and experimental design can be found in Soller (2004).

As in the Hidden Profile studies described above, the key knowledge elements needed to solve the OOA&D problems were distributed among the three students in each group before the problem solving session started. These three individual knowledge elements represented conceptual elements, such as, "Attributes common to a group of subclasses should be attached to the superclass, and will be inherited by each subclass". The distribution of knowledge elements was intended to reflect the natural distribution of knowledge among people with different expertise. While this experimental design does not preclude situations in which one student may know a concept while another has a deeply rooted misconception, it is perhaps less reflective of such situations because the student would need to have the misconception prior to the study.

The students were pre-tested on all three knowledge elements before the problem-solving session, and post-tested afterward. It was expected that the student given knowledge element #1 would get only pre-test question #1 correct, the student given knowledge element #2 would get only pre-test question #2 correct, and likewise for the third student. To ensure that each student understood his or her unique knowledge element, an experimenter reviewed the pre-test problem pertaining to each student's knowledge element before the group exercise. During the on-line problem-solving session that followed, the software automatically logged the students' conversation and actions. After the problem solving session, the subjects completed a post-test, which assessed the extent to which the students learned the two knowledge elements from their peers.

The problem-solving session logs were segmented by hand to extract the segments in which the students shared their unique knowledge elements. A total of 29 of these *knowledge sharing episodes* were manually identified, and each was classified as either an effective knowledge sharing episode (10) or a knowledge sharing breakdown (19). The manual segmentation procedure involved identifying the main topic of conversation by considering both the student dialog and workspace actions (such as creating or augmenting a new graphical OOA&D object), and the classification was based on an examination of the pre- and post-test scores. A sequence was considered a knowledge sharing breakdown if the knowledge element was discussed during the episode, but none of the receiving students demonstrated mastery of the concept on the post-test; otherwise, the sequence was considered effective if at least one of the participants learned the concept during the session. The 29 knowledge sharing episodes varied in length from 5 to 49 contributions, and contained both conversational elements and OOA&D actions. Ten sequences were identified as effective knowledge

Student	Subskill	Attribute	Text Chat
A	Request	Opinion	*Do you think* we need a discriminator for the car ownership?
A	*<Begins to construct a discriminator on the Collaborative Workspace>*		
C	Discuss	Doubt	*I'm not so sure*
B	Request	Elaboration	*Can you tell me more* about what a discriminator is
C	Discuss	Agree	*Yes, I agree* because I myself am not so sure as to what its function is
A	Inform	Explain	*Let me explain it this way*—A car can be owned by a person, a company, or a bank. I think ownership type is the discriminator.

Actual HMM Training Sequence

A–Request–Opinion
A–OOA&D–Action
C–Discuss–Doubt
B–Request–Elaboration
C–Discuss–Agree
A–Inform–Explain

Figure 9.4 Example of a logged knowledge sharing episode (above), showing system-coded subskills and attributes, and corresponding HMM training sequence (below).

sharing episodes, and 19 sequences were identified as examples of knowledge sharing breakdowns.

The top part of Figure 9.4 shows an example of one such episode. The italicized *sentence openers* in the figure were used by the system to automatically code the utterances' subskills and attributes which formed the basis for the HMM analysis. The bottom part of Figure 9.4 shows the corresponding sequence that was used to train the HMMs to analyze and classify new instances of knowledge sharing (described in the next section).

In a preliminary analysis, a prototype HMM classifier was able to determine (with 100% accuracy) which of the three students played the role of knowledge sharer during the identified knowledge sharing episodes (Soller & Lesgold, 2007). This analysis was performed because, if successful, it would allow the system to assign a special set of tags to the contributions of the knowledge sharer. In Figure 9.4, for example, the tags reserved for the knowledge sharer's contributions begin with the code "A–." The contributions of other two students were arbitrarily assigned the codes "B–" and "C–." Differentiating the roles of the knowledge sharer and recipients was thought to facilitate the system's assessment of the episodes' effectiveness.

Hidden Markov Modeling of Knowledge Sharing

Two 5-state Hidden Markov Models were trained using the MATLAB HMM Toolbox (available from Kevin Murphy at http://www.ai.mit.edu/~murphyk/Software/HMM/hmm.html). Five states were chosen because preliminary analysis results showed that 3, 4, and 6 state HMMs produced less favorable (although somewhat similar) results, and performance declined with 7 or more states. The first HMM was generated, as described previously, using only the 10 sequences of effective knowledge sharing interaction (this will be termed the effective HMM), and the second was generated using only the 19 sequences of ineffective knowledge sharing, or knowledge sharing breakdowns (the ineffective HMM). The ability of the HMMs to effectively model the behaviors exemplified by the observation sequences was tested using a modified "take-2-out" 58-fold cross-validation approach. Each of the observation sequences was replicated with actors B and C swapped so that the analysis would not reflect idiosyncrasies in the labeling of participants B and C. This resulted in a total of 58 episodes (or 29 pairs of episodes). Then, each test sequence and its B–C swapped pair were removed from the training set and tested against the two HMMs (representing effective and ineffective interaction) which were trained using the other 56 episodes.

Testing the models involved computing the probability of a new knowledge sharing sequence—one that is not used for training—given both models. The output given the effective HMM described the probability that the new test sequence was effective (as defined by the training examples), and the output given the ineffective HMM described the probability that the test sequence was ineffective (see Figure 9.5). The test sequence was

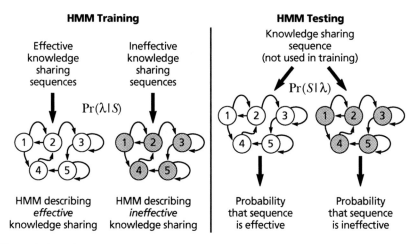

Figure 9.5 Schematic of procedure for training and testing the HMMs to assess the effectiveness of student knowledge sharing.

then classified as effective if it had a higher path probability through the effective HMM, or ineffective if its path probability through the ineffective HMM was higher. Procedures similar to this have been used successfully in other domains, such as gesture recognition (Yang, Xu, & Chen, 1997), and the classification of international events (Schrodt, 2000).

It is not necessarily intuitive that two probabilities, generated by models trained from different data sets, are comparable or even indicative of the effectiveness of a test sequence. The procedure discussed previously described how to obtain $Pr(S|\lambda)$, the probability of a test sequence given an HMM. If we would like to test the effectiveness of a sequence, we need to compare $Pr(S|\lambda_{eff})$ to $Pr(S|\lambda_{ineff})$. As long as the models are initially seeded using the same constraints, we can obtain the same result by comparing $Pr(\lambda_{eff}|S)$ to $Pr(\lambda_{ineff}|S)$. Formally, we can compute $Pr(\lambda|S)$ by Bayes' Rule:

$$Pr(\lambda|S) = \frac{Pr(S|\lambda)Pr(\lambda)}{Pr(S)}. \tag{9.8}$$

In comparing $Pr(\lambda_{eff}|S)$ to $Pr(\lambda_{ineff}|S)$, the probability of the test sequence, $Pr(S)$, is a constant because the same test sequence is run through both models; therefore, it can be eliminated. This leaves us with the comparison of $Pr(S|\lambda_{eff})Pr(\lambda_{eff})$ to $Pr(S|\lambda_{ineff})Pr(\lambda_{ineff})$. Because the models' λ_{eff} and λ_{ineff} are also constants across all of the test cases, and do not differ statistically significantly ($p = 0.65$), they too can be eliminated, leaving us with $Pr(\lambda|S) \approx (Pr(S|\lambda)$. The p statistic, obtained through a Kolmogorov-Smirnov test, tells us that the distributions of transition probabilities in the two models do not differ significantly (Fisher & van Belle, 1993). Because the HMMs remain constant for all of the test cases, it is reasonable to perform relative comparisons of $Pr(\lambda_{eff}|S)$ and $Pr(\lambda_{ineff}|S)$, although the absolute magnitudes of the differences between the models may not be significant. In summary, it may be more computationally intuitive to think of the analysis that follows as a process of comparing two HMMs—one effective and one ineffective—and determining which model best matches a given test sequence. But because this is essentially the same as the more conventional terminology in which we calculate the likelihood of a sequence, given a model, we have adopted the latter form.

As seen in Figure 9.6, 16 of the 20 effective knowledge sharing sequences were correctly classified by the effective HMM, and 27 of the 38 ineffective sequences were correctly classified by the HMM modeling knowledge sharing breakdowns. Overall, the HMM approach produced an accuracy of 74.14%, almost 25% above the baseline. The baseline comparison for this analysis is chance, or 50%, because there was a 0.5 chance of arbitrarily classifying a given test sequence as effective or ineffective, and the sample size was not large enough to establish a reliable frequency baseline.

	Effective HMM	Ineffective HMM	
Effective Test Sequences	16	4	0.8
Ineffective Test Sequences	11	27	0.7

Figure 9.6 Results of HMM analysis.

This analysis showed that HMMs are useful for identifying when group members are effectively sharing information, and when they are experiencing knowledge sharing breakdowns. A system based on this analysis alone could offer support and guidance about 74% of the time the students need it, which is better than guessing when students are having trouble, or basing intervention solely on students' requests for help. The next step is determining why students may be having trouble so that appropriate facilitation methods can be identified and tested. The following section takes a closer look at the differences between the effective and ineffective sequences in order to understand the qualitative differences.

Multidimensional Scaling of HMM Likelihoods

An HMM clustering approach (Juang & Rabiner, 1985; Smyth, 1997) was used to develop generalized models of effective knowledge sharing and breakdowns in knowledge sharing. The approach involved a combination of Hidden Markov Modeling, Multidimensional Scaling (Shepard & Arabie, 1979), and a self-organizing clustering routine. In the first step of this approach, each of the knowledge sharing episodes was used to train one HMM (in the traditional manner). This resulted in 29×2 paired HMMs, each pair representing a generalization of a particular knowledge sharing behavior.

Formally, each sequence, S_j, $1 \leq j \leq N$, was used to train one HMM, M_i, $1 \leq i \leq N$, $i = j$. For the effective case, $N_{eff} = 20$, and for the ineffective case, $N_{ineff} = 38$. Then, the log-likelihood of each sequence, S_j, given each of the HMMs, M_i, was calculated via the standard HMM testing procedure. This resulted in two matrices, one describing the log-likelihoods of the effective sequences given the effective models, $loglik_{eff}(S_j \mid M_i)$, and another describing the log-likelihoods of the ineffective sequences given the ineffective models, $loglik_{ineff}(S_j \mid M_i)$. The columns of these matrices described the likelihood of each of the sequences given a particular model, M_i; hence, similar HMMs should produce similar column vectors which we will call likelihood vectors. Given this observation, it would make sense to cluster these column vectors, and identify models that were most similar as model groupings. Traditional hierarchical clustering approaches, however, did not work well because the outlier data points caused the generation of single clusters from singleton data points. To deal with this problem, the data were analyzed using a Multidimensional Scaling (MDS) procedure in which the likelihood vectors were positioned in a multidimensional space that was divided into regions describing the groups of HMMs (Kruskal & Wish, 1978; Shepard, 1980).

The MDS approach was attractive for this research because each of the groupings found in the multidimensional space described a particular way in which group members effectively share new knowledge with each other, or experience breakdowns while attempting to share new knowledge with each other. The full algorithm to perform the MDS of HMM likelihoods is described in Soller (2004). Briefly, the standard MDS procedure was applied to the HMM log-likelihood matrices, such that $loglik(S_j \mid M_i) \rightarrow D_{ji}$, where $D_{ji} = d(L_{Mj}, L_{Mi})$ describes the Euclidean distance between the N HMM likelihood vectors in a 3-dimensional space (Kruskal & Wish, 1978). The likelihood vectors were then assigned to groups based on the closeness of the data points in the MDS scaled configurations.

The groups of scaled HMM likelihood vectors were verified using an iterative, self-organizing data analysis technique (ISODATA) along with a maximum distance threshold criteria (Looney, 1997). The maximum distance threshold enabled the algorithm to ignore those points that were too far away from any of the established clusters. The dataset that was analyzed was small compared to the number of different ways students may share new knowledge with each other. Even though some of the models in the dataset may represent single examples of certain types of interaction, only those models for which several examples exist can be reliably classified and analyzed. The additional maximum distance threshold criteria ensured that those models represented by only a single example would not be forced into a cluster.

Three groups of effective HMMs, and four groups of ineffective HMMs, were discovered (see Figure 9.7). Each grouping was compared to a qualitative analysis of the student activity in each of the groups. The episodes were first summarized blindly, without knowledge of the groupings. Then, the summarized episodes were compared to the clusters that were found computationally. The remainder of this section describes the sort of interaction that occurs when students attempt to share new knowledge with each other, as suggested by the computational procedure.

Figure 9.8 shows the four generalized models that were found from the groups of ineffective likelihood vectors (A_i, B_i, C_i, and D_i). In the first group (A_i), the sharer (student A) first proposes that the group discuss his Knowl-

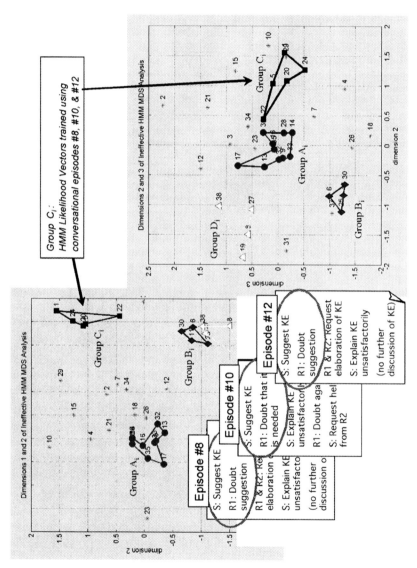

Figure 9.7 HMM likelihood vector clustering for knowledge sharing breakdown groupings.

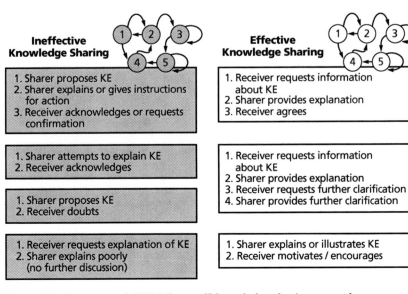

Figure 9.8 Summarized HMM "learned" knowledge sharing examples.

edge Element. The sharer then proceeds to either explain the Knowledge Element, or gives instructions to one of the receivers (students B or C) for applying the Knowledge Element concept to the exercise. The episode closes when the receiver(s) simply acknowledges, or request(s) confirmation of his actions. In the second group (B_i), the sharer first attempts to explain his Knowledge Element. This act is followed by only acknowledgement, and no further explanation. In the third group (C_i), the sharer proposes his Knowledge Element, and this act is followed by doubt on the part of the receivers. The blindly summarized knowledge sharing episodes for group C_i and the corresponding likelihood vector grouping in the multidimensional space is illustrated in Figure 9.7. In the fourth group (D_i), one of the receivers first requests an explanation of one of the Knowledge Elements, after which the sharer explains his Knowledge Element poorly, ending the discussion on the Knowledge Element (see Soller, 2004, for examples of knowledge sharing breakdowns).

Figure 9.8 also shows the three generalized models that were found from the groups of effective examples (A_e, B_e, and C_e). Generally, the discussions in which students effectively shared and learned each other's Knowledge Elements were marked by questioning, explanation, agreement, and motivation, whereas the discussions in which the students experienced breakdowns in knowledge sharing were marked by poor (inaccurate or incomplete) explanations, instructions for action, doubt, and acknowledgement.

This section described a longitudinal stochastic analysis approach that combines HMM and MDS with a threshold-based clustering method. The approach provided insight into the various ways that students may effectively share knowledge and the various ways that students may have trouble sharing new knowledge with each other. The analysis illustrated how effective knowledge sharing discussions were markedly different from discussions in which the students experienced knowledge sharing breakdowns. The results of this analysis could serve to inform and advise an instructor in selecting an appropriate facilitation strategy. The next section describes an application in which a different hybrid combination of longitudinal stochastic methods was used to model and assess cognitive development.

IMMEX COLLABORATIVE

IMMEX™ (Interactive Multi-Media EXercises) is a web-based multimedia scientific learning environment that combines iterative nonlinear machine learning algorithms to identify latent classes of student problem-solving strategies. The single-user version, which was developed at the University of California, Los Angeles, has been used in science classes across middle and high schools, universities, and medical schools in the U.S. over the past 12 years and has logged over 250,000 student problem-solving performances (Stevens & Palacio-Cayetano, 2003). A rich portfolio of over 100 problem sets in various disciplines has been developed, and is available online at http://www.immex.ucla.edu.

IMMEX Collaborative (shown in Figure 9.9), which was augmented at the University of Trento, Italy, also includes general purpose collaborative web navigation and synchronization facilities, and a structured chat interface (Ronchetti, Gerosa, Giordani, Soller, & Stevens, 2005). The IMMEX Collaborative environment is designed to help groups of students learn how to articulate hypotheses to each other (through a structured chat interface) and analyze laboratory tests while solving real-world problems. For instance, chemistry students learn how to discern the composition of unknown substances resulting from a chemical spill to determine if they are dangerous. The students use scientific inquiry skills to frame the problem, judge what information is relevant, plan a search strategy, select the appropriate physical and chemical tests to solve the problem (e.g., litmus, conductivity), and eventually reach a decision that demonstrates understanding. As the students work through the problems, the system logs their chemical and physical test selections, browser navigation actions, and chats. These actions then serve as the input vectors to self-organizing artificial neural networks (Kohonen, 2001) that are trained to recognize student problem-solving strategies.

Figure 9.9 IMMEX collaborative interface.

The strategies students use in solving scientific inquiry problems, in which they must search for and evaluate the quality of information, draw inferences, and make quality decisions, provide evidence of their knowledge and understanding of the domain. In this section, we show the utility of artificial intelligence methods, in particular Neural Networks and HMMs, for automatically identifying students' individual problem-solving strategies, and predicting their future strategies. If we can determine whether or not a student is likely to continue applying an inefficient problem-solving strategy, we may be able to determine whether or not the student will likely need help and guidance in the near future. Help might be provided through direct intervention by a teacher or computer-based coach, or indirect intervention by strategically setting up and mediating peer collaboration situations.

Item Response Theory (IRT) Modeling of Student Ability and Item Difficulty

Students provide evidence of the problem-solving strategies that they are using through the patterns of actions that they take while confronted with problems of varying levels of difficulty. The first step in developing metrics to assess student ability and problem-solving strategy development was to have students perform multiple problems that vary in difficulty. Estimates of their ability were initially obtained through IRT analyses, which describe the relative difficulty of problems and abilities of students. IRT relates characteristics of items (item parameters) and characteristics of individuals (latent traits) to the probability of a positive response (such as solving a case). Unlike classical test theory item statistics, which depend fundamentally on the subset of items and persons examined, IRT item and person parameters are invariant. This makes it possible to examine the contribution of items individually as they are added and removed from a test. It also allows researchers to conduct rigorous tests of measurement equivalence across experimental groups.

Using IRT, pooled student data were used to obtain a proficiency estimate for each student based on whether or not he solved each problem. The program Winsteps (Linacre, 2004) was used to compute proficiency scores and item difficulty estimates. Using the one-parameter logistic (1-pl) model as well as the two-parameter logistic (2-pl) model, Winsteps scales both the items and the individual examinees on the same logit (log-odds) scale:

$$\log\left[\frac{\Pr(x_j = 1)]}{\Pr(x_j = 0)}\right] = \theta_s - b_j. \qquad (9.9)$$

The overall θ_s is an estimated proficiency based on the number of correctly answered items in a set. The higher the student ability, θ, the higher the probability of getting a more difficult item correct. The item difficulties, b_j, are the difficulty estimates of each item. The IMMEX case item difficulties were determined by IRT analysis of 28,878 student performances. Cases included a variety of acids, bases, and compounds and the ability measures showed that the problem set presented an appropriate range of difficulties to provide good estimates of student ability.

The IRT analysis estimated a minimal amount of information about the students' cognitive thought processes because item score (a coarse measure) was all that was used; however, it provided the necessary foundation for the follow-on Neural Network analysis (described in the next section), which performs a more fine-grained analysis of students' cognition and problem solving.

Neural Network Modeling of Problem-Solving Strategies

Statistics for over 5000 individual problem-solving performances collected by the IMMEX system were used to train competitive, Self-Organizing

Maps (SOMs) (Kohonen, 2001). A SOM is a type of unsupervised Neural Network that learns to group similar observation vectors in such a way that the nodes physically near each other respond similarly to like input vectors (Kohonen, 2001). In our case, the neural network observation (input) vectors described sequences of individual student actions during problem solving (e.g., Run_Blue_Litmus_Test, Study_Periodic_Table, Reaction_with_Silver_Nitrate). The result of the Neural Network training was a topological ordering of neural network nodes according to the structure of the data, such that the distance between the nodes described the similarity of the students' problem-solving strategies. For example, the neural networks identified situations in which students applied ineffective strategies, such as running a large number of chemical and physical tests, or not consulting the glossaries and background information, and effective strategies such as balancing test selection with searching for background information. Other domain-specific problem-specific strategies included repeatedly selecting specific tests (e.g., flame or litmus tests) when presented with compounds involving hydroxides (Stevens, Soller, Cooper, & Sprang, 2004). From a statistical perspective, nonlinear SOMs are similar to nonlinear k-means clustering variants with constrained topologies.

The resulting SOM took the form of a 36-node Neural Network, derived from the 5,284 performances of university and high school chemistry students, that described the 36 different problem solving strategies used by the students. Each node of the network was represented by a histogram showing the frequency of items selected by students (Figure 9.10). For example, there were 22 tests related to Background Information (items 2–8), Flame Tests, Solubility and Conductivity (items 9–13), Litmus tests (items 14, 15), Acid and Base Reactivity (items 16, 17), and Precipitation Reactions (items 18–22).

Choices regarding the number of nodes and the different architectures, neighborhoods, and training parameters have been described previously (Stevens, Wang, & Lopo, 1996). The 36 Neural Network nodes are represented by a 6×6 grid of 36 graphs (see Figure 9.11). The nodes are numbered 1 through 36 left-to-right and top-to-bottom; for example, the top row is comprised of nodes 1 through 6. As the neural network is iteratively trained, the performances are automatically grouped into these 36 nodes so that each node represents a different generalized subset of the population. In this case, each subset describes a different problem solving strategy. These 36 classifications are observable descriptive classes that can serve as input to a test-level scoring process or be linked to other measures of student achievement. They may also be used to construct immediate or delayed feedback to the student or aggregated cognitive statistics for the instructor.

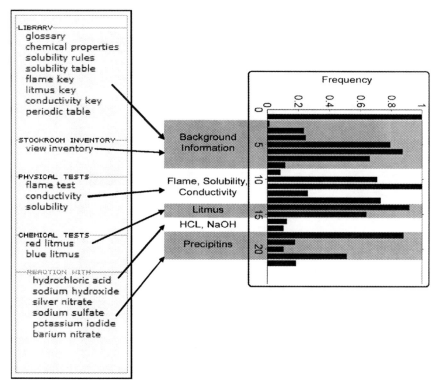

Figure 9.10 One Neural Network node describing the frequency of items selected by students at that node.

Many of the student performances that were grouped together at a particular node represent problem-solving strategies adopted by students who always selected the same tests (i.e., those with a frequency of 1). For instance, all Node 15 performances shown in the left-hand side of Figure 9.11 contain the items 1 (Prologue) and 11 (Flame Test). Items 5, 6, 10, 13, 14, 15, and 18 have a selection frequency of 60–90%, meaning that any individual student performance that falls within that node would most likely contain some of those items. Items with a selection frequency of 10–30% were regarded more as background noise than significant contributors to the strategy represented by that node.

The topology of the trained Neural Network provides information about the variety of different strategic approaches that students apply in solving IMMEX problems. First, it is not surprising that a topology is developed based on the quantity of items that students select. The upper right hand of the map (nodes 6, 12) represents strategies where a large number of tests are being ordered, whereas the lower left contains clusters of strategies

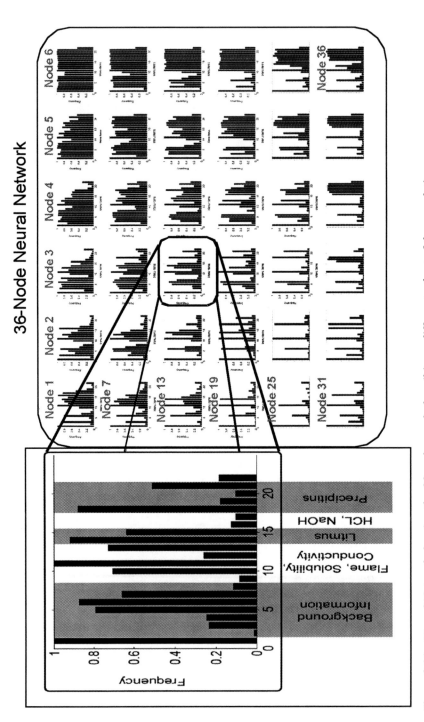

Figure 9.11 Neural Network showing the 36 nodes, each describing a different subset of the population.

where few tests are being ordered. There are also differences that reveal the quality of information that students use to solve the problems. Nodes situated in the lower right hand corner of Figure 9.11 (nodes 29, 30, 34, 35, 36) represent strategies in which students selected a large number of items, but no longer needed to reference the Background Information (items 2–9).

Each Neural Network node is associated with a corresponding solution frequency. The node's solution frequency describes the percentage of students at that node who successfully solved the problem. By linking the solution frequency to each of the Neural Network nodes, an indication of the efficiency of the different strategies can be obtained. Figure 9.12 shows the grayscale values for nodal solution frequencies overlaid on the 36 node Neural Network map. The darker shades indicate lower solution frequencies.

The figure shows that ordering all tests (nodes 5 and 6, upper right) or very few tests (node 25, lower left) are not efficient strategies. Effective strategies with the highest solution frequency were, for the most part, reflected by a balance of selecting background and test items. These were best visualized in the lower-left hand corner and the middle of the topology map and are exemplified by students making particularly useful associations among the most relevant tests for the problem at hand.

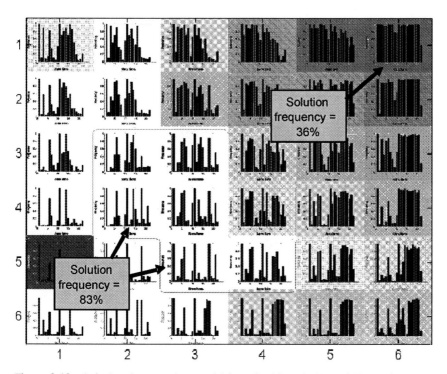

Figure 9.12 Solution frequencies overlaid on the 36 node Neural Network map.

Once the Neural Network is trained, and the strategies represented by each node are defined, new performances can be tested on the trained neural network, and the strategy (node) that best matches the new input performance vector can be identified. For instance, if a student were to order many different chemical and physical tests while solving a Hazmat (hazardous materials) case, his performance would be classified with the nodes of the upper right hand corner of Figure 9.11, whereas a performance in which the student ordered very few tests would be classified along the left side of the Neural Network map. Strategies defined in this way can be aggregated by class, grade level, school, or gender, and related to other achievement and demographic measures.

Hidden Markov Modeling of Problem-Solving Strategy Development

The Neural Network analysis described in the previous section provided point-in-time snapshots of students' problem-solving strategies and performance. In this section, we describe how longitudinal Hidden Markov Models were used to both model and predict strategic learning trajectories across time and problem sets.

IMMEX problem sets contain a number of isomorphic problems (5–60) for students to solve as they develop different chemistry skill sets. As students performed a series of cases from a problem set, learning trajectories were developed that indicate their progress. First, each student performance in the series was independently classified at the appropriate Neural Network node as described above. Second, the sequences of classified student performances became the input to train a Hidden Markov Model. Figure 9.13 shows the Neural Network node classifications for four performances of four students. The numbers in the node sequences listed on the right-hand side of the figure correspond directly to the Neural Network nodes numbered 1–36 in Figure 9.11.

By mapping these sequences to the performance characteristics at each node of the trained Artificial Neural Network (ANN), a profile of each student's progress can be generated. For example, the strategic approaches of students 1 and 3 evolved over time with practice, showing a reduced reliance on background information and progressively refined test selections. Other students showed less strategic adaptation and continued to use the same or similar strategies over time. While potentially informative, manual inspection and mapping of nodes to strategies is a time-consuming process. Certainly Markov Models provide an alternative approach for dynamically modeling this longitudinal information; however, the 1,296 possible transitions in a 36-node map renders the predictive power of this method less

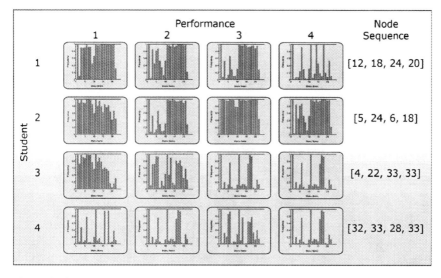

Figure 9.13   Neural Network node classifications for four performances of four students.

convincing. Instead, HMMs were used to extend our preliminary results to more generally model and predict student learning trajectories.

Figure 9.14 shows the overall hybrid Neural Network/HMM methodology, and Figure 9.15 shows an actual trained IMMEX HMM. The HMM training (observation) sequences were given by Neural Network classifications of different student problem-solving strategies, and the state transitions described the likelihoods of transitioning from one general problem-solving strategy set to another (e.g., on the next problem set). In parallel, this process trained the observation symbol probability distribution which describes the probabilities of each of the 36 problem-solving strategies (represented by the 36 Neural Network nodes) at each state. As a student completes a series of IMMEX problem sets, s/he will typically transit through several HMM states. At each state, the performance is modeled by (a) the general category of problem-solving strategies the student is currently applying (given by the HMM state), (b) his/her specific strategy (given by the HMM observation which is linked directly to the 6 × 6 ANN matrix), and (c) the next most likely strategy the student will apply (given by the HMM state transition matrix).

Figure 9.15 illustrates the state transition and observation symbol probabilities obtained from training the HMM with the performances of 1,790 students. The likelihood of transitioning from one state (generalized problem-solving strategy) to another is represented by the probabilities on the labeled arcs in the figure. The state transition probabilities for states 1 (0.99),

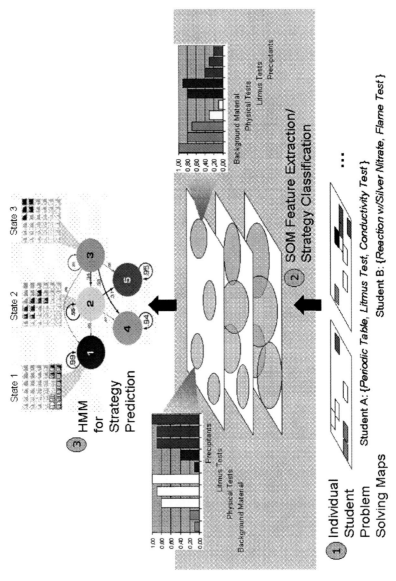

Figure 9.14 Individual problem-solving maps (step 1 at bottom of figure) are used by SOMs to identify students' problem-solving strategies (step 2 in middle of figure), and then input to the HMM to predict strategy shifts (step 3 at top of figure).

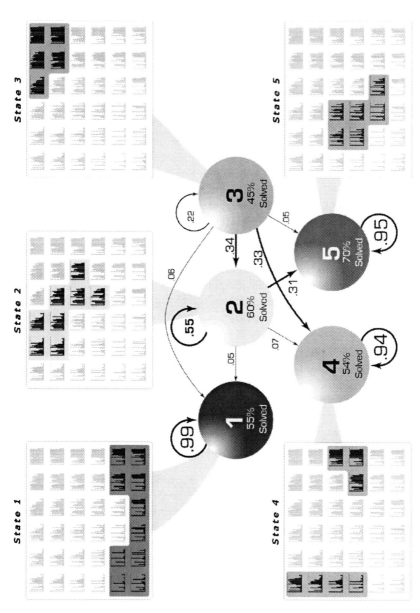

Figure 9.15 HMM including state transition probabilities and observation symbol probabilities given by SOMs.

4 (0.94), and 5 (0.95) suggest that these states are stable. Once students adopt strategies associated with these states, they are likely to continue to use them. In contrast, students adopting state 2 and 3 strategies are less likely to persist with those approaches and more likely to transition to applying other strategies. The highlighted nodes in each map indicate which nodes are most frequently associated with each state. The solution frequencies represent the correct answer on the first attempts.

The trained HMMs thus described patterns of students' strategy shifting over time, and could be used to describe and explain learning trajectories, and predict future problem-solving performances. For example, we might like to know whether or not a student is likely to continue using an inefficient problem-solving strategy, enabling an instructor to better assess whether or not the student is likely to need help in the near future.

The overall solution frequency for the testing dataset was 56%, and the solution frequencies between the states was significantly different ($\chi^2 = 131.6$, $p < .001$). State 3 had a lower than average solution frequency (45%), and State 5 had a higher than average solution frequency (70%). The solution frequencies at each state provided an interesting view of progress. For instance, if we compare the differences in solve rates shown with the most likely state transitions from the matrix shown in Figure 9.15, we see that most of the students who enter state 3 (with the lowest problem solving rate) will likely transit either to states 2 or 4. Those students who transit from state 3 to state 2 will show on average a 15% performance increase (from 45% to 60%) and those students who transit from state 3 to state 4 will show on average a 9% performance increase (from 45% to 54%). The transition matrix also shows that students who are performing in state 2 (with a 60% solve rate) will tend to either stay in that state, or transit to state 5, showing a 10% performance increase (from 60% to 70%). This analysis shows that students' performance is increasing and that by modeling with Neural Network and HMM methods, we are able to track and understand their learning trajectories.

In a previous section of this chapter, we explained how HMMs can be used to predict the likelihood of future behaviors. The prediction accuracy of the IMMEX HMM was tested by deleting the last known element from the longitudinal sequences of students performances and asking the HMM to predict the likelihood of the missing performance node. For each student performance within a sequence of performances, the most likely corresponding HMM state was calculated. For instance, Neural Network nodal sequence [6 18 1] mapped to HMM states (3 4 4), meaning that the student started out in state 3, moved to state 4, and then stayed in state 4. Then, the last sequence value was substituted by each of the 36 possible emissions, for instance [18 36 X] where X = 1 to 36. The best predicted value for X was the observation sequence that yielded the maximum path likelihood for the

	HMM accuracy (% correct predictions)
After 1st performance	67
After 2nd performance	75
After 3rd performance	83
After 4th performance	88
After 5th performance	86
After 6th performance	91

Figure 9.16 HMM accuracy in predicting future problem solving strategies.

corresponding state sequence, given the HMM. The most likely path probability for each of the 36 possibilities was then compared to the probability of the sequence with the "true" value.

Comparing the "true" values with the predicted values gives an estimate of the predictive power of the model. Figure 9.16 shows that as student complete more performances, the prediction power of the HMM increased. By performances 3, 4, and 5, students were repeatedly using similar strategies and by the 6th performance, the model achieved over 90% accuracy in predicting the students' next most likely problem-solving strategies.

The approach described in this section was used to predict students' future behaviors within the IMMEX scientific inquiry environment and provide targeted non-intrusive facilitation. The next section concludes this chapter by offering recommendations for future work.

SUMMARY AND FUTURE DIRECTIONS

This chapter presented a basic introduction to some popular stochastic analysis methods from an unbiased, unassociated disciplinary perspective. Examples of these methods were presented through two practical applications of longitudinal stochastic analysis to collaborative and cognitive training environments. The first application, EPSILON, applied a combination of Latent Mixed Markov Modeling and Multidimensional Scaling for modeling, analyzing, and supporting the process of online student knowledge sharing. These analysis techniques were used to train a system to dynamically recognize (a) when students are having trouble learning the new concepts they share with each other, and (b) why they may be having trouble. In the second application, IMMEX Collaborative, a combination of iterative nonlinear machine learning algorithms was applied to identify latent classes of student problem-solving strategies. The approach was used to predict students' future behaviors within a scientific inquiry environment and provide targeted non-intrusive facilitation.

When given enough data about a student's previous performances, the IMMEX HMM performed at over 90% accuracy when tasked to predict the most likely problem-solving strategy the student will apply next. Knowing whether or not a student is likely to continue to use an inefficient problem-solving strategy allows us to determine whether or not the student is likely to need help in the near future. Perhaps more interestingly, however, is the possibility that knowing the distribution of students' problem-solving strategies and their most likely future behaviors may allow us to strategically construct collaborative learning groups containing heterogeneous combinations of various behaviors such that intervention by a human instructor is required less often.

These two applications demonstrated that hybrid combinations of artificial intelligence and statistical mixture models can be used to perform new types of longitudinal analysis of learning and collaboration. Combinations of other types of models, such as Neural Nets, Decision Trees, and Bayesian Networks have already shown their utility in similar educational assessment applications (see, e.g., Mislevy, Steinberg, Breyer, Almond, & Johnson, 1999). Opportunities for exploration along these lines are unlimited. For example, the HMM path probabilities may be used as one factor, among others obtained statistically, that contributes to a weighted assessment function (Walker, Litman, Kamm, & Abella, 1997) for evaluating student interaction effectiveness. Weighted combinations of factors can also serve as feature vectors in decision trees, or input layers in neural networks.

The examples illustrated in this chapter are instances of an increasing global trend toward interdisciplinary research. As this trend continues to grow, research that takes advantage of the gaps and overlaps in analytical methodologies between disciplines will save time, effort, and research funds. We should not be surprised to discover that many analytic methods that are commonly applied within specific disciplines are more widely applicable and adaptable.

NOTE

1. The authors thank Greg Hancock and Karen Samuelsen for their invaluable help in preparing and reviewing this chapter. This work was supported by

the Institute for Defense Analyses Central Research Program, the National Science Foundation (ROLE 0528840, DUE 0429156, and GSE 0511045) and the U.S. Department of Education (R305H050052 and R303A980192). The opinions, assertions, and analyses in this chapter are those of the authors alone. They do not necessarily reflect official positions or views of any U.S. government entity, and they should not be construed as asserting or implying U.S. government endorsement of this content.

REFERENCES

Baum, L. (1972). An inequality and associated maximization technique in statistical estimation for probabilistic functions of Markov processes. *Inequalities, 3*, 1–8.

Baum, L., Petrie, T., Soules, G., & Weiss, N. (1970). A maximization technique occurring in the statistical analysis of probabilistic functions of Markov chains. *Annals of Mathematical Statistics, 41*, 164–171.

Bilmes, J. (1998). A gentle tutorial on the EM algorithm including Gaussian mixtures and Baum-Welch. ICSI Technical Report TR-97-021. Retrieved September 20, 2006, from ftp://ftp.icsi.berkeley.edu/pub/techreports/1997/tr-97-021.pdf

Brainerd, C. J. (1979). Markovian interpretations of conservation learning. *Psychological Review, 86*, 181–213.

De Boeck, P., & Wilson, M. (Eds.) (2004). *Explanatory item response models. A generalized linear and nonlinear approach.* New York: Springer.

Fisher, L., & van Belle, G. (1993). *Biostatistics: A methodology for the health sciences.* New York: Wiley.

Goodman, B., Linton, F., Gaimari, R., Hitzeman, J., Ross, H., & Zarrella, G. (2005). Using dialogue features to predict trouble during collaborative learning. *User Modeling and User-Adapted Interaction: The Journal of Personalization Research, 15*, 85–134.

Greeno, J. (1967). Paired-associate learning with short term retention: Mathematical analysis and data regarding identification of parameters. *Journal of Mathematical Psychology, 4*, 430–472.

Greeno, J., & Steiner, T. (1964). Markovian processes with identifiable states: General considerations and applications to all-or-none learning. *Psychometrika, 29*, 309–333.

Hollingshead, A. (1996). The rank-order effect in group decision making. *Organizational Behavior and Human Decision Processes, 68*, 181–193.

Juang, B., & Rabiner, L. (1985). A probabilistic distance measure for Hidden Markov models. *AT&T Technical Journal, 64*(2), 391–408.

Kintsch, W., & Morris, C. J. (1965). Application of a Markov Model for free recall and recognition. *Journal of Experimental Psychology, 69*, 200-206.

Kohonen, T. (2001). *Self Organizing Maps* (3rd ed.). New York: Springer.

Kruskal, J., & Wish, M. (1978). *Multidimensional scaling.* Newbury Park, CA: Sage Publications.

Langeheine, R., & van der Pol, F. (2002). Latent Markov chains. In A. McCutcheon (Ed.) *Advances in latent class models* (pp. 304–341). New York: Cambridge University Press.

Lavery, T., Franz, T., Winquist, J., & Larson, J. (1999). The role of information exchange in predicting group accuracy on a multiple judgment task. *Basic and Applied Social Psychology, 21*(4), 281–289.

Linacre, J. M. (2004). WINSTEPS Rasch measurement computer program. Chicago. Winsteps.com

Looney, C. (1997). *Pattern recognition using Neural Networks: Theory and algorithms for engineers and scientists.* New York: Oxford University Press.

McCulloch, W., & Pitts, W. (1943). A logical calculus of the ideas immanent in nervous activity. *Bulletin of Mathematical Biophysics, 5,* 115–133.

McCutcheon, A. (1987). *Latent class analysis.* Newbury Park, CA: Sage Publications.

Mennecke, B. (1997). Using group support systems to discover hidden profiles: An examination of the influence of group size and meeting structures on information sharing and decision quality. *International Journal of Human-Computer Studies, 47,* 387–405.

Miller, G. (1952). Finite Markov processes in psychology. *Psychometrika, 17,* 149–167.

Mislevy, R., Steinberg, L., Breyer, F., Almond, R., & Johnson, L. (1999). A cognitive task analysis, with implications for designing a simulation-based assessment system. *Computers and Human Behavior, 15,* 335–374.

Rabiner, L., (1989). A tutorial on Hidden Markov Models and selected applications in speech recognition. *Proceedings of the IEEE, 77,* 257–286.

Ronchetti, M., Gerosa, L., Giordani, A., Soller, A., & Stevens, R. (2005). Symmetric synchronous collaborative navigation applied to e-learning. *IADIS International Journal on WWW/Internet, 3,* 1–16.

Schrodt, P. (2000). Pattern recognition of international crises using Hidden Markov Models. In D. Richards (Ed.), *Political complexity: Nonlinear models of politics* (pp. 296–328). Ann Arbor, MI: University of Michigan Press.

Shepard, R. (1980). Multidimensional Scaling, Tree-fitting, and clustering. *Science, 210,* 390–398.

Shepard, R., & Arabie, P. (1979). Additive Clustering: Representation of similarities as combinations of discrete overlapping properties. *Psychological Review, 86,* 87–123.

Smyth, P. (1997). Clustering sequences with Hidden Markov Models. In M. Mozer, M. Jordan, & T. Petsche (Eds.) *Proceedings of the 1996 Conference on Advances in Neural Information Processing Systems 9* (pp. 648–654). MIT Press.

Soller, A. (2004). Computational modeling and analysis of knowledge sharing in collaborative distance learning. *User Modeling and User-Adapted Interaction: The Journal of Personalization Research, 14,* 351–381.

Soller, A., & Lesgold, A. (2007). Modeling the process of knowledge sharing. In U. Hoppe, H. Ogata, & A. Soller (Eds.) *The Role of Technology in CSCL: Studies in Technology Enhanced Collaborative Learning* (pp. 63–86). Springer.

Soller, A., Martínez-Monés, A., Jermann, P., & Muehlenbrock, M. (2005). From mirroring to guiding: A review of state of the art technology for supporting collaborative learning. *International Journal of Artificial Intelligence in Education, 15,* 261–290.

Stasser, G. (1999). The uncertain role of unshared information in collective choice. In L. Thompson, J. Levine, & D. Messick (Eds.), *Shared knowledge in organizations* (pp. 49–69). Hillsdale, NJ: Erlbaum.

Stevens, R., Ikeda, J., Casillas, A., Palacio-Cayetano, J., & Clyman, S. (1999). Artificial neural network-based performance assessments. *Computers in Human Behavior, 15,* 295–314.

Stevens, R., & Palacio-Cayetano, J. (2003). Design and performance frameworks for constructing problem-solving simulations. *Cell Biology Education, 2,* 162–179.

Stevens, R., Soller, A., Cooper, M., & Sprang, M. (2004). Modeling the development of problem-solving skills in chemistry with a Web-based tutor. *Proceedings of the 7th International Conference on Intelligent Tutoring Systems (ITS 2004).* Maceió, Brazil, 580–591.

Stevens, R., Wang, P., & Lopo, A. (1996). Artificial neural networks can distinguish novice and expert strategies during complex problem-solving. *Journal of the American Medical Informatics Association, 3,* 131–138.

Vermunt, J. (2007). A hierarchical mixture model for clustering three-way data sets. *Computational Statistics and Data Analysis, 51,* 5368–5376.

Visser, I., Maartje, E., Raijmakers, E. J., & Molenaar, P. (2002). Fitting Hidden Markov Models to psychological data. *Scientific Programming, 10,* 185–199.

Viterbi, A. (1967). Error bounds for convolutional codes and an asymptotically optimal decoding algorithm. *IEEE Transactions on Information Theory, 13,* 260–269.

Walker, M., Litman, D., Kamm, C., & Abella, A. (1997). PARADISE: A framework for evaluating spoken dialogue agents. *Proceedings of the 35th Annual Meeting of the Association of Computational Linguistics* (pp. 271–280). Madrid, Spain.

Wickens, T. D. (1982). *Models of behavior: Stochastic processes in psychology.* San Francisco, CA: W.H. Freeman and Company.

Winquist, J. R., & Larson, J. R. (1998). Information pooling: When it impacts group decision making. *Journal of Personality and Social Psychology, 74,* 371–377.

Yang, J., Xu, Y., & Chen, C. (1997). Human action learning via Hidden Markov Model. *IEEE Transactions on Systems, Man, and Cybernetics—Part A: Systems and Humans, 27,* 34–44.

CHAPTER 10

THE MIXTURE GENERAL DIAGNOSTIC MODEL

Matthias von Davier
Educational Testing Service
Center for Statistical Theory and Practice

Rule space methodology (Tatsuoka, 1983) and latent structure models with multiple latent classifications (Goodman, 1974a, 1974b; Haberman, 1979; Haertel, 1989; Maris, 1999) represent the most well-known early attempts at diagnostic modeling. The noisy-input deterministic-and (NIDA; Junker & Sijtsma, 2001; Maris 1999) is an example of a recently discussed diagnostic model. Similarly, the deterministic-input noisy-and (DINA) model, which is a constrained (multiple classification) latent class model has been discussed by several authors (Haertel, 1989; Junker & Sijtsma, 2001; Macready & Dayton, 1977). More recently, the unified model (DiBello, Stout, & Roussos, 1995), which lacks identifiability in its original parameterization, underwent modification and was recast as the reparameterized unified model (RUM; also referred to as the *fusion model* or the *ARPEGGIO system*; Hartz, Roussos, & Stout, 2002).

The general diagnostic model (GDM; von Davier, 2005a) is based on developments that integrate (located) latent class models (Formann, 1985; Lazarsfeld & Henry, 1968), multiple classification latent class models (Maris, 1999), and discrete multidimensional item response theory models (IRT: Lord & Novick, 1968; MIRT: Reckase, 1985) into one common framework. Von Davier (2005a) showed that the GDM contains several previous ap-

Advances in Latent Variable Mixture Models, pages 255–274

proaches in addition to some common IRT models as special cases. Similar to previous approaches to diagnostic modeling, GDMs describe the probability of a response vector as a function of parameters that describe the individual item response variables in terms of required skills and parameters that describe the respondents in terms of indirectly observed (latent) skill profiles. The item by skill requirements are in most diagnostic models recorded as a design matrix, which is often referred to as Q-matrix. This Q-matrix consists of rows representing a hypothesis of what combination of skills is needed to succeed or to obtain partial or full credit in response to a particular item. The hypothesized Q-matrix is either the result of experts rating items of an existing assessment (retrofitting) or comes directly out of the design of the assessment instrument, in which it served as a tool to design the items.

In this chapter, models referred to as the GDM (von Davier, 2005a; von Davier & Yamamoto, 2004a, 2004b) will be introduced and extended to mixtures and multiple-groups, which this chapter refers to under the title of the mixture general diagnostic model (MGDM). The MGDM extends the GDM to mixtures of discrete MIRT models (von Davier & Rost, 2006; von Davier & Yamamoto, 2006). Unidimensional mixture IRT models were previously described by Mislevy and Verhelst (1990), Kelderman and Macready (1990), and Rost (1990). Von Davier and Rost (1995) extended conditional maximum likelihood methods to mixture Rasch models for polytomous data, and von Davier and Yamamoto (2004b) described the mixture distribution generalized partial credit model (mixture GPCM), an extension of the GPCM (Muraki, 1992).

The extension of the GDM to multiple groups and/or mixtures of populations increases the utility of GDMs in that it allows one to estimate and test models in such settings. For example, the MGDM allows for complex scale linkages to compare assessments across populations (cf. von Davier & von Davier, 2004), and it allows one to test whether items are functioning the same in different populations. This can be done with either known populations (e.g., grades, cohorts) or with unknown subpopulations that need to be identified by the model. In both cases, MGDMs allow one to test whether different sets of items by skill parameters and/or different skill distributions have to be assumed for different subpopulations. This amounts to a generalized procedure that can be used to test for differential item functioning (DIF) on one item or on multiple response variables using multiple group or mixture models and to test such DIF models against models that allow additional skills for certain items in order to account for differences between subpopulations.

Diagnostic models typically assume a multivariate, but discrete, latent variable that represents the absence or presence, or more gradual levels, of multiple skills. These skill profiles have to be inferred through model assumptions with respect to how the observed data relate to the unobserved skill profile. The absence or presence of skills is commonly represented by a Bernoulli (0/1) random variable in the model. Given that the number of skills represented in the model is larger than in unidimensional models (obviously greater than 2, but smaller than 14 skills in most cases), the latent distribution of skill profiles needs some specification of the relations among skills in order to avoid the estimation of up to 2^{14}-1 = 16,383 separate skill pattern probabilities. The GDM (von Davier, 2005a) allows ordinal skill levels and different forms of skill dependencies to be specified so that more gradual differences among examinees can be modeled in this framework.

The following section will first introduce the GDM for dichotomous and partial credit data, and for binary as well as ordinal latent skill profiles. Second, the MGDM will be introduced. Third, scale linkage across multiple groups using GDMs will be discussed. Finally, examples of applications of the MGDM in large scale data analysis will be presented.

THE GENERAL DIAGNOSTIC MODEL FRAMEWORK

Von Davier and Yamamoto (2004a) developed a GDM framework, which uses ideas from MIRT, and from multiple-classification and located latent class models. The GDM is suitable for dichotomous items, for polytomous items, and for mixed items in one or more test forms. The GDM allows the modeling of polytomous skills, mastery/nonmastery skills, and pseudo-continuous skills. Von Davier (2005b) described the partial credit GDM and developed an expectation-maximization (EM) algorithm to estimate GDMs. In 2006, this algorithm was extended to facilitate the estimation of MGDMs, which was first applied to analyze data involving multiple populations from the National Asssessment of Educational Progress (Xu & von Davier, 2006).

General Diagnostic Models for Ordinal Skill Levels

This section introduces the GDM (von Davier & Yamamoto, 2004a) for dichotomous and polytomous data and ordinal skill levels. Diagnostic models can be defined by a discrete, multidimensional, latent variable θ; in the case of the MGDM, the multidimensional skill profile $\vec{a} = (a_1,...a_K)$ consists of discrete, user-defined, skill levels $a_k \in \{s_{k1},...,s_{kl},...,s_{kl_k}\}$. In the simplest (and most common) case, the skills are dichotomous (i.e., the skills will take on only two values, $a_k \in \{0,1\}$). In this case, the skill levels are interpreted as mastery (1) versus nonmastery (0) of skill k. Let $\theta = (a_1,...,a_K)$

be a K-dimensional skill profile consisting of K polytomous skill levels a_k, $k = 1, \ldots, K$.

The probability of a response x in the general diagnostic model is given by:

$$P(X_i = x | \vec{\beta}_i, \vec{q}_i, \vec{\gamma}_i, \vec{a}) = \frac{\exp\left[\beta_{xi} + \sum_{k=1}^{K} \gamma_{xik} h_i(q_{ik}, a_k)\right]}{1 + \sum_{y=1}^{m_i} \exp\left[\beta_{yi} + \sum_{k=1}^{K} \gamma_{yik} h_i(q_{ik}, a_k)\right]} \quad (10.1)$$

with K-dimensional skill profile $\vec{a} = (a_1, \ldots, a_K)$. The parameters β_{xi} may be viewed as item difficulties in the dichotomous case and as threshold parameters in the polytomous case, and the γ_{xik} may be interpreted as slope parameters. As is the case in item response theory, some restrictions on the $\Sigma_k \gamma_{xik}$ and the $\Sigma \beta_{xi}$ are necessary to identify the model. Von Davier and Yamamoto (2004a) showed that the GDM already contains a compensatory version of the fusion model (Hartz, Roussos, & Stout, 2002) as well as many common IRT models as special cases.

The Q-matrix entries q_{ik} relate item i to skill k and determine whether or not (and to what extent) skill k is required for item i. If skill k is required for item i, then $q_{ik} > 0$. If skill k is not required, then $q_{ik} = 0$.

The real functions $h_i(q_{ik}, a_k)$ are a central building block of the GDM. The function h_i maps the skill levels a_k and Q-matrix entries q_{ik} to the real numbers. In most cases, the same mapping will be adopted for all items, so one can drop the index i. The h mapping defines how the Q-matrix entries and the skill levels interact (von Davier, 2005a; von Davier, DiBello, & Yamamoto, 2006).

Examples of Skill Level Definitions

Assume that the number of skill levels is $S_k = 2$ and choose skill levels $a_k \in \{-1.0, +1.0\}$, or alternatively, $a_k \in \{-0.5, +0.5\}$. Note that these skill levels are *a priori* defined constants and not model parameters. This setting can be easily generalized to polytomous, ordinal skills levels with the number of levels being $S_k = m + 1$, m being an integer that determines the range of the levels in this case, and with a centering of levels such as $a_k \in \{b(0-c), b(1-c), \ldots, b(m-c)\}$ for some constants b and c. An obvious choice is $c = m/2$. So that $a_0 = -m/2$ and $a_m = m/2$.

Consider a case with just one dimension, say $K = 1$, and many levels, say $S_k = 41$, with levels of a_k being equally spaced (a common, but not a necessary choice),. In this case, the choice of constants $c = 20$ and $b = 0.2$ yields $a_k \in \{-4.0, \ldots, +4.0\}$. Hence, the GDM mimics a unidimensional IRT model, namely the generalized partial credit model (GPCM; Muraki, 1992). As a

consequence, this IRT-like version of the GDM requires constraints to remove the indeterminacy of the scale, just like IRT models do.

For GDMs with just a few levels per skill, such constraints may not be
needed. In the (most) common case of two levels per skill, the range of skill
levels is counterbalanced by the average of slope parameters. For example,
a GDM with $a_k \in \{-1.0, +1.0\}$ will produce slope parameters that are half the
size of those from a GDM that uses $a_k \in \{-0.5, +0.5\}$ as skill levels. This case
will not require constraints, as just one proportion determines the mean
and variance of a binary variable.

GENERAL DIAGNOSTIC MODELS
FOR PARTIAL CREDIT DATA

For a partial credit version of the GDM, choose $h_i(q_{ik}, a_k) = q_{ik}a_k$ with a binary
(0/1) Q-matrix. The resulting model contains many standard IRT models
and their extensions to confirmatory MIRT models using Q-matrices. This
GDM may be viewed as a multivariate, discrete version of the GPCM. For a
response, $x \in \{0,1,2,\ldots,m_i\}$, the model based probability in this GDM is:

$$P(X_i = x | \vec{\beta}_i, \vec{a}, \vec{q}_i, \vec{\gamma}_i) = \frac{\exp\left[\beta_{xi} + \sum_{k=1}^{K} x\gamma_{ik}q_{ik}a_k\right]}{1 + \sum_{y=1}^{m_i} \exp\left[\beta_{yi} + \sum_{k=1}^{K} y\gamma_{ik}q_{ik}a_k\right]} \qquad (10.2)$$

with k attributes (discrete latent traits), $\vec{a} = (a_1,\ldots,a_K)$, and a dichotomous
design Q-matrix $(q_{ik})_{i=1..I, k=1..K}$. These a_k are discrete scores determined before
estimation and can be chosen by the user. These scores are used to assign
real numbers to the skill levels, for example, $a(0) = -1.0$ and $a(1) = +1.0$
may be chosen for dichotomous skills.

For a vector of item responses, local stochastic independence (LI) is assumed, which yields:

$$P(\vec{X} = \vec{x} | \vec{\beta}, \vec{a}, Q, \vec{\gamma}) = \prod_{i=1}^{I} P(X = x_i | \vec{\beta}_i, \vec{a}, \vec{q}_i, \vec{\gamma}_i),$$

for a vector of item responses $\vec{x} = (x_1,\ldots,x_I)$, a Q-matrix Q, and a skill profile
$\vec{a} = (a_1,\ldots,a_K)$, as well as matrix-valued item difficulties $\vec{\beta}$ and slopes $\vec{\gamma}$. The marginal probability of a response vector is given by:

$$P(\vec{X} = \vec{x} | \vec{\beta}, Q, \vec{\gamma}) = \sum_{\vec{a}} \pi_{\vec{a}} \prod_{i=1}^{I} P(X = x_i | \vec{\beta}_i, \vec{a}, \vec{q}_i, \vec{\gamma}_i),$$

which is the sum over all skill patterns $\vec{a} = (a_1, \ldots, a_K)$, assuming that the discrete count density of the skill distribution is $\pi_{\vec{a}} = p(\vec{A} = \vec{a})$.

De la Torre and Douglas (2004) estimated the dichotomous version of this model, the linear logistic model (LLM; Hagenaars, 1993; Maris, 1999) using Markov chain Monte-Carlo (MCMC) methods. For ordinal skills with s_k levels, the a_k may be defined using $a(x) = x$ for $x = 0, \ldots, (s_k - 1)$ or $a(0) = -s_k/2, \ldots, a(s_k - 1) = s_k/2$. The parameters of the models as given in Equation 10.2 can be estimated for dichotomous and polytomous data, as well as for ordinal skills, using the EM algorithm.

An Example of a Simple Diagnostic Model

How do diagnostic models look? In the following example, there are two hypothesized skills, a dichotomous mastery/non-mastery skill $T1 \in \{-1,1\}$ and an ordinal skill $T2 \in \{-2,-1,0,1,2\}$ with five proficiency levels. In addition, there are seven observed variables, referred to as the item response variables in psychometric models and models for educational measurement. In this example, we assume that a mixed format set of three dichotomous items $X1 \ldots X3 \in \{0,1\}$ and four polytomous items $X4 \ldots X7 \in \{0,1,2,3\}$ is observed.

The Q-matrix, which relates items to the underlying skill variables, has two columns, one each for the two skills $T1$ and $T2$, and seven rows. The Q-matrix for this example may look like:

$$Q = \begin{pmatrix} 1 & 0 \\ 1 & 1 \\ 1 & 0 \\ 0 & 1 \\ 1 & 1 \\ 0 & 1 \\ 0 & 1 \end{pmatrix}, \tag{10.3}$$

which indicates that skill $T1$ is required for items $X1$, $X2$, $X3$, and $X5$, but not for the remaining items. Skill $T2$ is required for items $X2$, $X4$, $X5$, $X6$, and $X7$, but not for items $X1$ and $X3$. An illustration of Equation 10.3 is shown in Figure 10.1.

Models such as the one depicted in Figure 10.1 implicitly assume that the same structure holds for all examinees in the population from which the observations are sampled. More specifically, when using one Q-matrix as

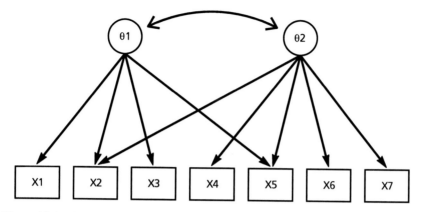

Figure 10.1 A graph of the example diagnostic model.

given in Equation 10.3 and the model equation as given in Equation 10.2, one assumes that this structure holds for all examinees in the population.

Mixtures of General Diagnostic Models

The GDM can also be extended to a mixture distribution IRT model (von Davier & Rost, 2006; see also the corresponding sections below). This allows for the estimation of this class of diagnostic model in different latent classes without prespecifying which observation belongs to which class. This provides the ability to check whether the same kind of skill-by-item relations holds for all the subjects sampled from a particular population. A multiple group version of the GDM can also be specified and estimated using the algorithm described below. This allows the estimation of diagnostic models using the GDM framework that contain partially missing grouping information (similar to the approach described by von Davier & Yamamoto, 2004b). For diagnostic models involving multiple observed groups or multiple unobserved populations (latent classes), parameter constraints can be specified that ensure scale linkages across these populations. The MGDM is:

$$P(X_i = x \mid \vec{\beta}_i, \vec{a}, \vec{q}_i, \vec{\gamma}_i, g) = \frac{\exp\left[\beta_{xig} + \sum_{k=1}^{K} x\gamma_{ikg} q_{ik}\theta(a_k)\right]}{1 + \sum_{y=1}^{m_i} \exp\left[\beta_{yig} + \sum_{k=1}^{K} y\gamma_{ikg} q_{ik}\theta(a_k)\right]},$$

with parameters as defined above and added group index g. This model allows the estimation of separate model parameters in the g separate groups. The groups may be defined by an observed group indicator variable; in this case, the above model is the diagnostic model equivalent of a multiple group IRT model (Bock & Zimowski, 1997). If the groups are unobserved and have to be inferred during estimation, the above model is a discrete mixture diagnostic model (see von Davier & Rost, 2006; von Davier & Yamamoto, 2006a).

The marginal probability of a response vector in the MGDM is:

$$P(\vec{X} = x | \vec{\vec{\beta}}, Q, \vec{\vec{\gamma}}) = \sum_g \pi_g \sum_{\vec{a}} \pi_{\vec{a}|g} \prod_{i=1}^{I} P(X_i = x | \vec{\vec{\beta}}_i, \vec{a}, \vec{q}_i, \vec{\vec{\gamma}}_i, g),$$

with cube-valued (classes $g \times$ items $i \times$ categories x) item difficulties:

$$\vec{\vec{\beta}} = (\beta_{gik})_{g=1..g; i=1..I; k=1..K},$$

and cube-valued (classes $g \times$ items $i \times$ skills k) slope parameters:

$$\vec{\vec{\gamma}} = (\gamma_{gik})_{g=1..g; i=1..I; k=1..K},$$

and a (0/1) Q-matrix Q. Let π_g denote the relative class or group sizes, and $\pi_{\vec{a}|g} = P(\vec{a} | g)$ denote the class or group specific distribution of skill patterns $\vec{a}$ in group g.

Figure 10.2 is a graph of a diagnostic model in multiple populations. This figure indicates that the item parameters and skill distributions are modeled separately in the different instances of the grouping variable g by providing a separate graph for each group. Instead of separate graphs for separable populations, groups, or classes, one may indicate the dependency of the model parameters on the group indicator by adding some new arrows to the diagnostic model graph in Figure 10.1. Figure 10.3 presents the multiple group variant in this manner. In this figure, the circles in shades of gray targeted by the *Group?Class* population indicator variable represent the dependency of item parameters on the population.

In Figure 10.3, all arrows originating from latent variables *T*1 and *T*2 include a grey circle that indicates the population dependency of the item parameters. Originating from a new variable (*Group?Class*), there are arrows that target these 'population dependency' indicators. In addition, the distribution of latent variables *T*1 and *T*2 are on the receptive end of arrows originating from the group indicator variable (*Group?Class*), indicating that the latent trait distributions for *T*1 and *T*2 may also vary across populations.

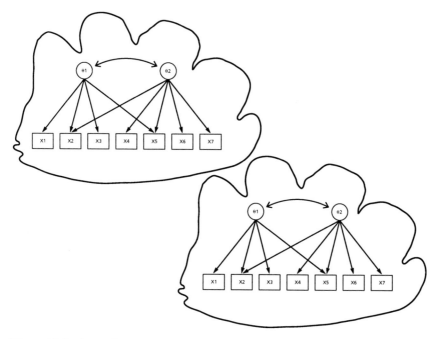

Figure 10.2   A graph of a multiple population or mixture diagnostic model.

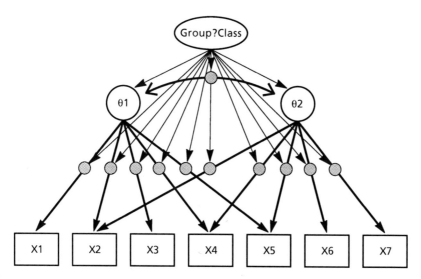

Figure 10.3   An alternative graph of a multi-group or mixture diagnostic model.

Multiple group and mixture models for item response data may be used to study how different two or more populations are by looking at the differences in the parameter sets from the model for different groups or subpopulations. These models are useful to separate samples into groups employing different strategies to solve items (Kelderman & Macready, 1990; Rost & von Davier, 1993). Researchers have used these models to identify response styles and faking (e.g., the distortion of responses to questionnaires in job applicant samples; Eid & Zickar, 2007; Rost, Carstensen, & von Davier, 1996, 1999). Rijmen and DeBoeck (2003) studied the relationship of mixture IRT models to MIRT (Reckase, 1985). More generally, mixture models can be used to test whether a unidimensional IRT model is appropriate for the data at hand (Rost & von Davier, 1995).

Scale Linkages across Mixture/Multiple Group Diagnostic Models

In the unconstrained case, all item parameters may differ across the subpopulations in an MGDM. This is not always desirable because comparisons across groups require that there is some common interpretation of the parameters involved. This is usually interpreted as meaning the parameters have to be on the same IRT scale. Scale linkage in IRT models enables one to compare ability estimates across different populations (see, e.g., Kolen & Brennan, 1995; von Davier & von Davier, 2004). The scale indeterminacy of IRT models makes these models invariant under appropriate linear transformations of the parameters involved, so that parameter estimates of common items can be transformed (or constrained) to match certain objectives. The objective to be met is either matching moments of the item parameters shared across forms or populations or setting equal the common items' parameters across forms or populations (von Davier & von Davier, 2004). This objective can be accomplished by employing constrained maximum likelihood estimation or by maximizing a modified likelihood that adds a penalty term or a Lagrange multiplier (Aitchison & Silvey, 1958).

In MGDMs, comparisons across subpopulations are made possible in the same way items are constrained in IRT scale linkages. The most stringent comparisons are made possible by assuming that the same item parameters hold for a set of common items across subpopulations. In a graphical depiction, arrows originating from the group indicator mean that the targeted parameter depends on the group indicator, while missing arrows mean that the targeted parameter is independent of the grouping indicator g (i.e., the missing arrows indicate that constraints on item parameters are to be equal across subpopulations). Figure 10.4 illustrates

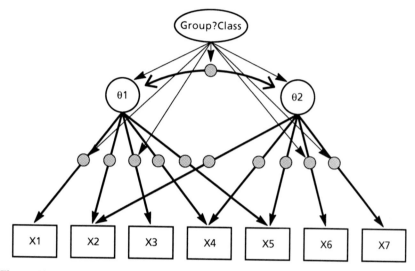

Figure 10.4 A mixture/multiple group general diagnostic model with equality constraints.

this sort of linkage in MGDMs. The items without a direct arrow originating from the ellipse labeled *group* are items *X*2, *X*4, and *X*5; these items have the same parameters across subpopulations. Items *X*1, *X*3, *X*6, and *X*7 have group-dependent parameters, which are indicated by arrows originating from the *Group?Class* ellipse. The same holds for the skill variables θ1 and θ2 as well as their covariance. The distribution of these variables and their relationship do not vary across subpopulations, which is indicated by an arrow originating from the *Group?Class* ellipse.

The *MDLTM* (Multidimensional Discrete Latent Trait Model) software (von Davier, 2005b) allows for the implemention of equality constraints on item pairs or multiple items in different subpopulations, as well as constraints that affect only difficulties or slopes in MGDMs. In addition, parameter constraints can be employed that fix item parameters to certain values, for example, to parameter values from previous calibrations. Other scale linkages such as the *mean-variance* methods used in unidimensional IRT (Loyd & Hoover, 1980; Marco, 1977) are also available for estimating linked GDMs in several populations by invoking corresponding key words in the *MDLTM* scripting language.

In addition to scale linkage methods that mirror traditional methods used in IRT, parameter constraints for MGDMs can be used to develop new methods of scale linkage and even new models within the class of MGDMs as outlined next.

DIFFERENT Q-MATRICES IN DIFFERENT POPULATIONS

The same skill by item structure implied by the Q-matrix might not be appropriate for all subpopulations. Imagine that different student groups receive test preparation from different vendors, so that some students are trained to use additional methods make sure their responses are correct. In that case, different Q-matrices might hold in different subpopulations since some student groups were trained to use this additional method (and may do so to with varying success), whereas other students most likely do not know about this method, since they have not been trained in using it. In the framework of MGMs, this can be implemented as follows using the methods of parameter constraints offered by *MDLTM:* Define a super Q-matrix with entries of 1 if a skill is needed for an item in at least one subpopulation, and set the Q-matrix to 0 only if the skill is not required for an item in all subpopulations. Then fix slope parameters to equal 0 for skills that are not needed in certain subpopulations for certain items. This ensures that no slope is estimated in these subpopulations as the slope has been set to equal 0. In these subpopulations, the corresponding skill (with the slope equaling 0 for certain items) does not contribute to items constrained in that way.

In the next step, the fit of these constrained models with unique Q-matrices across subpopulations may be compared to models that do not impose such constraints. This will provide evidence on how appropriate the assumptions are that lead to a specific constrained model.

STRONGEST FORM OF LINKAGE
ACROSS MULTIPLE POPULATIONS

Another important case of a constrained model for multiple populations is a multiple-group model where all common items are assumed to have the same parameters in all subpopulations. This means that while each common item may have a parameter that is different than other items in the same population; across populations (e.g., different administrations, different cohorts) the common item is assumed to have the same parameters. Only the ability distributions differ across subpopulations. For instance, the ability distribution in the example is $P(\theta 1, \theta 2 | g)$, where g stands for the group or population under consideration. This form of the model measures identical skills, allowing for different skill distributions across subpopulations.

The rationale for a multiple group model that includes just one set of item parameters is the assumption of measurement invariance, in the sense that the item's conditional response probability depends on a one-dimensional, person-specific variable only. Given the value of this variable (e.g., the skill, ability, or proficiency of an examinee) and knowing the item char-

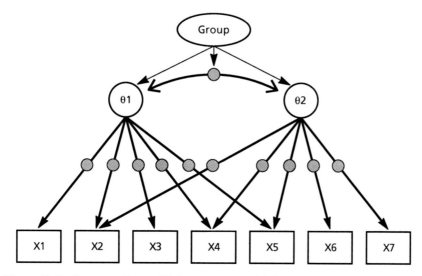

Figure 10.5 Strongest form of linkage across multiple populations.

acteristics or parameters, the response probability is determined, no matter to which group the examinee belongs. Figure 10.5 illustrates this form of equality constraint across subpopulations; note that the arrows originating from the *group* ellipse target the skill distribution variables only, and no arrow targets the grey bubbles representing the item characteristics. This measurement invariant MGDM assumes that item characteristics are exactly the same across groups, while allowing skill distribution differences across groups. Other models are easily obtained by varying the types of constraints presented in this chapter.

APPLICATIONS

GDMs have been applied in research studies conducted for different large-scale assessment programs. This section gives a brief summary of three applications to data from such programs.

General Diagnostic Models and English Language Testing

Von Davier (2005a) analyzed TOEFL® iBT pilot data with common IRT models and GDMs using expert generated Q-matrices. It was hypothesized that four skills each could be identified in the listening and reading sections of the TOEFL iBT pilot data. In contrast to this expectation, it was found that a unidimensional mixed two-parameter logistic (2PL)/GPCM IRT model fit the data as well as the GDM with four dichotomous mastery/nonmastery skills.

For reasons of parsimony, von Davier (2005a) concluded that the 2PL/GPCM was to be favored for both the listening and reading sections. Figure 10.6 shows the relation between the 2PL ability estimate and the skill mastery probabilities for the listening section data of this study. Figure 10.6 shows very similar results for the two forms of the TOEFL iBT (form A and form B) used in von Davier's (2005a) study. It is evident that all four skills have a rather strong relationship to the overall 2PL parameter estimate. The probability of skill mastery increases in a very systematic fashion with increasing 2PL parameter. The width of the four S-shaped plots is mainly a function of reliability of the skill mastery probability. If the skill is measured by many items, the S-shaped curve is more narrow; if few items are used to measure the skill, the S-shape is a little wider.

In additional analyses, *MDLTM* was used to test a unidimensional IRT model, a two-dimensional IRT model employing the 2PL/GPCM, and a GDM; each model contained all eight skills (four for reading, four for listening) in one Q-matrix and was composed of the joint listening and reading parts of the TOEFL iBT pilot data. It was found that the two-dimensional discrete IRT model estimated in the GDM framework provided the best data description in terms of balancing parsimony and model-data fit.

MGDMS FOR MATRIX SAMPLES OF ITEM RESPONSES

Xu and von Davier (2006) used a multiple-group GDM with large-scale survey data. In their example, gender and race/ethnicity were used as grouping variables. Xu and von Davier used data from the 2002 12th grade National Assessment of Educational Progress (NAEP) in reading and math (for the history of the national assessment, see Jones & Olkin, 2004). The reading data were modeled using MGDMs with up to three dimensions, and the mathematics data were modeled using MGDMs with up to seven (four content domains plus three complexity levels). Data from large scale surveys are extremely sparse in nature, so that the authors performed a parameter recovery study based on estimating GDMs in sparse samples of item responses.

The results are reported in detail in Xu and von Davier (2006). The parameter recovery results under different levels of sparseness of data support the feasibility of estimating GDMs under such sparseness conditions. Table 10.1 presents results of that study, making use of the average bias and the

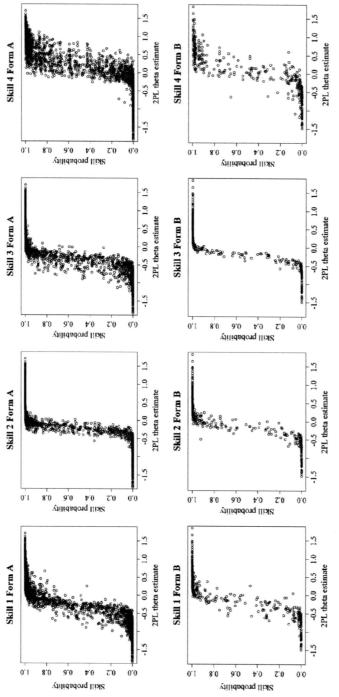

Figure 10.6 English language general diagnostic model, listening forms A and B.

TABLE 10.1 Bias and RMSE of General Diagnostic Model Item Difficulties and Slope Parameters and Skill Distributions Probability Estimates

		Percentage of missing data		
	Measure	10%	25%	50%
Item parameters	Average bias	0.001	0.002	0.005
	Average RMSE	0.071	0.083	0.119
Skill distribution	Average bias	0.000	0.000	0.000
	Average RMSE	0.004	0.004	0.007

root mean square error obtained under different degrees of data sparseness conditions.

The results reported by Xu and von Davier (2006) on the NAEP data showed that a multidimensional (M)GDM (both single group and multiple group versions of the GDM were tested) was found to fit the reading data consistently better than a unidimensional IRT model, whereas a unidimensional IRT model fit the math data better than a three-, four-, or even seven-dimensional GDM. This result has since been replicated using other, larger NAEP data sets and can be explained by the fact that the reading domains correlate less than the math subscales when defined by either content or complexity factors.

CONCLUSIONS AND OUTLOOK

This chapter introduces MGDMs and presents evidence for the utility of this class of models. So far, examples of successful applications of the GDM and its mixture generalizations come from data analyses aimed at identifying the necessary level of complexity needed to fit observed responses and exploring multiple group versus single group models as an example of scale linkages across multiple populations. Obvious next steps include the introduction of covariates for predicting skill distributions. One common way to do this is to extend the GDM using a latent regression model—a conditioning model in the language of NAEP and other large scale survey assessments (von Davier, Sinharay, Oranje, & Beaton, 2006). Figure 10.7 illustrates this model extension making use of the example used in previous figures.

Xu and von Davier (2006) developed parametric skill distribution models for GDMs. These parametric families of discrete skill distributions enable one to model the skill space more parsimoniously, so that models with larger skill counts are still estimable even when the sample sizes in the dif-

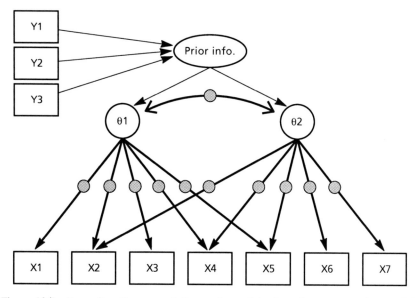

Figure 10.7 Extending the general diagnostic model using a latent regression model.

ferent subpopulations are not large. These extensions have been implemented in MDLTM and can be estimated with customary maximum likelihood methods. These developments are currently being studied using a variety of large scale data sets.

However, even with computationally efficient methods and fast computers that enable one to estimate complex models in reasonable time, the question of model complexity remains important. For this reason, research on model-data fit and the balance between parsimony of models is imperative (see Haberman & von Davier, 2006). For example, Huang and von Davier (2006) used background data from an international large-scale assessment of adult literacy. The results are based on data from approximately 47,000 adults assessed using cognitive adult literacy scales and background questionnaires. The goal of this study was to develop indicator variables using latent class models, GDMs, or common IRT models. In this study, the three types of models (GDM, unconstrained latent classes, IRT) fit the relatively short scales equally well. Measures of model-data fit made it evident that a distinction between discrete and continuous latent variables was difficult to make if only a few observed variables are used.

Mixture general diagnostic models are a useful tool for educational measurement research, since the level of generality of MGDMs allows for comparisons and model selection in a common framework. For model selection in practical large-scale data analysis, the ability to estimate and test a variety of models of different complexity within a common framework using standard maximum likelihood methods is an important advantage. However, as Haberman and von Davier (2006) pointed out, the availability of a wide range of model variants and the implied freedom to specify more or less complex latent variables makes careful consideration of the necessary level of complexity by the user of these models even more important.

NOTE

1. The chapter uses examples from joint work with Henry Braun, Alina von Davier, Xiaomin Huang, Xueli Xu, and Kentaro Yamamoto. The opinions presented in this chapter are the author's and not necessarily shared by ETS.

REFERENCES

Aitchison, J., & Silvey, S. D. (1958). Maximum likelihood estimation of parameters subject to restraints. *Annals of Mathematical Statistics, 29*, 813–829.

Bock, R. D., & Zimowski, M. F. (1997). Multiple group IRT. In W. J. van der Linden & R. K. Hambleton (Eds.), *Handbook of modern item response theory* (pp. 433–448). New York: Springer-Verlag.

De la Torre , J., & Douglas, J. A. (2004). Higher order latent trait models for cognitive diagnosis. *Psychometrika, 69*, 333–353.

DiBello, L. V., Stout, W. F., & Roussos, L. A. (1995). Unified cognitive/psychometric diagnostic assessment likelihood-based classification techniques. In P. D. Nichols, S. F. Chipman, & R. L. Brennan (Eds.), *Cognitively diagnostic assessment* (pp. 361-389). Hillsdale NJ: Erlbaum.

Eid, M., & Zickar. M. (2007). Detecting response styles and faking in personality and organizational assessments by mixed Rasch models. In M. von Davier & C. H. Carstensen (Eds.) *Multivariate and mixture distribution Rasch models.* New York: Springer.

Formann, A. K. (1985). Constrained latent class models: Theory and applications. *British Journal of Mathematical and Statistical Psychology, 38*, 87–111.

Goodman. L. A. (1974a). Exploratory latent structure analysis using both identifiable and unidentifiable models. *Biometrika, 61*, 215–231.

Goodman, L. A. (1974b). The analysis of systems of qualitative variables when some of the variables are unobservable. Part I: A modified latent structure approach. *American Journal of Sociology 79*, 1179–1259.

Haberman, S. J. (1979). *Qualitative data analysis: Vol. 2. New developments.* New York: Academic Press.

Haberman, S. J., & von Davier, M. (2006). A note on models for cognitive diagnosis. In C. R. Rao & S. Sinharay (Eds.), *Handbook of statistics: Vol. 26. Psychometrics* (pp. 1031–1038). Amsterdam: Elsevier.

Haertel, E. H. (1989). Using restricted latent class models to map the skill structure of achievement items. *Journal of Educational Measurement, 26*, 301–321.

Hagenaars, J. A. (1993). *Loglinear models with latent variables. Quantitative applications in the social sciences* (Vol. 94). Newbury Park: Sage.

Hartz, S., Roussos, L., & Stout, W. F. (2002). *Skills diagnosis: Theory and practice.* User manual for Arpeggio software. Princeton, NJ: Educational Testing Service.

Huang, X., & von Davier, M. (2006, April) *Comparing Latent Trait Models for Large-scale Survey Background Data.* Paper presented at the annual meeting of the National Council of Measurement in Education, San Francisco, CA.

Jones, L. V., & Olkin, I. (Eds.) (2004). *The nation's report card: Evolution and perspectives.* Bloomington, IN: Phi Delta Kappa Educational Foundation.

Junker, B. W., & Sijtsma, K. (2001). Cognitive assessment models with few assumptions, and connections with nonparametric item response theory. *Applied Psychological Measurement, 25,* 258–272.

Kelderman, H., & Macready, G. B. (1990). The use of loglinear models for assessing differential item functioning across manifest and latent examinee groups. *Journal of Educational Measurement, 27,* 307–327.

Kolen, M. J., & Brennan, R. J. (1995). *Test equating: methods and practices.* New York: Springer-Verlag.

Lazarsfeld, P. F., & Henry, N. W. (1968). *Latent structure analysis.* Boston: Houghton Mifflin.

Lord, F. M., & Novick, M. R. (1968). *Statistical theories of mental test scores.* Reading, MA: Addison-Wesley.

Loyd, B. H., & Hoover, H. D. (1980). Vertical equating using the Rasch model. *Journal of Educational Measurement, 17,* 179–193.

Macready, G. B., & Dayton, C. M. (1977). The use of probabilistic models in the assessment of mastery. *Journal of Educational Statistics, 2,* 99–120.

Marco, G. L. (1977). Item characteristic curves solutions to three intractable testing problems. *Journal of Educational Measurement, 14,* 139–160.

Maris, E. (1999). Estimating multiple classification latent class models. *Psychometrika, 64,* 187–212.

Mislevy, R. J., & Verhelst, N. D. (1990). Modeling item responses when different subjects employ different solution strategies. *Psychometrika, 55,* 195–215.

Muraki, E. (1992). A generalized partial credit model: Application of an EM algorithm. *Applied Psychological Measurement, 16,* 159–176.

Reckase, M. D. (1985). The difficulty of items that measure more than one ability. *Applied Psychological Measurement, 9,* 401–412.

Rijmen, F., & De Boeck, P. (2003). A latent class model for individual differences in the interpretation of conditionals. *Applied Psychological Measurement, 14,* 271–282.

Rost, J. (1990). Rasch models in latent classes: an integration of two approaches to item analysis. *Applied Psychological Measurement, 14,* 271–282.

Rost, J., Carstensen, C., & von Davier, M. (1996) Applying the mixed Rasch model to personality questionnaires. In J. Rost & R. Langeheine (Eds.), *Applications of latent trait and latent class models in the social sciences.* Münster: Waxmann

Rost, J., Carstensen, C. H., & von Davier, M. (1999). Sind die Big Five Rasch-Skalierbar? *Diagnostica, 45,* 119–127.

Rost, J., & von Davier, M. (1993). Measuring different traits in different populations with the same items. In R. Steyer, K. F. Wender, & K. F. Widaman (Eds.), *Psycho-*

metric methodology: Proceedings of the 7th European meeting of the Psychometric Society in Trier. Stuttgart: Gustav Fischer Verlag.

Rost, J., & von Davier, M. (1995). Mixture distribution Rasch models. In G. H. Fischer & I. W. Molenaar (Eds.), *Rasch models—Foundations, recent developments and applications.* (pp. 257–268). New York: Springer.

Tatsuoka, K. K. (1983). Rule space: An approach for dealing with misconceptions based on item response theory. *Journal of Educational Measurement, 20,* 345–354.

von Davier, M., (2005a). *A general diagnostic model applied to language testing data* (ETS Research Rep. No. RR-05-16). Princeton, NJ: Educational Testing Service.

von Davier, M., (2005b). *mdltm: Software for the general diagnostic model and for estimating mixtures of multidimensional discrete latent traits models* [Computer software]. Princeton, NJ: Educational Testing Service.

von Davier, M., DiBello, L., & Yamamoto, K. Y. (2006). *Reporting test outcomes with models for cognitive diagnosis* (ETS Research Rep. No. RR-06-28). Princeton, NJ: Educational Testing Service.

von Davier, M., & Rost, J. (1995). Polytomous mixed Rasch models. In G. H. Fischer & I. W. Molenaar (Eds.), *Rasch models: Foundations, recent developments, and applications* (pp. 371–379). New York: Springer-Verlag.

von Davier, M., & Rost, J. (2006). Mixture distribution item response models. In C. R. Rao & S. Sinharay (Eds.), *Handbook of statistics: Vol. 26: Psychometrics* (pp. 643–661). Amsterdam: Elsevier.

von Davier, M., Sinharay, S., Oranje, A., & Beaton, A. (2006). Marginal estimation of population characteristics: Recent developments and future directions. In C. R. Rao & S. Sinharay (Eds.), *Handbook of statistics: Vol. 26. Psychometrics* (pp. 1039–1056). Amsterdam: Elsevier.

von Davier, M., & von Davier, A. A., von. (2004). *A unified approach to IRT scale linkage and scale transformations* (ETS Research Rep. No. RR-04-09). Princeton, NJ: Educational Testing Service.

von Davier, M., & Yamamoto, K. (2004a, October). *A class of models for cognitive diagnosis.* Paper presented at the 4th Spearman conference, Philadelphia, PA.

von Davier, M., & Yamamoto, K. (2004b). Partially observed mixtures of IRT models: An extension of the generalized partial credit model. *Applied Psychological Measurement, 28,* 389–406.

von Davier, M., & Yamamoto, K. (2006). Mixture distribution Rasch models and hybrid Rasch models. In M. von Davier & C. H. Carstensen (Eds.), *Multivariate and mixture distribution Rasch models* (pp. 99–115). New York: Springer-Verlag.

Xu, X., & von Davier, M. (2006). *Cognitive diagnosis for NAEP proficiency data* (ETS Research Rep. RR-06-08). Princeton, NJ: Educational Testing Service.

PART III

CHALLENGES IN MODEL EVALUATION

CHAPTER 11

CATEGORIES OR CONTINUA?

The Correspondence Between Mixture Models and Factor Models[1]

Eric Loken and Peter Molenaar
The Pennsylvania State University

Over the last few years, mixture models have become increasingly popular as a way to describe and explain heterogeneity within populations (Bartholomew, 1987; McLachlan & Peel, 2000; Muthén, 2001; Richardson & Green, 1997). By assuming that the observed distribution is the marginal distribution of an unobserved mixture of qualitatively different subpopulations, researchers can model observed covariances as arising from simpler submodels. A trivial example of how mixture models are often a natural choice for scientifically meaningful description might involve observations of body height and hair length of a group of people. These data would likely show a negative correlation between height and hair length, with the obvious explanation that in a sample composed of women and men, on average, men are taller and women have longer hair; within each gender group there is unlikely to be much of a correlation.

While the above example may appear overly simple, it is in fact instructive. If gender were not recorded for the sample (i.e., if the gender variable were completely missing), then decomposition of the mixture is one way to recover information regarding qualitative differences within the sample.

Advances in Latent Variable Mixture Models, pages 277–297
Copyright © 2008 by Information Age Publishing

In fact, an early application of mixture models in statistics dealt with the identification of sample proportions of male and female halibut (Hosmer, 1973). The sex of halibut is difficult to determine without surgical methods, and so easily observed indicators of age and length were assumed to follow a mixture of bivariate normal distributions that allowed for non-intrusive classification.

Alternative analytical techniques can often provide similar statistical fit to the data, but, at least on the surface, differ radically in their description of the underlying reality. The above mentioned negative correlation between hair length and body height, for example, may also be modeled as occurring because both observed variables are connected to a latent factor. The common factor model posits that a set of observed variables are conditionally independent given a set (usually of much smaller dimension) of unobserved factors. It is perfectly reasonable, statistically, to explain a negative correlation among indicators with reference to a common factor. Although it may seem that gender is obviously categorical, especially when it is meant to refer to biological sex, there are indeed more continuous conceptions of gender identity (Bem, 1974; Dunne, Bailey, Kirk, & Martin, 2000); however, hair length and body weight are probably not the best indicator variables for these more continuous definitions.

For many scientific research questions, the determination of whether latent variables are best considered categorical (i.e., mixtures) or continuous (i.e., factor models) is less clear cut. Certainly there are many problems where it is logical to think in terms of categorical types (Meehl, 1992; Waller & Meehl, 1998). Biological sex, blood type, and simple genotypes may be relatively uncontroversial examples of qualitative differences. Researchers have also considered less "biological" phenomena, such as teaching styles (Aitkin, Anderson, & Hinde, 1981) and patterns of drinking (Muthén & Muthén, 1999). In the clinical literature, mixtures have been used to study depression (Sullivan, Kessler, & Kendler, 1998), schizophrenia (Kendler et al., 1997; Lenzenweger, 2006), nicotine withdrawal (Madden et al., 1997), ADHD (Hudziak et al., 1998), eating disorders (Bulik, Sullivan, & Kendler, 2000), child conduct disorder (Hudziak, Wadsworth, Heath, & Achenbach, 1999), social phobia (Kessler, Stein, & Berglund, 1998), and borderline personality disorder (Fossati, Maffei, Bagnato, Donati, Namia, & Novella, 1999).

What needs to be considered, however, is that successfully applying a mixture model does not immediately confirm the appropriateness of the model. A couple of research examples where mixture models were fruitfully applied, but where a factor-based approach could still be entertained, can be instructive here. One example is the study of infant temperament, where Kagan has advocated a typological approach (Kagan, 1994, 1998; Kagan, Reznick, & Snidman, 1988). Kagan's theory views temperament as a stable, biologically based response style. He has shown that patterns of infant reactivity to novelty at four months of age are predictive of childhood behavioral styles (Kagan, Snidman, & Arcus, 1998). His method of identifying infant temperament types is to divide infants into high and low reactive groups based on motor and crying reactivity in a laboratory procedure, and then to associate these types with behavioral inhibition through late childhood and adolescence.

Loken (2004) used latent class analysis to model Kagan's data (see also Stern, Arcus, Kagan, Rubin, & Snidman, 1994, 1995). With four observed indicators of the infants' motor reactivity, crying, smiling, and vocalizations (based on coding of videotapes during the laboratory procedure), Loken was able to find evidence for at least three latent classes, two of which corresponded very closely to the groups Kagan had identified as high and low reactive based on clinical (*a priori*) criteria.

In identifying the same two key subgroups, the statistical approach does provide some validation for Kagan's clinically-derived groupings. The latent class analysis operated exclusively on the observed data with no prior assumptions other than conditional independence, and thus the latent profiles were estimated on statistical grounds alone. Nevertheless, it is also true that other approaches to the data could easily be defended. A factor analysis of the four indicators could be used to determine what proportion of the variance was shared with a common factor structure. Such an analysis might also yield factor scores that would be predictive of inhibition at later points in development. The point is that the successful application of the latent class analysis does not in and of itself confirm that temperament is categorical in nature. Such a broad argument requires substantiation outside the statistical procedures.

A second example is the diagnosis of metabolic syndrome. With the rise in obesity, diabetes, and cardiovascular disease over the last quarter century, researchers have looked for an underlying set of factors that might account for observed covariation (Ford, 2003; Pladevall et al., 2006). Metabolic syndrome is a clinical syndrome diagnosed when an individual exceeds threshold on three or more indicators thought to be relevant to diabetes and cardiovascular disease, including blood pressure, weight circumference, glucose tolerance, triglyceride levels, and cholesterol levels (Ford, Giles, & Dietz, 2002).

The clinical literature on metabolic syndrome largely uses factor analysis to justify the relevant factors. The debate seems to center on whether one or more factors underlie the indicators. However, if the "syndrome" really were determined by a common factor, then it would seem more appropriate to diagnose it on the basis of a factor score rather than a set of cut-offs. An alternative analytical approach might be to posit an underlying typology (one or more syndromes, perhaps) associated with the observed indicators.

A latent profile analysis (Bartholomew, 1987), or mixture of normal distributions, might be appropriate to fit to the data, especially if the syndrome were indeed a disease state with distinct causal processes, and a unique progression not predictive from the indicators alone.

Ventura, Loken, and Birch (2006) took such an approach in a sample of adolescent girls and found evidence for four classes based on risk profiles for metabolic syndrome. One group was high on all risk indicators, and a second was low on all indicators. A third group showed risk factors related to hypertension (blood pressure, weight circumference) but low dyslipidemia risk (triglycerides, HDL cholesterol), while a fourth group had the opposite risk pattern. Ventura et al. were able to link the distinct profiles with family history data as well as with different developmental patterns of changes in body weight and fat mass, providing validation for the groupings. The mixture approach yielded insights into potentially qualitatively distinct risk profiles, as well as a convenient way to summarize differences on a number of related health outcomes. However, this is not enough to confirm the appropriateness of the mixture model approach versus the factor model. It is entirely likely that positing two underlying factors—one for hypertensive risk and one for dyslipidemia—might convey a similar scientific story.

Both the temperament and metabolic syndrome examples illustrate situations where the same data can be approached by researchers using what may ostensibly seem like very different analytic strategies. It is not controversial for us to suggest that analysis and interpretation generally have to be informed by theory and data, and that models should be chosen in the interests of science and should not determine science. But we wish to draw attention to an important issue. Even though mixture and factor models might seem very different in application because they have different points of departure, they usually use different software, and they tend to elicit different interpretations, the statistical models can be represented in such a way as to highlight striking similarities. This point is not new and has been raised by McDonald (1967; 2003), Bartholomew (1987), Molenaar and von Eye (1994), and others, but it bears repeating. It can be shown that a k group latent profile model can be represented as a $k-1$ factor model, identical up to first- and second-order moments. We will revisit the proof of the correspondence and show how the flexibility to move back and forth between mixture and factor representations can greatly facilitate understanding data. We provide a simple empirical example as an illustration, and discuss some implications for estimating and interpreting models.

It is worth taking a moment here to say that we are not talking about a so-called factor-mixture fusion. Recently, some researchers (Jedidi, Jagpal & DeSarbo, 1997; Lubke & Muthén, 2005; McLachlan, Peel, & Bean,

2003; Muthén, 2007) have talked about the convergence of mixture and factor models. For these researchers, convergence largely means moving both types of analysis into the same model (and sometimes then the same software). For example, the most common latent profile model (see below) assumes conditional independence given group membership. But conditional independence might seem overly restrictive, and it might make sense to posit that within latent groups the indicators have some residual correlations, thereby positing a within-group factor structure. The latent profile model could be expanded to accommodate such within-group structure, leading to a mixture of factor models. Another example is the latent growth mixture model that posits separate growth models (which can be thought of as factor models) across distinct subgroups. We view these developments as important contributions because they remind us of the variety of structures that can be built into modeling, and they also move toward common software packages for estimating composite models. However, they do not address the more fundamental question we raise concerning the choice to model a factor structure or a mixture in the first place.

THE COMMON FACTOR MODEL

The correspondence of the common factor and latent profile models can be efficiently highlighted by reviewing the definitions of the two models. In the common factor model, a set of p indicator variables, distributed as multivariate normal, are represented as conditionally independent given a set of m latent factors. Observed variables can be seen as regressed on the latent variables with regression weights λ_{ij} representing the factor loading of variable i on the jth factor. The error term, ε_i, represents the contribution of specific factors and measurement error to variable i that is not explained by the common factor structure.

The variance-covariance of the observed variables Σ can therefore be represented in the following manner:

$$\Sigma = \Lambda\Phi\Lambda^T + \Theta \tag{11.1}$$

Here Λ represents the $p \times m$ matrix of factor loadings, and Φ represents the $m \times m$ variance-covariance matrix of the factor scores. Finally, Θ represents the variance-covariance matrix of the error terms, which is diagonal under the assumption of conditional independence among the observed variables given the factor structure. Below we show the regression model implied by the factor and error structure. We do this in anticipation of showing a similar representation of the latent profile model:

$$Y_{1i} = \lambda_{11}F_{1i} + \lambda_{12}F_{2i} + \ldots + \lambda_{1m}F_{mi} + \varepsilon_{1i}$$
$$Y_{2i} = \lambda_{21}F_{1i} + \lambda_{22}F_{2i} + \ldots + \lambda_{2m}F_{mi} + \varepsilon_{2i}$$
$$\ldots \quad \ldots \quad \ldots \quad \ldots \quad \ldots$$
$$Y_{pi} = \lambda_{p1}F_{1i} + \lambda_{p2}F_{2i} + \ldots + \lambda_{pm}F_{mi} + \varepsilon_{pi}$$

The main point of this review is that given the construction of the model, and assuming without loss of generality that the observed variables have been centered, the variance-covariance matrix summarizes all that is necessary to know about the observed variables to fit the factor model. Fitting the factor model then requires standard structural equation modeling (SEM) software to find the loadings and error variances that provide the best fit to the observed variance-covariance matrix. Maximum likelihood estimation proceeds by finding the estimates that maximize the log-likelihood:

$$LL(Y \mid \Lambda, \Phi, \Theta) = -\frac{1}{2}n\left[\log \mid \Sigma \mid + \mathrm{tr}(S\Sigma^{-1})\right], \tag{11.2}$$

where S denotes the sample covariance matrix based on n observations.

THE LATENT PROFILE MODEL

At first pass, the latent profile model (Bartholomew, 1987) seems quite different. Unlike the factor model, there is no assumption that the observed variables are multivariate normal. (In fact, as we will see below, it is often implied that this absolutely must not be the case.) However, for the latent profile model, the latent groups' data are assumed to be distributed as multivariate normal. Often it is assumed the variables are independent given latent group, which makes for a very simple structure. In a latent profile model with k hypothesized groups, the observed variables are assumed to be derived from the sum of k multivariate normals, weighted by the k group probabilities π_i (which must sum to 1):

$$Y \sim \pi_1 N(\mu_1, \Sigma_1) + \pi_2 N(\mu_2, \Sigma_2) + \ldots + \pi_k N(\mu_k, \Sigma_k). \tag{11.3}$$

Thus the likelihood is given by:

$$L(Y \mid \pi, \mu, \Sigma) = \prod\left[\pi_1 N(\mu_1, \Sigma_1) + \ldots + \pi_k N(\mu_k, \Sigma_k)\right], \tag{11.4}$$

and maximum likelihood estimation of the parameters is usually carried out using an EM algorithm (Dempster, Laird, & Rubin, 1977). If there are p observed variables, and k groups, then there are $2pk + (k-1)$ estimated parameters: $2pk$ for the mean and variance of each observed variable conditional on group membership, and $k-1$ for the group probabilities that must sum to one. This model is called a latent profile model because the focus and interpretation is often on the pattern of conditional means for the latent groups. Note that under the assumption of conditional independence, all the within-group covariance matrices are diagonal.

Although the latent profile model is not estimated by explicitly trying to reproduce the observed variance-covariance matrix, the final estimates do imply a variance-covariance matrix in a manner very similar to the factor model. The implied first- and second-order moments can be reconstructed as follows. The expectation of the observed variables is the weighted sum of the group means. Once again, if we assume without loss of generality that the observed variables have been centered, the expected squares and cross-products of the observed variables are represented as below:

$$E(y_i) = \sum_k \pi_k \mu_{ik} \tag{11.5}$$

$$E(y_i^2) = \sum_k \left(\pi_k \mu_{ik}^2 + \pi_k \sigma_{ik}^2 \right) \tag{11.6}$$

$$E(y_i y_j) = \sum_k \pi_k \mu_{ik} \mu_{jk} \tag{11.7}$$

Because the variables are centered, the marginal means given by (11.5) are all zero, and the second moments represent the sum of the weighted conditional means squared, along with the within class variance. The net result is that the implied variance-covariance matrix of the data given estimates for the group probabilities, the conditional means, and the conditional variances, can also be described in matrix form by Equation 11.1 (repeated here):

$$\Sigma = \Lambda \Phi \Lambda^T + \Theta,$$

where Λ represents the $p \times m$ matrix of conditional means, Φ represents the $m \times m$ diagonal matrix where each ith element of the diagonal is the ith group probability. Here Θ is a diagonal matrix of the weighted sum of the conditional variances.

To make the comparison even more direct, we rewrite our description of the mixture model to emphasize the parallel with the factor model. Comparing the equations below to the equations describing the factor model, it becomes apparent that by replacing "factor loading" with "conditional mean," "factor score" with "group membership," and "uniqueness" with "pooled within-group error," the same basic structure for first- and second-order moments is achieved across the models:

$$Y_{1i} = \mu_{11}F_{1i} + \mu_{12}F_{2i} + \ldots + \mu_{1m}F_{mi} + \varepsilon_{1i}$$
$$Y_{2i} = \mu_{21}F_{1i} + \mu_{22}F_{2i} + \ldots + \mu_{2m}F_{mi} + \varepsilon_{2i}$$
$$\ldots \quad \ldots \quad \ldots \quad \ldots \quad \ldots$$
$$Y_{pi} = \mu_{p1}F_{1i} + \mu_{p2}F_{2i} + \ldots + \mu_{pm}F_{mi} + \varepsilon_{pi}$$

The major difference between the two representations comes in defining the distribution of the latent factor/mixture score. For the factor model, F_{1i} represents the score on the first factor for a particular respondent, and the set of m factor scores are assumed to have a joint multivariate normal distribution. In the case of the mixture model, the F can be seen to have either a multinomial distribution or a Dirichlet distribution. In the multinomial distribution, one and only one of the F_{ji} is a one, and the rest are zeroes. Furthermore, the distribution of the error term is dependent on the class that i is in—but the overall variance "within classes" can be summarized by the weighted sum of the within class variances.

One subtlety is that, as written, the model above describes an inadmissible factor solution. Because the "factor scores" sum to one, the columns are collinear. Nevertheless, we will retain this representation because it is convenient to illustrate the similarity. The non-identifiability of the model can be addressed either with nonlinear constraints, or by projecting down to a $k-1$ dimensional factor space.

The most exciting benefit of being able to express the latent profile and common factor models in a way that emphasizes equivalence up to first- and second-order moments is that it allows for greater flexibility in reading and interpreting results of analyses. Typically, the results of a factor analysis are presented in the familiar form of a factor loading matrix, and typically a mixture model is presented in the form of a plot or table of conditional means and variances. It is rarely obvious to a reader how to translate back and forth. With the above representations in mind, a researcher can readily make a translation to answer the question, "How might this factor/mixture analysis have looked if it had been run the other way?" We present an empirical example below to illustrate this point.

Empirical Example

We offer two analyses of data from a questionnaire given to college students about their perceptions of adolescents, first conducting a typical exploratory factor analysis and then carrying out a mixture model analysis. The data were gathered in a manner similar to a study by Buchanan and Holmbeck (1998), and were part of a larger study examining the perceptions of adolescents. Respondents were asked to rate on a scale of 1 to 10 how likely it was for an adolescent to display a given attribute. For the purposes of this example we restrict our analysis to a smaller set of nine attributes: *Confused, Considerate, Depressed, Emotional, Generous, Hardworking, Helpful, Intelligent,* and *Tests Limits.* There were 194 respondents in the sample.

An exploratory factor analysis of the data would proceed by assuming that some set of k common factors can serve to explain the covariances among the nine observed variables, as seen in Table 11.1. Using a maximum likelihood extraction, a two-factor orthogonal model (reported in correlation metric) provides a reasonably good fit to the data ($\chi^2 = 30$, $df = 19$, $p = .05$). Table 11.2 provides the standardized factor loadings after a varimax rotation.

TABLE 11.1 Variance-Covariance Matrix

	1	2	3	4	5	6	7	8	9
1. Confused	2.98								
2. Considerate	−.02	2.82							
3. Depressed	1.89	−.08	4.56						
4. Emotional	1.36	−.03	1.63	2.39					
5. Generous	.00	1.93	.17	.09	2.66				
6. Hardworking	.06	1.60	.04	.10	1.79	2.86			
7. Helpful	−.04	1.68	−.03	−.02	1.82	1.89	2.60		
8. Intelligent	.18	.43	.37	.32	.51	.53	.61	1.91	
9. Tests Limits	.86	−.28	1.12	.73	−.07	−.07	.05	.46	2.31

TABLE 11.2 Standardized Factor Loadings After Varimax Rotation

	F_1	F_2	Uniqueness
Confused	.012	.711	.495
Considerate	.772	−.064	.399
Depressed	.028	.714	.489
Emotional	.033	.697	.513
Generous	.854	.015	.270
Hardworking	.777	−.001	.396
Helpful	.831	−.034	.308
Intelligent	.288	.180	.885
Tests Limits	.011	.475	.774
Factor Variance	1	1	

286 E. LOKEN and P. MOLENAAR

The interpretation of the factor model is that the items are reflective of two underlying dimensions, perhaps a prosocial dimension represented by *Considerate, Generous, Hardworking,* and *Helpful,* and a dimension associated with negative emotionality (i.e., the storm and stress of adolescence). A possible correlation between the two factors could also be estimated, but we consider only the orthogonal model here as this is an exercise to demonstrate the correspondence with the latent profile model.

To approach these data from a mixture perspective and consider a latent profile model, we would proceed in a different manner. We would view the population of raters as composed of a mixture falling into k subgroups, each group with its own means and variances on the nine indicators. We might successively fit larger numbers of groups (i.e., values of k) until the model appears to provide a good fit to the data.

There are a great number of issues to be considered in fitting mixtures using maximum likelihood. These include choosing good starting values, assessing convergence, navigating local maxima, and determining the best choice for k. We do not attempt to discuss these issues here. Rather, for these data we take a very naïve approach and fit successively models with $k = 1$, 2, and 3 latent profile classes. For each value of k we estimated approximately 20 models each time starting from a new set of initial values. As k increased the model fit improved considerably. There were multiple local maxima at $k = 3$ classes, so we settled on the best fitting one as selected using the information criteria measures AIC and BIC. (We stopped at $k = 3$ because, on the face of it, there was no benefit in fit to be gained by adding a 4th class—see below for more involved discussion.)

The results of a latent profile analysis like this one would often be represented with a graph of the conditional means, as seen in Figure 11.1. This graph is a nice way to represent visually the profiles and allows for convenient interpretation. In this case, we see that one group is especially low on the variables *Considerate, Generous, Hardworking,* and *Helpful;* another group is high on those variables; and one group has average scores on all the variables. The interpretation of such a model is that there are three kinds of raters, some who view adolescents as prosocial, some who view them as not prosocial, and some who do not rate them high or low one way or the other.

So far, the two approaches seem to have very little in common. Two very different models were estimated using different estimation techniques, and in the way the factor and latent profile models were reported, there is little apparent overlap. However, if we take a step back and consider framing the latent profile results slightly differently, we should recognize something familiar. The first factor in the factor analysis was the prosocial factor. Another way to think about the three latent profile groups is to view them as three points on the first latent dimension (low, medium, and high). This is

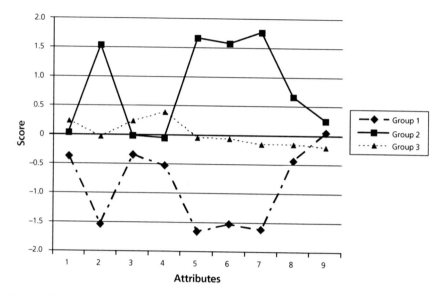

Figure 11.1 Conditional means for 3-group latent profile model.

not necessarily obvious when looking at the profiles in Figure 11.1, but it becomes much more so if we present the mixture results in a table format more similar to the way factor analysis results are presented.

In Table 11.3, the conditional means are presented in a matrix parallel to factor loadings. If they were factor loadings from a covariance analysis, we would interpret the first column as a factor parallel to (but pointing in an opposite direction as) the second factor, and the third factor as one with essentially no loadings at all. In short, this looks suspiciously like a one-factor solution.

Indeed, if we were to carry out a one-factor model, the pooled within-group variance from the latent profile analysis is similar to the pattern of uniqueness seen when a one-factor model is applied to the observed covariance matrix. A one-factor model has high loadings on the four prosocial variables, and very small loadings on the others. Therefore, the one-factor model has large communalities for the four prosocial variables, and large error variances for the others. Now, reconsider Table 11.3. Viewing the sums of the squared conditional means as "communal variance," or variance explained by the group structure, we see that for the four prosocial variables the communality is large. Conversely, for the other five variables, the sum of the squared conditional means is very small, and the largest proportion of variance falls in the pooled within-group error. The best fitting three-class model has an implied covariance structure that is very similar to that implied by the one-factor model. Recognizing this, it becomes clear that

TABLE 11.3 Latent Profile Means, Variances, and Group Probabilities

	Group 1	Group 2	Group 3	Pooled within variance
Confused	−.37	.02	.23	2.91
Considerate	−1.54	1.53	−.04	1.46
Depressed	−.34	−.02	.23	4.48
Emotional	−.53	−.06	.39	2.23
Generous	−1.66	1.66	−.05	1.07
Hardworking	−1.53	1.56	−.06	1.48
Helpful	−1.61	1.76	−.16	.96
Intelligent	−.43	.65	−.16	1.71
Tests Limits	.05	.25	−.21	2.26
Group Probabilities	.28	.29	.43	

the three-group mixture can be viewed as representing three "cut-points" on the first extracted latent factor. This is the kind of interpretive flexibility that we think researchers should find profitable when recognizing the similarities between models positing categorical and continuous underlying variables.

IMPLICATIONS FOR THE SIMILARITIES BETWEEN FACTOR AND MIXTURE MODELS

We divide our discussion of the implications into two main sections. First, we discuss implications of what has been shown so far for improving our understanding of mixture and factor models and for getting good estimates. Second, we discuss the significance of the fact that factor solutions fitting variance-covariance matrices are only identified up to a rotation of the factor loadings. If there is a correspondence between the factor and mixture models, is it also the case that mixture solutions are only identified up to a rotation of the conditional means? This idea has previously been discussed by Molenaar and von Eye (1994).

First we must emphasize that just because a k factor model can be rewritten as an equivalent mixture model (up to first- and second-order moments), it does not follow that the model with optimal fit as a mixture is also the model with optimal fit as a factor model. Consider the adolescent ratings discussed above. Although the mixture model can be written as in Table 11.3 to highlight the implied variance-covariance matrix, the maximum likelihood solution for the three-group mixture is not identical to the solution to the two-factor model. In fact, when the estimates from the mixture model are entered as hard constraints into an SEM program to force a three-factor model, the fit is poor. On the other hand, the unrestricted two-factor solution provides an excellent maximum likelihood fit to the variance-covariance matrix.

The reason for this is of course that the mixture model likelihood (Equation 11.3) is not the same as the likelihood for the factor model (Equation 11.1). The mixture model is not expressly trying to optimize the fit of the first- and second-order moments; in this example, the maximum likelihood three-class solution does not even provide a good fit to the variance-covariance matrix. So the general point is not that mixture models and factor models are identical—it is that a given factor model can be rewritten as a mixture model that implies identical first- and second-order moments (and vice versa). However, the optimal $k - 1$ factor model that maximizes the fit to the observed variance-covariance matrix is not necessarily identical to the optimal k group mixture that maximizes the mixture likelihood.

We think that there are more lessons to be learned from the correspondence of the models. Interesting insights can assist with estimating and interpreting the models. For example, it is not uncommon in the mixture model literature to see solutions where the number of classes k is actually quite close to the number of observed variables p. It would not be surprising to see, for example, seven or more groups estimated on the basis of nine observed variables like those in our example. However, realizing that this seven-group mixture can be recast as a six-factor model with identical fit to the variance-covariance matrix, immediately makes a very important point clear: a six-factor model, without further constraints, is not identified with only nine observed variables. Mixture models of increasing complexity and size can be estimated without concerns about running out of degrees of freedom, so it is easy to miss the fact that the "equivalent" factor model is over-saturated with infinite solutions to fitting the second-order moments. The implication is that, especially as the size of mixture models increase (in terms of the number of groups and estimated parameters), the model fit must be heavily determined by the higher order moments of the data. We find that this fact is not transparent to the user of mixture model software, and that it certainly gives us pause for reflection.

There is another very practical lesson to be learned from fully appreciating the mixture-factor correspondence. Just as we showed that representing final estimates of the mixture solution in a certain format can make it very easy to appreciate the correspondence to a factor model, we can also use the best fitting factor model to facilitate fitting the mixture. A very difficult task in estimating mixtures is to explore the likelihood sufficiently in order to be confident that a global maximum has been achieved. When fitting a three-class mixture to the adolescent ratings we found many different local maxima after starting the algorithm from a variety of locations. We chose our starting values at "random," but this is a risky thing to do in such a large parameter space. Researchers ultimately want a set of reasonable starting values to probe for the global solution in the likelihood. But randomly choosing starting values is at best a hit and miss procedure, and at worst extremely wasteful because many of the randomly chosen starting points lie in poor or inadmissible regions of the solution space so the algorithm diverges. Thinking about the variance-covariance matrix, it is easy to see how randomly chosen starting values for the mixture model could imply negative estimates for the within-group variance. If the start values for the means are chosen to imply greater between-group variance than the marginal variance for that variable, then this would create a negative variance estimate for the error if a factor model were estimated. When carrying out a factor analysis it would be foolish to choose an initial communality greater than the observed variance of the variable; however, with purely random starting values for the conditional group means of a mixture model it is possible to do exactly this.

But even supposing that a researcher is fully aware of the connection between the implied first- and second-order moments due to the start values, and makes sure to have some constraints in generating random initial estimates so as not to start in dead end regions of the parameter space, there is still very little guidance in the mixture model world as to what might constitute good starting values that are likely to lead to an optimal solution. When we analyzed the three-group mixture above, we encountered multiple local maxima when initiating EM from a variety of randomly chosen start values. This is often an indication that the mixture solution is being pushed "too far," perhaps analogous to fitting too many factors to a dataset and getting unstable solutions difficult to reproduce using different estimation methods. We made a few half-hearted attempts to fit a four-group latent profile model, but once again saw multiple maxima, and no immediate indication that a large improvement in fit over the three-class model was possible.

However, upon realizing that the best fitting three-group solution provided a poor fit to the variance-covariance structure, and seeing that it really represented three points along the one-factor model, we saw what would be an obvious choice for new start values. Given that the two-factor model provides superior fit over the one-factor model, a natural choice for starting values for a four-group mixture would be to place four groups "high" and "low" on the two-factor solution. So we started a single run of EM with mean profiles under the four possible combinations of "high" and "low" on the two factors as given in Table 11.2. The solution converged very quickly, yielding a four-group model of clearly superior fit to the best three-class model found previously. The drop in deviance, as measured by $-2LogL$, was 224 with 19 degrees of freedom. Both the AIC (6,373 vs. 6,189) and BIC (6,556 vs. 6,431) clearly favored the new four-class solution.

We believe that the above result is a very significant one for mixture model estimation. Searching for an optimal solution in high dimensional space can be a difficult procedure that is often carried out in an *ad hoc* manner. Indeed, our own *ad hoc* runs with random starting values led us to many distinct local three-group solutions, and even more in the four-group case. Without seeing much benefit to pushing the analysis to four groups, we were willing to settle for the best three-group solution that we found. However, with a single run starting with conditional means placed along the dimensions defined by the factor model that optimizes the fit to the variance-covariance matrix we immediately landed on a vastly superior solution. It was from realizing that our mixture model failed to provide a good fit to the variance-covariance matrix that we first came to doubt the three-class solution, and it was by bringing our start values into line with the best factor model that we found the best fitting mixture. We think that researchers using mixture models would be well served to be aware of the variance-covariance structure implied by their choice of start values and by their final solutions, and to use this correspondence to greatly improve their chances of finding better fitting parameter estimates.

ROTATIONAL INDETERMINACY

We now take up an interesting question raised by Molenaar and von Eye (1994) after they explored the correspondence between mixture and factor models. It is well-known that any orthogonal factor solution is only determined up to an orthogonal rotation of the factors. Is it therefore also possible to "rotate" a mixture model solution and find sets of loadings that yield equivalent implied variance-covariance matrices?

Molenaar and von Eye (1994) showed that this was indeed possible. Starting with the equation for the implied matrix, they devised a method to generate new sets of class probabilities and conditional group means that would yield the same marginal means and implied covariances. The transformation is not exactly the same as the standard rotation of an orthogonal factor model. The trick is to preserve the factor variance matrix as diagonal with trace equal to 1. We can begin by taking an orthonormal transformation matrix $\mathbf{T}$. As a first step, define $\Omega^{1/2}$ as a diagonal matrix where the ith element of the diagonal is equal to the square root of the diagonal of Φ multiplied by the ith column of $\mathbf{T}$ (recall that Φ contains the factor variances when Equation 11.1 arises from a factor model, and group probabilities in the reframing of the mixture model). In short, Ω now represents a newly transformed matrix of group probabilities—it is diagonal with trace = 1. The reproduced covariance matrix can now be written as:

$$\Sigma = \mathbf{A}\Phi^{1/2}\mathbf{T}\Omega^{-1/2}\Omega\Omega^{-1/2}\mathbf{T}^{\mathsf{T}}\Phi^{1/2}\mathbf{A}^{\mathsf{T}}. \tag{11.8}$$

It is clear that if $\mathbf{B} = \mathbf{A}\Phi^{1/2}\mathbf{T}\Omega^{-1/2}$, the equation has the form $\mathbf{B}\Omega\mathbf{B}^{\mathsf{T}}$; that is, a new set of conditional means and group probabilities has been found to imply the same variance-covariance structure. The algorithm presented by Molenaar and von Eye (1994) generates an infinite number of mixture solutions that provide identical fit to the variance-covariance matrix as $\mathbf{T}$ can be any orthonormal transformation matrix.

But to argue that mixture model solutions are in general not unique is to overinterpret the above result. Bartholomew and Knott (1999) mentioned the work of Molenaar and von Eye and stated that "this means that any set of latent classes we identify by a latent class solution is not unique"(p. 155). While it is true that a mixture model solution that matches a specific factor model structure is not unique with regard to the implied variance-covariance matrix, it is not the case that the infinite set of such solutions provide similar fit to the mixture model likelihood, which is, after all, the relevant metric.

To illustrate, we take the three-group solution from Table 11.3 of the adolescent rating data example. An infinite number of three-group solutions with equal implied variance-covariance matrices can be generated by applying the algorithm in Equation 11.8. However, while all those solutions provide equal fit to the factor likelihood, the solution in Table 11.3 stands as the optimal solution for maximizing the mixture likelihood. A good example of why the rotated solutions do not provide equivalent fit can be seen by examining a rotated solution given in Table 11.4.

Although the solution in Table 11.4 implies the same covariance structure as the solution in Table 11.3, and is therefore in some sense similar, it is obvious that it does not fit the data equally well. Group one, with estimated marginal probability of .01, contains very low means on the prosocial variables. The prosocial means are in fact all below −10 which is not even possible given that the responses were on a 10 point scale centered at the mean. It is theoretically possible to reproduce the marginal means by incorporating a class with .01 weight outside the parameter space, and similarly to approximate marginal variance of the variable. But clearly there is no sense in fitting a model to the data that posits a class with size .01 in a region where there exists no data. Understandably, the fit to the mixture model likelihood of the solution in Table 11.4 is vastly inferior to the fit of the solution in Table 11.3. Therefore, it is more appropriate to say that the latent class solutions are not unique with respect to covariance structure rather than to say that the solutions *per se* are not unique.

TABLE 11.4   Latent Profile Solution After "Rotation" of First Two Columns

	Group 1	Group 2	Group 3	Pooled within variance
Confused	−1.47	−.14	.23	2.91
Considerate	−10.39	.25	−.04	1.46
Depressed	−1.25	−.15	.23	4.48
Emotional	−1.87	−.25	.39	2.23
Generous	−11.22	.28	−.05	1.07
Hardworking	−10.44	.27	−.06	1.48
Helpful	−11.28	.37	−.16	.96
Intelligent	−3.53	.20	−.16	1.71
Tests Limits	−.51	.17	−.21	2.26
Group Probabilities	.01	.56	.43	

SUMMARY

Despite a number of apparent differences in analysis and interpretation, and despite a long history of debate about types versus dimensions in psychology, it is worth remembering that factor models and mixture models are just two forms of latent variable models. In one the latent variable is considered continuous, and in the other categorical. As both models are intended to fit real-world data, it is relevant in both circumstances to investigate the model's implied variance–covariance structure. As has been shown before (Bartholomew, 1987; McDonald, 1967, 2003; Molenaar & von Eye, 1994), a k-group mixture (or latent profile) model can be redescribed as factor model with $k − 1$ factors that is identical up to first- and second-order moments.

In this chapter we have given an illustrative example, and in particular shown how to represent the model parameters to emphasize the correspondence. By placing the conditional means in a matrix similar to a factor loading matrix, and aggregating the pooled within-group variance, we represented the mixture model in a way that highlights the between and within decomposition of the variance. With means posing as factor loadings, within-group error posing as uniquenesses, and group probabilities posing as factor variances, the familiar equation of factor analysis $\Sigma = \Lambda\Phi\Lambda^T + \Theta$ also yields the reproduced covariance matrix for the mixture model.

We believe that rewriting the mixture model to look like a factor model is a valuable exercise, one that should be undertaken regularly to evaluate new solutions. The purpose is to recognize immediately what the corresponding factor model is. As we saw with the adolescent data, a three-group mixture that was accepted by us as probably the best fit turned out to correspond only to a one-factor model. From factor analyzing the data it was known that at least a two-factor model was needed. The implication was that a four-class model with greater correspondence to the two-factor solution would have to have better overall fit.

The point is not that factor and mixture models are fully interchangeable. They are not. The maximum likelihood solution for a mixture model is unlikely to provide optimal fit to the variance–covariance matrix. And likewise, the maximum likelihood estimates for a factor model, when rewritten as a mixture, are unlikely to provide optimal fit to the mixture model likelihood. However, even though there is no direct mapping between the optimal mixture and factor models for a given set of data, there is a general correspondence among the better and worse fitting solutions within each type. The correspondence is rooted in the fact that both models are explaining the same variance in a given set of data, even if they posit a different underlying structure.

One very real benefit in appreciating the factor-mixture correspondence is in efficient estimation of mixtures. Although degrees of freedom are rarely an issue in estimating mixtures, it is very helpful to remember that in fitting mixtures with too many classes, the equivalent factor model may be hugely overdetermined. If so, the researcher does not simply face the problem of rotational indeterminacy, he or she may also face the problem of severe multimodality.

Random start values are popular in mixture modeling (e.g., Bauer & Curran, 2003), but a simple check can determine if the initial values are even permissible. If the start values imply a covariance structure that would require negative pooled within-groups variance in order for the communality of the variable not to exceed 1, it is quite possible the mixture estimation algorithm will fail to converge. Start values are also important in finding optimal solutions, as shown when it took just one run of the EM algorithm, starting from a strategically chosen set of start values based on the two-factor model, to find a vastly superior fitting four class solution.

One interesting area for future work will be investigating the possibility to estimate mixtures using standard SEM software. The best fitting factor model lends an initial insight, but as Molennar and von Eye (1994) pointed out, the conditional variances are only identified up to the pooled within-group variation. Furthermore, there is the problem of rotational indeterminacy, the need for nonlinear constraints, and the need to incorporate information regarding higher order moments. Even if getting at the final estimates for a mixture model using standard SEM approaches proves too difficult, however, it is nevertheless clear that such efforts can help improve current methods for solving mixtures.

NOTE

1. This material is based upon work supported by the National Science Foundation under Grant No. 0352191.

REFERENCES

Aitkin, M., Anderson, D., & Hinde, J. (1981). Statistical modeling of teacher styles. *Journal of the Royal Statistical Society A, 144,* 419–461.

Bartholomew, D. J. (1987). *Latent variable models and factor analysis.* London: Griffin.

Bartholomew, D. J., & Knott, M. (1999). *Latent variable models and factor analysis.* New York: Oxford University Press.

Bauer, D. J., & Curran, P. J. (2003). Distributional assumptions of growth mixture models: Implications for over-extraction of latent trajectory classes. *Psychological Methods, 8,* 338–363.

Bem, S. (1974). The measurement analysis of psychological androgyny. *Journal of Consulting and Clinical Psychology, 42,* 155–162.

Buchanan, C. M. & Holmbeck, G. M. (1998). Measuring beliefs about adolescent personality and behavior. *Journal of Youth and Adolescence, 27,* 607–627.

Bulik, C. M., Sullivan, P. F., & Kendler, K. S. (2000). An empirical study of classification of eating disorders. *American Journal of Psychiatry 157,* 886–895.

Dempster, A. P., Laird, N. M., & Rubin, D. B. (1977). Maximum likelihood from incomplete data via the EM algorithm (with discussion). *Journal of the Royal Statistical Society B, 39,* 349–374.

Dunne, M. P., Bailey, M. J., Kirk, K. M., & Martin, N. G. (2000). The subtlety of sex-atypicality. *Archives of Sexual Behavior, 29,* 549–565.

Ford, E. S. (2003). Factor analysis and defining the metabolic syndrome. *Ethnicity and Disease, 13,* 429–437.

Ford, E. S, Giles, W. H., & Dietz, W. H. (2002). Prevalence of the metabolic syndrome among US adults: findings from the third National Health and Nutrition Examination Survey. *Journal of the American Medical Association, 287,* 356–359.

Fossati, A., Maffei, C., Bagnato, M., Donati, D., Namia, C., & Novella, L. (1999). Latent structure analysis of DSM-IV borderline personality disorder criteria. *Comprehensive Psychiatry, 40,* 72–79.

Hosmer, D. W. (1973). A comparison of iterative maximum-likelihood estimates of the parameters of a mixture of two normal distributions under three different types of sample. *Biometrics, 29,* 761–770.

Hudziak, J. J., Heath, A. C., Madden, P. F., Reich, W., Bucholz, K. K., Slutske, W., et al. (1998). Latent class and factor analysis of DSM-IV ADHD: A twin study of female adolescents. *Journal of the American Academy of Child and Adolescent Psychiatry, 37,* 848–857.

Hudziak, J. J., Wadsworth, M. E., Heath, A. C., & Achenbach, T. M. (1999). Latent class analysis of child behavior checklist attention problems. *Journal of the American Academy of Child and Adolescent Psychiatry, 38,* 985–991.

Jedidi, K., Jagpal, H. S., & DeSarbo, W. (1997). Finite-mixture structural equation models for response-based segmentation and unobserved heterogeneity. *Marketing Science, 16,* 39–59.

Kagan, J. (1994). *Galen's prophecy.* New York: Basic Books.

Kagan, J. (1998). The biology of the child. In W. Damon (Series Ed.) & N. Eisenberg (Vol. Ed), *Handbook of child psychology: Vol. 3. Social, emotional, and personality development* (5th ed., pp. 177–235). New York: Wiley Press.

Kagan, J., Reznick, J. S., & Snidman, N. (1988). Biological bases of childhood shyness. *Science, 240,* 167–171.

Kagan, J., Snidman, N., & Arcus, D. (1998). Childhood derivatives of high and low reactivity in infancy. *Child Development, 69,* 1483–1493.

Kendler, K. S., Karkowski-Shuman, L., O'Neill, F. A., Straub, R. E., MacLean, C. J., & Walsh, D. (1997). Resemblance of psychotic symptoms and syndromes in affected sibling pairs from the Irish Study of High-Density Schizophrenia Families: Evidence for possible etiologic heterogeneity. *American Journal of Psychiatry, 154,* 191–198.

Kessler, R. C., Stein, M. B., & Berglund, P. (1998). Social phobia subtypes in the National Comorbidity Survey. *American Journal of Psychiatry, 155,* 613–619.

Lenzenweger, M. (2006). Schizotaxia, schizotypy, and schizophrenia: Paul E. Meehl's blueprint for the experimental psychopathology and genetics of schizophrenia. *Journal of Abnormal Psychology, 115,* 195–200.

Loken, E. (2004). Using latent class analysis to model temperament types. *Multivariate Behavioral Research, 39,* 625–652.

Lubke, G. H., & Muthén, B. O. (2005). Investigating factor mixture models. *Psychological Methods, 10,* 21–39.

Madden, P. A., Buucholz, K. K., Dinwiddie, S. H., Slutske, W. S., Bierut, L. J., Statham, D. J., Dunn, M. P., Martin, N. G., & Heath, A. C. (1997). Nicotine withdrawal in women. *Addiction, 92,* 889–902.

McDonald, R.P. (1967). Nonlinear factor analysis. *Psychometric Monographs No 15.*

McDonald, R. P. (2003). A review of multivariate taxometric procedures. *Journal of Educational and Behavioral Statistics, 28,* 77–81.

McLachlan, G. J., & Peel, D. (2000). *Finite mixture models.* New York: Wiley.

McLachlan, G. J., Peel, D., & Bean, R. W. (2003). Modelling high-dimensional data by mixtures of factor analyzers. *Computational Statistics 7 Data Analysis, 41,* 379–388.

Meehl, P. E. (1992). Factors and taxa, traits and types, differences of degree and differences of kind. *Journal of Personality, 60,* 117–174.

Molenaar, P. C. M., & Von Eye, A. (1994). On the arbitrary nature of latent variables. In A. Von Eye & C. C. Clogg (Eds.), *Latent variables analysis* (pp. 226–242). Thousand Oaks, CA: Sage.

Muthén, B. (2001). Latent variable mixture modeling. In G. A. Marcoulides & R. E. Schumacker (Eds.), *New developments and techniques in structural equation modeling* (pp. 1-33). Mahwah, NJ: Erlbaum.

Muthén, B., & Muthén, L. (1999). Integrating person-centered and variable-centered analysis: Growth mixture modeling with latent trajectory classes. *Alcoholism: Clinical and Experimental Research, 24,* 882–891.

Pladevall, M., Singal, B., Williams, L. K., Brotons, C., Guyer, H., Sadurni, J., et al. (2006). A single factor underlies the metabolic syndrome: A confirmatory factor analysis. *Diabetes Care, 29,* 113–122.

Richardson, S., & Green, P. J. (1997). On Bayesian analysis of mixtures with an unknown number of components. *Journal of Royal Statistical Society Series B, 59,* 731–792.

Stern, H. S., Arcus, D., Kagan, J., Rubin, D. B., & Snidman, N. (1994). Statistical choices in temperament research. *Behaviormetrika, 21,* 1–17.

Stern, H. S., Arcus, D., Kagan, J., Rubin, D. B., & Snidman, N. (1995). Using mixture models in temperament research. *International Journal of Behavioral Development, 18,* 407–423.

Sullivan, P. F., Kessler, R. C. & Kendler, K. S. (1998). Latent class analysis of lifetime depressive symptoms in the National Comorbidity Survey. *American Journal of Psychiatry, 155,* 1398–1406.

Ventura, A. K., Loken, E., & Birch, L. L. (2006). Risk profiles for metabolic syndrome in a nonclinical sample of adolescent girls. *Pediatrics, 118,* 2434–2442.

Waller, N. G., & Meehl, P. E. (1998). *Multivariate taxometric procedures: Distinguishing types from continua.* Thousand Oaks, CA: Sage.

CHAPTER 12

APPLICATIONS AND EXTENSIONS OF THE TWO-POINT MIXTURE INDEX OF MODEL FIT

C. Mitchell Dayton
University of Maryland, College Park

A primary focus of statistical analysis is on selecting an appropriate model for data. In most cases, this involves significance tests, confidence intervals, information measures, posterior odds ratios and/or similar procedures that, in one sense or another, are aimed at providing a basis for selecting a "best" approximating model. Given that a model (or, set of models) has been selected, it is of interest to consider whether or not that model is "reasonable." For example, based on information measures such as the Akaike Information Criterion (AIC) or Bayesian Information Criterion (BIC), a mixture of two Poisson processes may provide better fit to a set of observed frequencies than does a single Poisson process. Although this may be of interest to a researcher from a theoretical perspective, it does not convey any sense of the reasonableness, from a descriptive perspective, of the two-component mixture. For reasons such as this, the field of applied statistics has always offered the researcher a variety of descriptive measures under rubrics such as correlation coefficients, measures of association, strength-of-effect indices, and the like.

Advances in Latent Variable Mixture Models, pages 299–316
Copyright © 2008 by Information Age Publishing
299

Rudas, Clogg, and Lindsay (RCL; 1994) proposed a new and novel measure of model fit that is based directly on the theory of mixture models. Although not founded on conventional notions of strength of association, their two-point mixture index of fit has wide applicability for evaluating the fit of models for frequency data with potential extensions to broader classes of models. In simplest terms, the RCL index, known as π^*, is the minimum proportion of cases that must be removed from a data set so that a theoretical model of interest *fits the frequency data perfectly*. Thus, the population is conceptualized as a mixture of two components—one component that is consistent with the theoretical model of interest and one component that is "outside the model." It should be noted that the model of interest can be any theoretical model for frequency data including conventional and mixture item-response models, latent class models, and so forth. Some additional papers by the developers of this index include Clogg, Rudas, and Xi (1995), Rudas and Zwick (1997), Rudas (1999) and Rudas (2002).

There are very few historical antecedents for the RCL index other than the intrinsically unscalable latent class model proposed by Goodman (1975) in the context of Guttman scaling of attitude items. A Guttman scale with three Yes/No items, for example, might comprise the permissible patterns {No, No, No}, {Yes, No, No}, {Yes, Yes, No}, and {Yes, Yes, Yes}. Goodman's model posits two components in the population: a scalable component in which responses conform exactly to the Guttman scale and an unscalable component in which responses to the attitude items are random and independent. A distinct feature of this model is that scalable respondents display error-free responses and, as a result, impermissible Guttman response patterns such as {No, Yes, No} or {No, No, Yes} arise entirely from the unscalable class. Dayton & Macready, 1980, proposed a related model with response errors for scalable respondents.

In the remainder of this chapter, I summarize the theory behind the RCL index, apply the index to a variety of conventional applications such as latent trait and latent class analysis, and then consider extensions that have promise when continuous variables, rather than discrete variables, are of interest. This extension to continuous variables is an original contribution to this currently active area of research.

THEORETICAL BACKGROUND OF π^*

Let P be the true probability distribution for the proportions of cases in cells representing discrete frequency data. Assume that a theoretical model, H, specifies expected proportions for these cells. The two-point mixture model proposed by RCL can be represented as:

$$P = (1-\pi)\Phi + \pi\Psi \tag{12.1}$$

where Φ is the probability distribution specified by model H, and Ψ is an arbitrary, unspecified probability distribution. The mixing parameter, $0 \le \pi \le 1$, represents the proportion of the population that is not consistent with, or is not explained by, the model, H. Thus, the RCL conceptualization is that the population is divided into two components, one of which exactly conforms to the theoretical model, H, and one that represents the remainder of the population. In fact, Equation 12.1 is true for any model and for any frequency data. However, the RCL index of fit, π^*, is the *minimum* value of π for which Equation 12.1 is true. That is:

$$\pi^* = \inf\left\{\pi \mid P = (1-\pi)\Phi + \pi\Psi, \Phi \in H\right\} \tag{12.2}$$

Thus, π^* can be interpreted as representing the minimum proportion of cases that the researcher must omit in order to provide perfect fit for the model, H, to the remaining cases. RCL proved the following properties for π^*:

1. π^* is unique; that is, for a given frequency table, there is one-and-only-one value that satisfies Equation 12.2;
2. π^* is defined on the $(0,1)$ interval; this contrasts with several other measures that have been presented for contingency tables where the range of the measure depends upon the marginal frequencies in the table;
3. for nested models, π^* decreases in magnitude for increasingly complex models; while this property is not unique to π^*, it does mean that nested models can be directly compared;
4. π^* is invariant to multiplicative transformation of the frequencies (e.g., doubling all frequencies in a cross-tabulation).

This latter property is especially interesting because it means that π^* is invariant to changes in sample size, although, of course, the sampling variance of estimates of π^* becomes smaller as sample size increases.

It should be noted that π^* stands in contrast to familiar goodness-of-fit procedures based on observed and expected frequencies such as the Pearson chi-square statistic. For these measures, the sums of observed and expected frequencies are constrained to be equal and expected proportions may be larger than, equal to, or smaller than observed proportions. In contrast, both components of Equation 12.1 are non-negative and, thus, the component associated with the hypothesis, H, cannot exceed the true proportion.

As is true for most descriptive measures of model fit or association, there is no absolute standard for an "acceptable" level of fit across different situations. RCL remarked that 10% (i.e., $\pi^* = .10$) is reasonable in the context of a specific 4×4 contingency table. However, one should note that 10% for the first example they present is only about 59 respondents but, for their second example, it is about 2,526 respondents. My own experience with this index for a variety of frequency models suggests that 5% to 10% (i.e., $\pi^* = .05$ to .10) is a reasonable range of values for models representing acceptable fit.

ESTIMATION OF π^*

Estimation of π^* involves simultaneously estimating the parameters associated with the model, H, as well as the mixing parameter itself. Except for the simplest cases (e.g., a 2×2 contingency table of frequencies; see below) there is no closed-form expression for the estimate of π^* and, in fact, conventional iterative computational procedures do not apply. A method suggested by RCL entails a guided search that, at each step, sets the value of π^* at a constant and derives maximum likelihood (ML) estimates of the parameters in the components of Equation 12.1 using an expectation-maximization (EM) algorithm. Because π^* is treated as known, the process simplifies to maximizing the likelihood based on the components of the model. For a frequency model, maximum likelihood estimation is equivalent to minimizing the value of the likelihood ratio chi-square goodness-of-fit statistic, G^2. The estimation process starts with a small value (e.g., .005) for π^*, derives ML estimates for the components of the model and, then, increments π^* by a small constant (e.g., .005) with re-estimation for the model H at each step. At some step (and beyond), the value of G^2 becomes 0 (nearly) and this can be taken as the final estimate of the fit index, $\hat{\pi}^*$. Specific computational details for this approach are provided by RCL, and a FORTRAN program, Mixit, is available (Xi, 1994) for $R \times C$ contingency tables.

An alternate approach to estimating π^* is based on nonlinear programming (NLP) techniques as described by Xi (1994). Additional details of the NLP approach, including technical details and numerical issues related to NLP, were presented by Xi and Lindsay (1996). Also, Dayton (2003) presented examples based on NLP where the computations were done using Microsoft Excel. The Excel function, SOLVER, is a readily available optimization routine that implements the so-called GRG2 code originally developed by Lasdon, Waren, Jain, and Ratner (1978). For non-linear problems, this routine uses finite-differences for repeated computation of the Jacobian (first-derivative) matrix for the objective function and constraints with respect to the unknown parameters in the model. For the purpose of estimating π^*, the objective function that is minimized (actually convergent to 0) is G^2 and the constraints include setting the upper limits on expected frequencies equal to observed frequencies as well as any needed restrictions on the parameters of the model in H (e.g., non-negativity restrictions). The practical advantages of using NLP include the fact these routines are readily available in spreadsheet programs and mathematical programming languages such SAS IML, Matlab and Gauss. Also, convergence is more rapid than for the EM algorithm and complex programming can, in general, be avoided given that only the model *per se* need be specified. However, the limitations of computations based on NLP include the fact that, for complex models, convergence to a local optimum may occur and, as is also true for the EM algorithm, solutions can be found for models that have no unique solution (i.e., for non-identified models). This latter problem occurs because these algorithms may impose implicit constraints on the solution that are not necessarily obvious to the analyst.

For the special case of independence models for 2×2 contingency tables, RCL provided the following simple estimates for π^* and for the expected frequencies associated with π^*. Let the observed cell frequencies for the cross-tabulation of variables A and B, be represented as *a*, *b*, *c* and *d* with total sample size equal to n:

	B1	B2
A1	*a*	*b*
A2	*c*	*d*

Then, assuming $ad > bc$, the estimate is

$$\hat{\pi}^* = \frac{ad - bc}{an}$$

with the expected cell frequencies given respectively by the following functions of the observed frequencies: $\{a, b, c, bc/a\}$.

For an independence model in a two-way (or, higher-order) contingency table, the existence of 0 observed frequencies in one or more cells requires that a corresponding row (or, column) estimated proportion be equal to 0. In consequence, the expected frequencies are equal to 0 for the entire row (or, column) of the table. Among the approaches to avoiding this undesirable result are: (a) replace 0 cell frequencies with small, flattening values (e.g., .1 or .5); or, (b) treat the 0 as a structural 0 and explicitly model the structure. At present, little is known about how these options affect the estimation and properties of π^*. However, ignoring 0 observed frequencies can be expected to result in overestimation of π^*. In practice, a range of flattening constants, say from .1 to 1.0, can be used in separate solutions to assess their impact on the estimated value of π^*.

CONFIDENCE INTERVAL FOR $\hat{\pi}^*$

RCL presented a method for estimating a lower confidence bound for π^*. In general, $\hat{\pi}^*$ can be expected to overestimate its true value of π^* (i.e., to be positively biased) because $\hat{\pi}^*$ cannot be negative. Furthermore, all values of $\hat{\pi}$ greater than $\hat{\pi}^*$ are associated with models providing perfect fit to the frequency data. Following the logic presented by RCL, a 95% lower bound, $\hat{\pi}_L^*$, can be computed by locating the value of π^* that results when the likelihood-ratio G^2 fit statistic is equal to the 90th percentile point of a central chi-square distribution with one degree of freedom. In particular, this value is 2.70, which is equal to the square of the 95th percentage point of the unit normal distribution, 1.645. For two-way tables, the program Mixit calculates $\hat{\pi}_L^*$ by the same iterative procedure used to determine $\hat{\pi}^*$. Clogg, Rudas, and Xi (1995) suggested that the effect of sample size on the estimator, $\hat{\pi}^*$ is indicated by the width of the confidence interval, $\hat{\pi}_L^* - \hat{\pi}^*$.

For applications involving frequency tables more general than two-way tables, the standard error for $\hat{\pi}^*$ can be estimated using the jackknife as demonstrated by Dayton (2003). In this context, the jackknife is a "leave-out-one" technique that requires J re-estimations for a J-cell frequency table. For the J-cell table, let the frequencies be n_j with total sample size equal to n. The general computational procedure for the jackknife is: a) for the jth cell, with observed frequency, n_j, reduce the cell frequency to $n_j - 1$; b) compute the estimate, $\hat{\pi}_j^*$, from the data with the reduced cell frequency using any appropriate computational approach; c) repeat the above step for each cell of the frequency table; d) weight the J estimates by corresponding cell frequencies; and, e) compute the estimated standard error:

$$S_J = \sqrt{\left(\frac{n-1}{n}\right)\sum_{j=1}^{J} n_j (\hat{\pi}_j^* - \hat{\pi}^*)^2}$$

where $\hat{\pi}^*$ is the estimate based on the complete frequency table. A one-sided, lower confidence bound can then be calculated in the usual manner, that is, $\hat{\pi}^* - Z_{1-\alpha} S_J$ (see Dayton, 2003, for additional computational details and Lohr, 1999, for a fuller discussion of the jackknife).

EXAMPLES WITH FREQUENCY DATA

General Social Survey (GSS) Sibling Data

The public files for the GSS contain responses to an item indicating the number of siblings reported by respondents. The frequency distribution for a sample of 1,505 respondents is summarized in Table 12.1 with a plot presented in Figure 12.1. The appearance of the plot, combined with the fact the responses are counts, suggest fitting a Poisson distribution of the form

$$P(y) = \frac{\lambda^y \cdot e^{-\lambda}}{y!} \ .$$

TABLE 12.1   GSS Number of Siblings Distribution

# Sibs	Count	Proportion
0	74	.049
1	235	.156
2	276	.183
3	237	.157
4	209	.139
5	118	.078
6	80	.053
7	81	.054
8	58	.039
9	47	.031
10	34	.023
11	22	.015
12	11	.007
13	9	.006
14	5	.003
15	3	.002
16	1	.001
17	2	.001
18	1	.001
19	0	.000
20	0	.000
21	1	.001
22	0	.000
23	0	.000
24	0	.000
25	0	.000
26	1	.001
Total	1,505	1.000

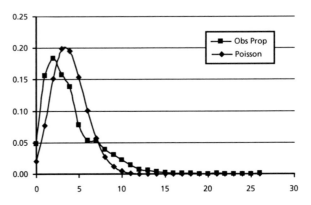

Figure 12.1 Poisson fitted to Sibling Data.

The rate parameter, λ, has a maximum likelihood estimator equal to the mean number of siblings which, for this case, is 3.93. The fitted distribution is also shown in Figure 12.1. The apparently poor fit is confirmed by $G^2 = 586.96$ with 10 degrees of freedom (expected values were fit to a collapsed 12-cell table with combined frequencies for numbers of siblings 11 and above; this avoids small expected frequencies but has negligible impact on estimates). Computations for π^* result in the considerably lower estimated rate parameter of 2.68, based on omitting 28.4% of the observations (i.e., $\hat{\pi}^* = .284$). The original distribution, the best-fitting Poisson distribution, and the Poisson distribution associated with the $\hat{\pi}^*$ computations are shown in Figure 12.2 (note that the two fitted Poisson distributions are not directly comparable as they are based on different sample sizes). Using the jackknife, the standard error for $\hat{\pi}^*$ is estimated as .038 with lower confidence bound equal to $.284 - 1.645(.038) = .221$.

The poor fit of the single Poisson distribution (as indicated by G^2 and π^*), as well as the heavy tail of the empirical distribution, suggest that a mixture of two (or more) Poisson processes might provide a more suitable model. Figure 12.3 displays the mixture of two Poisson distributions with rate parameters estimated as 2.64 and 7.81 in a mixture of 3:1. The apparently good fit is supported by a G^2 value of 11.22 with 8 degrees of freedom (again, based on the 12-celled frequency distribution). For this mixture, only 8.1% of the cases need to be omitted to provide a model with perfect fit. The Poisson rate parameters for the mixture associated with $\hat{\pi}^*$ are 2.63 and 7.74 in the same 3:1 mixture and the lower 95% confidence bound, using a jackknife estimate as above, for $\hat{\pi}^*$ is only .019.

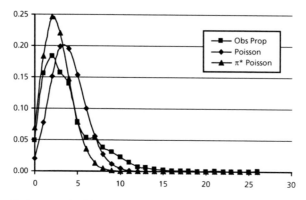

Figure 12.2   Poisson and π* Poisson fitted to Sibling Data.

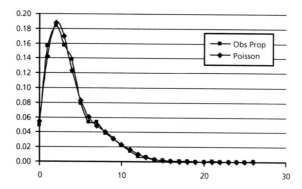

Figure 12.3   Mixture of Two Poissons fitted to Sibling Data.

Achievement Test Items

Test items that are scored on a 0/1 (incorrect/correct) basis can be represented by a large variety of psychometric models. Item response theory (IRT) encompasses many of these models. In general terms, IRT relates the probability of a correct response on a test item to an underlying, hypothetical latent variable (e.g., "ability"). This latent variable can be continuous, discrete or some relatively complex hybrid of these two types. The specific model connecting the item responses to the latent variable defines an item characteristic curve (ICC). In this section, I illustrate the use of $\hat{\pi}$ * to compare the fit of two models representing different classes of IRT. The data, shown in Table 12.2, are the first five mathematics achievement items

TABLE 12.2 Response Patterns for Five Mathematics Achievement Items

A	B	C	D	E	Frequency	Proportion
0	0	0	0	0	1,614	.123
1	0	0	0	0	594	.045
0	1	0	0	0	375	.029
1	1	0	0	0	262	.020
0	0	1	0	0	89	.007
1	0	1	0	0	109	.008
0	1	1	0	0	50	.004
1	1	1	0	0	99	.008
0	0	0	1	0	1,296	.099
1	0	0	1	0	1,132	.086
0	1	0	1	0	568	.043
1	1	0	1	0	810	.062
0	0	1	1	0	335	.026
1	0	1	1	0	662	.050
0	1	1	1	0	285	.022
1	1	1	1	0	936	.071
0	0	0	0	1	108	.008
1	0	0	0	1	86	.007
0	1	0	0	1	53	.004
1	1	0	0	1	82	.006
0	0	1	0	1	22	.002
1	0	1	0	1	52	.004
0	1	1	0	1	29	.002
1	1	1	0	1	61	.005
0	0	0	1	1	328	.025
1	0	0	1	1	387	.029
0	1	0	1	1	274	.021
1	1	0	1	1	566	.043
0	0	1	1	1	131	.010
1	0	1	1	1	389	.030
0	1	1	1	1	277	.021
1	1	1	1	1	1,066	.081
Total					13,127	1.000

that appeared on a 17-item test administered to a large sample ($n = 13,127$) of high school students. Given this extremely large sample size, virtually any IRT model fitted to the responses will show significant lack of fit using conventional procedures such as chi-square goodness-of-fit tests. Hence, it becomes of interest to see whether or not models provide reasonable representation in terms of descriptive measures.

The first model that was estimated is a three-class latent class model in which it is posited that the population is composed of subgroups of students responding correctly at different rates. Larger numbers of latent classes can be fitted but the choice of three was to allow for an interesting comparison with the Rasch model, as described below. These subgroups (classes) are unobserved (latent) and each class has a unique conditional probability for a correct response to each of the five items. That is, each latent class has a unique set of item difficulty parameters. In addition to these item difficulties, the proportions in the classes are unknown and must be simultaneously estimated (see Dayton, 1999). In common with most IRT models, a basic assumption of latent class analysis is that responses to items are independent within latent classes, that is, that local independence holds. Using notation by Goodman (1974), for five items, A through E, and T latent classes defining the latent class variable X, the probabilistic latent class model for the response $\{i, j, k, l, m\}$ to items A through E is:

$$\pi_{ijklm}^{ABCDE} = \sum_{t=1}^{T} \pi_t^X \pi_{it}^{\bar{A}X} \pi_{jt}^{\bar{B}X} \pi_{kt}^{\bar{C}X} \pi_{lt}^{\bar{D}X} \pi_{mt}^{\bar{E}X}.$$

The proportion in the tth latent class is

$$\pi_t^X \text{ with } \sum_{t=1}^{T} \pi_t^X = 1.$$

Conditional on membership in the tth latent class, the probability for the observed response $\{i, j, k, l, m\}$ to items A through E is:

$$\pi_{ijklmt}^{\overline{ABCDEX}} = \pi_{it}^{\bar{A}X} \pi_{jt}^{\bar{B}X} \pi_{kt}^{\bar{C}X} \pi_{lt}^{\bar{D}X} \pi_{mt}^{\bar{E}X}.$$

For dichotomously scored items, the item conditional probabilities may be monotonic across the latent classes in the sense that there is an ordering for the classes (say, 1, 2, 3) such that $\pi_{11}^{\bar{A}X} \geq \pi_{12}^{\bar{A}X} \geq \pi_{13}^{\bar{A}X}$, $\pi_{11}^{\bar{B}X} \geq \pi_{12}^{\bar{B}X} \geq \pi_{13}^{\bar{B}X}$, and so forth. This may occur naturally in estimating the parameters for a model or be imposed as an ordering condition during the solution. A more rigid condition for a solution is double monotonicity which, in addition to the above, requires that there is an ordering for the items (A, B, etc.) such that $\pi_{11}^{\bar{A}X} \geq \pi_{11}^{\bar{B}X} \geq \pi_{11}^{\bar{C}X} \geq \pi_{11}^{\bar{D}X} \geq \pi_{11}^{\bar{E}X}$, and so forth, for the remaining latent classes. In effect, this means that the ICCs are increasing (actually, non-decreasing) and do not intersect.

Profiles for an unrestricted three-class latent class solution for the five achievement items are shown in Figure 12.4 where it appears that monotonicity, but not double-monotonicity, holds. That is, all five sets of item conditional probabilities increase across the classes although the items are not

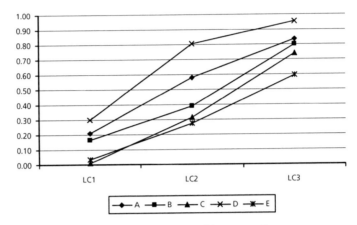

Figure 12.4 Latent Class Profiles for Math Achievement Items.

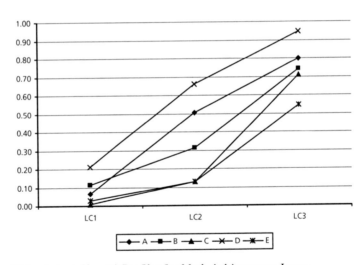

Figure 12.5 Latent Class π* Profiles for Math Achievement Items.

in uniform order (e.g., the profiles for items C and E cross; whether this is a significant departure from double-monotonicity was not investigated).

The proportions in the latent classes are estimated to be .249, .490 and .261, respectively. The value of $\hat{\pi}*$ is estimated as .0388, with the 95% lower confidence bound estimated as .0364 using the jackknife standard error. Profiles for conditional item probabilities associated with the solution for $\hat{\pi}*$ are shown in Figure 12.5 based on estimated latent class proportions of .207, .442 and .351, respectively. Although only a small proportion of cases has been omitted and the item profiles appear quite similar to the original solution, the relative proportions estimated for the latent classes have been impacted quite heavily.

In contrast to the latent class model, the Rasch model posits an underlying continuous latent variable along which both items and respondents are scaled. The model for the probability of a correct response by respondent i to item j can be written as

$$P_{ij} = \frac{e^{\theta_i - \delta_j}}{1 + e^{\theta_i - \delta_j}},$$

where θ_i is the respondent's ability parameter and δ_j is the parameter for item difficulty (or, easiness, but this is merely a scaling issue). The underlying notion is that the odds for a correct response are the product of parameters associated with the respondent and item; re-expressing the relation in exponential form and applying a logistic transform results in the Rasch model above. There is an interesting mathematical relation between latent class models and the Rasch model. Specifically, the Rasch model, as conceptualized and estimated by conditional ML, is equivalent to a restricted latent class model. In particular, for J items, a suitably restricted latent class model with *strictly more than $J/2$* classes provides the same fit to item responses as does the Rasch model (Lindsay, Clogg, & Grego, 1991). In the present context, a restricted three-class latent class model is equivalent to a Rasch model for five items. The restrictions on the latent class model require that the item conditional probabilities are ordered and fall along parallel logistic functions. A computer program (PRASCH) incorporating these restrictions is presented by Grego (1993).

Estimated Rasch model profiles for the five achievement items, with their distinctive logistic form, are displayed in Figure 12.6. Comparing these profiles with the latent class profiles in Figure 12.4 illustrates the more flexible nature of the latent class model.

The estimated value of π^* for the Rasch model is .128 with estimated, jackknife standard error of only .001. Note that this π^* estimate is more than three-times as large as the value found for the three-class latent class model. This can be interpreted as meaning that the more highly restricted parametric IRT represented by the Rasch model provides substantially worse fit to these achievement data than the non-parametric IRT model represented by the three-class latent class model. These results, in general, are consistent with the respective likelihood-ratio goodness-of-fit statistics for the two models. The value from the three-class analysis is 57.82 based on 14 degrees of freedom whereas the value from the Rasch analysis is 222.27 based on $(5 - 1)(5 - 2) = 12$ degrees of freedom. As expected, given the very large sample size, both chi-square statistics suggest lack of fit. However,

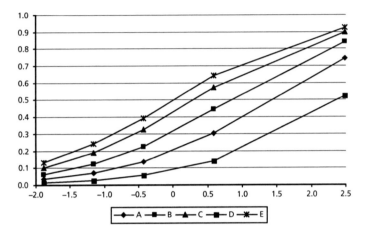

Figure 12.6 Rasch Model Profiles for Math Achievement Items.

there is substantially better fit for the latent class model compared to the more highly constrained Rasch model.

EXTENSION TO CONTINUOUS VARIABLES

In general, there does not appear to be a simple extension of the RCL two-point mixture fit index to models based on continuous variables unless some notion of "error" is included in the formulation. For example, in the case of simple linear regression, a linear model with perfect fit would consist of the collection of points falling along a straight line with any two distinct points in the sample defining a possible line. However, by allowing some structured degree of misfit by analogy with confidence intervals, it is possible to create methods that are in the same spirit as π^* but more appropriate for regression models (see Low, undated). Consider the simple linear regression model for bivariate X, Y data: $E(Y_i) = \beta_0 + \beta_1 X_i$. Absolute residuals, $|Y_i - E(Y_i)| = |Y_i - \beta_0 - \beta_1 X_i|$, greater than 0 indicate lack of fit of the model to the data. Let the index, π^*_ε, be defined as the proportion of the population in which the regression coefficients $\beta_{0\varepsilon}$ and $\beta_{1\varepsilon}$ satisfy the condition: $-\varepsilon \le Y_i - \beta_{0\varepsilon} - \beta_{1\varepsilon} X_i \le \varepsilon \ \forall \ X_i, Y_i$. In practice, following an approach suggested by Low (undated), an iterative procedure can be employed as follows: a) compute the usual least-squares estimates for the regression coefficients and calculate residuals; b) find the largest absolute residual and omit the corresponding case from the sample; c) repeat a) and b) with successively reduced sample size, noting the value of the multiple coefficient of determination, R^2, at each cycle. For some $n \ge 2$, the value $R^2 = 1$

will be achieved. A plot of R^2 versus the proportion of omitted cases (i.e., π_ε^* for some defined value of ε) at each cycle provides a useful schema for characterizing the loss of data required to achieve any specified level of correlation between X and Y. In principle, this method generalizes easily to multiple regression, logistic regression and related regression methods.

I illustrate this method with a small data set that is included with SPSS 14.0. The data comprise 15 observations for mathematics scores defined on a three-point scale and language skill scores defined on a four-point scale. Using language scores to predict mathematics scores, the coefficient of determination, R^2, for the total sample equals .378. Figure 12.7 displays the scattergram, coefficient of determination, and proportion of omitted cases across five steps, where the first step is for the total sample. Based on the maximum residual of 1.74 at the first step, one observation out of 15 (6.7%) was removed with a resulting R^2 of .709, a dramatic increase. This corresponds to setting the maximum absolute error, ε, at 1.74 with the result that $\hat{\pi}_\varepsilon^* = .067$. As shown in Figure 12.8, for steps 3 through 5 the percent omitted and R^2 values were (26.7%, .818), (33.3%, .878), and (46.7%, 1.00), respectively. With larger, and more realistic, data sets the increments to R^2 can be expected to be less dramatic. Also, case-by-case omissions based on residuals can be replaced by more efficient strategies such as omitting cases in subsets based on ranges of absolute standardized residuals.

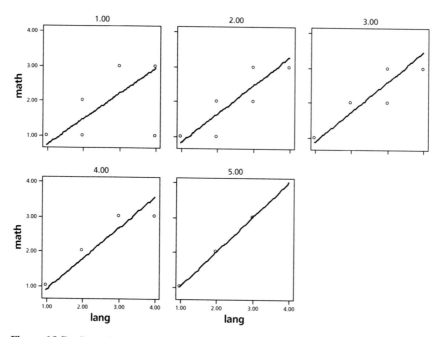

Figure 12.7   Stepwise Extreme Residual Deletions for Small Data Set.

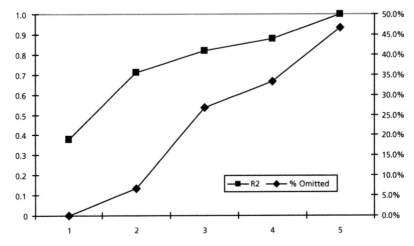

Figure 12.8 Summary of Stepwise Extreme Residual Deletions for Small Data Example.

I use a 5% random sample from the NELS data set to illustrate a more realistic situation for simple linear regression although these analyses do not take into account the complex sampling design on which NELS is based. The data set comprises 1,220 complete data cases for standardized reading achievement and mathematics achievement scores with the coefficient of determination being .477, or somewhat less than 50% "shared" variance. The criterion for standardized residuals for case omission at each step, which was set at 1.8 in this demonstration, is relatively arbitrary and can be adapted for specific data sets. Figure 12.9 displays the step-by-step R^2 values (left ordinate) and percent of omitted cases (right ordinate). It appears that omitting about 10% of the cases raises R^2 to approximately .65, whereas it takes an omission rate above 25% to achieve about 80% "shared" variance, after which there is substantially diminishing returns. As for π^* in general, the interpretation of these results is not based on any set standard but, rather, provides a descriptive background against which to judge the strength of the observed and potential associations among variables.

These methods are easily adapted to more complex regression models with multiple predictors, non-linear functions of predictors, categorical dependent variables (e.g., logistic regression) and so forth. Also, as noted by Rudas (1999) and Low (undated), the regression criterion can be generalized beyond least-squares. In particular, because the emphasis is on residuals, it would be natural in some applications to consider L_∞ regression that is based on a criterion of minimizing the maximum residual rather than minimizing a sum of squared residuals (Gonin & Money, 1989). This is an area that poses computational challenges and, clearly, requires additional research.

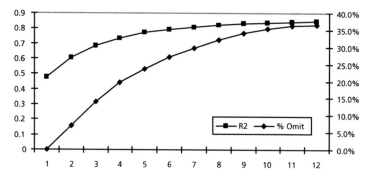

Figure 12.9   Summary of Stepwise Extreme Residual Deletions for Large Data Example.

REFERENCES

Clogg, C. C., Rudas, T., & Xi, L. (1995). A new index of structure for the analysis of models for mobility tables and other cross-classifications. In P. Marsden (Ed.), *Sociological Methodology* (pp. 197–222). Oxford: Blackwell.

Dayton, C. M. (1999). *Latent Class Scaling Analysis.* Sage University Papers Series on Quantitative Applications in the Social Sciences, 07-126. Thousand Oaks, CA: Sage.

Dayton, C. M. (2003). Applications and computational strategies for the two-point mixture index of fit. *British Journal of Mathematical & Statistical Psychology, 56,* 1–13.

Dayton, C. M., & Macready, G. B. (1980). A scaling model with response errors and intrinsically unscalable respondents. *Psychometrika, 45,* 343–356.

Gonin, R., & Money, A. H. (1989). *Nonlinear Lp-norm estimation.* New York: Marcel Dekker.

Goodman, L. A. (1974). Exploratory latent structure analysis using both identifiable and unidentifiable models. *Biometrika, 61,* 215–231.

Goodman, L. A. (1975). A new model for scaling response patterns: An application of the quasi-independence concept. *Journal of the American Statistical Association, 70,* 755–768.

Grego, J. M. (1993). PRASCH: a FORTRAN program for latent class polytomous response Rasch models. *Applied Psychological Measurement, 17,* 238.

Lasdon, L. S., Waren. A. D., Jain, A., & Ratner, M. (1978). Design and testing of a generalized reduced gradient code for nonlinear programming, *ACM Transactions on Mathematical Software, 4,* 34–49.

Lindsay, B., Clogg, C. C., & Grego, J. (1991). Semiparametric estimation in the Rasch model and related models, including a simple latent class model for item analysis. *Journal of the American Statistical Association, 86,* 96–107.

Lohr, S. L. (1999). *Sampling: Design and Analysis.* Pacific Grove, CA: Duxbury Press.

Low, A. (undated). L_{∞} regression and mixture index of fit. Unpublished paper; www.math.uni-klu.ac.at/stat/Tagungen/Ossiach/Low.pdf

Rudas, T. (1999). The mixture index of fit and minimax regression. *Metrika, 50,* 163–172.

Rudas, T. (2002). A latent class approach to measuring the fit of a statistical model. In J. Hagenaars & A. McCutcheon (Eds.), *Applied Latent Class Analysis,* Cambridge University Press.

Rudas, T., Clogg, C. C., & Lindsay, B. G. (1994). A new index of fit based on mixture methods for the analysis of contingency tables. *Journal of the Royal Statistical Society, Series B, 56,* 623–639.

Rudas, T., & Zwick, R. (1997). Estimating the importance of differential item functioning. *Journal of Educational and Behavioral Statistics, 22,* 31–45.

Xi, L. (1994). *The mixture index of fit for the independence model in contingency tables.* Master of Arts paper, Department of Statistics, Pennsylvania State University.

Xi, L., & Lindsay, B. G. (1996). A note on calculating the π^* index of fit for the analysis of contingency tables. *Sociological Methods & Research, 25,* 248–259.

CHAPTER 13

IDENTIFYING THE CORRECT NUMBER OF CLASSES IN GROWTH MIXTURE MODELS

Davood Tofighi and Craig K. Enders
Arizona State University

Growth mixture modeling (GMM; Muthén, 2001, 2002, Muthén & Shedden, 1999) has become an increasingly popular tool for exploring heterogeneity in developmental research in the social sciences. GMM has recently been used to study a variety of developmental processes, including depression (Stoolmiller, Kim, & Capaldi, 2005), reading skills (Parrila, Aunola, Leskinen, Nurmi, & Kirby, 2005), religiousness over the life span (Greenbaum, Del Boca, Darkes, Wang, & Goldman, 2005; McCullough, Enders, Brion, & Jain, 2005), smoking (Abroms, Simons-Morton, Haynie, & Chen, 2005), community intervention (Segawa, Ngwe, Li, & Flay, 2005), and poverty and health (McDonough, Sacker, & Wiggins, 2005).

GMM offers several advantages over traditional latent growth modeling (LGM). For example, LGM assumes that the population being studied is homogeneous in terms of the shape of their growth trajectories. Although individuals may differ from the average growth trajectory via random variation in their intercepts or slopes (or other functional elements), it is assumed that a common growth form (e.g., linear) holds for all cases. In contrast, GMM allows for heterogeneity in the growth trajectories. This heterogeneity is represented by a latent categorical variable that defines

Advances in Latent Variable Mixture Models, pages 317–341
Copyright © 2008 by Information Age Publishing
All rights of reproduction in any form reserved.

k classes of individuals, each of which are potentially described by a unique set of growth model parameter values. For example, the k classes might differ with respect to their fixed effects (i.e., average growth trajectories), variance components (i.e., intercept or slope variances, level-1 residual variances), or both.

Latent class growth analysis (LCGA; Nagin, 1999; Nagin & Tremblay, 2001) is closely related to GMM, and has also been used in a variety of substantive areas. Like GMM, LCGA allows for k latent trajectory classes, such that each class may have a different growth form. Unlike GMM, however, the LCGA model assumes that individual heterogeneity is completely captured by the mean growth trajectories of the k latent classes. Whereas GMM allows one to model class-specific variance components (e.g., intercept variance, slope variance), the LCGA model views within-class deviations from the average trajectory as random error (Bauer & Curran, 2004). In the remainder of this chapter we focus on enumerating the number of latent classes in the GMM context, and do not consider LCGA models.

Extracting the correct number of classes is one of the most challenging tasks in a GMM analysis. In cases where the researcher has no *a priori* knowledge about the number of latent classes represented in the data, the analysis proceeds in a fashion that resembles cluster analysis (e.g., increasing numbers of classes, or clusters, are sequentially extracted, and the fit of the k-class model is compared to that of the $k-1$ class model). However, this process is not necessarily straightforward. For example, Bauer and Curran (2003) noted that nonnormally distributed repeated measures may lead to the extraction of multiple classes when only a single class exists in the population. In a related work, Bauer and Curran (2004) showed that model misspecification (e.g., misspecifying the within-class covariance structure) can also lead to incorrect inferences regarding the number of classes. In addition, it has been suggested that incorporating covariates may play an important role in enumerating classes (Muthén, 2004).

A number of statistical tests and fit indices can be used to guide the extraction process.[1] Early GMM applications relied almost exclusively on information-based indices such as the Bayesian Information Criterion (BIC; Schwartz, 1978), while more recent applications have utilized the nested model likelihood ratio test outlined by Lo, Mendell, and Rubin (2001). In addition, a bootstrapped likelihood ratio test (BLRT; McLachlan, 1987; McLachlan & Peel, 2000) and goodness of fit tests based on model-implied skewness and kurtosis values (Muthén, 2003) were recently implemented in the M*plus* software package (Muthén & Muthén, 2006). To date, we are aware of only a single study that examined the performance of selected fit indices in the context of GMM (Nylund, Asparouhov, & Muthén, in press), but the primary focus of that work was on latent class analysis. As such, the purpose of the research presented in this chapter was to conduct a comprehensive Monte Carlo study to evaluate the performance of nine different fit indices that can be used to enumerate the number of latent classes in a GMM analysis. The details of this simulation are given later in the chapter.

DESCRIPTION OF STATISTICAL TESTS AND FIT MEASURES

The measures we examined in this study can be roughly grouped into three categories: information-based criteria, nested model likelihood ratio tests, and goodness of fit measures. Specific details about each of the tests we examined are provided below.

Information-Based Indices

Many of the early GMM applications relied heavily on information-based indices such as the BIC to determine the number of classes. We consider the performance of five such indices in this study: the BIC, a sample size adjusted BIC (SABIC) proposed by Sclove (1987), Akaike's Information Criterion (AIC; Akaike, 1987), the consistent AIC (CAIC) proposed by Bozdogan (1987), and a sample size adjusted CAIC (SACAIC). These indices are comprised of two parts: the log likelihood of the postulated model, and some collection of penalty terms that take model complexity into account. The information-based criteria generally favor models that produce a high log likelihood value while using relatively few parameters, and are scaled such that a lower value represents better fit.

The BIC is one of the most commonly used information-based indices, and is based on the log likelihood (LL) of the postulated model, the number of parameters (p), and sample size (N), as follows:

$$BIC = -2\,LL + p\ln(N).\qquad(13.1)$$

The BIC is scaled so that it favors models with a large log likelihood, few parameters, and smaller sample sizes (i.e., the penalty for model complexity increases as the sample size increases). It should be noted that BIC is consistent (Haughton, 1988), meaning that it tends to select the correct model more frequently as sample size increases. Sclove (1987) suggested a sample size adjustment for BIC where N is replaced by $N' = (N+2)/24$. Adding the sample size adjustment serves to reduce the sample size penalty, and should lead to better performance when the model has either a large number of parameters or a small sample size (Yang, 2006). We refer to this adjustment as the sample size adjusted BIC (SABIC) throughout this manuscript.

The AIC is also based on the log likelihood and the number of estimated parameters, and is defined as follows:

$$AIC = -2LL + 2p. \tag{13.2}$$

The AIC is not consistent (Woodruffe, 1982), as it does not choose the correct model more frequently as the sample size increases. Bozdogan (1987) remedied this deficiency, and derived a consistent version of AIC as follows:

$$CAIC = -2LL + p \ (\ln[N]+1). \tag{13.3}$$

The CAIC is quite similar to BIC, but invokes a larger penalty term for model complexity. Finally, we examined a sample size adjusted CAIC where N is replaced by $N' = (N+2)/24$ (the same adjustment applied to the BIC). This index is referred to as the SACAIC.

Nested Model Tests

In addition to the information-based indices, we examined the performance of a nested model likelihood ratio test. Nested model likelihood ratio tests (i.e., chi-square difference tests) are employed in a wide variety of methodological and applied arenas, and can be used to compare the relative fit of two models that differ by a set of parameter restrictions. More formally, two nested models can be compared using negative two times the log likelihood difference (denoted here as simply LR) as follows:

$$LR = -2(LL_{Restricted} - LL_{Full}), \tag{13.4}$$

where LL_{Full} is the log likelihood value for the full model, and $LL_{Restricted}$ is the log likelihood for the nested model with restrictions (e.g., fewer parameters). Under certain conditions, the LR is distributed as a chi-square with degrees of freedom equal to the number of restrictions imposed on the nested model (i.e., the difference in the number of estimated parameters between the two models).

In the context of GMM, the LR is used to test the fit of a k-class model (i.e., the full model) versus a $k-1$ class model with one fewer latent class (i.e., the restricted model). The problem with this approach is that LR is not asymptotically distributed as a chi-square in this case, because the mixing proportion for one of the classes in the restricted model (i.e., the $k-1$ class model) is fixed at zero. Said differently, the class probabilities for one of the k classes must be fixed at the boundary of the parameter space (i.e., zero), resulting in a violation of the regularity conditions necessary for the *LR* to be asymptotically distributed as a chi-square (Everitt, 1981; McLachlan & Peel, 2000).

Lo, Mendell, and Rubin (2001) derived an approximate reference distribution for the *LR* in the mixture context that is a weighted sum of chi-squares, and we henceforth refer to this simply as the Lo-Mendell-Rubin (LMR) test. These authors also proposed an *ad hoc* adjustment to the *LR* that was designed to improve the accuracy of the resulting inferences (the adjusted LMR, or ALMR). The null hypothesis for the LMR and ALMR is that the restricted model with $k - 1$ classes fits the data as well as the full model with k classes. As such, a small probability value indicates that the $k - 1$ class model should be rejected in favor of the model with at least k classes. It should be noted that the LMR depends on multivariate normality of the outcomes, conditional on the covariates in the model, and may favor a model with too many classes when this assumption is violated (Muthén, 2003). The performance of the LMR and ALMR was virtually identical in our simulations, so we focus on the LMR for the remainder of this chapter.

A significance test for the *LR* can also be generated using bootstrap resampling (McLachlan, 1987; McLachlan & Peel, 2000). In this case, the *LR* is evaluated against an empirical reference distribution. In order to obtain an appropriate null distribution, *B* bootstrap samples are generated from a mixture distribution defined by the maximum likelihood estimates associated with the $k - 1$ class model. Next, the k and $k - 1$ class models are fit to each bootstrap sample, and the LR_b values are accumulated, forming an empirical null distribution. An approximate probability value is subsequently obtained by computing the proportion of LR_b values that exceed the *LR* from the original analysis. When the $k - 1$ class model is incorrect, the *LR* should be large relative to the LR_b values obtained from the resampling procedure, and the resulting probability value will be small. As such, a small probability value indicates that the $k - 1$ class model should be rejected in favor of the model with at least k classes. This test was very recently implemented in the M*plus* software package, so we were not able to systematically examine its performance. We encourage readers to consult a recent paper by Nylund et al. (in press) for a comprehensive investigation of the bootstrap test.

Goodness of Fit Tests

Goodness of fit tests based on multivariate skewness and kurtosis have recently been proposed in the literature (Muthén, 2003), and are available in the M*plus* software package; throughout this paper we refer to these tests as the Multivariate Skewness Test (MST) and Multivariate Kurtosis Test (MKT). These tests are analogous to the goodness of fit test used in structural equation models, but compare the multivariate skewness and kurtosis values implied by the k-class model to those obtained from the sample data.[2] With more than one class, the distribution of the test statistic becomes complex (or unknown), so an empirical sampling distribution for the multivariate skewness and kurtosis statistics is generated using 200 Monte Carlo replications. A low probability value suggests that the implied moments from the k-class model differ from their sample counterparts, whereas a larger probability value is indicative of adequate model fit. Strictly speaking, these tests are goodness of fit tests, and do not compare models with different numbers of mixture components. Nevertheless, the behavior of MST and MKT has not been studied, so it was of interest to examine whether these tests could accurately enumerate the number of latent classes.

METHODS

The population model used in this study was a 3-class GMM, where two classes (Class 1 and 2) exhibited quadratic trends, and one class (Class 3) was linear. The following formulae are expressed using multilevel notation (Singer & Willett, 2003), and the data generation model is also displayed graphically in Figure 13.1 using standard path diagram conventions. The level-1 (repeated measures) model for class k was:

$$y_{ij}^k = \pi_{0i}^k + \pi_{1i}^k \left(TIME_j \right) + \pi_{2i}^k \left(TIME_j^2 \right) + \varepsilon_i^k, \qquad (13.5)$$

where y_{ij}^k was the outcome variable for a case i at time j, π_{0i}^k was the intercept of the true change trajectory, π_{1i}^k was the linear slope of the true change trajectory, π_{2i}^k was the quadratic curvature of the true trajectory, and ε_i^k was the level-1 residual for case i.[3] The values of $TIME_j$ were the same across all cases, and ranged from zero to six with a unit increment.

The level-2 (person-level) model was as follows:

$$\begin{cases} \pi_{0i}^k = \gamma_{00}^k + \gamma_{01}^k x_{1i} + \gamma_{02}^k x_{2i} + \zeta_{0i}^k \\ \pi_{1i}^k = \gamma_{10}^k + \gamma_{11}^k x_{1i} + \gamma_{12}^k x_{2i} + \zeta_{1i}^k \\ \pi_{2i}^k = \gamma_{20}^k \end{cases} \qquad (13.6)$$

where x_{1i} and x_{2i} were level-2 covariates (i.e., predictors of linear slope and quadratic curvature), γ_{00}^k, γ_{10}^k, and γ_{20}^k were level-2 means (because the covariates were centered at zero), and γ_{01}^k, γ_{02}^k, γ_{11}^k, and γ_{12}^k were class-specific regression coefficients. The values of these coefficients were chosen such that the covariates accounted for 15% of the intercept and slope variation

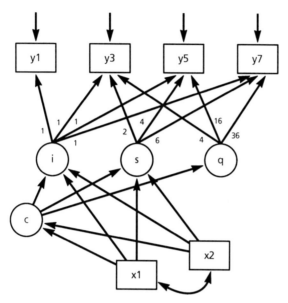

Figure 13.1 Path diagram of the growth mixture model used for the data generation and analyses.

in Class 1, and 2% and 7% of the variation in the growth factors in Classes 2 and 3, respectively. These proportions of explained variance roughly correspond with Cohen's (1988) effect size benchmarks in the multiple regression context (e.g., 7% approximates a medium effect size for R^2), but we chose these values somewhat arbitrarily. Finally, ζ_{0i}^k and ζ_{1i}^k are level-2 residuals that captured the variation between individuals in level-1 intercepts and slopes within class k, respectively. In other words, each class had non-zero variation in the intercepts and slopes, but had no variation in the curvature component. In our experience, the quadratic variance term is "exotic" in that sense that it can rarely be estimated, even when quadratic fixed effects are present (e.g., McCullough et al., 2005).

A graphical depiction of the mean growth trajectories for the 3-class population model is shown in Figure 13.2. These growth trajectory shapes were chosen after reviewing several published substantive applications of GMM, with the goal that the artificial data might reasonably represent common data structures in psychology and the behavioral sciences (e.g., Schaeffer, Petras, Ialongo, Poduska, Kellam, 2003). For example, Class 1 can be thought of as a "problem class" of individuals with elevated, but relatively stable, levels of some problem behavior such as drinking or antisocial behavior. Class 2 can be characterized as an "increaser class" of cases that start relatively low, but increase in severity as time passes. Finally,

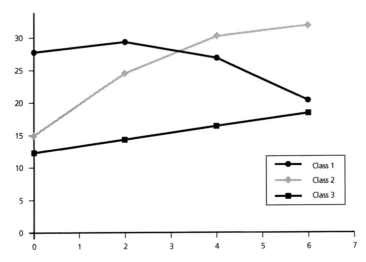

Figure 13.2 Average growth trajectories for the 3-class population model.

Class 3 might be characterized as a "zero class" characterized by low and stable outcome scores.

A brief discussion of the population model is warranted before proceeding. A potentially dizzying array of model characteristics could be manipulated in a GMM simulation study. Because relatively few GMM simulations have been published to date, we felt it was important to select a population model that was reasonably representative of models found in the applied research literature. As such, the specific population parameters were chosen after a careful review of several GMM applications. First, our review of the literature indicated that the number of extracted classes is typically between 2 and 4 (e.g., Chassin, Pitts, & Prost, 2002; Li, Duncan, & Hops, 2001; Mc-Cullough et al., 2005; Schaeffer et al., 2003; Szapocznik et al., 2004; White, Pandina, & Chen, 2002). The extraction of more than four classes was rare, except when the within-class variance components were assumed to be zero (i.e., LCGA analyses), so we felt that a 3-class population model was quite representative.

Next, we chose to vary the shape of the estimated growth trajectories across classes. Again, we felt that this facet of the population model accurately represented published GMM applications, as it is frequently the case that the estimated growth trajectory for one class may approximate a linear trend, but may be quadratic in another class (e.g., Barrett & White, 2002; McCullough et al., 2005; Schaeffer et al., 2003). As noted previously, we chose to simulate non-zero intercept and linear variance components, but fixed all quadratic variance components to zero; the magnitude of the variance components was allowed to vary across classes, such that each class had a unique covariance matrix.

Manipulated Factors

Five factors were manipulated in this study: the number of repeated measures, sample size, separation of the latent classes, the mixing percentages, and within-class distribution shape.

First, the number of repeated measures took on values of 4 and 7. In the former case, the *TIME* variable (i.e., the fixed loadings shown in Figure 13.1) took on values of 0, 2, 4, and 6, while in the latter case *TIME* scores were integer values ranging between 0 and 6. This parameterization allowed us to use the same set of population parameters for both conditions; in effect, we generated data sets with the same number of repeated measures, but ignored the odd-numbered factor loadings when performing the analyses that involved four repeated measures.

Second, the sample size factor took on values of 400, 700, 1000, and 2000. Again, these values were chosen after a careful review of substantive GMM applications. The studies we reviewed varied dramatically with respect to sample size, such that Ns were positively skewed, and ranged between 110 and 5833 (e.g., Chung, Maisto, Cornelius, & Martin, 2004, used an N of 110; Szapocznik et al., 2004, had an N of 209; Schaeffer et al., 2003, utilized 297 subjects; Chassin et al., 2002, used an N of 446; and Ellickson, Martino, & Collins, 2004, had a sample of 5833 cases). The sample size values we examined represent a range of values between approximately the 25th and 75th percentiles of the sample size distribution in the published studies we reviewed.

Third, we varied the separation of the latent classes, and manipulated the variance components to create what we refer to henceforth as "high separation" and "low separation" conditions. The variance components for the high separation model were roughly patterned after a study of aggressive behavior among elementary school boys (Schaeffer et al., 2003). After some exploration with a single data set comprised of 100,000 cases, we selected within-class variance parameters that produced an average posterior probability of approximately .90 for each class (in computing this average, cases were first assigned to a single class based on their highest probability). To put the high separation condition in further perspective, the intercept for Class 1 (the highest class) differed from that of Class 2 (the middle class) and Class 3 (the lowest class) by approximately 2.40 and 2.96 standard deviation units, respectively, while Class 2 and Class 3 differed by approximately .55 standard deviation units.[4] The low separation condition was generated by increasing the magnitude of the within-class variance parameters, while holding the growth factor means constant. In this case, the average posterior probability was roughly .80. The intercept for Class 1 (the highest class) differed from that of Class 2 (the middle class) and Class 3 (the lowest class) by approximately 1.90 and 2.30 standard deviation units, respectively, while Class 2 and Class 3 differed by approximately .44 standard deviation units. Note that different degrees of separation could have been obtained by holding the within-class variance estimates constant, while varying the mean differences across classes. We initially experimented with both techniques, and ultimately decided to hold the class means constant.

To visually illustrate the high and low separation conditions, a sample of individual fitted trajectories for each class is shown in Figures 13.3a and 13.3b. Note that the average trajectories shown in Figure 13.2 were identical in both conditions, but the regression of the growth factors on the covariates changed in order to keep the proportion of explained variation constant in the high and low separation conditions. We emphasize that our definition of "high" and "low" separation is somewhat subjective, and is based solely on prior experience with these models (e.g., McCullough et al., 2005).

Fourth, two sets of mixing percentages of classes were implemented: 20%, 33%, 47%, and 7%, 36%, 57%, for Classes 1, 2, and 3, respectively. Finally, we varied the within-class distribution shape. In the normative condition, the within-class distribution was multivariate normal. We also created a nonnormal case where univariate skewness (S) and kurtosis (K) were set to unity within each class. Although these values are not necessarily extreme, pilot testing indicated that larger values of S and K produced excessive convergence problems and parameter estimates that were substantially biased.

Data Generation

We generated 1000 replications within each design cell using the IML procedure in SAS. The within-class covariance matrices for the data generation process were obtained by requesting the model-implied covariance matrices from an initial M*plus* run where all model parameters were fixed at their population values. We first generated matrices of random normal variates using the RANNOR function in SAS, and subsequently transformed these data matrices to the desired covariance and mean structure using Cholesky decomposition. The distribution shape of the artificial data was created using methods outlined by Vale and Maurelli (1983). This procedure was repeated for each of the three latent classes, and the full data matrix was obtained by vertically concatenating the class-specific data matrices. We verified that the data generation process produced the desired param-

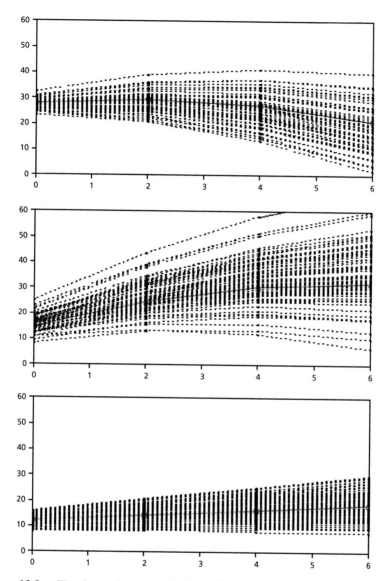

Figure 13.3a   Fitted growth trajectories from the high separation condition.

eter values by fitting the properly specified 3-class model to the generated data and inspecting the resulting parameter estimates.

The computational burden for some of the tests we examined (e.g., MST, MKT, LMR) was excessive, and precluded the use of a full factorial design. Instead, we used a design similar to that of Beauchaine and Beauchaine (2002). Briefly, we defined a "normative" condition that was based

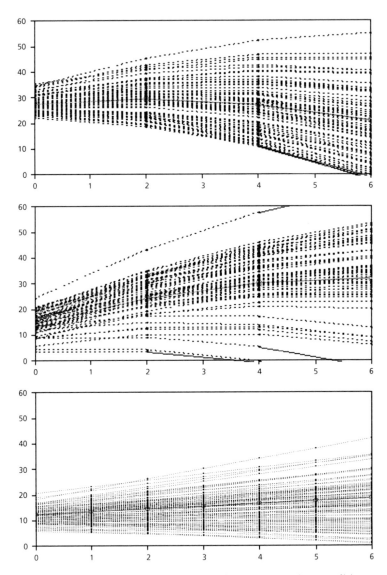

Figure 13.3b Fitted growth trajectories from the low separation condition.

on the following combination of the design cells: 4 repeated measures, $N = 1,000$, high class separation, mixing percentages of 20%, 33%, 47%, and within-class normality. We then proceeded to vary each independent variable while holding the remaining variables constant at their normative values. For example, we generated 1,000 replicates for each of the four sample size conditions, but the remaining design cells were fixed at the values described above. We chose the values of the normative conditions to represent the "best case scenario." For example, in examining the impact of mixing percentages (i.e., varying the mixing percentages while holding all other factors constant), we wanted the extraction process to be minimally affected by sample size, distribution shape, and mixing percentages, so the normative value of N was set at 1000, the within-class distributions were all normal, and the mixing percentages were large in each class, so as to avoid difficulties associated with extracting a class with very few cases; a similar logic was applied when choosing the normative values for the other design cells. Although not ideal, this analytic procedure was a practical necessity given the computational burden involved in computing MST, MKT, and LMR. In adopting this approach, we are assuming that the magnitude of any interaction effects is zero or of no practical consequence.

Analysis Procedure

To mimic the procedure that one might use in applied practice, mixture models with between two and four classes were fit using M*plus* 4 (we assumed that the fit indices would uniformly reject a single-class model). For each run, the values of the fit indices described above were stripped from the M*plus* output files, and were saved for further analysis. It was of interest to determine whether the inclusion of covariates substantially improved the ability to detect the correct number of latent classes, so we analyzed each data set twice: once with covariates, and once without covariates. Recall that the data generation process included two covariates (e.g., see the population model in Figure 13.1), so the runs where the covariates were excluded represent a model misspecification.

The process of determining the number of latent classes varied across fit indices. Specifically, the information-based indices are scaled such that a lower value (closer to zero) reflects an improvement in fit. As such, a k-class model was retained when the value of the index associated with the k-class model was lower than that of both the $k - 1$ and $k + 1$ class models (e.g., a 3-class model would be retained if the BIC decreased when going from a 2- to a 3-class model, but increased when a 4-class model was extracted). In contrast, MST and MKT are goodness of fit tests, such that a non-significant probability value indicates that the model-implied skewness and kurtosis do not differ from the corresponding sample moments. For example, a 3-class model would be retained in a situation where the 2-class model produced a significant MST (or MKT), but the corresponding 3-class model was non-significant. Finally, the LMR is significant when the k-class model provides better fit than the $k - 1$ class model. In this case, a 3-class model would be retained when the 3-class test was significant but the corresponding 4-class test was not.

Studying the behavior of the LMR posed some methodological challenges. As described above, the LMR is a nested model test, where the fit of the k-class model is compared to the fit of a nested $k-1$ class model. The difficulty in studying this test results from the fact that the ordering of latent classes is arbitrary. M*plus* implements the LMR by discarding the first class in the k-class solution, and uses the remaining classes to compute the log likelihood for the $k-1$ class solution. Because the first class is always discarded, the value of the LMR test depends on the ordering of the classes. For example, when fitting the 3-class model, there are three different 2-class models that could be used to compute the LMR. In order to study the behavior of the LMR, it was necessary to ensure that the test statistics for the 2-, 3-, and 4-class models were mutually consistent (e.g., the two classes that were extracted in the 2-class solution need to be the same two classes that are used for the nested model test in the 3-class solution, and so on). Consistent with the M*plus* user's guide (Muthén & Muthén, 2006), we used starting values to order the classes such that the first class was the smallest one, and the last class was the largest one. However, the use of starting values did not always ensure that the classes were ordered properly. In most cases, remedying this problem required a time-consuming process whereby the 3- and 4-class models were estimated multiple times in an attempt re-order the classes. A comparison of log likelihood values dictated when the correct ordering of classes had been achieved (e.g., if the 2-class log likelihood matched the log likelihood value obtained from the nested model generated from the 3-class solution, the classes were ordered properly).

Outcome Measure

Our primary interest was to determine the frequency with which the correct number of latent classes could be identified using the fit indices and statistical tests described above. As such, the outcome variable was simply the proportion of replications that a particular fit index correctly enumerated the number of latent classes. A secondary concern was whether the indices had a tendency to over- or under-extract the true number of classes, so this was also examined.

RESULTS

A number of the 4-class solutions failed to converge, so we were not able to obtain fit indices from these replications. One option for handling this problem was to simply discard the failed replicates and base the analyses on the replicates that produced a proper solution for the 2-, 3-, and 4-class models. We chose a tack that more closely resembled the decision making process in a practical application of mixture modeling. Specifically, after finding that the 4-class model failed to converge, it seems likely that a researcher would retain and interpret the 3-class class model. Thus, in cases where the 4-class model failed to converge, we classified a fit index as correctly identifying the proper number of latent classes, provided that the index was favorable toward the 3-class model (e.g., the 3-class BIC was lower than the 2-class BIC). Of course, the convergence of the 4-class model had no bearing in cases where a given index unequivocally favored the 2- or 3-class model. For example, there were cases where the 3-class BIC exceeded the 2-class BIC, thereby rendering the 4-class solution irrelevant for that particular case. Similarly, the p value for MST and MKT was greater than .05 in 100% of the 3-class replicates, so the convergence of the 4-class model did not matter. In general, only the LRT and the information-based criteria were affected by this choice.

It should be noted that the number of repeated measures (4 or 7) had a relatively minor impact on class enumeration. As such, these results are omitted for the sake of brevity. The impact of the remaining design factors is discussed below.

Sample Size

The influence of sample size varied dramatically across the fit measures we studied. To illustrate, Table 13.1 gives the proportion of replications in which the 3-class model was correctly identified. Note that the other design factors were held constant at the following values: within-class normal data, high class separation, 4 repeated measures, and mixing percentages of 20%, 33%, and 47%.

Focusing on the top portion of Table 13.1 (covariates excluded from the extraction process), it is clear that the SABIC accurately enumerated the number of latent classes, and did so across a wide range of sample sizes; at $N = 400$, the SABIC correctly pointed to 3 classes in 81% of the replications, and the accuracy improved to 96% at $N = 700$. The LMR also provided an accurate assessment of the number of latent classes, but was somewhat less accurate than the SABIC in small samples; at $N = 400$ and 700, LMR correctly enumerated the classes 57% of the time, and 86% of the time, respectively.

In general, the remaining information-based measures performed poorly, and extracted too few classes. For example, the BIC was quite sensitive to sample size, and performed poorly in smaller samples; at $N = 400$,

TABLE 13.1 Proportion of Correctly Identified 3-Class Models by Sample Size

Index	Sample Size			
	400	700	1000	2000
No Covariates				
BIC	.04	.36	.84	1.00
SABIC	.81	.96	.99	.99
AIC	.77	.78	.79	.76
CAIC	.01	.16	.64	.99
SACAIC	.52	.91	.99	1.00
LMR	.57	.86	.91	.88
MST	.01	.01	.01	.04
MKT	.02	.05	.11	.27
Covariates Included				
BIC	.01	.02	.19	.99
SABIC	.54	.79	.95	.99
AIC	.63	.36	.26	.23
CAIC	.01	.01	.04	.93
SACAIC	.14	.49	.88	1.00
LMR	.25	.70	.89	.94
MST	.01	.01	.01	.02
MKT	.04	.06	.07	.34

Note: Sample size was varied while holding other design factors constant as follows: Within-class normal data, high class separation, 4 repeated measures, and mixing percentages of 20%:33%:47%.

the BIC pointed to 3 classes in only 4% of the replications. The BIC only achieved adequate accuracy in cases where N exceeded 1,000. In general, our results do not support the use of the information-based indices, except for the SABIC.

MST and MKT nearly always favored the 2-class model, provided that the within-class distribution shape was normal. These results were consistent across the design factors were studied, except for the distribution shape factor. As such, no further discussion of these indices is warranted in this section of the chapter.

Class Separation

Table 13.2 gives the proportion of replications in which the 3-class model was correctly identified, and does so for the high and low separation condi-

TABLE 13.2 Proportion of Correctly Identified 3-Class Models by Class Separation

| | Class Separation | | | |
| | Low | High | Low | High |
Index	No Covariates		Covariates Included	
BIC	.11	.84	.01	.19
SABIC	.88	.99	.53	.95
AIC	.77	.79	.41	.27
CAIC	.04	.64	.01	.04
SACAIC	.64	.99	.15	.88
LMR	.78	.91	.55	.89
MST	.01	.01	.01	.01
MKT	.01	.11	.01	.07

Note: Sample size was varied while holding other design factors constant as follows: Within-class normal data, $N = 1000$, 4 repeated measures, and mixing percentages of 20%:33%:47%.

tions. Note that the other design factors were held constant at the following values: within-class normality, $N = 1000$, 4 repeated measures, and mixing percentages of 20%, 33%, and 47%.

Not surprisingly, class separation had a rather dramatic impact on the ability to correctly enumerate the number of classes, in that identifying the correct number of classes was made easier when the trajectories were well-separated. Consistent with the previous results, the SABIC and LMR were the most accurate indices. Even when the classes were not well-separated, the SABIC chose the correct model in 88% of the replications; this is compared to 99% when class separation was high. As before, the LMR was somewhat less accurate, and correctly enumerated the classes in 78% of the replications, as compared to 91% when classes were well-separated. The poorly separated classes had the largest effect on the BIC and the CAIC, and these indices performed poorly, even at $N = 1000$; the BIC and CAIC correctly pointed to the 3-class model in 11% and 4% of the replications, respectively.

Mixing Percentages

Table 13.3 gives the proportion of replications in which the 3-class model was correctly identified, and does so for two different sets of mixing percentages. Note that the other design factors were held constant at the fol-

TABLE 13.3 Proportion of Correctly Identified 3-Class Models by Class Mixing Percentage

| | Class Mixing Percentage | | | |
| | 20:33:47 | 7:36:57 | 20:33:47 | 7:36:57 |
Index	No Covariates		Covariates Included	
BIC	.84	.12	.19	0
SABIC	.99	.88	.95	.55
AIC	.79	.79	.27	.49
CAIC	.64	.03	.04	0
SACAIC	.99	.64	.88	.17
LMR	.91	.68	.89	.43
MST	.01	.01	.01	.14
MKT	.11	.01	.07	0

Note: Sample size was varied while holding other design factors constant as follows: Within-class normal data, $N = 1000$, 4 repeated measures, and high class separation.

lowing values: within-class normality, $N = 1000$, 4 repeated measures, and high class separation.

The mixing percentages had a substantial bearing on class enumeration. It is probably not surprising that the accuracy of the indices decreased when one of the classes (Class 1) was comprised of only 7% of the cases. Nevertheless, the performance of the fit measures was consistent with the previous results, such that the SABIC and LMR most frequently identified the true 3-class model. The SABIC had surprisingly high accuracy when the mixing percentages were fixed at 7%, 36%, and 57%, and identified the correct model in 88% of the replications. Again, the LMR was somewhat less accurate, and correctly enumerated the classes in 68% of the replications.

Within-Class Distribution Shape

Table 13.4 gives the proportion of replications in which the 3-class model was correctly identified, and does so for both the normal and nonnormal distribution conditions. Note that the other design factors were held constant at the following values: $N = 1000$, 4 repeated measures, high class separation, and mixing percentages of 20%, 33%, and 47%.

The relatively mild levels of nonnormality that we imposed within each class ($S = 1$ and $K = 1$) had a negative impact on the ability to accurately identify trajectory classes. In this situation, there were no indices that stood

TABLE 13.4   Proportion of Correctly Identified 3-Class Models by Within-Class Distribution Shape

| | Within-Class Distribution Shape | | | |
| | Normal | Nonnormal | Normal | Nonnormal |
Index	No Covariates		Covariates Included	
BIC	.84	.41	.19	.55
SABIC	.99	.41	.95	.58
AIC	.79	.41	.27	.58
CAIC	.64	.40	.04	.51
SACAIC	.99	.41	.88	.58
LMR	.91	.35	.89	.48
MST	.01	.04	.01	.02
MKT	.11	.48	.07	.44

Note: Sample size was varied while holding other design factors constant as follows: $N = 1000$, 4 repeated measures, mixing percentages of 20%:33%:47%, and high class separation.

out on the basis of their accuracy. The indices that accurately enumerated the classes in the previous conditions (the SABIC and LMR) now correctly identified the 3-class model in only 41% and 35% of the replications, respectively. Most the other indices gave comparable performance. As discussed below, the poor performance of the fit measures owes to the fact that within-in-class nonnormality consistently led to the extraction of too many classes. This finding is consistent with that of Bauer and Curran (2003).

Including Covariates During Extraction

As described previously, the extraction process was performed twice: once with covariates, and once without covariates. Tables 13.1 through 13.3 contain a very clear message: the inclusion of covariates uniformly and substantially hampered the ability to correctly enumerate the classes, particularly when the sample size was less than 1000. To illustrate, consider the lower panel of Table 13.1. When covariates were omitted from the analysis model, the SABIC correctly extracted 3 classes in 81% of the replications ($N = 400$). In contrast, the 3-class model was correctly identified 54% of the time when the analysis model included two covariates. A similar pattern of results was observed for the LMR; at $N = 400$, the LMR correctly identified the 3-class model in 25% of the replications where covariates were included in the analysis model, as compared to 57% when the covariates were excluded.

In considering these results, it should be noted that model complexity increased rather dramatically when covariates were included in the analysis. Recall that the data were generated such that the covariates accounted for a proportion of the within-class variation in the intercepts and slopes, but also influenced latent class membership. Additionally, the effects of the covariates on the growth factors were class-specific, such that each latent class had unique slope coefficients. As such, the properly specified model that incorporated covariates included a large number of additional parameters relative to the misspecified model with no covariates. For example, the 3-class model required the estimation of 16 additional regression coefficients (4 regressions per class, and 4 regressions relating the latent categorical variable to the covariates), plus class-specific covariances among the predictors. Thus, it is important to interpret our results with some caution, as future studies need to clarify the role that model complexity plays in the decision to include covariates in the extraction process.

Extraction Errors

The tabled results give some indication of how frequently one might expect to correctly enumerate the number of latent classes, but gives no indication about the types of errors that were committed (i.e., extracting too few or too many classes). When errors were made, it was generally the case that the 2-class model was favored, although the LMR had the tendency to favor the 4-class model once the sample size reached $N = 1000$. The notable exception occurred when the within-class distribution was nonnormal. In this case, all of the indices we studied extracted too many classes. This is probably not surprising, and is consistent with previous research (Bauer & Curran, 2003).

DISCUSSION

The purpose of this study was to provide a comprehensive evaluation of nine different fit indices that can be used to enumerate trajectory classes in GMM analyses. All of the indices we studied are readily available in commercial software packages such as M*plus*, or can be computed easily using information given on the computer output (e.g., the SACAIC).

With few exceptions, there were two indices that consistently extracted the correct number of latent classes: the SABIC and LMR (note that the performance of the ALMR was virtually identical to that of the LMR in all cases we studied). The SABIC generally identified the correct model in at least 80% of the replications, and many design cells exceeded 90% accuracy. Interestingly, we set no threshold on how much of a decrease in the SABIC was needed in order to favor a k-class model over a $k-1$ class model. That is, we adopted a strategy whereby a reduction of *any* magnitude provided evidence in favor of the k-class model, as long as the value of the SABIC increased (again, by any amount) when fitting the $k+1$ class model. In cases where the SABIC did not identify the correct model, it tended to extract too few classes, and might be viewed as conservative on those grounds. Note that our results are consistent with those of Yang (2006), who found that the SABIC was quite accurate in the context of latent class analysis. Consistent with the Yang study, our results provided little evidence to support the use of other information-based criteria.

The LMR also accurately enumerated the number of classes, but consistently did so at a lower rate than the SABIC. In cases where the LMR did not identify the correct model, the type of error was dependent on the sample size. Specifically, when N was less than 1000, the LMR tended to extract too few classes, but it extracted too many classes as N increased. As described previously, some caution is necessary when using the LMR, because the arbitrary ordering of the classes can yield a set of nested model tests that are mutually inconsistent (e.g., the 2-classes that are retained for computation of the 3-class LMR may not be the same two classes that were extracted when fitting a 2-class model). The M*plus* user's guide (Muthén & Muthén, 2006, p. 518) suggests using starting values to order the classes, such that the last class is the largest class.

MST and MKT consistently favored a 2-class model, except when the data were nonnormal. However, we caution that the performance of these two indices may be model-specific, and will likely depend on the exact configuration of the mixture classes. For example, we conducted an initial pilot study that had a slightly different data generation model, such that the lowest class (the "zero" class) had very little intercept and slope variation. In this case, MST performed slightly better than the LMR, and accurately enumerated the trajectory classes across a wide set of conditions. More research is needed to understand the performance of these measures.

The fact that the inclusion of covariates appeared to be detrimental to class enumeration was surprising, particularly given recent recommendations that covariates be included during the extraction process (e.g., Muthén, 2004). To be clear, the influence of covariates on class extraction was dependent on sample size. In fact, there appeared to be some benefit of including covariates, but this was only evident at $N = 2000$. For example, Table 13.1 shows that the LMR correctly identified the 3-class model in 94% of the replications, as opposed to 88% when covariates were excluded. It may not be a coincidence that the negative impact of including covariates began to diminish at $N = 1000$. The population values for the regression of the latent categorical variable on the covariates were chosen after conducting preliminary power analyses, such that the power associated with these regressions was approximately 80% in the $N = 1000$ condition. Because of the relatively small effect size, it appeared that the power loss due to increasing model complexity far outweighed the benefit of including covariates, at least in the two smallest sample size conditions. It is again important to reiterate that our population model was very complex, and allowed virtually every parameter to vary across classes. This level of complexity is often unnecessary in GMM applications, so the inclusion of covariates may ultimately prove beneficial under much smaller sample sizes than those used here. In the interim, we feel that our results should be interpreted rather cautiously, and that further studies should attempt to clarify the role that covariates play in the enumeration process.

At this point in time, few studies have thoroughly investigated class enumeration in the GMM context. Some of the recommendations from our study (e.g., the use of the SABIC) are consistent with latent class studies (Yang, 2006), while other findings (e.g., the poor performance of the BIC) are inconsistent with GMM research (Nylund et al., in press). Model complexity is one potential explanation for these inconsistencies, and is a factor that should be systematically examined in future studies. As alluded to previously, our population model probably represents an endpoint on the complexity continuum, as virtually every parameter was allowed to vary across classes. One the one hand, it was reassuring to find that classes could be correctly enumerated using an N of 1000, even when employing a model as complex as ours. On the other hand, it is not clear whether our results will generalize to less complex models that might be found in applied practice.

The use of a complex model with many class-specific parameters does appear to have some practical benefit for extracting classes. Our initial attempts at extracting 4 classes largely resulted in local or improper solutions that were highly sensitive to the starting values we used. In fact, a 4 class model with no constrained parameters produced at least one negative variance in 100% of the initial replications (we ultimately had to use a highly restricted 4 class model in order to avoid local or improper solutions). When employing a flexible model with many class-varying parameters, the single best predictor of over-extraction may be the presence of negative variance estimates or solutions that change dramatically across different sets of random starting values. In this sense, a complex model such as ours is probably conservative, and naturally prevents one from extracting too many classes. However, this is unlikely to be the case for more parsimonious models (e.g., LCGA models), so the reliance on fit indices becomes an important issue that needs to be studied further.

In sum, it was our intent to conduct a comprehensive simulation study of several fit indices that can be used to enumerate the number of latent classes in a GMM analysis. Our results indicated that the SABIC and LMR were quite useful in this regard, and functioned well across a variety of experimental conditions. However, we recommend some caution when interpreting our results, as our population model may be substantially more complex than other models found in applied practice. Ultimately, it seems unlikely that any single study will completely inform or resolve the issue of class enumeration. Rather, we suspect that the performance of the fit indices we studied may depend on a number of model-specific characteristics, making one-size-fits-all recommendations difficult. Until the results from more studies accumulate, we recommend that class enumeration decisions be made after considering a variety of evidence.

NOTES

1. Throughout the remainder of this chapter we use the term *fit index* to refer to both statistical significance tests (e.g., Lo, Mendell, & Rubin, 2001) and descriptive indices such as the BIC.
2. Computations for the model-implied skewness and kurtosis values can be found in the M*plus* technical appendices.
3. Note that the π symbol is *not* being used to denote the mixing proportion in this chapter, as is otherwise commonly done.
4. The pooled standard deviation was obtained by averaging the variance of the manifest variables across classes at the initial time point. Expressing the intercept differences in standard deviation units is akin to a standardized mean difference, or Cohen's *d*, at the initial assessment point.

REFERENCES

Abroms, L., Simons-Morton, B., Haynie, D. L., & Chen, R. (2005). Psychosocial predictors of smoking trajectories during middle and high school. *Addiction, 100,* 852–861.

Akaike, H. (1987). Factor analysis and AIC. *Psychometrika, 52,* 317–332.

Barrett, A. E., & White, H. R. (2002). Trajectories of gender role orientations in adolescence and early adulthood: A prospective study of the mental health effects of masculinity and femininity. *Journal of Health and Social Behavior, 43,* 451–468.

Bauer, D. J., & Curran, P. J. (2003). Distributional assumptions of growth mixture models: Implications for overextraction of latent trajectory classes. *Psychological Methods, 8,* 338–363.

Bauer, D. J., & Curran, P. J. (2004). The integration of continuous and discrete latent variable models: Potential problems and promising opportunities. *Psychological Methods, 9,* 3–29.

Beauchaine, T. P., & Beauchaine, R. J., III (2002). A comparison of maximum covariance and *k*-means cluster analysis in classifying cases into known taxon groups. *Psychological Methods, 7,* 245–261.

Bozdogan, H. (1987). Model selection and Akaike's information criterion (AIC): the general theory and its analytic extensions. *Psychometrika, 52,* 345–370.

Chassin, L., Pitts, S. C., & Prost, J. (2002). Binge drinking trajectories from adolescence to emerging adulthood in a high-risk sample: Predictors and substance abuse outcomes. *Journal of Consulting and Clinical Psychology, 70,* 67–78.

Chung, T., Maisto, S. A., Cornelius, J. S., & Martin, C. S. (2004). Adolescents' alcohol and drug use trajectories in the year following treatment. *Journal of Studies on Alcohol, 69,* 105–114.

Cohen, J. (1988). *Statistical power analysis for the behavioral sciences* (2nd ed.). Hillsdale, NJ: Erlbaum.

Ellickson, P. L., Martino, S. C., & Collins, R. L. (2004). Marijuana use from adolescence to young adulthood: Multiple developmental trajectories and their associated outcomes. *Health Psychology, 23,* 299–307.

Everitt, B. S. (1981). A Monte Carlo investigation of the likelihood ratio test for the number of components in a mixture of normal distributions, *Multivariate Behavioral Research, 16,* 171–180.

Greenbaum, P. E., Del Boca, F. K., Darkes, J., Wang, C., & Goldman, M. S. (2005). Variation in the drinking trajectories of freshmen college students. *Journal of Consulting and Clinical Psychology, 73,* 229–238.

Haughton, D. (1988). On the choice of a model to fit data from an exponential family. *The Annals of Statistics, 16,* 342–355.

Li, F., Duncan, T. E., & Hops, H. (2001). Examining developmental trajectories in adolescent alcohol use using piecewise growth mixture modeling analysis. *Journal of Studies on Alcohol, 62,* 199–210.

Lo, Y., Mendell, N. R., & Rubin, D. B. (2001). Testing the number of components in a normal mixture. *Biometrika, 88,* 767–778.

McCullough, M. E., Enders, C. K., Brion, S. L., & Jain, A. R. (2005). The varieties of religious development in adulthood: A longitudinal investigation of religion and rational choice. *Journal of Personality and Social Psychology, 89,* 78–89.

McDonough, P., Sacker, A., & Wiggins, R. D. (2005). Time on my side? Life course trajectories of poverty and health. *Social Science and Medicine, 61,* 1795–1808.

McLachlan, G. J. (1987). On bootstrapping the likelihood ratio test statistic for the number of components in a normal mixture. *Applied Statistics, 36,* 318–324.

McLachlan, G. J., & Peel, D. (2000). *Finite mixture models.* New York: Wiley.

Muthén, B. (2001). Latent variable mixture modeling. In G. A. Marcoulides & R. E. Schumacker (Eds.), *New developments and techniques in structural equation modeling* (pp. 1–33). Mahwah, NJ: Erlbaum.

Muthén, B. (2002). Beyond SEM: General latent variable modeling. *Behaviormetrika, 29,* 81–117.

Muthén, B. (2003). Statistical and substantive checking in growth mixture modeling: Comment on Bauer and Curran (2003), *Psychological Methods, 8,* 369–377.

Muthén, B. (2004). Latent variable analysis: Growth mixture modeling and related techniques for longitudinal data. In D. Kaplan (Ed.), *Handbook of quantitative methodology for the social sciences* (pp. 345–368). Newbury Park, CA: Sage.

Muthén, L. K., & Muthén, B. O. (2006). Mplus user's guide [Computer software and manual], (4th Ed.). Los Angeles: Muthén & Muthén.

Muthén, B., & Shedden, K. (1999). Finite mixture modeling with mixture outcomes using the EM algorithm. *Biometrics, 55,* 463–469.

Nagin, D. S. (1999). Analyzing developmental trajectories: A semi-parametric, group based approach. *Psychological Methods, 4,* 139–157.

Nagin, D. S., & Tremblay, R. E. (2001). Analyzing developmental trajectories of distinct but related behaviors: A group-based method. *Psychological Methods, 6,* 18–34.

Nylund, K. L., Asparouhov, T., & Muthén, B. (in press). Deciding on the number of classes in latent class analysis and growth mixture modeling: A Monte Carlo simulation study. *Structural Equation Modeling: A Multidisciplinary Journal.*

Parrila, R., Aunola, K., Leskinen, E., Nurmi, J., & Kirby, J. R. (2005). Development of individual differences in reading: Results from longitudinal studies in English and Finnish. *Journal of Educational Psychology, 97,* 299–319.

Schaeffer, C. M., Petras, H., Ialongo, N., Poduska, J., & Kellam, S. (2003). Modeling growth in boys' aggressive behavior across elementary school: Links to later criminal involvement, conduct disorder, and antisocial personality disorder. *Developmental Psychology, 39,* 1020–1035.

Schwartz, G. (1978). Estimating the dimension of a model. *The Annals of Statistics, 6,* 461–464.

Sclove, L. S. (1987). Application of model-selection criteria to some problems in multivariate analysis. *Psychometrika, 52,* 333–343.

Segawa, E., Ngwe, J. E., Li, Y., & Flay, B. R. (2005). Evaluation of the effects of the Aban Aya youth project in reducing violence among African American adolescent males using latent class growth mixture modeling techniques. *Evaluation Review, 29,* 128-148.

Singer, J. D., & Willett, J. B. (2003). *Applied longitudinal data analysis.* New York: Oxford University Press.

Stoolmiller, M., Kim, H. K., & Capaldi, D. M. (2005). The course of depressive symptoms in men from early adolescence to young adulthood: Identifying latent trajectories and early predictors. *Journal of Abnormal Psychology, 114,* 331–345.

Szapocznik, J., Feaster, D. J., Mitrani, V. B., Prado, G., Smith, L., Robinson-Batista, C., et al. (2004). Structural Ecosystems Therapy for HIV-seropositive African American women: Effects on psychological distress, family hassles, and family support. *Journal of Consulting and Clinical Psychology, 72,* 288–303.

Vale, C. D., & Maurelli, V. A. (1983). Simulating multivariate nonnormal distributions. *Psychometrika, 48,* 465–471.

White, H. R., Pandina, R. J., & Chen, P-H. (2002). Developmental trajectories of cigarette use from early adolescence into young adulthood. *Drug and Alcohol Dependence, 65,* 167–178.

Woodruffe, M. (1982). On model selection and the arcsine laws. *The Annals of Statistics, 10,* 1182–1194.

Yang, C. C., (2006). Evaluating latent class analysis models in qualitative phenotype identification. *Computational Statistics & Data Analysis, 50,* 1090–1104.

CHAPTER 14

CHOOSING A 'CORRECT' FACTOR MIXTURE MODEL

Power, Limitations, and Graphical Data Exploration

Gitta H. Lubke[1] and Jeffrey R. Spies
University of Notre Dame

BUILDING A FACTOR MIXTURE MODEL

Factor mixture models are designed for multivariate data obtained from a possibly heterogeneous population consisting of one or more clusters of subjects (Arminger, Stein, & Wittenberg, 1999; Dolan & van der Maas, 1998; Heinen, 1996; Jedidi, Jagpal, & DeSarbo, 1997; Lubke & Muthén, 2005; Muthén & Shedden, 1999; Vermunt & Magidson, 2003; Yung, 1997). A cluster of subjects is loosely defined as a homogeneous subpopulation with a common cluster-specific mean vector and covariance structure. Differences among clusters may involve mean differences and/or differences regarding (some aspect of) the covariance structure. For instance, in one of the clusters a single factor may explain covariances among observed items whereas in a second cluster two factors may be needed. Alternatively, one

Advances in Latent Variable Mixture Models, pages 343–361
Copyright © 2008 by Information Age Publishing

cluster may have considerably higher means on the observed variables than another cluster. In the context of this chapter, the nature of these differences is usually unknown. Furthermore, it is not known which individual belongs to which cluster, or how many clusters there are in the population. In addition, the number of continuous latent variables underlying the responses on the observed variables within each cluster may be unknown. In the most challenging case, the only information available when starting to build a model are the observed data.

The process of building a factor mixture model can be broken down into three parts. In each part, one or more assumptions are made which might be violated.

Part 1: Mixture Distributions and the Correspondence between Component Distributions and Clusters of Subjects

If a population is heterogeneous and consists of several clusters, then it may be suboptimal to model the data obtained from this population using a distribution with a mean vector and covariance matrix that is common for all subjects. Rather, each cluster can be modeled with a cluster-specific distribution. Mixture distributions provide the necessary flexibility. A mixture distribution consists of a finite number of component distributions each of which can have component-specific parameters. For instance, a mixture distribution may consist of two multivariate normal component distributions with component-specific mean vectors. Capitalizing on this flexibility, factor mixture models are models for mixture distributions with a user specified number of components. If the population is known to consist of two clusters of subjects, then a model for two mixture components may be specified.

However, the number of clusters in the population is often not known, and it is common practice to fit and compare models using mixture distributions with an increasing number of mixture components. When conducting such a model comparison it is important to realize the following. As stated above, the response patterns in each cluster of subjects can be adequately modeled using a mixture component for each of the clusters. However, mixture distributions are not only used to model data from heterogeneous populations. A mixture of normal components can also be used, for instance, to approximate non-normal distributions of data from a homogeneous population (e.g., skewed distributions, see Figure 14.1, left or right panel). Here, the number of mixture components used for the approximation does not necessarily have a conceptual meaning. Because of this alternative use of mixture distributions, it is not necessarily correct to deduce that a population

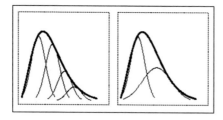

Figure 14.1 Approximation of non-normal distributions with normal components.

consists of, say, 3 clusters if a 3-class model provides the best fit to the data. Such an interpretation of model fitting results is only unproblematic if a) none of the model assumptions is violated, and if b) there is sufficient power to distinguish among the clusters. With respect to the first requirement, if it is *incorrectly assumed* that the data within each cluster are multivariate normal and a mixture of multivariate normals is used to model these data, then some of the mixture component distributions might only serve to account for the non-normality within cluster, with the result that the total number of mixture components of the best fitting model does not necessarily correspond to the number of clusters in the population (see for instance, Bauer & Curran, 2003, and the discussion thereof). The second requirement is a matter of effect size very similar to a multi-group situation in which detection of mean differences depends on the size of the mean difference and the sample size. Both requirements will be discussed in more detail below.

As shown in the next sections, most violations of model assumptions can result in a lack of a correspondence between the number of mixture components and the number of clusters of subjects in the population. Although ideally a mixture component corresponds to a specific cluster of subjects, this is not necessarily the case. Some of the confusion regarding this much discussed weakness of mixtures might also be due to the fact that components and clusters of subjects are often interchangeably referred to in the mixture literature as "latent classes." Although a bit contrived, the term *latent class* is avoided in this chapter. Instead, we use either *cluster of subjects* or *mixture component* in order to clearly distinguish between characteristics of the subjects on the one hand and the distribution used to model their data on the other.

In the following description of the general model, capital letters are used to indicate random variables, whereas lower case letters are used to indicate scores on the random variables. Further, observed variables are denoted as **Y**, probability distributions as $f(\cdot)$, the number of mixture components as $k = 1,\ldots,K$, and the proportion of component k as π_k where

$$\sum_{k=1}^{K} \pi_k = 1.$$

The first part of building a mixture model can be formalized as

$$f(\mathbf{y}) = \sum_{k=1}^{K} \pi_k f_k(\mathbf{y}) \tag{14.1}$$

Equation 14.1 shows that the joint distribution is a weighted sum of the K component distributions. For instance, if component k is small relative to other components, then this is reflected in a small proportion π_k. As a result, small components contribute less than larger components to the joint distribution. When building a mixture model, the researcher specifies a model for a specific number of mixture components. Hence, a possible error at this point is to specify a model for an incorrect number of components.

Part 2: Making Specific Distributional Assumptions

The next step is to make assumptions regarding the type of component distributions. In the case of factor mixture models, component distributions are assumed to be multivariate normal with mean vectors μ_k and covariance matrices Σ_k. As the subscript k indicates, the means and covariance matrices can be component specific. Let φ be a vector containing all parameters of the joint distribution, that is, $\pi_1, \ldots, \pi_K, \mu_1, \ldots, \mu_K, \Sigma_1, \ldots, \Sigma_K$, then:

$$f(\mathbf{y}; \varphi) = \sum_{k=1}^{K} \pi_k f_k(\mathbf{y}; \mu_k, \Sigma_k) \tag{14.2}$$

The assumption regarding multivariate normality of $\mathbf{Y}$ might be violated in practice. Note that different distributional assumptions regarding $f_k(\cdot)$ can affect the number of components K. An example would be the case where $\mathbf{Y}$ has a skewed distribution in a population with a single cluster (i.e., a single homogeneous population). Mixtures of normal components can be used to approximate a wide range of non-normal distributions including skewed distributions (Pearson, 1894, 1895). Increasing the number of components usually leads to better approximations. In addition, the choice of restrictions on component parameters may affect the number of components necessary to approximate the target distribution. This is illustrated in Figure 14.1. If variances of the component distributions are restricted to be equal, more components are needed than when variances are allowed to vary (see also McLachlan & Peel, 2000).

Another example illustrating that restrictions on component parameters can affect K is to assume that the Σ_k in Equation 14.2 are diagonal. This is the assumption of local independence, in which case Equation 14.2 would represent a latent profile model with K classes. If the off-diagonal elements of any of the Σ_k are non-zero in the population, fitting models assuming local independence can result in choosing K larger than the true number of clusters in the population (Lubke & Neale, 2005).

The most important point is that mixtures of normal component distributions can be used to approximate non-normal distributions, which implies that the number of components K in Equation 14.1 and Equation 14.2 does not necessarily correspond to K clusters of subjects in the population. Secondly, restrictions on parameters of the component distributions can also affect K when fitting models to data.

Part 3: Structuring the Component Distributions

The third step of building factor mixture models consists of imposing a *factor structure* on the mean vector and covariance matrix of observed variables of each mixture component. Let $\mathbf{v}$, $\boldsymbol{\alpha}$, $\boldsymbol{\Lambda}$, $\boldsymbol{\Psi}$, and $\boldsymbol{\Theta}$ indicate measured variable intercepts, factor means, factor loadings, factor covariance matrices and error matrices, respectively. The factor structure imposed on the kth component can then be denoted as:

$$\boldsymbol{\mu}_k = \mathbf{v}_k + \boldsymbol{\Lambda}_k \boldsymbol{\alpha}_k \tag{14.3}$$

$$\boldsymbol{\Sigma}_k = \boldsymbol{\Lambda}_k \boldsymbol{\Psi}_k \boldsymbol{\Lambda}_k^{\mathrm{T}} + \boldsymbol{\Theta}_k. \tag{14.4}$$

Because restrictions on component parameters can lead to using a mixture distribution with too many components, it would be ideal to compare models without imposing any restrictions on the component specific mean vectors and covariance matrices. Unfortunately, such an approach is usually not feasible in practice. Unrestricted models for large numbers of observed variables (e.g., questionnaire data) very often do not converge. Imposing a structure on the covariance matrices and mean vectors is therefore necessary to decrease the number of estimated parameters. Not surprisingly, imposing a factor structure relies on additional assumptions that can lead to further errors. The additional assumptions are the same as when fitting conventional factor models, namely that a) items are linearly regressed on factors, b) factors and errors are normally distributed resulting in normally distributed outcome variables, c) there are zero correlations between factors and errors, and d) errors have zero autocorrelations.[2]

The description thus far shows that as the model gets more complex, more assumptions are made resulting in a corresponding list of potential violations of these assumptions. It should be noted that several violations may occur at the same time, leading to a potential confound which could prove difficult to disentangle. Given these complications, for what type of research goals are factor mixture models useful? And under what conditions does fitting factor mixture models lead to satisfactory results in the sense that an adequate model is chosen when comparing a set of alternative models? These two questions are addressed in the following sections.

IMPLICATIONS OF THE LIMITATIONS
OF MIXTURE MODELING FOR DIFFERENT TYPES
OF RESEARCH QUESTIONS

As already mentioned, researchers often reason that if a model for a mixture distribution with K components emerges as the best fitting model in a model comparison, then the data stem from a population with K distinct clusters of subjects. However, if any of the model assumptions are violated, then this correspondence might not hold. Skewed data from a single cluster of subjects can be fitted using models for mixture distributions with several normal components. Equally, a nonlinear item-factor relation such as an increase of a factor loading with increasing factor scores can result in choosing a mixture model for more components than clusters in the population (Lubke & Neale, submitted). In this chapter we would like to argue that it depends on the type of research question as to whether this type of incorrect model choice, which is also known as 'overextraction of classes,' actually leads to incorrect decisions on a conceptual level. The following two examples illustrate the argument.

In psychiatric research, it is a much discussed topic whether individual differences in disorders such as Attention Deficit/ Hyperactivity Disorder (ADHD) should be conceptualized in terms of different subtypes (e.g., inattentive, hyperactive/impulsive, and combined subtypes), or in terms of continuous severity differences (Lubke et al., 2007). This question can be addressed by comparing the fit of factor mixture models for several components (corresponding to the different subtypes) to the fit of a factor model for a single component. Obviously, for this type of research question the direct correspondence between the number of mixture components and the number of clusters of subjects is essential and the adequacy of the model assumptions should be carefully considered. When questionnaire data are analyzed, prior information concerning the factor structure of the data is clearly helpful. Doubt concerning any of the model assumptions will weaken the conclusions drawn from the model comparison.

The second example also comes from the field of psychiatry and concerns the use of factor mixture models to single out potentially affected subjects for differential treatment. To determine a positive or negative diagnosis, it is common practice to use arbitrarily chosen cut-offs on total scores from questionnaires such as depression inventories (e.g., the CES-

D or BDI, Beck, Steer, & Brown, 1996; Radloff, 1977). As an alternative, factor mixture models can be fitted to questionnaire data to discriminate between a high-scoring cluster of potentially affected subjects and a lower scoring cluster of unaffected subjects. The factor mixture model approach can lead to superior results due to the fact that the factor structure of the questionnaire and measurement errors are taken into account. In such an application of factor mixture models it does not necessarily matter whether the high scoring subjects form a qualitatively distinct cluster or whether they correspond to the tail of a skewed distribution of a single continuous trait. In this case, the correspondence between the mixture components of the fitted model and the distinct clusters of subjects in the population is less essential. Obviously, a conceptual interpretation of model fitting results has to take this possibility into account.

SIMULATION RESULTS: MODEL COMPARISONS AND CORRECT MODEL CHOICE

As shown above, model violations such as skewness of Y or non-linear item-factor relations can result in the lack of a correspondence between the number of mixture components and clusters of subjects in the population. This section focuses on the question of whether it is possible to discriminate between alternative models if none of the assumptions are violated. The importance of this question lies in the fact that adequate model performance under ideal conditions is a necessary basis for the use and further development of factor mixture models. In other words, trying to find solutions for the limitations described above only makes sense if correct model choice is possible with reasonable sample sizes in the absence of violations of assumptions.

Results of two large simulation studies are summarized which investigate the conditions under which a model with the correct number of components and factor structure is chosen when fitting a set of alternative models. Although it can be expected that choosing the correct model is easier if mean differences between clusters of subjects are large, exactly how large does the effect size have to be to be able to distinguish between the clusters? How many subjects are needed to have sufficient power to discriminate between alternative models? These and other questions concerning the conditions under which factor mixture models perform adequately can be addressed in simulation studies in which the data generating process is under the control of the researcher.

The two simulation studies aim at providing some idea of what to expect when using factor mixture models to explore potential population heterogeneity. The first study, a detailed description of which is in Lubke and

Neale (2006), examines whether it is possible to distinguish between different types of models including conventional exploratory factor models, latent profile models (i.e., latent class models for continuous rather than categorical outcomes), and factor mixture models based on commonly used measures of goodness of fit. The data to which these different model types are fitted are multivariate normally distributed within component. The second study (Lubke & Neale, submitted) differs in that the response formats of the observed variables examined include categorical (i.e., 5-point Likert scale) as well as binary.

The data generating models in both studies are conventional factor models with 1, 2, and 3 factors (which are equivalent to factor mixture models for a single component), latent profile (or latent class) models with $K = 2$ and $K = 3$ (which are equivalent to factor mixture models with zero factors within component), and factor mixture models for $K = 2$ and 1 or 2 factors within component. The set of models that is fitted to each of these different data types is the same, resulting in a full factorial design of data generating and fitted models.

The procedure in both studies is to generate a large number of individual data sets under each model type and to fit the alternative models to each of the individual data sets. For each individual data set, the fitted models are then compared using the AIC, BIC, the sample size adjusted BIC, CAIC, and the adjusted likelihood ratio test statistic as measures of goodness-of-fit (Akaike, 1974, 1987; Bozdogan, 1987; Lo, Mendell, & Rubin, 2001; Schwarz, 1978). All analyses were carried out using the software program M*plus* (Muthén & Muthén, 2006). Aggregating over the individual data sets generated under a particular model, one can then compute the proportion of correct model choice for each of the fit indices for that particular data generating model type. The proportion correct can be regarded as a measure of how reliably alternative models can be distinguished when fitted to a certain data type. If, for example, the data generating model (i.e., the "true model") is a 2-class latent class model, and fitting a 2-class latent class model has much higher proportions than any of the other fitted models, then correct model choice for this data type is apparently unproblematic. The setup of the two simulation studies also allows for the computation of average fit measures for each fitted model. Average fit measures show which of the alternative models are close competitors and which of the alternative models can be easily distinguished. If, say, the average BIC of the fitted 2-class latent class model is closer to the average BIC of the 3-class latent class model than to the average BIC of the 2-factor model, then the 3-class latent class model is a competitor whereas the factor model can be easily distinguished from the true 2-class latent class model.

The general pattern of results of the two simulations can be summarized as follows:

- limiting the set of alternative fitted models to latent profile (or latent class) models with increasing numbers of components can lead to accepting models with too many components if the data generating model has one or more underlying factors;
- limiting the set of fitted models to conventional exploratory factor models with an increasing number of factors can lead to accepting models with too many factors if the data generating model has more than a single mixture component;
- choosing the correct model is generally unproblematic if the set of fitted models includes different model types, and if fit indices and parameter estimates are considered jointly; and
- having 5-point scale Likert outcomes instead of normally distributed outcomes results in a slight decrease in power to distinguish among models.
- having binary outcomes instead of normally distributed outcomes also decreases the power to distinguish among models.

Regarding the third point above, that the joint consideration of fit indices and parameter estimates better leads to correct model choice, the results of one data generating model are presented in more detail. The particular data generating model was chosen because the results were less clear than for other data types. The generating model is a latent profile model (i.e., normally distributed outcomes within component) with 2 mixture components and 10 observed variables. Outcomes are independent within component (i.e., local independence). The components are separated by a multivariate Mahalanobis distance equal to 1.5 or 3. As for the number of subjects, using a prior class probability of 0.5, subjects are assigned to either class 1 or 2 based on a value drawn from the uniform distribution for each subject; this procedure leads to approximately 200 subjects within each class. As mentioned above, the fitted models are exploratory factor models with 1, 2, and 3 factors, latent profile (or latent class) models for 2 or 3 components, and factor mixture models for 2 components with 1 or 2 factors.

Proportion of correct model choice and average results are shown in Tables 14.1 and 14.2. The adjusted likelihood ratio test (Lo et al., 2001) and different information criteria (e.g., AIC, BIC) are used as measures of goodness of fit. Table 14.1 shows the proportion that the fitted 2-class latent profile model was chosen as the best model (i.e., "first choice") and the proportion this model had second best fit indices (i.e., "second choice"). Table 14.2 shows the average fit statistics only for fitted models that could not be clearly rejected based on the fit indices (i.e., close competitors).

As can be seen in Table 14.1, the proportion of correct model choice when comparing the fitted models is excellent when mixture components

TABLE 14.1 Proportions of Latent Profile Data Sets in Which the Correct Model Would Be Chosen as the First or Second Best-Fitting Model

	logL-val	AIC	BIC	saBIC	CAIC	aLRT
			Small Class Separation			
1st choice	0.06	0.11	0.00	0.14	0.00	0.97
2nd choice	0.52	0.34	0.60	0.50	0.33	—
			Larger Class Separation			
1st choice	0.06	0.12	0.97	0.77	0.97	1.00
2nd choice	0.56	0.73	0.00	0.20	0.00	—

Note: The log likelihood value is abbreviated as "logL-value," sample size adjusted BIC as "saBIC," and the adjusted likelihood ratio test as "aLRT." A proportion of .11 indicates that when fitting the correct model the corresponding information criterion had a minimum value 11% of the time when comparing all fitted models. The value in the column of the aLRT is the proportion the aLRT was indicating the necessity of the second class.

TABLE 14.2 Average Fit Statistics Computed for All Generated Data Sets

	logL-value	AIC	BIC	saBIC	aLRT
		Small Class Separation			
LPMc2	–4,484.82	9,051.63	9,215.28	9,085.19	0.01
LPMc3	–4,458.66	9,041.32	9,288.79	9,092.06	0.47
F1c1	–4,496.85	9,053.70	9,173.45	9,078.25	NA
F1c2	–4,452.22	9,026.45	9,269.93	9,076.37	0.60
		Larger Class Separation			
LPMc2	–4,599.16	9,280.33	9,443.98	9,313.88	0.00
LPMc3	–4,573.00	9,270.00	9,517.47	9,320.74	0.43
F1c2	–4,577.46	9,276.91	9,520.39	9,326.83	0.06

Note: Latent profile models for j mixture components are designated LPMcj, and factor mixture models with i factors for j components are designated Ficj. A proportion of .11 indicates that the information criteria of the correct model had a minimum value 11% of the time when comparing all fitted models. Each value in the aLRT column is the average p-value.

are well separated, but very low for the smaller separation. Even as the second choice, the proportions for the different fit indices are not acceptable. Table 14.2 shows which models were the close competitors. It shows that the factor models with a single factor and one or two components have

slightly lower average information criteria. In practice, fit indices, although important, are not the only information used when deciding which model provides the best fit to the data. Researchers would also consider whether parameter estimates fall into acceptable ranges. In the simulation, factor loadings and the percentage of explained variance of the observed variables were very low for all fitted factor models. For instance, for the fitted single factor model for a single component (i.e., a conventional single factor model), the observed variable R^2 averaged over the 100 data sets of this data type ranged between 0.02 and 0.23 for the ten observed variables, with an average standard deviation of 0.04. In addition, on average, the factor mixture model for two components is not supported by the aLRT. Therefore, when considering fit indices and parameter estimates jointly and comparing a set of different models, the correct model without underlying continuous factors would be the most likely choice.

In sum, a comparison of different types of models under the conditions chosen in the two simulation studies (i.e., no model violations) leads to good results for normally distributed outcomes and $N = 75$ within component if components are well separated. Smaller separation requires larger samples. Finally, a comparison of these results to the results of the Likert scale outcome variables shows a slight decrease in power to discriminate among components, while binary response outcome variables result in a more clear reduction in power.

Although these results are reassuring, two main limitations of using factor mixture models to explore potential population heterogeneity remain. First, the reliance on model assumptions, although unavoidable in a modeling context, can be problematic when using factor mixture models in a model comparison. As we have seen in the previous sections, any violation of model assumption could lead to a lack of a correspondence between mixture components and clusters of subjects in the population. Depending on the type of research question, the lack of a correspondence may weaken the interpretation of results on a conceptual level. Second, in an empirical study the number of alternative models may be much larger than in the above simulations. An increase of the number of potential clusters in the population can drastically increase the number of alternative models, leading to a situation in which multiple testing might become problematic. To reduce the number of competing models it would be desirable to know the approximate number of clusters and factors in the population. However, this information is usually not available in an exploratory setting. The following section demonstrates that both issues can benefit from visualizing the observed data using a tool called HDTreeV, or High Dimensional Tree Visualization (Spies & Boker, 2006).

HDTreeV

Background

The previous sections have illustrated that discovering and understanding relations in multidimensional data can be problematic, especially if the underlying structure is largely unknown. Traditionally, exploratory data analysis (EDA) has been used to discover patterns and garner substantive understanding of data by emphasizing the use of graphical representations (Behrens, 1997). However, methods for visualizing data beyond two or three dimensions are rarely used, as most mathematical and statistical packages provide only basic 3-dimensional plotting.

With the exception of visualization tools that extend 3-dimensional plots to 4 or 5 dimensions through motion, point shape, and color, most multidimensional displays represent data as icons, where variables map onto components of the icon. Examples of icons that map data onto lengths and angles of components have included glyphs (Anderson, 1960), profiles, stars, and polygons (Siegel, Goldwyn, & Friedman, 1971). A graph is generally considered successful if the relations it presents can be comprehended quickly and efficiently; this can be accomplished effectively by considering the properties of human perception and cognition. Capitalizing on the human ability to perceive and remember variations in the human face, Chernoff (Chernoff, 1973) introduced the use of cartoon faces to represent data by mapping variables onto the shape and size of facial features, such as the mouth, nose, eyebrows, and eyes. It should be noted that, although using a familiar object to integrate many variables is advantageous, Chernoff's faces can be overinterpreted or even misleading in that if, for example, frowns do not pertain to a negative qualitative assignment, the display becomes counterintuitive. The Exvis system (Grinstein, Pickett, & Williams, 1989) takes advantage of another inherent human quality: visual texture perception. By densely displaying icons on screen, textural gradients and contours are formed, indicating potentially interesting structures in data.

HDTreeV combines the power of using familiar objects (i.e., trees) with the human ability to detect change in patterns, thus creating a visualization tool effective in deciphering relations in multidimensional data (Spies & Boker, 2006). The overall shape of the trees as they occur in nature is the outcome of potentially complex relations among many variables; however, humans have the innate ability to categorize trees by reducing this complexity to simple categorical terms, like "oak trees" and "maple trees." These distinctions among trees can also be made in the virtual world by generating trees using Lindenmayer systems, or L-systems, which is the mathematical theory of plant development often used in computer graphics to render realistic flora. By manipulating aspects of how components are rewritten, cat-

egorically different trees can be created. Although the L-system algorithm is not specifically implemented in HDTreeV, the idea is similar: the shape of trees whose components are based upon data should provide a holistic view of the potentially complex relations that exist in that data. If there are group differences in given data set, then a graphical representation in HDTreeV should result in categorically different trees.[4]

Mapping of Response Patterns

Similar to other icon-based visualization techniques, in HDTreeV the responses of a given subject on multiple observed variables (e.g., questionnaire items) are represented as an individual icon, in this case a tree. Trees in HDTreeV have a trunk and bifurcating branches. A response on a single observed variable is mapped either onto a branch length or onto an angle determining the bifurcation, as can be seen in Figure 14.2. In the example shown, there are two subjects measured on seven variables. This produces two trees, one for each subject. Across subjects, the responses on the observed variables are mapped on the components of each tree—trunk, angles, and branch lengths—in the same order. For example, variable X_1 is mapped onto the length of the trunk of the tree, X_2 is the angle from vertical of the first branch, X_3 is the length of third branch, continuing through variable X_7 which is mapped to the length of the outermost branch. The order in which variables are mapped to components can also be randomly assigned, generating different views of the same data. After trees are generated for a given data set, they can be moved and sorted on the screen using a mouse.

It is in this way that the shape of a tree is dependent upon the data, and thus it is proposed that trees that look similar but are visually distinguishable from other sets of similar looking trees might belong to quantitatively

	X_1	X_2	X_3	X_4	X_5	X_6	X_7
Subject 1	x_{11}	x_{21}	x_{31}	x_{41}	x_{51}	x_{61}	x_{71}
Subject 2	x_{12}	x_{22}	x_{32}	x_{42}	x_{52}	x_{62}	x_{72}

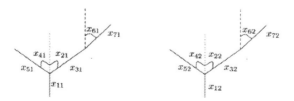

Figure 14.2   HDTreeV representation for two subjects measured on seven variables.

distinguishable groups. These differences may very well not be solely based on the comparison of one component between trees, for if this were the case, simply plotting a histogram of that variable would reveal group differences. It is by viewing the data holistically as trees that complex relations can be seamlessly accommodated. Most importantly, *no assumptions are made regarding the underlying structure of the data.* HDTreeV simply represents a vector containing the responses of a subject on multiple variables as a tree by mapping each individual response on a given part of the tree. Higher scores on a given variable will result in a longer branch or larger angles between branches. This is repeated for all subjects in the same order such that trees corresponding to subjects with similar response patterns will look similar. Systematic differences in response patterns will become visually evident as differentially shaped trees.

Examples

The following example is a classic data set often used in discriminant analysis, cluster analysis, and the testing of multivariate visualization techniques. It is the iris data set, which contains a sample of 150 flowers from three species of iris collected by Anderson (1935) and originally published by Fisher (1936). There are 50 observations of each species (setosa, versicolor, and virginica) measured on sepal length, sepal width, petal length, and petal width. Figure 14.3 shows the histograms of each of these four variables. Using HDTreeV, these variables were mapped onto tree components as previously described. One such mapping is show in Figure 14.4. Although

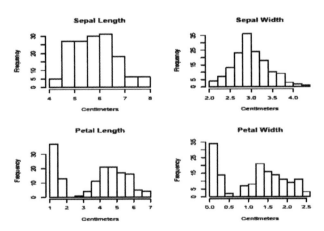

Figure 14.3 Histograms for four variables in a sample of 150 flowers from three species of iris.

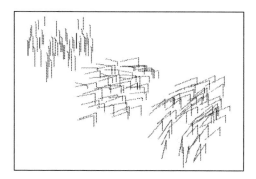

Figure 14.4   HDTreeV representations of 150 flowers of flowers from three species of iris.

not obvious from the histograms, the three species of iris are immediately discernible when visualized using HDTreeV and sorted on screen.

The next example is more complex, using the responses of a subset of subjects on a questionnaire designed to measure Attention Deficit/Hyperactivity Disorder (ADHD). The subjects are part of the 1985–86 Northern Finnish Birth Cohort.[3] The questionnaire is the Strengths and Weaknesses of ADHD and Normal behaviors (SWAN; Swanson et al., 2001), which consists of 18 items. Half of the items measure inattentiveness, while the other half measures hyperactivity/impulsivity. The full data set has been analysed using factor mixture model comparisons (Lubke et al., 2007). The aim of this analysis was to determine whether ADHD should be conceptualized in terms of different subtypes (i.e., inattentive, hyperactive/impulsive, and combined subtypes) or in terms of one or more underlying continua of severity (gradual differences in inattentiveness and/or hyperactivity/impulsivity). Genders were analyzed separately due to known differences in prevalence of ADHD and potential differences in subtype proportions. The best fitting model for both genders turned out to be a 2-factor model with 2 mixture components. The larger component was clearly the low scoring unaffected part of the sample whereas the smaller high scoring component contained possibly affected subjects. Within component, there was substantial variability on two factors measuring inattentiveness and hyperactivity/impulsivity; however, there was no evidence favoring qualitatively different subtypes (Lubke et al., 2007).

For the representation in HDTreeV, a subset of the male data was created such that 25 subjects were randomly selected from the low scoring majority, and 30 subjects were randomly selected from the high scoring minority. Potentially affected subjects are over-represented in order to more easily detect different types of affected subjects if present.

The screen shots in Figures 14.5 and 14.6 show considerable variation in shapes of the trees representing the 55 subjects in the subset, but no clear clustering of four different types (e.g., unaffected, inattentive, hyperactive/impulsive, and combined subtypes). The labels in Figure 14.5 correspond to the assigned component membership resulting from fitting a 2-factor/2-component factor mixture model (1 = potentially affected, 2 = unaffected). The dual digit labels in Figure 14.6 relate to the within-class factor scores on the inattentiveness (first digit) and hyperactivity/impulsivity factors (second digit). To create the labels, factor scores were categorized using

Figure 14.5 HDTreeV representation of 55 response patterns on 18 ADHD items.

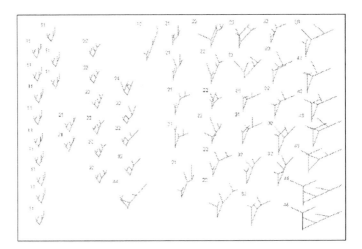

Figure 14.6 Different labeling of the same response patterns shown in Figure 14.5.

four equally spaced intervals, with higher numbers indicating higher scores on the factors. Comparing the two figures one can see that the potentially affected second class has higher factor scores than the unaffected majority class. In addition, higher factor scores correspond to larger trees. Even though the trees are representations of *observed* scores, this correspondence is expected due to positive within-class factor loadings. The graphical representation underscores that only a part of the variability in observed scores can be allocated to subjects belonging to either a non-affected majority class or a potentially affected class. A substantial part of the variability seems to be caused by more gradual differences between subjects.

The example of the ADHD data demonstrates the usefulness of a graphical representation of the observed data. Without having to rely on tenability of model assumptions or measures of goodness of fit, a tool such as HDTreeV allows one to inspect the data for clustering and/or gradual variation. Based on such an inspection, a restricted set of models can be chosen and subsequently fitted to the data. In addition, outcomes of model fitting such as factor scores and class assignments can be used to label the visual representation of the individual response patterns in order to evaluate the correspondence of model fitting results and observed data.

CONCLUDING REMARKS

Factor mixture modeling constitutes a flexible framework allowing for the comparison of a wide variety of different model types. If exploration of potential heterogeneity is the goal of a model comparison, restricting the set of fitted models to a particular model type (e.g., conventional latent class or exploratory factor models) can lead to accepting models with too many components or factors. In the absence of model violations, choosing the correct model when fitting a set of alternative model types depends mainly on the separation among the clusters, the sample size, and the response format. One of the most important limitations of using factor mixture models is the potential lack of a correspondence between the number of component distributions used when specifying a model and the number of clusters of subjects in the population. The structure of this particular problem may be recognized as a weakness that is inherent to model fitting in general. Although data might be adequately represented by a model, deducing that the best fitting model describes the data adequately is always prone to alternative explanations. This general weakness is exacerbated in more complex models that are based on a larger number of assumptions.

To address the specific issue of the number of clusters of subjects, it can be helpful to graphically represent the data. Mapping individual response patterns of the subjects on icons such as trees does not rely on any assumptions concerning a particular underlying structure or distribution of the data. Clustering of subjects should be evident in similar looking icons, and should be distinguishable from gradual differences. Although further research along these lines is clearly needed, graphical representations of the data may prove to be very useful to assess the validity of model assumptions.

NOTES

1. The research of the first author was supported by MH65322 (NIMH) and AG027360-01 (NIA).
2. Additional restrictions of elements of the parameter matrices in Equations 3 and 4, similar to those imposed in multigroup models, are necessary to achieve identifiability.
3. We would like to thank Marjo-Riitta Jarvelin, University of Oulu, Oulu, Finland, for making the data available.
4. Information about HDTreeV can be found on http://sourceforge.net/projects/hdtreev

REFERENCES

Akaike, H. (1974). A new look at statistical model identification. *IEEE Transactions on Automatic Control, AU-19*, 719–722.

Akaike, H. (1987). Factor analysis and AIC. *Psychometrika, 52*, 317–332.

Anderson, E. (1935). The irises of the gaspe peninsula. *Bulletin of the American Iris Society, 59*, 2–5.

Anderson, E. (1960). A semi-graphical method for the analysis of complex problems. *Technometrics, 2*, 387–392.

Arminger, G., Stein, P., & Wittenberg, J. (1999). Mixtures of conditional mean and covariance structure models. *Psychometrika, 64*, 475–494.

Bauer, D. B., & Curran, P. J. (2003). Distributional assumptions of growth mix true models: Implications for overextraction of latent trajectory classes. *Psychological Methods, 8*, 338–363.

Beck, A. T., Steer, R. A., & Brown, G. K. (1996). *Beck Depression Inventory: Second Edition manual,* San Antonio, TX: The Psychological Corporation.

Behrens, J. T. (1997). Principles and procedures of exploratory data analysis. *Psychological Methods, 2*, 131–160.

Bozdogan, H. (1987). Model selection and Akaike's Information Criterion (AIC): The general theory and its analytical extensions. *Psychometrika, 52*, 345–370.

Chernoff, H. (1973). The use of faces to represent points in k-dimensional space graphically. *Journal of the American Statistical Association, 68*, 361–368.

Dolan, C. V., & van der Maas, H. L. J. (1998). Fitting multivariate normal finite mixtures subject to structural equation modeling. *Psychometrika, 63*, 227–253.

Fisher, R. A. (1936). The use of multiple measurements in taxonomic problems. *Annals of Eugenics, 7*, 179–188.

Grinstein, G., Pickett, R., & Williams, M. G. (1989). *Exvis: An exploratory visualization environment. Graphics Interface '89*, 254–261.

Heinen, T. (1996). Latent class and discrete latent trait models: *Similarities and differences.* Thousand Oaks, CA: Sage Publications, Inc.

Jedidi, K., Jagpal, H. S., & DeSarbo, W. S. (1997). Finite mixture structural equation models for response based segmentation and unobserved heterogeneity. *Marketing Science, 16,* 39–59.

Lo, Y., Mendell, N., & Rubin, D. B. (2001). Testing the number of components in a normal mixture. *Biometrika, 88,* 767–778.

Lubke, G. H., & Muthén, B. O. (2005). Investigating population heterogeneity with factor mixture models. *Psychological Methods, 10,* 21–39.

Lubke, G. H., Muthén, B. O., Moilanen, I., McGough, J. J., Loo, S. K., Swanson, J. M., et al. (2007). Subtypes vs. severity differences in Attention Deficit Hyperactivity Disorder in the Northern Finnish Birth Cohort (NFBC). Manuscript accepted for publication in the *Journal of the American Academy of Child and Adolescent Psychiatry.*

Lubke, G. H., & Neale, M. C. (2006). Distinguishing between latent classes and continuous factors: Resolution by maximum likelihood? *Multivariate Behavioral Research, 41,* 499–532.

Lubke, G.H., & Neale, M.C. (submitted). *Distinguishing between latent classes and continuous factors: A follow-up addressing categorical outcomes and model violations.*

McLachlan, G. J., & Peel, D. (2000). *Finite mixture models.* New York: Wiley.

Muthén, B. O., & Shedden, K. (1999). Finite mixture modeling with mixture outcomes using the EM algorithm. *Biometrics, 55,* 463–469.

Muthén, L. K., & Muthén, B. O. (2006). *Mplus version 4.0* [Computer program]. Los Angeles, CA: Muthén & Muthén.

Pearson, K. (1894). Contributions to the mathematical theory of evolution. *Philosophical Transactions of the Royal Society of London. A, 185,* 71–110.

Pearson, K. (1895). Contributions to the mathematical theory of evolution. II. Skew variation in homogeneous material. *Philosophical Transactions of the Royal Society of London. A, 186,* 343–414.

Radloff, L. S. (1977). The CES-D Scale: A new self-report depression scale for research in the general population. *Applied Psychological Measurement, 1,* 385–402.

Schwarz, G. (1978). Estimating the dimensions of a model. *Annals of Statistics, 6,* 461–464.

Siegel, J. H., Goldwyn, R. M., & Friedman, H. P. (1971). Pattern and process in the evolution of human septic shock. *Surgery, 70,* 232–245.

Spies, J. R., & Boker, S. M. (2006). *HDTreeV: A multidimensional visualization tool.* In preparation.

Swanson, J., Schuck, S., Mann, M., Carlson, C., Hartman, C., Sergeant, J., et al. (2001). Categorical and dimensional definitions and evaluations of symptoms of ADHD: The SNAP and SWAN ratings scales. Available at http://www.adhd.net.

Vermunt, J. K., & Magidson, J. (2003). Latent class models for classification. *Computational Statistics & Data Analysis, 41,* 531–537.

Yung, Y. F. (1997). Finite mixtures in confirmatory factor analysis models. *Psychometrika, 62,* 297–330.

ABOUT THE CONTRIBUTORS

Tihomir Asparouhov is a member of the M*plus* team. His main research interest is in numerical algorithms for latent variable model estimation. His research has appeared in a diverse mix of journals including *Structural Equation Modeling: A Multidisciplinary Journal, Communications in Statistics, Econometric Theory*, and the *Proceedings of the American Mathematical Society*.

C. Mitchell Dayton is Professor and Chair in the Department of Measurement, Statistics and Evaluation at the University of Maryland. For more than 30 years, he has pursued a research interest in latent class analysis and in 1999 he published a Sage book dealing with latent class scaling models. Recently, he has focused on model comparison procedures with a special interest in approaches based on information theory and Bayes factors. His research has appeared in journals such as *The Journal of The American Statistical Association, Psychometrika, American Statistician, Multivariate Behavioral Research, Applied Psychological Measurement, Journal of Educational and Behavioral Statistics, British Journal of Mathematical and Statistical Psychology, Psychological Methods*, and *Journal of Educational Measurement*.

Karen Draney received her Ph.D. in Education from the University of California at Berkeley in 1996, specializing in educational measurement, psychometrics, and applied statistics. Her dissertation, entitled "The polytomous saltus model: A mixture model approach to the diagnosis of developmental differences," received the American Psychological Association Division 5 Dissertation Award. She is currently an associate director for the Berkeley Evaluation and Assessment Research (BEAR) center in the Graduate School of Education at the University of California at Berkeley. In addi-

Advances in Latent Variable Mixture Models, pages 363–370
Copyright © 2008 by Information Age Publishing
All rights of reproduction in any form reserved.

tion to her current project, entitled "Developing a research-based learning progression for the carbon cycle," a collaborative project with Michigan State University, she is also the managing editor for the journal *Measurement: Interdisciplinary Research and Perspectives*. Her research interests include the development of assessments for, and the analysis of data from, complex educational and psychological issues, such as embedded assessment, cognitive development, and problem solving.

Craig K. Enders is Associate Professor at Arizona State University. His research interests involve methodological issues related to analyses with missing data, longitudinal modeling, and growth mixture modeling. His research has appeared in journals such as *Educational and Psychological Measurement, Psychological Methods, Structural Equation Modeling: A Multidisciplinary Journal, Multivariate Behavioral Research*, and *Applied Measurement in Education*. He is a past officer of the structural equation modeling special interest group of the American Educational Research Association. He has served on the editorial board of several methodological and applied journals, including *Educational and Psychological Measurement* and *Psychological Methods*, and has been an ad hoc reviewer for several other leading methodological journals.

Brian P. Flaherty is Assistant Professor in the Department of Psychology at the University of Washington. His research interests involve categorical and longitudinal statistical models, often within the context of substance use and dependence. His work has appeared in journals such as the *Multivariate Behavioral Research, International Journal of Behavioral Development*, and *Drug and Alcohol Dependence*. He has guest edited two journal issues and has been an ad hoc reviewer for several leading journals and conferences, as well as a grant reviewer.

Judith Glück is Professor of developmental psychology at the University of Klagenfurt. She completed her doctoral degree at the University of Vienna, where she also worked as an Associate Professor until 2006, and was a postdoc in Paul Baltes' center for life span psychology at the Max Planck Institute for human development in Berlin from 1999 to 2002. Her research interests include the psychology and measurement of wisdom, the self in old age, autobiographical memory, the development of spatial abilities across the life span, and statistical methods for analyzing longitudinal data (with a focus on item response modeling). She has published several book chapters and journal articles on item response models for longitudinal data.

Gregory R. Hancock is Professor in the Department of Measurement, Statistics and Evaluation at the University of Maryland, College Park, and the Director of the Center for Integrated Latent Variable Research (CILVR). His research has appeared in such journals as *Psychometrika, Multivariate*

Behavioral Research, British Journal of Mathematical and Statistical Psychology, Structural Equation Modeling: A Multidisciplinary Journal, Psychological Bulletin, Journal of Educational and Behavioral Statistics, and *Educational and Psychological Measurement.* He is the past chair of the structural equation modeling special interest group of the American Educational Research Association. He also serves on the editorial boards of several methodological and applied journals.

Frauke Kreuter is Assistant Professor in the Joint Program in Survey Methodology at the University of Maryland. Her research interests include interviewer effects and nonresponse in household surveys, systematic measurement error in survey reports, and growth mixture modeling for non-normal outcomes. She has published several books on data analysis using Stata. Her work has appeared in journals such as the *Journal of Official Statistics.*

Marc Kroopnick is a doctoral candidate in the Department of Measurement, Statistics & Evaluation at the University of Maryland, College Park. He is the past chair of the Graduate Student Issues Committee of the National Council on Measurement in Education. His research interests include structural equation modeling, item response theory, test equating, and standard setting. He currently works as a research assistant for Cisco Systems Inc. in support of their network academy and certification testing program assessments.

Roy Levy is Assistant Professor in the Measurement, Statistics, and Methodological Studies Program in the Division of Psychology in Education at Arizona State University. Prior to his current position, he received his Ph.D. from the University of Maryland in Measurement, Statistics & Evaluation and was a Harold Gulliksen Psychometric Fellow at Educational Testing Service. He has published work on Bayesian network psychometric models, item response modeling, structural equation modeling, adaptive testing, and assessment design. His current research interests include methodological investigations and applications in item response theory, structural equation modeling, latent class analysis, and Bayesian networks, focusing on issues of dimensionality, data-model fit, model comparisons, and Bayesian approaches to inference and psychometric modeling for simulation based assessments.

Eric Loken is Assistant Professor in the Department of Human Development and Family Studies in the College of Health and Human Development, Pennsylvania State University. He studies continuous latent variable models, such as factor and structural equation models, and categorical latent variable models such as mixture models. He also works in the area of item response theory with applications to educational measurement. His focus is usually on the application of Bayesian methods.

Gitta H. Lubke is Assistant Professor in the Psychology Department at the University of Notre Dame. Her research interests include applications of latent variable modeling and purely methodological topics. Her current applied research is mainly in the field of psychiatric genetics, with a focus on the question whether a disorder is best described in terms of qualitatively different subtypes or in terms of a continuous underlying risk factor. The methodological topics are in the areas of measurement invariance, factor mixture modeling, latent class analysis, longitudinal analysis, analysis of categorical data, and genetic statistics. Her work has appeared in journals such as *Multivariate Behavioral Research, Structural Equation Modeling: A Multidisciplinary Journal, Psychological Methods,* and *Twin Research and Human Genetics.*

Katherine E. Masyn is Assistant Professor in the Department of Human and Community Development at the University of California, Davis. Her areas of specialization are discrete time survival analysis, latent variable growth modeling, and finite mixture modeling. Her work has applied in the areas of prevention science, childhood aggression, alcohol and substance abuse, and teacher retention in urban school settings. She has been published in the *Journal of Educational and Behavioral Statistics.*

Robert J. Mislevy is Professor in the Department of Measurement, Statistics and Evaluation at the University of Maryland. He joined the EDMS department in 2001, after 16 years at Educational Testing Service where he was a Distinguished Research Scientist in the Division of Statistics and Psychometrics Research. His research interests center on applying recent developments in statistical methodology and cognitive research to practical problems in educational and psychological measurement. He has received numerous awards including the Raymond B. Cattell Early Career Award for Programmatic Research, the National Council of Measurement in Education's Triennial Award, and the National Council of Measurement's Award for Career Contributions to Educational Measurement. He has been president of the Psychometric Society and was nominated as a Fellow of the American Psychological Association. He has served as a member on two committees of the National Academy of Sciences concerning assessment instruction and cognitive psychology, and was a primary author of final report of the National Assessment Governing Board's Design Feasibility Team.

Peter C. M. Molenaar is Professor of Human Development at The Pennsylvania State University. The general theme of his work concerns the application of mathematical theories to solve substantive psychological issues. Some more specific elaborations of this theme are: 1. Application of mathematical singularity theory (in particular catastrophe theory) to solve the longstanding debate about the reality of developmental stage transitions. 2. Application of nonlinear multivariate statistical signal analysis techniques to solve the problem of mapping theoretical models of cognitive information-processing onto dynamically interacting EEG/MEG neural sources embedded in spatio-temporally coherent backgrounds. 3. Application of mathematical-statistical ergodic theory to study the relationships between intra-individual (idiographic) analyses and inter-individual (nomothetic) analyses of psychological processes. 4. Application of advanced multivariate analysis techniques in quantitative genetics. 5. Application of adaptive resonance theory (ART neural networks) to study the effects of nonlinear epigenetical processes. Use of mathematical biological models of self-organization. 6. Application of optimal control theory to guide psychological and disease processes in person-specific ways.

Bengt O. Muthén is Professor Emeritus at the Graduate School of Education & Information Studies at UCLA. He was the 1988-89 President of the Psychometric Society. He currently has an Independent Scientist Award from the National Institutes of Health for methodology development in the alcohol field. He is one of the developers of the M*plus* computer program, which implements many of his statistical procedures. His research interests focus on the development of applied statistical methodology in areas of education and public health. Applications in education concern achievement development while public health applications involve developmental studies in epidemiology and psychology. Methodological areas include latent variable modeling, analysis of individual differences in longitudinal data, preventive intervention studies, analysis of categorical data, multilevel modeling, and the development of statistical software.

Daisy Rutstein is a doctoral student in the Department of Measurement, Statistics & Evaluation at the University of Maryland, College Park. She has done work in structural equation modeling and her current interests also include Bayesian networks and assessment design. She currently works with Cisco Systems, Inc. as a research assistant, offering support for their network academy and certification testing program assessments.

Karen M. Samuelsen is Assistant Professor in the Department of Educational Psychology and Instructional Technology's program in Research, Evaluation, Measurement, and Statistics (REMS) and Evaluation at the University of Georgia. She is also the past Assistant Director of the Center for Integrated Latent Variable Research (CILVR) at the University of Maryland. She has been the project manager on a federally funded research grant and was awarded an NSF grant to examine computer-based performance assessments for middle school science. Her research has included the examination of differential item functioning within a mixture model context.

Amy Soller is a Research Staff Member in the Science and Technology Division at the Institute for Defense Analyses. She holds a B.S. in Electrical Engineering, and a Ph.D. in Artificial Intelligence from the University of Pittsburgh. Her research involves applying artificial intelligence methods to analyze and assess human performance, learning, and collaboration, and performing independent assessments on national security issues concerning training and education, performance support, information sharing, and distributed collaboration technology. Previously, she worked as a Senior Artificial Intelligence Engineer at the MITRE Corporation where she led a crisis management technology integration project and developed an intelligent tutoring system for intelligence analysts. She has also worked as a project manager at the Institute for Research in Science and Technology in Italy and as an independent educational technology consultant. She sits on a number of editorial and scientific advisory boards, has co-edited a textbook on collaborative learning technology, and has published over 50 peer reviewed articles.

Christiane Spiel is Professor of Educational Psychology and Evaluation and department head at the Faculty of Psychology, University of Vienna. She is founding dean of the faculty of psychology, president of the European Society for Developmental Psychology and of the DeGEval – Evaluation Society, member of the supervisory board of the University of Hannover, member of various international advisory and editorial boards. In several projects she works together with the Austrian Federal Ministry of Education. She has received several awards for research, university teaching, and university management, and has published more than 150 original papers. She has directed many external funded projects and organized several international conferences. Her research topics are on the border between educational psychology and evaluation. Specific research topics are: Bullying and victimization, integration in multicultural school classes, lifelong learning, assessment of deductive reasoning competences, change measurement, and evaluation and quality management in the educational system.

Jeffrey R. Spies is a graduate student at the University of Notre Dame in a Joint Ph.D. program in Quantitative Psychology and Computer Science. His current research interests include developing methods of time-series analysis and visualization techniques for multidimensional data. He is the developer of HDTreeV, a multidimensional visualization tool, for which he received the SGI Award for Computational Science and Visualization in 2005.

Ron Stevens is Professor of Microbiology, and member of the Brain Research Institute at the UCLA School of Medicine, and has engaged in both basic research and educational research for 20 years. His current interests are the use of machine learning tools and electroencephalography (EEG) to model the acquisition of scientific problem solving skills. The educational software tools developed by the IMMEX project have received multiple research and corporate awards including the New Researcher Award from the Association of American Medical Colleges (1992), a Masters of Innovation award from Zenith Corporation (1992), a nomination from the Computerworld-Smithsonian Institute's "A Search For New Heroes" competition (1994) and an award of excellence from the 2001 Minnesota Learning Software Design Competition. Over 500 teachers and 140,000 students have participated in IMMEX-related activities.

Davood Tofighi is a Ph.D. student in the quantitative psychology department at Arizona State University. His main research interests include multilevel modeling, mediation, and growth mixture modeling. His research has appeared in journals such as *Psychological Methods*. His current research involves deriving covariances among the coefficient estimates in a single mediator model under various conditions.

Matthias von Davier is a Principal Research Scientist at Educational Testing Service (ETS). He developed WINMIRA, a stand-alone software program for estimating and testing a number of probabilistic models including dichotomous and polytomous mixed Rasch models. His work has appeared in journals such as *Psychometrika* and *Applied Psychological Measurement*, and has chapters in such books as *Rasch Models: Foundations, Recent Developments, and Applications* (Gerhard H. Fischer & Ivo W. Molenaar, Eds.) and *Applications of Latent Trait and Latent Class Models in the Social Sciences* (Jürgen Rost & Rolf Langeheine, Eds.). He recently edited a volume on multivariate Rasch models and mixture distribution Rasch models (Matthias von Davier & Claus H. Carstensen, Eds.).

Mark Wilson is Professor in the area of Policy, Organization, Measurement, and Evaluation at the University of California, Berkeley, where his interests focus on measurement and applied statistics. His work spans a range of issues in measurement and assessment from the development of new statistical models for analyzing measurement data, to the development of new assessments in subject matter areas such as science education, patient-reported outcomes, and child development, to policy issues in the use of assessment data in accountability systems. He has recently published three books, *Constructing Measures: An Item Response Modeling Approach, Explanatory Item Response Models: A Generalized Linear and Nonlinear Approach*, and *Towards Coherence Between Classroom Assessment and Accountability*. He was recently the chair of a National Research Council committee on assessment of science achievement, which produced a report entitled: *Systems for State Science Assessment*. He is founding editor of a new journal, *Measurement: Interdisciplinary Research and Perspectives*.